Jewish Studies and Israel Studies in the Twenty-First Century

Lexington Studies in Modern Jewish History, Historiography, and Memory

Series Editor:
Carsten Schapkow, University of Oklahoma

Modern Jewish history is an essentially interdisciplinary field. This series aspires to transcend disciplinary and methodological boundaries, welcoming original scholarship that advances our understanding of the modern Jewish experience. The series will cover all geographical areas and all periods in modern Jewish history by welcoming scholarly contributions including cultural history, intellectual history, transnational Jewish history, global Jewish history, and memory studies. We welcome original monographs and edited volumes as well as English-language translations of manuscripts originally written in other languages.

Titles in the Series

Jewish Studies and Israel Studies in the Twenty-First Century: Intersections and Prospects, Edited by Carsten Schapkow and Klaus Hödl
Modern Spain and the Sephardim: Legitimizing Identities, by Maite Ojeda-Mata
Eastern European Jewish American Narratives, 1890–1930: Struggles for Recognition, by Dana Mihailescu

Jewish Studies and Israel Studies in the Twenty-First Century

Intersections and Prospects

Edited by Carsten Schapkow
and Klaus Hödl

LEXINGTON BOOKS
Lanham • Boulder • New York • London

Das Land Steiermark
→ Wissenschaft und Forschung

Published by Lexington Books
An imprint of The Rowman & Littlefield Publishing Group, Inc.
4501 Forbes Boulevard, Suite 200, Lanham, Maryland 20706
www.rowman.com

6 Tinworth Street, London SE11 5AL

Copyright © 2019 by The Rowman & Littlefield Publishing Group, Inc.

All rights reserved. No part of this book may be reproduced in any form or by any electronic or mechanical means, including information storage and retrieval systems, without written permission from the publisher, except by a reviewer who may quote passages in a review.

British Library Cataloguing in Publication Information Available

Library of Congress Cataloging-in-Publication Data

ISBN: 978-1-7936-0509-2 (cloth : alk. paper)
ISBN: 978-1-7936-0511-5 (paper : alk. paper)
ISBN: 978-1-7936-0510-8 (electronic)

∞™ The paper used in this publication meets the minimum requirements of American National Standard for Information Sciences Permanence of Paper for Printed Library Materials, ANSI/NISO Z39.48-1992.

Contents

1 Introduction   1
Carsten Schapkow (University of Oklahoma)

Part I: Defining the Field

2 David Ben-Gurion, the Bible, and the Case for Jewish Studies and Israel Studies   15
Alan Levenson

3 Meta-Halacha and Real Life: Using Jewish Thought Methodology in Solving Religion and State Issues in Contemporary Israel   31
Yossi Ben-Harush

Part II: Defining the Borders of Israel Studies

4 Israel, Palestine, and Holy Land Studies in Post-Soviet Territory: Views, Trends, and Prospects   45
Dzmitry Shavialiou

5 Israel in the Mirror of Iran: An Iranian Approach to Jewish and Israeli Messianism   73
Amir Rezaeipanah

6 Turkish Jews' Perspectives on Israel   101
Özgür Kaymak

7 Israel Studies, the Jewish Challenge   121
Yakov M. Rabkin and Yaacov Yadgar

Part III: The Place of Israel Studies Contested?

8 Israel Studies, Intersectonality, and the Changing American College Scene — *Aharon Klieman* — 133

9 Intersections between Israel Studies and Israel Education: Language-Use and Educational Programming — *Shlomit Attias* — 157

Part IV: The Middle Eastern Angle

10 Jewish Studies as Transdisciplinary Middle East Studies: Notes from Tunisia — *Achim Rohde* — 175

11 Methodological Canaanism: The Case for a Rupture between Jewish Studies and Israel Studies — *Johannes Becke* — 199

Part V: The Future of Israel Studies

12 Thinking Big: Connecting Classical Jewish Studies, Jewish Studies Past, Present, Presence, and Israel Studies — *Dani Kranz* — 217

13 Intersections of Jewish Studies and Israel Studies: Israeli Haredim — *Tryce Hyman* — 247

Index — 275

About the Contributors — 285

Chapter One

Introduction

Carsten Schapkow (University of Oklahoma)

There is an ongoing and growing interest in the academic field of Israel Studies internationally.[1] Since the Association for Israel Studies was founded in 1985, Israel Studies as a multidisciplinary field has engaged in research on the history, politics, society, and culture of the modern state of Israel. Emerging in the United States, and also in Israel (with its peculiar place within the context of Jewish and General History in Israel), Israel Studies today is also present in Europe and beyond in places such as the University of Graz in Austria. It was here that the 2018 conference "Intersections between Jewish Studies and Israel Studies in the 21st Century" was held with conference participants of junior and more senior academic levels from Israel, Canada, Great Britain, the United States, Austria, Germany, Belorussia, and China. The conference was made possible by a generous grant from the government of Styria with additional funding from the Israel Institute, Washington, DC; the Department of History and the Schusterman Center for Judaic and Israel Studies at the University of Oklahoma; the City of Graz; and the University of Graz. Many thanks for the manifold logistic help goes to Susanne Korbel and Lukas Nievoll (both University Graz) who both helped to make the conference a success. Financial support for the publication of this volume was provided by the University of Graz and the Office of the Vice President for Research at the University of Oklahoma.

A big thank you goes to Tryce Hyman whose splendid work as the copy editor really helped this volume to improve in content and stature.

The conference organizers, Klaus Hödl from the Center for Jewish Studies at Karl-Franzens University Graz and Carsten Schapkow from the Schusterman Center for Judaic and Israel Studies at the University of Oklahoma, were not so much interested in Israel Studies per se but in the complex dynamic and intersections with its "older brother": Jewish Studies.[2] This was due to the fact that Hödl and Schapkow both teach classes in areas of Jewish Studies and Israel Studies to a diverse student body, the majority of them non-Jewish. While it is generally agreed upon that Jewish Studies focuses on topics pertinent to Jewish cultures and relations between Jews and non-Jews, Israel Studies addresses a variety of questions dealing with Israel's vibrant and diverse society, which encompasses many groups, both Jewish and non-Jewish, whose visions of the State of Israel are complex and multidimensional. Added to that, courses on Jewish Studies and Israel Studies topics experience high enrollment—cutting against the apparent trend of declining student enrollment in history-related courses more generally. One might add that this also has to do with popular depictions of Israeli society in movies, such as *Synonymes*, by Israeli director Nadav Lapid—a film which won the Golden Bear for Best Film at the Berlinale Film Festival in Berlin in February 2019. The movie clearly addresses questions of identity politics through the main character, an Israeli ex-soldier who wants to get rid of his Israeli identity, speaking to questions of belonging and loyalty beyond Israeli society and individuals and instead as a global phenomenon.

In the Call for Papers for the conference the organizers asked interested scholars whether a shift can be seen currently from Jewish Studies to Israel Studies. When looking back at the history of both fields, there are a few important similarities or analogies between Jewish Studies and Israel Studies, which we described as "intersections." I will introduce a few of these intersections here that will be discussed in more detail within the contributions of the volume.

Whereas Israel Studies is only a few decades old, Jewish Studies—which celebrated its two hundredth anniversary in 2018—goes back to the inception of the Berlin-based *Verein für die Geschichte und Kultur der Juden* and Leopold Zunz's imperative essay "Etwas Über die Rabbinische Literatur" ["Something on Rabbinic Literature"] in 1818.[3] The goal of the members of the *Verein* was to integrate Jewish Studies as a field of philological and historical research into university curricula in Prussia first of all. However, this aim was ignored by both the Prussian state administrators and the non-Jewish educated majority at large mainly for one reason: for a state like Prussia, it was not acceptable to integrate Jewish Studies as a subject of study at the university because Jewish assimilation should be encouraged and Jewish particularity—through studying matters Jewish—should be prevented. Therefore, Jewish Studies was never formally introduced into the canon of university teaching and scholarship but instead could only exist outside academia in rabbinical seminars and other Jewish institutions carried out exclusively by Jews. Scholars of the Science of Judaism began studying Judaism in secular—or more precisely, historical—terms and moved away from traditional Jewish scholarship focused on the interpretation of Jewish texts only. This was meant to foster integration of the Jews into non-Jewish majority society by reaching out and not keeping themselves apart from non-Jewish majority society which developed into a key goal since the *Haskalah* took shape. This was more than an important step, it was a revolution, one which ultimately led to the integration of the Jewish population at large but did *not* integrate Jewish Studies at German universities as the founding father of the Science of Judaism had envisioned.

Today, the situation looks very different. Not just in the United States but also in Europe, Jewish Studies and Israel Studies are part of university curricula. In the United States primarily Jewish donors ensure the thriving of Jewish and Israel Studies as academic fields. In Germany and Europe, for instance, the state supports these areas of research and study financially. Critical voices regarding private funding are concerned that private money will have, or already has had, implications on how research on Israel is carried out when also recognizing an increasing influence of pro-Israel foundations and think tanks on the field of Israel Studies. As a matter of fact, since 1967, a growing hostility within Middle Eastern Departments toward Israel[4] led as a response to an increase in funding from Jewish donors and has seen even more flourishing of Israel Studies Centers in particular since the turn of the twenty-first century. This raises a variety of questions for and from scholars and the general public about whether there is any interference with academic freedom or on how content is delivered and discussed in a classroom setting. Criticism, however, prevailed regarding the engagement of pro-Israel foundations and think tanks. Clearly, think tanks and foundations sponsor Israel Studies and Jewish Studies and without their financial contribution these institutions would most likely not exist. A one-sided pro-Israel approach based on the support of these organizations was expressed most passionately by Aaron Hughes as "the thorny issue of identity politics" in an article for the Chronicle of Higher Education in 2014.[5] Even if one does not agree with Hughes's overall argument,[6] though some did, his criticism highlights the important and difficult-to-parse "question of objectivity" in terms of content and agencies in both fields—Jewish Studies and Israel Studies. This includes the key question of whether they indeed do "belong" together or not. Indeed, even before Hughes published his essay, Michael Kotzin and Elie Rekhes had argued in 2013 that Israel Studies should not be about advocacy but about scholarship.[7] Nevertheless, in their view Israel Studies is mainly or simply about "connecting Jewish Students with their Jewish identity."[8] Additionally, there is the reality of a growing number of non-Jewish academics and students studying these fields. An emerging number of students in the classroom today do not have any personal connection to either Jewish Studies or Israel Studies, which is a tendency that will most likely continue and will therefore have a very significant impact on both areas of study in the years to come. So, how can we explain the rising interest of non-Jews on Israeli history in places like Graz, where the students are overwhelmingly non-Jewish/non-Israeli? Ambivalent and hybrid identity concepts play a crucial role, and they will continue to do so also regarding the instructors who teach these classes.

The relationship and engagement between Israel and the Diaspora, including self-images of Israel and the Diaspora can already be found in Jewish Studies with its goal to integrate Jewish history and thus the Jewish experience into the canon of general history by establishing a mind-set which understands Jewish history and Jews as contributors to general history and society. Scholars of the Science of Judaism developed forms of belonging through the historical experience which were set in context to the emerging nation-states in nineteenth-century Europe by precisely these scholars. As a consequence, and through the analysis of Jewish history, most importantly loyalty to the emerging nation-states was expressed and Judaism developed into a denomination in the private sphere and was not perceived as a religion first and foremost any longer. Jews developed a feeling of being at home in the Diaspora and only in the liturgy did Israel, in a very modified way, keep a central place. The relationship between Israel as a modern state and Jews living in the Diaspora today seem to replicate questions of loyalty and belonging once again.

But beyond that, a good number of faculty and students—depending on the context and country—are also neither Jewish nor citizens of Israel. Are their goals and intentions different when it comes to Israel Studies? And what about comparative perspectives including ambivalent or hybrid concepts of identities, including identity politics, in the context of contemporary migration, citizenship, transnationalism, and Diaspora (politics) with Israeli expats and non-Jewish immigrants in Israel? Notably, a survey conducted by the Jewish Agency from April until June 1995 offered findings that 58 percent of Israelis saw themselves first and foremost as Jews before seeing themselves as Israelis. For 75 percent of those surveyed in 1995, Judaism was perceived as the key factor of their identity.[9]

Moreover, is the "place" of Israel Studies in need for being evaluated/debated/questioned and even contested as Johannes Becke and Achim Rohde suggest in this very volume? Can Israel no longer be seen as a Western outpost in the Middle East, but instead as a regional power in the Middle East and has thus the study of Israel to be recontextualized in "cognate" fields such as Middle Eastern Studies? To rename Israel Studies to Israel-Palestine Studies, as it has been argued on some occasions, would not really be helpful. Quite the contrary. Undoubtedly, Israel Studies is much more, and in particular right now with an emergence of Jewish and Israel Studies not just in Europe but also in Asia, than a pro-Israel study group, because non-Jewish minorities, who largely contributed to the well-being of the state, and the conflict are a steadfast component of Israel Studies. This very diversity of Israeli society was recently portrayed in the *Israel Institute Magazine*.[10]

Part I of the volume, Defining the Field: Bible Studies and Beyond, opens with a chapter by Alan T. Levenson (University of Oklahoma). Levenson explores "David Ben Gurion, the Bible, and the Case for Jewish Studies and Israel Studies" and as one bridge between two fields increasingly in competition for talent and funding. This was not always the case, as Levenson makes clear when analyzing the deep skepticism by scholars of the *Wissenschaft des Judentums* regarding critical historical Bible Studies. Since the beginnings of Zionism, however, the Bible had served as a repository of national history and literature in the land of Israel. At its peak in the 1950s–1960s, the Bible served as a linchpin for Israeli national identity politics. Israeli high school students still study *Tanach* and soldiers still receive Bibles upon induction. In his chapter, Levenson sheds light on Zionist thinkers like Ahad Ha'Am, Vladimir Ze'ev Jabotinski, and David Ben-Gurion—whose "The Bible is our Mandate" remains in the public sphere up to this very day. Their readings of the Bible facilitated the connection of the people to the land based not on a religious standpoint but instead as a tool for conflict resolution. Or, in David Ben Gurion's own understanding: reading the Bible was seen as a powerful instruction manual for how the Jewish state ought to negotiate military, economic, and even diplomatic challenges in the years to come.

Yossef Yaacov (Yossi) Ben-Harush (Hebrew University of Jerusalem) offered a complementary reading to Levenson's focus on the Bible as a secular guiding line. Ben-Harush's chapter "Meta Halacha and Real Life: Using Jewish Thought Methodology in Solving Religion and State Issues in Contemporary Israel" analyzes Haredi authors' halachic or theological text usage to understand a contemporary situation. Ben-Harush provides an overview on how Israeli society has engaged in recent years in several disputes with the Ultra-Orthodox (Haredi) community regarding the state of Shabbat, the Western Wall, and conversion to Judaism and its implications for the right of return. In his chapter, Ben-Harush asks two questions: Are these debates strictly political? and can we find—by exploring and understanding the theology of the Haredi community—an answer with a larger scope? Ben-Harush proposes that reading the conflict between religion and state issues through the eyes of text-based research would allow adding another level of discourse to the state's sometimes shallow discussion on and with the Haredim. One of the cases he presents is Rabbi Shlomo Amar's reading of a medieval text written by Rabbi Yitzchak Arama (ca. 1420–1494), which can help to bring more insight to these contemporary debates (i.e., questions of "objectivity" regarding "holiness" and the "public sphere" for instance) through the lenses of Jewish Thought Methodology.

Part II of the volume, Defining the Borders of Israel Studies begins with a chapter by Dzmitry Shavialiou (Belarusian State University), "Israel, Palestine, and Holy Land Studies in Post-Soviet Territory: Views, Trends, and Prospects." Shavialiou provides an overview on the emergence and development of Jewish and Israel Studies from the late 1980s to the mid-2010s, focusing on trends and prospects of the academic discipline within the Former Soviet Union (FSU). The chapter outlines two stages: 1) from the late 1980s to the late 1990s, and 2) from the early 2000s to the present. Three regional schools of today's Israel studies in Russia and the Ukraine are outlined—the "Moscow School," the "Nizhniy Novgorod School," and the "Odessa School."

The chapter by Amir Rezaeipanah (Shahid Behesti University Tehran) "Israel in the Mirror of Iran. An Iranian Approach to Jewish and Israeli Messianism" is concerned with the particular contexts impacting Iranian-Shiite understanding of Jewish Studies and Israel Studies. In his assessment, such scholarship in Iran is centered on political theology and messianism and is affected by some of the existing sources and bases and are thus prone to many structural mistakes and errors. Accordingly, the historical heritage of Islam toward Jewishness and *Bani-Israel*, centered as it is on the holy Quran, provides some bases for an unrealistic and dark view of both the Jewish religion and its people. After the establishment of political Islam in Iran, and the hegemony of the revolutionary elites in 1979, this historical heritage was revived and appeared in an ideological and pragmatic form. The attitude and viewpoint of the revolutionary elites in Iran was articulated on three levels: ideological, strategic, and diplomatic. This took the form of othering and activism toward the nature of Israel, especially in the realms of the religious, the political, and the social. The existence of an alternative, called *Mahdaviat*, is another effective context in the Iranian understanding of Israeli and Jewish political theology and messianism. These issues affect even the Iranian-Jewish diaspora, called the *Kalimis,* and stimulated two conservative and radical paradigms in studying the Iranian approach to Israeli and Jewish Studies. Some categories and problems affected by this approach and context include the duties and missions of the believers and the Jews; the nature and functions of the state; the holy land; emancipation, redemption, and salvation; sacred or holy suffering, and the acceptance of hardship. Rezaeipanah's chapter investigates these categories comparatively as the axes of difference between Israeli and Jewish iterations of theology and messianism.

Özgür Kaymak's (Istanbul University) chapter focuses on "Turkish Jews' Perspectives on Israel," particularly their citizenship practices, through a detailed analysis of their relationship with Israel, through the kind of symbolic/social capital they have to the state, which is an understudied area in Turkish Jewish Studies and Israel Studies. Although there has been a remarkable increase in research on non-Muslim minorities in recent years, scholarly works focusing on the sociology of daily life of non-Muslims are limited. The vast majority of the extant research concerning political engagement in Turkey has centered on general understandings of the opinions and behaviors of the broader Turkish population; however, these studies have been heavily weighted in terms of the engagement of the majority Turkish population and have largely ignored the legal, social, and economic barriers that directly influence the structures and realities of ethnic and racial minority citizenship practices. Considering this gap in the literature, Kaymak's chapter aims to answer questions about the perceptions Jews of Istanbul have regarding Israel. In so doing, Kaymak also contributes to the identity and citizenship studies in minority literature. It is intended to be a substantial beginning and an invitation to other scholars to further advance this area of inquiry. The author sees her results as a perspective, rather than as a truth-claim. The data collected through her fieldwork is presented in the context of the theories of citizenship, nationalism, and diaspora.

The lunch discussion between Yaacov Yadgar (University of Oxford) and Yakov M. Rabkin (Université de Montréal) summarizes the proceeding of a panel held at the conference "Intersections between Jewish Studies and Israel Studies in the 21st Century." It was agreed upon by the two speakers that arguments for the intersections between Jewish and Israel Studies can already be seen in the historical foundations of Zionism. Without a proper knowledge of Jewish History in Russia, for instance, the powerful impact Zionism had on Russian Jewry cannot be studied and properly understood. Also, questions of identity (politics) regarding Jewishness and Israeliness clearly intersect between the two fields of research. Both speakers argue that the State of Israel has no clear definition of Jewishness. The increasing trend to prefer nationalism of the Jews over Israel also as a non-Jewish collective speaks to that point. One might add, that this very special situation is embedded in the peculiar situation after the Holocaust that left Jewish life in Europe devastated and in more than just a simple response helped to create a new type of self-confident new Jew born in Israel, the *Sabra*. The neglect of the Diaspora was key to it but today Holocaust remembrance, although still crucial, even seems to unfold many hidden layers in Israel when we look at emigration from Israel to Europe or the United States and more recent books on Holocaust commemoration and Israel today show.[11] Ultimately, in the opinion of the speakers, Israel Studies must become more contemporary and inclusive.

In Part III of the volume, The Place of Israel Contested?, Aharon Klieman's (Tel Aviv University) chapter "Israel Studies, Intersectionality, and the Changing American College Scene" questions the prospects of a growing academic discipline devoted to the study of modern Israel in the United States. He presents, instead, a grim picture of today's American campus scene where Israel-related studies are increasingly under attack, thrust on the defensive, and may actually be regressing. Klieman cites the growing list of ugly and distinctly unacademic incidents at United States colleges and universities, and proceeds to elaborate on three worrisome trends. First, the politicized and poisoned campus environment marked by the disruption of contemplative academic study and serious course work by extracurricular campus activism, characterized by anti-Israel protests, violent demonstrations, and the intimidation of professors. Second, these provocations and the purposeful linking of anti-Israel sentiment with anti-Zionism, anti-Judaism, and anti-Semitism are having a decidedly divisive effect upon Jewish students and faculty over how to respond tactically, and whether to support or fault Israel. Third, in an effort to deflect criticism, college administrators tend increasingly to favor "softer" subjects like Hebrew literature and the Israeli arts over controversial yet core course offerings such as the Israeli-Arab conflict and peace process, or Israeli foreign policy. Should these present trends continue, Klieman contends, American universities are going to be hard-pressed to sustain, let alone expand, degree programs, visiting Israeli scholar appointments, research funding, speakers' forums, centers and institutes focused on teaching, researching, and writing about contemporary Israel. Arguably, however, one potentially positive development is the forced intersection between what have traditionally too often been regarded as independent fields of study. Jewish Studies, Israel Studies, and Middle East Studies in reality do overlap as well as impact meaningfully on each other, and therefore merit administrative steps at more closely integrated programs for the benefit of students and scholars alike.

Shlomit Attias (Levinsky College of Education Tel Aviv), in her chapter "Intersections between Israel Studies and Israel Education: Language-use and Educational Programming," argues that since its first emergence in the American Jewish Education system at the beginning of the 2000s, Israel Education has been developed and categorized as a distinct pedagogic field about Israel. Like Israel Studies, it also focuses on modern Israel society, history, and politics. Despite their different field of operation, Israel Studies in academia and Israel Education in Jewish schools, both seem to exhibit similar meaning-making processes that involve politicization and identity politics. Based on her long-term ethnographic study of Israel Education in the United States and Australia, Attias argues, that in certain perspectives and to some degree, the complex dynamics between Israel Studies and Jewish Studies can be observed also between the new field of Israel Education and the established field of Jewish Education in American and Australian Jewish schools. Therefore, she proposes to expand the discussion on the place and multifaceted meaning of Israel Studies by looking also at its sister field Israel Education. Attias points to shifts in the place of Israel within Diaspora Jewish educational discourse and programming, and highlights Israel Education as a crisis-motivated field that reveals complex changes in the place of Israel both in that educational discourse and beyond the confines of the classroom; changes that are influenced by and shape Diaspora-Israel relations and Diaspora local reality. Through elaboration of this subject,

Attias hits upon the concept of promoting a worldwide Jewish identity with and through Israel (Studies).

Part IV of the volume, The Middle Eastern Angle, begins with Achim Rohde's (University of Marburg) chapter "Jewish Studies as Transdisciplinary Middle Eastern Studies: Notes from Tunisia." Rohde questions the place of Israel Studies in academia today. Rather than discussing the pros and cons for consolidating and enlarging the disciplinary container of Jewish Studies to encompass an emerging Israel Studies, Rohde argues in favor of blurring the disciplinary contours of scholarship on both Jews/Judaism and Israel. Instead, scholars should address them both as highly innovative fields of knowledge production that are necessarily intertwined with various other disciplinary configurations in the humanities and social sciences. According to Rohde, German history and contemporary German society cannot be adequately addressed by scholars without considering the Jewish dimensions therein. This is true for Israel Studies as well, given the location of Israel in the Middle East. Scholarship on the Middle East and North Africa increasingly addresses Jewish topics as an integral aspect of this field. The chapter exemplifies this approach by introducing Rohde's current research project on Jews in Tunisia after the revolution of 2011. He highlights that Arab-Jewish identities have been preserved in the case of Tunisia.

Johannes Becke's (Hochschule für Jüdische Studien Heidelberg) chapter "Methodological Canaanism: The Case for a Rupture between Jewish Studies and Israel Studies" is based on his personal teaching experiences at the Center for Jewish Studies in Heidelberg and a critical reading of the ideological writings of the Young Hebrews (Canaanites). The chapter makes the case for a systematic rupture between the two fields. Jewish Studies with its typical focus on religious texts and Diasporic statelessness in the West fails, according to Becke, to provide students of the State of Israel with the necessary tools to study the politics, culture, and society of a sovereign state in the Middle East. While students of Israel require a solid understanding of Jewish-Diasporic history, Becke argues, their language and methodological training needs to be reoriented toward Middle Eastern Studies. In order to explore the Zionist project in its regional environment, students of Israel Studies need more Arabic and less Yiddish—and a class on Kurdish nationalism rather than one on the German-Jewish *Haskalah*. Becke provides a number of suggestions for how Israel Studies can be integrated more closely into Area Studies, Global Studies, and naturally Middle East Studies, ranging from comparative classes and integrated language training to joint MA degrees in Middle East Studies. He raises the question of how to escape the narrative of what Becke terms "Israeli exceptionalism" (right now). Clearly, Becke situated Israel Studies not in an Ashkenazi-Centered framework but situated it in the Middle East. According to him Israel Studies would be better suited in Area Studies departments and not in Humanities departments, which was not appreciated by all of the conference participants. More importantly, Becke asked about the kind or type of Israel scholars in the field are talking about.

Part V of the volume, The Future of Israel Studies, includes two chapters. In the first, Dani Kranz (Bergische Universität Wuppertal) focuses on the continued separation between Jewish Studies and Israel Studies within German academia, despite the intricate link between the two fields. This structure mirrors the relationships, past and present, of studies of diasporic Jews and Israeli Jews. Yet, Kranz elaborates, diaspora Jews and Israeli Jews interact with each other as often as they are shaped by local contexts: diaspora Jews can turn into Israeli Jews, and Israeli Jews can become diasporic; movements and flows indeed define the issue. Beginning with historic links of Jewish Studies to Israel Studies, via possible borders of each field, her chapter endeavors to engage Jewish Studies and Israel Studies. It seeks to question issues that support exclusionary tropes, and it seeks to establish intersections by approaching Jewish Studies and Israel studies through transdisciplinary debates. Besides the tropes of diaspora versus Israel, disciplinary boundaries come to the fore, which can be fruitfully negotiated. Yet, Jewish Studies and Israel Studies are also impacted by *Realpolitik*, which influences the study of each, and which manifests in specific structures and topics: by this token Kranz's chapter advises an endeavor to lift surreptitious discourses and connect regions, disciplines, and foci. While historical studies remain a key area in both Jewish Studies and Israel studies, these already indicate links, which studies of specific locations, contexts, and within other disciplines, empirical and nonempirical, support further analysis, and moreover allow for meta-analyses that indicate an entangled future.

In the concluding chapter, Tryce Hyman (University of Oklahoma) elaborates on practical considerations of the intersections between Jewish Studies and Israel Studies. He argues that the two fields are too interrelated to be effectively divorced, and that in certain instances one field might be rendered unintelligible in the absence of the other. He uses Israeli Haredim as a case in point—demonstrating that Jewish Studies frameworks are vital in identifying phenomena found among Israeli Haredim. However, the Israeli context of their lives, namely as a Jewish minority within a *Jewish majority society*, carries analysis beyond the ken of a general Jewish Studies framework and into the realm of Israel Studies.

Finally, Hyman considers the relationship between Israel Studies and geographically cognate fields like Middle Eastern Studies. He acknowledges the reality that these fields will likely remain formally separated for as long as the Israel-Palestine conflict persists, as their current separation and even generation are themselves a reflection of that conflict. Be that as it may, Hyman notes a growing trend of informal and organic integration between the fields in response to shifting academic needs.

The editors of this volume hope that its contents will serve to illustrate that the ongoing and growing interest in Israel Studies must be analyzed and understood in its relationship to Jewish Studies. Only this will allow scholarship to reflect on not only their intersections, but also on the prospects of both fields in the realms of both research and teaching. This will become ever more vital in an increasingly globalized world with shifting concepts, borders, and identity concepts.

NOTES

1. See the following recent publications for further insight: Eliezer Ben-Rafael and Julius H. Schoeps, Yitzhak Sternberg, and Olaf Glöckner (eds.), *A Handbook of Israel Major Debates* (Berlin: De Gruyter, 2016); Andreas Lenhardt (ed.), *Judaistik im Wandel. Ein halbes Jahrhundert Forschung und Lehre über das Judentum in Deutschland* (Berlin: De Gruyter, 2016); Ilan Troen and Donna Robinson (eds.), "Special Issue: Zionism in the 21st Century," *Israel Studies* 19, no. 2 (2014); Michael Kotzin and Elie Rekhes, "The State of Israel Studies: An Emerging Academic Field," in *The Bloomsbury Companion to Jewish Studies*, Dean Philipp Bell (ed.) (London: Bloomsbury, 2013), 317–48.

2. Ra'anan S. Boustan, Oren Kosansky, and Marina Rustow (eds.), *Jewish Studies at the Crossroads of Anthropology and History: Authority, Diaspora, Tradition* (Philadelphia: University of Pennsylvania Press, 2011).

3. Leopold Zunz, "Etwas über die rabbinische Literatur. Nebst Nachrichten über ein altes bis jetzt ungedrucktes hebräisches Werk (1818)," in *Gesammelte Schriften*, vol. 1, Leopold Zunz and the Curatorium der Zunzstiftung (eds.) (Hildesheim: G. Ohms, 1976 [Berlin: L. Gerschel, 1875–76]), 1–31; for a general overview regarding the two hundredth anniversary, see Mirjam Thulin and Markus Krah, "Disciplining Jewish Knowledge: Cultures of *Wissenschaft des Judentums* at 200," *Pardes* 24 (2018): 9–16.

4. Martin Kramer, *Ivory Tower on Sand. The Failure of Middle Eastern Studies in America* (Washington, DC: The Washington Institute for Near East Policy, 2001).

5. Aaron Hughes, "Jewish Studies Is Too Jewish," *The Chronicle of Higher Education*, March 24, 2018. https://www.chronicle.com/article/Jewish-Studies-Is-Too-Jewish/145395.

6. Abraham Socher and Alan Arkush, "Who Gets to Define Jewish Studies?" *The Chronicle of Higher Education*, May 5, 2014. https://www.chronicle.com/article/Who-Gets-to-Define-Jewish/146267.

7. Kotzin and Rekhes, "The State of Israel Studies," 325.

8. Kotzin and Rekhes, "The State of Israel Studies," 327.

9. Michael Wolffsohn and Tobias Grill, *Israel. Geschichte, Politik, Gesellschaft, Wirtschaft* (Opladen: Verlag Barbara Budrich, 2016), 34.

10. See *Israel Institute Magazine*, Winter 2017.

11. See for instance Yishai Sarid, *Mifletzet Ha-Zikaron* [The Memory Monster] (Tel Aviv: Am Oved, 2017).

BIBLIOGRAPHY

Ben-Rafael, Eliezer, Julius H. Schoeps, Yitzhak Sternberg, and Olaf Glöckner (eds.). *A Handbook of Israel Major Debates*. Berlin: De Gruyter, 2016.

Boustan, Ra'anan S., Oren Kosansky, and Marina Rustow (eds.). *Jewish Studies at the Crossroads of Anthropology and History: Authority, Diaspora, Tradition*. Philadelphia: University of Pennsylvania Press, 2011.

Hughes, Aaron. "Jewish Studies Is Too Jewish." *The Chronicle of Higher Education*. March 24, 2018. https://www.chronicle.com/article/Jewish-Studies-Is-Too-Jewish/145395.

Israel Institute Magazine. Winter 2017.
Kotzin, Michael and Elie Rekhes. "The State of Israel Studies: An Emerging Academic Field." In *The Bloomsbury Companion to Jewish Studies*, edited by Dean Philipp Bell, 317–48. London: Bloomsbury, 2013.
Kramer, Martin. *Ivory Tower on Sand. The Failure of Middle Eastern Studies in America.* Washington, DC: The Washington Institute for Near East Policy, 2001.
Lenhardt, Andreas, (ed.). *Judaistik im Wandel. Ein halbes Jahrhundert Forschung und Lehre über das Judentum in Deutschland.* Berlin: De Gruyter, 2016.
Sarid, Yishai. *Mifletzet Ha-Zikaron* [The Memory Monster]. Tel Aviv: Am Oved, 2017.
Socher, Abraham, and Alan Arkush. "Who Gets to Define Jewish Studies?" *The Chronicle of Higher Education.* May 5, 2014. https://www.chronicle.com/article/Who-Gets-to-Define-Jewish/146267.
Thulin, Mirjam, and Markus Krah. "Discipling Jewish Knowledge: Cultures of *Wissenschaft des Judentums* at 200." *Pardes* 24 (2018): 9–16.
Troen, Ilan, and Donna Robinson (eds.). "Special Issue: Zionism in the 21st Century." *Israel Studies* 19, no. 2 (2014).
Wolffsohn, Michael, and Tobias Grill. *Israel. Geschichte, Politik, Gesellschaft, Wirtschaft.* Opladen: Verlag Barbara Budrich, 2016.
Zunz, Leopold. "Etwas über die rabbinische Literatur. Nebst Nachrichten über ein altes bis jetzt ungedrucktes hebräisches Werk (1818)." In *Gesammelte Schriften*, Vol. 1, edited by Leopold Zunz and the Curatorium der Zunzstiftung, 1–31. Hildesheim: G. Ohms, 1976 [Berlin: L. Gerschel, 1875–76].

Part I

Defining the Field

Bible Studies and Beyond

Chapter Two

David Ben-Gurion, the Bible, and the Case for Jewish Studies and Israel Studies

Alan Levenson

This past year, the College of International Studies at the University of Oklahoma promoted a trip to Israel/Palestine. As director of a program in Judaic and Israel Studies, I found myself immersed in rather intense conversations. Once again, I was reminded that few issues pertaining to Jews—not Holocaust Denial, not Antisemitism, whether Alt-Right or Far Left, not Christian Supersessionism, certainly not the issue of intermarriage or the collapse of the Jewish "middle," as sociologist Steve Cohen calls it—stir contention as quickly as this one.[1] What I had not expected from this conference, and I sincerely thank Professors Klaus Hödl and Carsten Schapkow for organizing it, was the argument that Jewish Studies and Israel Studies ought to be separated altogether. Indeed, I had spent much of the flight to Graz doodling Venn diagrams imagining the way participants might visualize the "intersections." Although an intellectual case can be made for separating Jewish Studies and Israel Studies, let me say that as much as I might personally benefit from this divorce, I do not think it is "good for the kids," and I am sure the custody battles would be nasty.[2] Would a teacher who favors this divorce, for instance, offer a survey of Jewish history that excludes contemporary Israel, the second largest and fastest growing Jewish population? That strikes me as an artificial outcome. So the question becomes: should an Israel Studies teacher exclude Jewish history as content? In the following pages, I want to offer some thoughts on the Bible as a natural offspring of Jewish Studies and Israel Studies that may offer a good point of contact. Before that, however, I would like to make a methodological point.

Historians incline toward more data, more context, and widely varied perspectives. When evaluating Greco-Roman or Israelite history, or ancient history generally, the pall of doubt invariably clouds scholarly findings on these grounds. The Peace of Callias between the Delian League and Persia, 449 BCE, largely accepted as fact, relies on a meager handful of sources, was challenged as a fabrication by one ancient historian, and glaringly left unmentioned by Thucydides, whose account of the fifty-year break between the Persian and Peloponnesian Wars constitutes the scholarly gold standard. The Siege of Jerusalem in the reign of King Hezekiah in 701/700 BCE seems like one of the most reliable events in ancient Israel, attested by three biblical accounts (Isaiah, Kings, Chronicles), but more importantly, by an opposing perspective; namely, the Assyrian records of Sennacherib. By the standards of modern historiography, this data set looks pretty unimpressive. All numerical claims coming from ancient historians should be treated with extreme skepticism: did two to three million pilgrims come to Jerusalem for Passover as Josephus claims in *The Jewish War*? No modern historian accepts that literally, yet all are glad for the Josephan narrative.

As with facts, so with perspectives. The historian's preference for more facts is matched by the historian's preference for more frames of reference and methodologies: social, economic, political, cultural, and intellectual perspectives, to name a few. In recent decades, more rigorous terms, such as "performative" or "situational" have been employed in order to highlight the elements of contingency, and avoid essentialist assumptions, but good historians have long emphasized the complexity of events. Whence this proclivity? It ultimately stems, partly, from the simple observation that the human condition is a complex one and thus the diversity of human experience demands diverse explanatory vehicles.

My little homily aims at rejecting the idea, voiced by some conference participants, that Middle East Studies *alone* will serve to place Israel in its proper context. Without doubt, Middle East Studies offers an irreplaceable context, and the various examples broached, both political and cultural, show this. Comparisons of Israel to the wide variety of ethno-dominant states, of the structures of successful states versus failed states in this region, pilgrimages in the Tunisian-Arabic-Jewish culture (elucidated by Dr. Achim Rodhe), other regional "misfits" like the Kurds and the Yazidis; the MENA experience generally; all of these contexts help greatly to fully understand contemporary Israel.[3] Parenthetically, *The Jew in the Modern World*, the most widely used sourcebook for *Jewish* history, acknowledges this expanded perspective. While remaining largely Eurocentric, Paul Mendes-Flohr and Jehuda Reinharz wisely added a section on the Mizrachi-Sephardi experience to its third revised and expanded edition.[4] In Israel itself, the Biton Commission has sought to rectify the underrepresentation of MENA communities in the history books and in the educational system. Thus, the

Middle Eastern context for understanding Israel should be a given intellectually. "Area Studies," as Heidelberg's Dr. Johannes Becke argues, *might* well prove the best location for Israel Studies rather than a traditional Humanities context.[5] My qualification about this claim is more professional than intellectual. I fear for graduate students who present a paper at their first MESA conference, or apply for that first Middle East Studies job, thinking that objective scholarly analysis of Israel will *not* be an immediate disqualifier. Obviously, regional context matters for understanding any nation, Israel included. But it should also be a given that developments within Jewish history and historiography, when it comes to understanding Israel, sometimes matter too. I am not championing the kind of teleological A to Z ("Abraham to Zionism") course that I taught to what are now called "heritage students," in the last century, when I was myself a graduate student.[6] Scholars have moved beyond that—in the Humanities as well as in Area Studies. Nevertheless, for me, the shock of hearing a scholar dismiss the European Haskalah as irrelevant to Israel Studies was profound, not the least, because Zionist architects from Peretz Smolenskin to David Ben-Gurion and beyond, acknowledged their debt to the Maskilim as providing the necessary secularizing and politicizing elements to forge their own Zionist ideologies. To employ a metaphor mathematical rather than marital: the Venn diagram of Jewish Studies and Israel Studies may overlap either more or less depending on the particular inquiry; one can, arguably, talk about Israel's economic or environmental policies without reference to Moses Mendelssohn; in intellectual or religious history, however, one must acknowledge significant overlap (intersection) between Jewish Studies and Israel Studies. The predecessors of the state who conceptualized Zionism and the founders of the state (and nobody would dismiss as unimportant this "*dor ha-kiyyuum*") drew deeply from the well of the Haskalah as well as from non-Jewish nineteenth-century ideologies.

This last point may be illustrated through the bibliocentrism of David Ben-Gurion (1886–1973), Israel's founding father.[7] A preliminary comment: is the Bible part of Jewish Studies? Yes, if one includes the use and reuse of the biblical anthology by Jews over the centuries.[8] Is the Bible part of contemporary Israeli culture? Yes, if one listens to Israeli high schoolers muttering curses at exam time or reads the literature from professional Israeli scholars (think: Zakovitch and Shinan, *That's Not What the Good Book Says*) or ambitious Israeli politicians (think: Yair Lapid, *My Heroes*). Better yet, take the case of David Ben-Gurion's promotion of the Bible as a linchpin for modern Israeli identity formation, a subject that has been well-documented and well-qualified.[9] As Shabtai Teveth noted, Ben-Gurion left a literary record which makes differentiating the oft-repeated and the essential difficult.[10] In response to the views of the "Canaanites" who denied any continuity between Hebrew and Jew, Ben-Gurion stressed the history of the Jewish people. Against attempts to rehabilitate rabbinic literature, Ben-Gurion absurdly underestimated the creativity of the Jewish diaspora. In other words, like any politician, Ben-Gurion spun his story differently depending on the context.

Ben-Gurion did not organize the Tanach-heavy school curriculum of 1953–1954, which showed the impact of his "statism" doctrine.[11] Ben-Gurion never pretended to be a Bible scholar and made a show of deferring to academics. Nevertheless, as a result of his unparalleled prestige, his stance regarding the Bible becomes more than a historical curiosity. As a representative of the Second Aliyah, for whom the first person plural was always the most natural voice, Ben-Gurion's relationship to the Bible tells us much about Israeli identity in its formative years. Michael Keren's *Ben-Gurion and the Intellectuals* summed it up:

> This was one area in which Ben-Gurion clearly dominated the "charismatic center." Not only did he play a personal role in the promotion of activities, such as the international bible contest, or bible study groups (one of which met in his home on a biweekly basis), he also determined, to a great extent, the subject matter to be discussed. [A question such as what motivated the Hebrew to go to the land of the Canaan portrayed the return to Canaan as a major biblical event to be studied and debated. Military officers turned amateur archaeologists, and journalists engaged in the writing of long essays on questions such as how many kings Joshua actually overpowered.] Prophetic statements were incorporated into political language, often as a substitute for genuine public ethics. Ben-Gurion himself used biblical quotations in every speech. These quotations not only decorated his speeches but often served as sources of political insight.[12]

I will examine Ben-Gurion's impact in four steps. First, I examine Ben-Gurion's hopelessly conflicted idea of secular biblical authority. Second, I discuss the tension between biblical humanism versus biblical nationalism. Third, I highlight his radical view of the superiority of biblical over rabbinic Judaism. Fourth, I analyze Ben-Gurion's hostility toward biblical source criticism. Finally, I reflect on Ben-Gurion's personal role in forwarding the Bible as part of Israeli national identity, which subsequent scholars have tended to see as a "rise and fall" tale.[13]

DILEMMAS OF SECULAR BIBLICAL AUTHORITY

While Ben-Gurion's interest in the Bible as a basis for national identity emerged after 1948, its utility must have been latent in Ben-Gurion's mind much earlier.[14] Israel Tabenkin, another member of the Second Aliyah, contended that every pioneer had a copy of the Tanach that was used as a field guide to the old-new land and as an inspirational text. In a similar vein, cited in Shapira, Aharon Meged wrote:

> The Bible was learned and read in the country not as a religious book, but as a literary work of genius, as a linguistic treasure filled with gems, as a historical source, as a geographic and archaeological guidebook, as a fount of wisdom, as a clarion call to idealism and social justice. From the first and in retrospect—the Bible was forging the bond between the people and their ancestral land.[15]

Even if Tabenkin and Meged exaggerate, the Second Aliyah clearly expended much energy integrating the Bible into their various ideologies. Ben-Gurion consistently named Harriet Beecher Stowe's *Uncle Tom's Cabin* and Abraham Mapu's biblical novel *The Love of Zion* as the two books which made the greatest impression on him politically. The former taught him the value of freedom; the latter, love of homeland.[16] Ben-Gurion spoke for his generation when he claimed, "I am not religious, nor were the majority of the early builders of modern Israel believers. Yet their passion for this land stemmed from the Book of Books. That is why the socialists of the Bilu movement named themselves with reference to Ezra. And it is why, though I reject theology, the single most important book in my life is the Bible."[17]

A contrast can be drawn between Ben-Gurion and that of his perennial opponent, Vladimir Jabotinsky. Jabotinsky, a Russian cosmopolitan turned militant nationalist, had an interest in the Bible too, but when he addressed the British High Commission of 1936, better known as the Peel Commission, his argument rested solely on the relative benefit and relative suffering that both sides would experience.[18] The Arabs had a *desire* for another state, Jabotinsky conceded, but Jews had an existential *need* for one. By contrast, Ben-Gurion told the Commission, "The Bible is our Mandate," a clever play on the notion of the Jewish people's initial right to the land of Israel, as well as a reminder of the religious motivations behind Britain's bestowal of the Balfour Declaration. Twelve years later, the Israeli Declaration of Independence echoed Ben-Gurion's version of Israel's right to a state as being, in part, biblically based. Dramatically delivered by Ben-Gurion from the Tel Aviv Museum at 4:00 p.m. on May 14, 1948, as the British Mandate ended and as the civil war between Jews and Arabs escalated to a regional conflict, the Declaration's opening sentences validated the specific Jewish stake to the land and the universal gift of the Jews: "The Land of Israel was the birth place of the Jewish people. Here their spiritual, religious and political identity was shaped. Here they first attained to statehood, created cultural values of national and universal significance and gave to the world the eternal Book of Books."[19] This brings us to the first set of contradictions in Ben-Gurion's Bible.

When Ben-Gurion told the British that "the Bible is our Mandate," it is easy to dismiss this claim as mere rhetoric. Had Ben-Gurion been a pious Jew, this statement to would be self-explanatory. If God promised the Jewish people the Land of Israel, then took it away for bad behavior, God could give it back when it suited Him, just as Rashi had commented to Genesis 1:1. Ben-Gurion often expressed messianic aspirations for the new state, and had his own ideas about redemption. He was no Rashi, however, and his idea of redemption was far removed from either that of Rashi or today's settlers. If Ben-Gurion was closer to Spinoza than Rashi theologically, how then could the Bible be a "mandate" for the Zionist movement or as a claim to rightful possession of any part of the land of Israel? For Ben-Gurion, Jewish longevity, influence, and national self-consciousness were inextricable from the Bible's legacy. The Bible stamped Jewish character, yet was itself a creation of the Jewish people. Since the Bible remains in the realm of the human, however, it is necessarily temporal, not eternal. How can any ancient classic (Homer's *Iliad* or Virgil's *The Aeneid*) bestow political rights in a contemporary context? Ben-Gurion spoke frankly of the Bible's origins:

> The Bible, in my humble opinion, is the creation of the Jewish people, and did not come to it from outside. [I also do not accept the explanation that Job was translated from another language.] Without a doubt the Bible was one the chief factors in the molding of the image of our people; but this factor came from within the people. The greatness of the Bible is the greatness of the spirit of the Jewish people; it is the fruit of its spirit, the fruit of the great men of our people.[20]

But what created the Jewish people and how to account for their genius in creating the Bible? To this objection, Ben-Gurion offers the stock nineteenth-century answer: the Jews possessed a spirit of genius in the ethical arena, just as the Greeks possessed a genius for literature, or the Romans for laws. The claim that the Jewish people possessed an ethical "genius," was made explicitly by Abraham Geiger, who agreed that the biblical era represented a highpoint in Jewish creativity and humanism. Ahad Ha'am also inclined to this view of high ethical standards as a national characteristic. Centuries of relative Jewish powerlessness, combined with nineteenth-century nationalist rhetorical impulse fueled this line of argument. In retrospect, it is much easier to maintain purity of aims when one is not engaged in struggle, as Zionism was and as Israel is. This leads to a second source of ambivalence for Ben-Gurion, that of biblical humanism versus biblical nationalism.

BIBLICAL HUMANISM VS. BIBLICAL NATIONALISM

Among the many contrasting views of Ahad Haam and Berdichevsky, one difference can be isolated as the former's preference for the Latter Prophets with its soaring ethical dicta, and the latter's preference for the Former Prophets with its essentially political-military narrative. On the one hand, Ben-Gurion never tired of praising the humanistic values of the Bible. One member of his famed Bible study group at his kibbutz home of Sde Boker in the 1960s recalls the biblical quotes that were inscribed on Ben-Gurion's coffee table: "Nation Shall Not Lift Sword Against Nation," "Love Thy Brother As Thyself," and so forth. He cited the high-minded ethics of the Latter Prophets in numerous addresses and clearly considered the synthesis of spirituality and physicality desirable, as Ahad Haam had argued in "Flesh and Spirit." Ben-Gurion also followed Ahad Haam in his belief in an eternal Jewish essence; both men were drawn to vague, organistic metaphors of the Jewish people's survival through the history of "national uniqueness."[21] Ben-Gurion sided with Ahad Haam in his unwillingness to accept that the secularization of the Jewish people necessarily entailed a de-Judaizing of that people, a prospect that Berdichevsky, Brenner, and the "Canaanites" embraced. For Ben-Gurion and Ahad Haam, Israelite and Jewish history displayed consistency, though as Jewish nationalists, both considered the diaspora setting of most of that history inferior. Ben-Gurion differed from Ahad Haam on the issue of biblical historicity. For Ahad Haam, the reality of even so central a figure as Moses was a peripheral concern. Not so Ben-Gurion, for whom the basic historicity of the Bible was required as a basis of national guidance. Ben-Gurion adopted aspects of Ahad Haam's reading of Moses, but rejected his "postmodern" concession.[22] Writing in 1982, Benjamin Beit Hallahmi (Haifa University) complained, "Most Israelis today, as a result of Israeli education, regard the Bible as a source of reliable historical information of a secular, political kind. The Zionist version of Jewish history accepts most biblical legends about the beginnings of Jewish history, minus divine intervention. Abraham, Isaac and Jacob are treated as historical figures. The descent into Egypt and the Exodus are phases in the secular history of a developing people, as is the conquest by Joshua. The Biblical order of events is accepted, but this interpretation is nationalist and secular."[23]

Ben-Gurion cited the Bible as a text of conflict resolution, a use that would be dismissed by both Palestinian Arabs and Revisionists, albeit for entirely different reasons. As a principal formulator of statism, Ben-Gurion also deployed the Bible as a text that could solve class conflict, or at least, ease the tensions between worker and owner, an important element in the transition of Zionism from class-movement to nation.[24] The utility of the Bible for current day problems, may be found in Ben-Gurion in an obsessively "presentist" manner, as if the Bible obviously applied to the 1950s.[25]

Nevertheless, as Anita Shapira has argued, as the national struggle between Jews and Arabs exacerbated, the parable of national struggle in the Bible loomed larger and larger. Joshua, the biblical character with whom Ben-Gurion most closely identified, conquered the land of Canaan in the traditional account. With the possible exception of the book that comes right after it (Judges) there is no more martial and violent book in the Hebrew Bible. Ben-Gurion went so far as to say that he considered Joshua greater than Moses, who, after all, prepared the nation for the Promised Land, but did not lead them into it. Yet Ben-Gurion's evaluation of Joshua's accomplishment is noteworthy precisely because it would certainly have been possible to read the story of Joshua, and the Bible overall, as praising brute force, "a wall of iron," in Jabotinsky's phrase. Ben-Gurion does not do that. As a matter of fact, the heart of Joshua's accomplishment, in his eyes, is to be found in the book's final chapter, where Joshua established a unified Hebrew nation on the basis of mutual agreement:

> Chapter 24 in Joshua, with the possible exception of several verses which were added later, is one of the principal and most important documents—if not the most important, in the history of the life of our people. . . . This chapter bears the stamp of historical truth and isn't adorned with miracles and supernatural feats. This is a lofty dialogue between the nations leader—its political and spiritual leader—and the nation's most prominent people from every stratum of society.[26]

Ben-Gurion's democratic tendencies checked his admiration for conquest and the *Realpolitik* of the political right. His secularism checked any impulse to celebrate Israel's victory as God-given. The relative absence of God as an actor in Joshua 24 where God is invoked by the Israelites, but as standard of national fealty, probably attracted Ben-Gurion, and the consensual nature of the social compact in Joshua 24 is far-removed from the dynamics of the covenant at Sinai. Unlike the miraculous events at Sinai, which had limited utility for the modern nation, the covenant renewal at Schechem had plenty of relevance. Thus, what drew Ben-Gurion to this chapter above all is pretty clear: the nation was created by consent of governed and from the bottom up, not the top down. Jews are not the Chosen people; they are, however, the choosing people.[27]

At least in theory, Ben-Gurion believed that right, not might, should guide Arab-Jewish relations. In practice, his record is much cloudier, and one suspects that Ben-Gurion projected an ideal situation on the past to compensate for a murkier present. Ben-Gurion professed wildly inflated views of the Bible's current applicability and moral clarity:

> Anyone carefully perusing the Bible will find a solution to the two crucial problems of humankind in our time: the problem of capital and labor in society and the problem of war and peace among the nations.[28]

Modern readers of the Bible have accomplished a great deal in regard to creating a meaningful text. But the Bible in our time has not stopped economic privation or ended bloodshed—in the Middle East or anywhere else.

BIBLE AS CREATIVE HIGHPOINT IN JEWISH HISTORY

Like most Zionists, Ben-Gurion believed that the Bible represented a highpoint in Jewish creativity. In a response to an issue of *Davar*, Ben-Gurion took umbrage at the suggestion that the *Midrash*, a running rabbinic commentary to the Bible, could actually surpass the original text itself in creativity or literary quality. In "The Bible Is Illumined by Its Own Light," Ben-Gurion revealingly commented that "large segments of orthodox Judaism relate negatively to the Bible and see it as an almost heretical book. In any case, the Talmud, the Responsa and the Midrashim are closer to their hearts."[29] While "rabbinic" literature did occupy most of the advanced school years in a traditional yeshiva, by dint of both its size and technical difficulty, it would be perverse to present the Orthodox view of the Bible as a heretical book—unless, of course, one meant that the Orthodox viewed the academic, secular study of the Bible as heretical—an entirely different charge. When Ben-Gurion goes on to attack Rashi and traditional commentary as abstract (*mufshat*) and detached from the realia of the Bible, Ben-Gurion is simply drawing up lines of battle: on the one side, Zionist, Israelo-centric, and biblical; on the other, Orthodox, diasporic, and rabbinic. Nobody familiar with Rashi, as Ben-Gurion surely was, could characterize him as "abstract." Rashi used illustrations, contemporary French synonyms, simple math and a slew of other explanatory devices to render what he took to be the teachings of Torah. But Ben-Gurion believed that traditional Judaism lacked the one critical element to unpacking the biblical text properly, a national orientation toward the text:

> Without a familiarity with the environment, there can be no understanding of the Bible.... During the exile the image of our people was distorted, and the image of the Bible twisted. Christian Bible scholars, with Christian and anti-Semitic motives, turned the Bible toward Christianity. Even Jewish commentators were uprooted from the environment of the Bible—from its spiritual and physical climate—have not yet been able to understand the book of Books properly. Only now that we have again become a free nation on its own soil, and can again breathe in the air which surrounded the Bible at its creation, has the time come, it appears to me, to deal with the essence of the truth of the Bible historically and geographically, as well as religiously and culturally.[30]

And again, from the same essay:

> The rebirth of Israel and the War of Independence placed the bible before me in a new light. After I delved into it, considering the facts of the War of Independence and the settlement of Israel in our day, questions were raised within me to which biblical commentators in Israel throughout the generations had not paid sufficient attention, because to them the concepts nation, tribes, conquest war, geography, Israel, settlement, and mother tongue were abstract concepts.[31]

We will return to the pointed attack on Christian interpreters. For now, let us fully register this deprecation of Jewish exegetical tradition. I would stress both the pragmatic elements of this formulation, namely, the appearance of a free nation under its own governance; and, the more mystical ones, namely, the connection between a people and its native soil as the sole factor enabling creativity.

Ben-Gurion's laudation of the Bible over the rabbinic literature was standard Zionist fare, but the lengths to which Ben-Gurion took this dichotomy invited rebuttal. An article in *Davar* praising Midrash infuriated Ben-Gurion. Avraham Kariv, author of *Seven Pillars of Biblical Wisdom*, could hardly be accused of lacking enthusiasm for the Bible, but he too found Ben-Gurion's assessment of rabbinic literature lacking. Ben-Gurion's subsequent debate with the author Hayim Hazaz revealed clearly the weakness of Ben-Gurion's elevation of the Bible.[32] Hazaz argued, on historical grounds, that rabbinic literature provided the real link between generations of Jews; whatever the Zionist movement did to reinvigorate the biblical past, the link had been the rabbinic traditions, not longing for Zion. Hazaz rejected the idea that the Bible exhausted the spiritual resources of Judaism; famously, philosopher Yeshayahu Leibowitz charged Ben-Gurion with "bibliolatry." Ben-Gurion rejected the idea that love of Tanach was idolatry by any name, but he also backpedaled somewhat, agreeing with Hazaz that without the Mishnah one could not know Hebrew.[33] That concession could have been a major one: the Mishnah was written in Hebrew, in the land of Israel, and after the destruction of Jewish sovereignty. In other words, the Mishnah straddled the border between biblical and rabbinic and challenged his dichotomy of Jewish history. Ben-Gurion was a politician not a logician: he did not pursue the example.

On occasion, Ben-Gurion dated "Zionism" from the destruction of the Second Temple: "From when can one date the Jewish return to Israel? One can say, therefore, without being accused of mysticism that the Jewish return to autonomy in Israel really dates from the fall of Jerusalem and Masada in the eighth decade of the Common Era."[34] But elsewhere, he strikes a more radical note. For Ben-Gurion, the Maccabean dynasty was short-lived and impressive mainly as a national refusal to assimilate; Masada and the bar

Kochba revolt were outright defeats. Ben-Gurion found the Second Commonwealth on a far lower level than the first. Abraham, Moses, David, and, above all, Joshua were Ben-Gurion's heroes. Although Ben-Gurion lavished praise on the Persian Era King Cyrus for allowing the restoration of Jewish sovereignty, and conceded that the religious consolidation of Israel took place in the Persian period, his main interest was in Nehemiah's account of the combination of labor and defense needed to rebuild the walls of Jerusalem. Granted, this speech was given to the IDF on the theme of the army's role in educating the nation, but Ben-Gurion's preference for early events in Israel's history is consistent. Rather radically, Ben-Gurion imagined a nation interruptus, in which the entire Jewish people treaded water from 586 BCE all the way to the beginning of Zionism. It might be mentioned that this explicit preference for First Temple over Second Temple is found in both Spinoza and Mendelssohn. Ben-Gurion's admiration for Spinoza was boundless, though his attempts to rescind Spinoza's excommunication, unsuccessful.

BEN-GURION, HIGHER CRITICS, ISRAELITE AUTOCHTHONY

We have examined Ben-Gurion's extreme elevation of the biblical past. But there are other Jewish elements in Ben-Gurion's orientation to the Bible, if only in his animosity toward German Protestant Bible scholarship. Today, scholars agree that Julius Wellhausen and Source Critics generally possessed a negative view of what they derogatorily called "Spätjudentum." The Jewish response to this attack on the Mosaic nature of the Torah and the so-called degeneration of Second Temple Judaism was transcontinental; in Israel, it included Cassuto, Segal, Kaufmann, and that pioneering archaeologist, Eliezer Sukenik, who called for a "Jewish archaeology." All these rejected the academic characterization of Judaism in the centuries before Jesus as "spent."

Although Segal and Cassuto wrote books confuting Source Criticism, the most sustained rejoinder to its findings may be found in Yehezkel Kaufmann (1889–1963).[35] Kaufmann made maximalist claims for the antiquity of Israel's presence in the land and for the autochthonous nature of Israel's faith. Kaufmann poured his monumental learning into his multivolume *History of the Israelite Faith* and his meditation on the diaspora, *Exile and Estrangement*. His influence on Israeli Bible scholarship in Ben-Gurion's era and at New York's Jewish Theological Seminary in the immediate post–World War II years can hardly be overestimated. Steven Geller has highlighted Kaufmann's dialectical relationship with Wellhausen. On almost every point, whether dating individual documents, assessing the nature of Israelite faith, or judging Israel's dependence on external cultures, Kaufmann dissented vigorously from Wellhausen. Indeed, by the end of his career Kaufmann was still battling Wellhausen, largely oblivious to ascent of very different methods in the field of Bible, including Form Criticism and the study of oral traditions. Kaufmann wrote in modern Hebrew and not until Moshe Greenberg translated and condensed Kaufmann's biblical magnum opus into *History of Israelite Religion*, giving it a second lease on life for English-only readers, did Kaufmann's conceptions begin to receive much scholarly treatment, much of it beyond the interest of the general reader.[36] But a few highlights of Kaufmann's approach are worth noting. As Nahum Sarna wrote:

> Most important for Kaufmann's thesis is his conclusion that the "Torah book" was fixed before the organization of the prophetic literature had worked its decisive influence upon the people. For Kaufmann, the implications of all this for the history of the religion of Israel are clear. The Torah becomes, once again, the starting point for historical inquiry. The sources do furnish us with genuine traditions about the times with which they purport to deal. Monotheism appears as a popular national phenomenon pervading the earliest traditions and molding the earliest institutions of Israel. This, indeed, is the very core of Kaufmann's thesis, the elaboration of which takes up the more than 2,500 pages of the as yet unfinished Hebrew original.[37]

Ben-Gurion accurately identified himself as a Kaufmann disciple,[38] despite their numerous disputes over particulars. When it came to highlighting the connection of the people Israel and the land of Israel, Ben-Gurion went even further than his teacher. Ben-Gurion held radical views of both Abraham and Exodus:

> My first assumption is that the Jewish people or the Hebrew people was born in Israel and grew up in Israel even before the days of Abraham, as one of the nations of Canaan, and, at that time was scattered in the south, central sector, and the north with its spiritual and political capital in Shechem. But, in my opinion, only a few families, among the most highly ranked, descended into Egypt. The remaining masses of the children of Israel remained among the peoples of Canaan.[39]

Even Kaufmann never claimed that that there were Hebrews in the land before Abraham, or that most Israelites never went down to Egypt but rather, remained in Canaan. But any approach to the Bible that did not consistently reaffirm its status as a Zionist mandate ultimately had no appeal to Ben-Gurion; at the end of the day, his reading of the Bible was tendentiously political.

This particular reading of the early history of the nation ignited a firestorm. On May 12, 1960, Ben-Gurion called a press conference to report these speculations on ancient Israel, and after *The Jerusalem Post* dutifully reported these remarks, the National Religious Party moved a motion of non-confidence, accusing Ben-Gurion of lending support to the "Canaanites." Ben-Gurion tried to prove an Exodus of about six hundred people through biblical arithmetic, genealogical analysis, and the rendering of the Hebrew word *elef* as "family" rather than "thousand."[40] His eagerness to enter into the nitty-gritty of Bible scholarship was typical. Ben-Gurion, insatiable bibliophile and late-night reader, liked to be thought of as an *intellectual*. Yet his interests were ultimately practical, not academic. How would Israel sustain itself in its years of formation and ingathering? How could a small state sustain itself economically and forge diplomatic alliances? How did the Jewish people survive indefinite hostility? These questions, asked repeatedly by Ben-Gurion of the Bible, were blatantly driven by the imperatives of the present—there is little sense of an unfolding academic discourse.

In conclusion, Ben-Gurion's role in forwarding the centrality of the Bible should not be underestimated. The Bible study group at Kibbutz Sde Boker was a serious and sincere meeting of professors, Bible-enthusiasts, and family favorites. As recalled by Haim Gevaryahu, the group met every fortnight for a couple of hours, usually until Paula Ben-Gurion announced that her husband needed his rest. The symbolism of the nation's founding father spending his time surrounded by fellow intellectuals studying the Jewish mandate corresponds to that of the founding generals excavating the Jewish patrimony. One struggles to imagine a modern parallel. Thomas Jefferson assembling fellow Virginians at Monticello to pore over the words of Jesus seems plausible; Jefferson did, after all, author a New Testament with the "superstitious" sections removed. But imagining Bismarck at Berlin, studying Luther with a cohort of Prussian Junkers? This fictional scene boggles the imagination. Consider again the no-confidence vote prompted by Ben-Gurion's claims of a limited Exodus. If Angela Merkel declared Otto the Great overrated, or Emmanuel Macron called the Merovingians louts, who would care? What other nation would be so *bookish* about its identity?

NOTES

1. In Hebrew, one simply refers to "the situation" ("ha-matzav") a word both canonical and euphemistic. As to addressing the relative importance of this issue in the wider region, I leave that question open to others more competent than I.

2. I take it as axiomatic that Israel is necessary for the health of world Jewry, and I take it as equally axiomatic that a healthy Jewry is essential for Jewish Studies. As to the debate between Jewish Studies and Judaic Studies, also raised at the conference, the preferences for one or the other term are well known and not worth rehashing.

3. Relatively recent usages such as MENA (Middle East and North Africa) and Islamicate Jewry are welcome terminological attempts to encompass the entirely of the Jewish experiences in this region.

4. Reinharz and Mendes-Flohr, it should be noted, made many other sage additions and rearrangements in this third edition of *JMW*—the most relevant to our topic being the decision *not* to end the anthology with Zionism and the Holocaust, clearly an antiteleological move, but rather, with the section "Jewish Identity Challenged and Redefined," which one could argue is the only "constant" for the modern period.

5. I disagree with the implication that Jewish Studies is headed toward an enclave or a cul de sac. To judge from the training of scholars, the membership composition, and the topics at the annual Association of Jewish Studies, the field—in America at least—looks less and less like an enclave and more like any other branch of the Humanities, as well it should. I will confess to a smidgen of nostalgia for the time where everyone at AJS, and in the field, had studied a little Bible and knew a little Hebrew. But my point is that the caricature of the AJS as a preserve of male-only ex-yeshiva students is exactly that, a caricature, not reality. For the sexism and ethnocentrism—implicit and explicit—that once prevailed at AJS, I have no nostalgia whatsoever.

6. See the special issue of *Shofar* (32, no. 4 [Summer 2014]) on a different approach to teaching the introductory course in Jewish Studies.

7. The following example draws from my book *The Making of the Modern Jewish Bible* (Rowman & Littlefield, 2011, paperback 2016), but will serve to illustrate the points made above. Also, to address a particular lacuna, I have not yet read the new biography by Tom Segev, *David Ben-Gurion: A State at Any Price* (New York: Farrar Strauss, and Giroux, 2018), but Segev's works have been uniformly superb, and important.

8. His assertion that the Bible is part of Jewish history comes from a teacher (me) who must constantly remind undergraduates that Judaism is not equivalent to the religion of ancient Israel, and that ancient Israelites differ from contemporary Israelis.

9. Michael Keren, Anita Shapira, Yaakov Shavit, Uriel Simon, and Yael Zerubavel have all addressed the role of the Bible in Israeli identity formations searchingly. Dan Kurzman's older, and less critical, *Ben-Gurion. Prophet of Fire* (New York: Simon and Schuster, 1983) subdivided his biography into three sections (Moses/Joshua/Isaiah), titled each chapter from a verse of Scripture, and explicitly described the Bible as Ben-Gurion's inspiration from youth onward. Kurzman probably overstated matters. But the more circumspect Shabtai Teveth noted that Ben-Gurion attended a "modern" primary school by shtetl standards and presumably learned Bible and Hebrew. See Shabtai Teveth, *Ben-Gurion. The Burning-Ground, 1886–1948* (Boston: Houghton Mifflin, 1987), 12–13.

10. Teveth, *Ben-Gurion*, xi–xv.

11. Yaacov Shavit and Mordecai Eran, *The Hebrew Bible Reborn: From Holy Scripture to Book of Books* (Berlin: Walter de Gruyter, 2007), 494n44. By 1956, the Bible in state-secular Israeli middle-schools occupied four to five hours/week, thirty weeks per year, but also departed from Ben-Gurion's preferences in that it increased the attention paid to the Pentateuch, and encouraged some recognition of the weekly order of Torah readings.

12. Michael Keren, *Ben-Gurion and the Intellectuals: Power, Knowledge and Charisma* (DeKalb, IL: Northern Illinois University Press, 1983), 105.

13. Shapira, Simon, Amit, Shavit all stress the relative abandonment of the Bible in the 1970s and beyond to the nationalist right and to other sources of Jewish identity. In my nonexpert view, this contrast has been somewhat overestimated; the Tanach still exists as an important element in Israeli culture.

14. Anita Shapira, "The Bible and Israeli Identity," *AJS Review* 28 (2004): 11–42; "Ben-Gurion and the Bible: The Forging of an Historical Narrative?" *Middle Eastern Studies* 33, no. 4 (1997): 645–74; *New Jews/Old Jews* (Hebrew) (Tel Aviv: Am Oved, 1997); *The Bible and Israeli Identity* (Jerusalem: Hebrew University Press, 2005).

15. Shapira, "The Bible and Israeli Identity," 21n41.

16. Ben-Gurion found the Bible relevant to America's racial question: "Had the Americans heeded Amos, they never would have adopted slavery and would be avoiding all the racial tensions at present in America." Jews had it easier than African-Americans, "Thanks to our Bible, the Jewish reinsertion into a creative stream of human history, as realized by the return to Israel, has been relatively easy" (*Recollections* [London: Macdonald, 1970], 125–28).

17. Ben-Gurion, *Recollections*, 121.

18. Arthur Hertzberg, *The Zionist Idea* (Philadelphia: JPS, 1997), 559–70; On Jabotinsky, see Michael Stanislawski, *Zionism and the fin de siècle* (Berkeley: University of California Press, 2001), 116–238.

19. Nili Wazana, *All the Boundaries of the Land: The Promised Land in Biblical Thought in Light of the Ancient Near East* (Winona Lake, IN: Eisenbrauns, 2013). Wazana has pointed out that the Bible emphatically presents Israelites as immigrants not indigenous residents.

20. Jonathan Kolatch (ed.), *Ben-Gurion Looks at the Bible* (New York: Jonathan David, 1972), 49; see also Mordechai Kogan (ed.), *Ben-Gurion and the Tanach* (Beer Sheva, 1989).

21. Kolatch, *Ben-Gurion Looks at the Bible*, 34.

22. Both Ben-Gurion and Ahad Haam regarded Moses as a positive model. See Arnold Band, "The Ahad Ha-Am and Berdyczewski Polarity," in *At the Crossroads: Essays on Ahad Haam*, Jacques Kornberg (ed.) (Albany: SUNY, 1993), 49–59.

23. Nur Masalha, *The Bible and Zionism. Invented Traditions, Archaeology and Post-Colonialism in Israel-Palestine* (London-New York: Zed Books, 2007), 21. While Zionism did lean on the Bible, the Jewish debate was principally internally directed, at least before 1967.

24. Mitchell Cohen, *Zion and State. Nation, Class and the Shaping of Modern Israel*, 2nd ed. (New York: Columbia University Press, 1992).

25. David Ben-Gurion: "In this respect, the Book of Genesis is most revealing. Christian Gospel begins with the birth of Jesus; the Koran with Mohammed. Torah, however, doesn't start either with Moses or even Abraham, the original Jew, the man who traveled from Chaldea into unknown territory beyond the Euphrates River thereby becoming a pioneer and the first 'Hebrew' or 'man who crossed over' the river. Torah begins with creation and we are told that six days after conceiving the light, the grass, and all the animals, on the final day of genesis a man and a woman were made and they were in the image of God. Of course speaking personally as one who is non-religious, I believe that theology reverses the true sequence of events. To me it is clear that God was created in the image of man as the latter's explanation to himself of the mystery of his own earthly presence." [Kolatch, *Ben-Gurion Looks at the Bible*, 15; Ben-Gurion, *Recollections*, 19.]

26. Kolatch, *Ben-Gurion Looks at the Bible*, 238.

27. Ben-Gurion, *Recollections*, 125–28. And again: "Truly in chapter 24 of the Book of Joshua we hear that Israel chose God, and not the other way around. It is inconceivable that this chapter was inserted later, because no one would dare to contradict the accepted tradition that God chose the Israelites, and to fabricate a story that the people chose God. But it is understood that the people did choose God—was captivated by a faith in one God—it became a chosen people by virtue of having been the one and only nation which for many hundreds of years believed in one God."

28. Kolatch, *Ben-Gurion Looks at the Bible*, 108–35.

29. Kolatch, *Ben-Gurion*, 44.

30. Kolatch, *Ben-Gurion*, 53.

31. Kolatch, *Ben-Gurion*, 13.

32. Shapira, *The Bible and Israeli Identity*, 139–57.

33. Shapira, *The Bible*, 144.

34. Kolatch, *Ben-Gurion Looks at the Bible*, 1–43.

35. Thomas Krapf, *Yehezkel Kaufmann* (Berlin: Institut Kirsche und Judentum, 1990).

36. Leo Schwartz's successful anthology *Great Ages and Ideas of the Jewish People* (1956) assigned the essay on the biblical period to Kaufmann, whose views were even more out of the scholarly mainstream by then than when he originally published them.

37. Nahum Sarna, "From Wellhausen to Kaufmann," *Midstream* 7, no. 3 (1961): 64–74, 68.

38. Shavit and Eran, *The Hebrew Bible Reborn*, 459.

39. Ben-Gurion, "The Eternality of Israel," Government Annual 1953, cited in Shavit and Eran, *The Hebrew Bible Reborn*, 484.

40. Keren, *Ben-Gurion and the Intellectuals*, 100–103; Shavit and Eran, *The Hebrew Bible Reborn*, 455–59.

BIBLIOGRAPHY

Band, Arnold. "The Ahad Ha-Am and Berdyczewski Polarity." In *At the Crossroads: Essays on Ahad Haam*, edited by Jacques Kornberg, 49–59. Albany: SUNY, 1993.
Ben-Gurion, David. *Recollections*. London: Macdonald, 1970.
Cohen, Mitchell. *Zion and State. Nation, Class and the Shaping of Modern Israel*. 2nd ed. New York: Columbia University Press, 1992.
Hertzberg, Arthur. *The Zionist Idea*. Philadelphia: JPS, 1997.
Keren, Michael. *Ben-Gurion and the Intellectuals: Power, Knowledge and Charisma*. DeKalb, IL: Northern Illinois University Press, 1983.
Kogan, Mordechai (ed.). *Ben-Gurion and the Tanach*. Beer Sheva, 1989.
Kolatch, Jonathan (ed.). *Ben-Gurion Looks at the Bible*. New York: Jonathan David, 1972.
Krapf, Thomas. *Yehezkel Kaufmann*. Berlin: Institut Kirsche und Judentum, 1990.
Kurzman, Dan. *Ben-Gurion. Prophet of Fire*. New York: Simon and Schuster, 1983.
Levenson, Alan J. *The Making of the Modern Jewish Bible: How Scholars in Germany, Israel and America Transformed an Ancient Text*. Lanham, MD: Rowman & Littlefield, 2011.
Masalha, Nur. *The Bible and Zionism. Invented Traditions, Archaeology and Post-Colonialism in Israel-Palestine*. London-New York: Zed Books, 2007.
Sarna, Nahum."From Wellhausen to Kaufmann." *Midstream* 7, no. 3 (1961): 64–74.
Shapira, Anita. "Ben-Gurion and the Bible: The Forging of an Historical Narrative?" *Middle Eastern Studies* 33, no. 4 (1997): 645–74.
———. *New Jews/Old Jews* [Hebrew]. Tel Aviv: Am Oved, 1997.
———. "The Bible and Israeli Identity." *AJS Review* 28 (2004): 11–42.
———. *The Bible and Israeli Identity*. Jerusalem: Hebrew University Press, 2005.
Shavit, Yaacov, and Mordecai Eran. *The Hebrew Bible Reborn: From Holy Scripture to Book of Books*. Berlin: Walter de Gruyter, 2007.
Stanislawski, Michael. *Zionism and the fin de siècle*. Berkeley: University of California Press, 2001.
Teveth, Shabtai. *Ben-Gurion. The Burning-Ground, 1886–1948*. Boston: Houghton Mifflin, 1987.
Wazana, Nili. *All the Boundaries of the Land: The Promised Land in Biblical Thought in Light of the Ancient Near East*. Winona Lake, IN: Eisenbrauns, 2013.

Chapter Three

Meta-Halacha and Real Life

Using Jewish Thought Methodology in Solving Religion and State Issues in Contemporary Israel

Yossi Ben-Harush

One of the most recurrent topics in Israeli society today is the issue of "church and state," and the contradictions each exhibits from time to time. This issue arises regularly, bringing secular and religious elements within Israeli society into some manner of conflict.

As is well known, in Israel the "church" and the state are deeply intertwined.[1] Due to agreements made by the religious parties and the government over the years, and due to the religious context of Israeli society, the public sphere is constantly beset by these topics.

Most of the thought given to this issue by the general public in the political realm is based on sociological and political thought. It is commonly believed that if we will apply negotiation techniques these issues will be solved.[2] Unfortunately, none of the solutions put forth so far by politicians and writers have led to much progress toward the goal of resolving the underlying tensions that feed the ongoing clashes between "church" and state. This chapter attempts to offer a different path for approaching these issues, and, perhaps, hopefully, may even help precipitate a change of mindset regarding them.

To address this issue from the academic point of view: the discipline known as "Jewish Thought" or "Jewish Studies" has allowed us, paraphrasing Foucault, to create an archaeology of the Jewish Text.[3] After almost two hundred years of reading Jewish texts systematically and academically, we can now excavate the sources, influences, and the way each author perceives the world in nearly every Jewish Text. Furthermore, in recent years academics have perfected this system of textual analysis and, having done so, are bringing it to bear with great effect on texts scholars had never considered analyzing before.

In reading contemporary text from a close perspective, we can identify the sources an author chooses to implement in his text, the reasons for this implementation, and the way an author understands these sources. We can even discern what bigger idea may underlie the written text.[4] This becomes even more crucial if we are dealing with a halakhic text. The sources chosen by halakhic authors, and the ways they decide to interpret them, show us their way of thinking and reveals meta-halakhic and theological aspects of their thought. In the halakhic realm, the "Archeology of Text" is more difficult—but has larger implications on everyday life.

We, the scholars, have perfected this system. Yet, can we, following Foucault, use the knowledge generated by this system of analysis to make statements about the current sociopolitical situation?

The answer to this question must be affirmative. As experts in Jewish texts, scholars can and should weigh in on current conversations, based on our familiarity with the sources that underlie this discussion. Our knowledge and connection to Jewish civilization gives us a distinct voice in contemporary Jewish discourse. We can engage in the discussion and better understand the different positions.

Naturally, I believe that this engagement can and will be fruitful in relaxing some of the tensions that plague relations between Jews, Judaism, and the secular state of Israel. This scholarly voice is one which many of the parties would be interested in hearing and may create a common ground with the potential to develop further.

To push this claim further: this a direction Jewish Studies must take to remain relevant. Academic scholars of the "ivory tower" have a responsibility to enter the broader world, using the techniques and systems that they have acquired to solve issues impacting the society they live in. As I will try to show in this chapter, I believe that this was the original plan for "Jewish Studies" as a discipline.

THE CURRENT SITUATION AND THE ROLE OF THE ACADEMIA

There are many reasons why the secular-religious status quo in Israel, established even before statehood itself, has become less stable in recent years. The Haredization of many fields within the Jewish State operates on the one hand, while an openness to varied Jewish perspectives on the "Jewish" way of living operates on the other. Secular Jews in Israel are also reclaiming their right to the public Jewish sphere and are bothered by what is going on today in Israel from the religious perspective now more than ever. Of course, the involvement of American Jewry in those issues is critical as well. Diaspora Jews are looking at the Land of Israel, wishing to claim their right to the culture and options Israel gives to Jews.

The opening of grocery stores on Shabbat; the new section in the Western Wall for non-orthodox Jews, and the recruitment of Haredi youth into the army have become issues discussed in the news media and Knesset Committees. NGOs and other organizations are targeting these issues, hoping to establish a new secular-religious status quo or at least to change the existing one.

Can academic scholars, as text readers, make a difference in this escalated discourse? Yes, they can, and they must. Indeed, now is the most critical time for us to intervene in the discussion. We should try to extract new knowledge that may help us better understand the disagreements. We have already done so for many years with other texts. We crafted the art of understanding every philosophical hint in the *Guide to the Perplexed* and every allegory in the *Zohar*, so why not here? Modern-day Jewish writers use the same terminology and methods of interpretation in their texts because they are, in their eyes, carrying on the same formulas used by previous generations. We should read the text like always and then share our conclusions. If we have the technique (and we do), we need to try implementing it with other texts and try to excavate a fruitful conclusion.

One example demonstrates the case. Before illustrating this example, however, we must acknowledge the difficulties of the approach introduced here.

First, this is a very narrow perspective of the entire situation in Israel. Texts will not reveal the political psychology and inner interests of the different groups involved. Furthermore, a text is always just what the author wanted to share with the world, and we never know what else he or she thought or said on other occasions or thought to themselves.

Second, of course, is that scholars may read and interpret a text incorrectly. This challenge is intensified by the all too real fear that the author misunderstood the sources they relied on. A quoted passage might mean "x" and the author used it with the understanding that it means "y"; the author can misquote and so on, while we as scholars might misinterpret the author through our understanding of the sources they relied on.

In contemporary Jewish writing this is a common phenomenon we are struggling with. Writers today trust the understanding of their predecessors and consider it somewhat holy. A misunderstanding in the past becomes an almost permanent mistake. This may lead the researcher to wrong conclusions, and, instead of helping, the scholar may hurt and perhaps offend the different parties.

Third, and this is a broader problem, we do not have enough distance from our subject of interest. When we address a current topic, it is very difficult to stay objective. The realm of humanities has always tried to stay objective, and here we are forcing it to say something about an issue that might affect everyone involved and have an immediate impact on the Israeli society. Such closeness to the situation can manipulate the reading of the text. Some may say that we will be using another method to say the same thing and that we are forcing academia into politics.

The difficulties I just mentioned are true of any textual analysis methodology, but here it seems those difficulties are especially pronounced. The texts we are dealing with are not a fully elaborated theological manifesto—rather it is a loose collection of compressed and indoctrinated response answers or pamphlets. It becomes a greater task to extract a thesis or a coherent idea from these dense texts when you put these difficulties into consideration.

However, sometimes we need a "fresh view" on issues that seem unsolvable. Even if it is just a small crack or just a mind-teaser, sometimes it is worth the change of perspective. Here I am walking the footsteps of Benjamin Brown, who called this kind of textual study "revealing the unscientific theology."[5] Even if we lack a coherent position on a topic, we need to invest ourselves and use all the knowledge we must come up with something valuable. I believe that we can see the greater ideology of the author from these cracks in the text. If we get familiar with the ideology, we can better understand the set of values and the mind-set the Haredi sector brings to the table of Isreali society.

This notion of understanding the set of values expressed in the writing of a Halachic text, through what remains unwritten, is not new. It has been used extensively by contemporary writers on the subject of Meta-Halacha.[6] For the sake of this chapter, I will describe Meta-Halacha as the set of ideas and beliefs an author holds in mind while writing a Halachic answer or essay. Researchers have used various academic tools to reveal the Meta-Halachic notions in halachic texts, and my work here follows after them. One scholar who has influenced this analysis greatly is Ariel Picard—one of the first to use sociological and cultural aspects in the deconstruction of a text.[7] By implementing this methodological system, Picard was able to expose the deeper meaning of some of most commonly known Halachic texts in the twentieth century.

Furthermore, the idea of influencing Jewish culture by using Jewish text is not new. Since at least the early days of the *Wissenschaft des Judentums* movement Jewish academic writers wanted to reshape the Jewish public sphere by employing Jewish texts. This idea is most clearly described in the introduction to Zunz's famous book *On the Sermons*.[8] Zunz describes his study as one that needs to impact the way that Judaism lays itself out.[9]

In this chapter I would like to follow these two notions, and combine them, in order to achieve a new way to deal with these burning issues. I would like to expose the meta-halachic ideas behind some of the Rabbinical writers on the "church and state" situation in Israel—and by doing so try to change the way we look at those issues.

THE NONORTHODOX SECTION IN THE WESTERN WALL AND THE SODOM SIN

The example illustrated in this chapter focuses on a problem many Israelis believe is among the most prominent within the secular-religious status quo debate: the new section in the Western Wall Plaza and one of the leading figures in the Rabbinical politic sphere—Rabbi Shlomo Moshe Amar. Rabbi Amar is currently the Chief Rabbi of Jerusalem and the former Sephardic Chief Rabbi of Israel. He has spoken very loudly against the new section in the Western Wall on many occasions.

This is an issue that has impacted Israeli society and its relationship with American Jewry for several years. In 2013, the Israeli government assigned a part of the Western Wall Plaza for nonorthodox denominations to pray and conduct religious rituals. By doing so, the government fulfilled a longtime demand from mostly American Jews. This was a major political and public debate that involved lobbying on many sides. Orthodox Rabbis, such as Rabbi Amar, were asked about this decision and, as expected, they strongly objected.

On one occasion, Rabbi Amar published an open letter addressing his strong resentment. Many important Rabbis signed the letter when it was released.[10] This letter made headlines in Israel because Rabbi Amar wrote a controversial remark in it. Rabbi Amar suggests that it is better to let a demolition company destroy the Western Wall entirely than to give non-Orthodox denominations of Judaism a place to pray near it. This harsh statement, though shocking, will not be this chapter's primary focus. I would like to discuss something that fewer readers noticed or paid attention to. It is a reference that Rabbi Amar makes in the middle of the letter, easily missed in a cursory reading. The reference is to a medieval text written by Rabbi Isaac Arama.

Rabbi Arama, or "Baal Ha'Akeda," after his great book *Akedat Yitzchak*, was a famous preacher in the fifteenth century who lived in Spain for most of his life.[11] His book is considered one of the important voices of medieval Jewry in Spain and in other places after the Alhambra Decree from March 31, 1492.

Rabbi Amar's reference is to one of Rabbi Arama's sermons regarding the divine punishment of Sodom.[12] In the middle of this sermon, Rabbi

Arama describes a compelling case within the communities surrounding his own. In those communities, brothels employing Jewish women were established, and the members of the community wished to embrace them and support them financially.[13] Interestingly enough, their motivation was a halakhic one. They reasoned that it was better for Jewish men to have sexual encounters with single, halakhically pure Jewish women rather than with non-Jewish women or, even worse, married women. After these communities came up with this idea, they began asking the Rabbis around them for approval. Word of this got to Rabbi Arama, and he opposed it, going so far as to give this phenomenon the appellation of a "Sodom Sin."

The most interesting part of Arama's writing on the topic is that his major problem (for which he calls this a "Sodom Sin") was not the normalization of prostitution in the community but the idea that community institutions would approve it. He was bothered by the nerve of the community to ask for rabbinical approval. For him, this kind of sin is unbearable. He writes: "Those who do not understand why this is wrong don't understand the divine wisdom and have no part in the godly Torah."[14]

According to Rabbi Arama, some things in life are just wrong according to the Torah even if it seems that Halacha might permit them. He does not say that this is wrong because of the moral aspects, but rather that there is a Divine Wisdom given to those who understand the deeper meaning of the Torah and this Wisdom will not permit these things to happen. If the community does not understand why the brothels are wrong—they don't possess this wisdom. Rabbi Arama doesn't lecture the people supporting the brothels by saying that they are engaged in a morally impaired deed. Rather, he insists that they have no part in the Torah even though they come in the name of Halacha.

Returning to Rabbi Amar's invocation of this sermon in his open letter on the Western Wall: Amar quotes this sermon deliberately and means something by doing so. Rabbi Amar is not comparing the new section of the Western Wall to the establishment of community-run brothels. Rather, he makes what he thinks is a critical point about religious affairs in Israel today. By quoting the sermon, Rabbi Amar is saying that the situation in the Kotel is not a halakhic problem but is in fact a problem with the religious community in Israel allowing something that does not correlate with divine wisdom.

The term here is fascinating. "Divine Wisdom" is not the Halacha or the interpretation of a canonical text, but rather some kind of knowledge which those who are familiar with the divine possess.

In his responsa book, Rabbi Amar quotes the same text from "Baal Ha'Akeda" regarding a different issue.[15] Therein, he is asked about giving a Kashrut certification only for weekdays for restaurants that serve seven days and by that desecrating the Shabbat. Rabbis in the Northern part of Israel decided to give these restaurants a Kashrut Certification with the intention of helping them make a living from Kashrut keepers during the week and non-Kashrut keepers during the weekend, thereby providing Kashrut keepers with more dining options, and incentivizing the restaurants to remain committed to Kashrut laws.

In this case too, Rabbi Amar refers to the concept of "Divine Wisdom":

> We can create a situation where those restaurant owners are not violating the Shabbat. We can find a halakhic solution, but this is also not in correlation with the Divine Wisdom. We, as the Orthodox establishment—cannot allow this to happen.[16]

Rabbi Amar says that this will create contempt for the Orthodox establishment, and people would think that a Kashrut certification is something to be toyed with. Some days it is there, and on the weekends it's not.

DA'AT TORAH AND THE CHANGE IN ATTITUDE

Now, after focusing on this reference, what can be learned from this discussion? First, we can say that that Rabbi Amar seems to recognize that the issue at stake in the Kotel affair is not a halakhic issue. Maybe it lives in the realm of "Divine Wisdom." The Western Wall Plaza is not a synagogue, and not even a holy place, in halakhic terms. Even if we say it is—praying in this place according to non-Orthodox custom should not interfere with such holiness. The issue here isn't about synagogue laws, but rather the problem of the Orthodox public sphere and its presentation.

To see what the problem really is, we need to discern what exactly is this "Divine Wisdom," which caused Rabbi Amar to make such a bold statement, is based on. To better understand this term, we need to explore another which is a close relative of "Divine Wisdom"—"Daat Torah."

Daat Torah is a term which has evolved considerably since its first appearance in the Talmud. After scholar Benjamin Brown's comprehensive article on the subject,[17] we can say that Daat Torah is somewhat of a mystical power that the wise Rabbis are believed to possess which allows them to rule not only on issues regarding Halacha, but also on any and all other matters that come before them. This wisdom is what allows them to give a halakhic answer to nonhalakhic issues.

This is what Rabbi Amar wishes to accomplish here. He wants us, his readers, to know that even though the Halacha is neutral about the new section in the Western Wall, his Halakhically attuned mind nonetheless has a precise answer.

In his Responsa book, Rabbi Amar clearly says that after Baal Ha'Akeda wrote his opinion on the matter, his way of ruling can be used as a halakhic method. Meaning that even though Divine Wisdom is not a basic halakhic tool, following Arama's ruling—it is. The weight of this argument is the same as any other halakhic argument, and we can use it to determine what would be the Rabbi's opinion.

Now, following this brief venture into the realm of the philosophy of the Halacha in Rabbi Amar's writings—what can we say about the issue at hand? What can we add to the discussion about the new section at the Western Wall?

First, I think we need to change our attitude toward it. From my analysis, we can conclude that this is not a dispute between Orthodox Jewry and other Jewish denominations. It is a dispute, in Rabbi Amar's eyes at least, between the Orthodox establishment and those who try to challenge it. The issue here is not who is challenging but rather what is challenged.[18] Here, we can see what Haredi look at as the "Public Sphere." It is not, as more commonly thought, the democratic realm in which we all debate. Rather, as per Haredi conception, it is the community of those who follow godly orders.

Second, the recent attempts to reconcile with those who oppose the new section has been based on political assumptions. It was believed that the Haredi Community would agree to a settlement if they were to be given some political or financial benefits. After considering the situation as I have formulated it here, I think that we need to change that mind-set as well.

This, at least for some, is not a political issue. It is a struggle over the core values of what the community is and is not willing to do. Treating the Haredi position on the matter as if Haredim see the matter as a political bargaining chip harms the process. Try imagining yourselves being told that the basis for your community can be bought with enough money—not only would you refuse, we would perceive the offer itself as a grave insult.

Here we need to dive into the term "political" in this context. When I state that this is not a political issue, I mean this is not only a partisan issue that is used to leverage the interest of the Haredi sector in Israel. It is also an argument about the Haredi voice in wider Israeli discourse. The term "political" is translated differently in the Haredi sphere due to the above-mentioned concept of "Daat Torah." If the Rabbis who rule regarding Kashrut laws are the same ones who determine how we should treat military recruitment laws in Israel, such politics thus (and this is key) become a part of the halakhic way of life. For the Haredi community, Rabbi Amar's ruling, and those of many other Rabbis alongside him, about any aspect of political status, is another way to obey to what God wants.

Third, the Kotel argument is not merely local to our time and place. Some, like Rabbi Amar, see those who push for compromise as part of a long tradition of rivals or their unwitting accomplices who wished to pull the rug from underneath the foundations of the Jewish community's strength. This issue is a fundamental and even existential one, and decisions here will be remembered for years to come.

What is described here regarding Rabbi Amar's view on the Western Wall crisis can be implemented in other debates that involve religion and state. We have an abundance of texts involving almost every issue that correlates with secular-religious status quo. These texts are not being studied or dealt with anywhere outside the Haredi community. Those texts are not being the subject of close and careful readings which try to show the "unscientific theology" and what the author wanted to show us.

In those texts, rabbis and other religious influencers are showing the world what they think and feel about this issue; how those opinions are based on the hermeneutical legacy of the Jewish tradition through which they argue; and what are the things they are willing to negotiate and what are the things they won't move an inch from.

Recently I was given the opportunity to read some responsa produced by various rabbis regarding the gender separation of Haredi academic classrooms.[19] I firmly believe that by reading such responsa and analyzing them carefully, academics can come to many important conclusions which might help us to better discuss the issue.

Does Rabbi Amar's affiliation with the Sephardic element of Orthodox Jewry change the way he looks at these issues? I would claim that the exact opposite in this case. The notion of "Daat Torah," in its broad sense, comes from the Ashkenazi worldview. In the Ashkenazi world, the rabbis led the way in every aspect and ruled in matters not connected directly to the Halacha. Researchers have shown the origins of this notion in the Askenazi Responsa in the eighteenth century.[20] The idea that every political contemporary question should be dealt with using halakhic tools is something that Rabbi Amar embraced from his Ashkenazi partners. In the Sephardic Jewish world, the rabbis usually deal with Halacha and its implication. Even the Sephardic Meta-Halacha does not usually relate to concepts outside the Halachic realm.[21] As I mentioned, I do not think that Rabbi Amar would've ruled differently without looking out to the Ashkenazi world; however, the way he writes and how he uses the sources to manifest a meta-halakhic concept seem to be borrowed from the Ashkenazi world. When Rabbi Amar quotes the story from Ba'al HaAkeda, he seeks to manifest an antireform notion. This notion derives from the Asknazi world and his struggle from reform Jews over the years.

CONCLUSION

To conclude, in this chapter I have presented the implementation of a method excavating meta-halachic ideas and beliefs on contemporary political and sociological issues. I have tried to show that contemporary texts may be a worthwhile target for the sort of methods and approaches applied to older ones, with possibilities for change in the current discussion as a resultant upshot. My attempt here was to create somewhat of a methodology and back it up with a theoretical framework that shows that text-based discussion can change our perspective on the secular-religious status quo problems in Israel. I have tried to demonstrate my thesis by showcasing an open letter written by one of the prominent rabbis in Israel today and his influence in his halakhic writings.

Exposing the written halachic text and showing the subtextual meaning of it has been done before. But trying to use the result of this revelation in the ongoing discourse of Israeli society was not tried sufficiently until now. I believe that we, in some way, owe this implementation to the scholars throughout the years who really believed that investing in Jewish studies research should change the way that Jewish culture, the Jewish people, and the Jewish state behave and progress.

While it remains to be seen how effective the methodology I have demonstrated here would be in dealing with broader issues, the paradigm shift proposed is greatly needed. We, as scholars, need to look at things differently than we are used to. Currently, the role of the researcher is to reach out and use his skills to shine light on contemporary debates. This will allow academics to use their knowledge and methodology in current issues and become a more relevant group of voices in the discourse. By doing so, we may achieve the goal we always looked for—the creation of vibrant and important studies which will affect our lives.

NOTES

1. See, for example, Daniel Statman, "Judaism and Democracy: The Current Debate," in *On Liberty: Jewish Perspectives*, Daniel Frank (ed.) (London: Curzon, 1999), 129–49.

2. I have been told by some of the engaged parties that only "political tactics" will help in this situation.

3. Michel Foucault, *The Archeology of Knowledge* (New York and London: Routledge, 2002), 151–52.

4. See Nissan Rubin, "Teoryut Sociologiyout-Antropologiyout KeMisgeret LeParshanut Textim" [Sociological and Anthropological Theories as a Framework for Textual Interpretation], in *Halacha, Meta Halacha Ve'Philosofyia* [Halacha, Meta Halacha and Philosophy] (Jerusalem: Van Leer, 2001), 98–21.

5. Alan Brill, "Review of Benny Brown's Book on the Hazon Ish by Etkes," *The Book of Doctrines and Opinions*, June 26, 2012. https://kavvanah.wordpress.com/2012/06/26/review-of-benny-browns-book-on-the-hazon-ish-by-etkes/

6. The origin of this term is Eliezer Goldman. Ever since, it has been used broadly to describe what I am discussing here. See Alexander Kaye, "Eliezer Goldman and the Origins of Meta-Halacha," *Modern Judaism* 34, no. 3 (2014): 309–33.

7. Ariel Picard, *Halacha Ba'olam Hadash* [Halacha in the New World] (Jerusalem: Hartman, 2012).

8. Leopold Zunz, *Ha'Drashut BeYisrael* [On the Sermons] (Jerusalem: Bialick, 1982), 33–39.

9. See Scholem's critique about the loss of influence of Jewish Studies on the society: Gershom Scholem, "Mitoch Hirhurim al Chochmat Yisrael" [Contemplations on Wissenschaft des Judentums], in *Dvarim Bego* [Selected Essays] (Tel Aviv: Am Oved, 1982), 385–403.

10. See Amar, Open letter (Psak Din), March 2, 2016.

11. Yitzchak Arama, *Akeydat Yitzchak* [The Binding of Issac], trans. Eliyahu Munk (New York: Lambda Publishers, 2001).

12. Arama, *Akeydat Yitzchak*, 142–56.

13. Arama, *Akeydat Yitzchak*, 147 (the translator does not translate this part of the sermon but rather mentions it shortly).

14. Translated by author.

15. Shlomo Amar, *Shema Shlomo* [The Hearings of Shlomo], vol. 4 (Bnei Brak: Shema Shlomo, 2001), 133–42.

16. Arama, *Akeydat Yitzchak*, 147.

17. Benjamin Brown, "Jewish Political Theology: The Doctrine of Daat Torah as a Case Study," *Harvard Theological Review* 107 (July 2014): 255–89.

18. As a side note I will say that I do not believe that Rabbi Amar is considering the Chief Rabbinate of Israel as the establishment. I think that he still, like many other Haredi rabbis—even though they hold rabbinical positions in the state of Israel—believes that the Haredi community in Israel is the actual center of Orthodox establishment and power.

19. I hope to address to this issue in a different essay.

20. See Moshe Samet, *Hadash Asur Min HaTorah* [The New Is Forbidden by the Torah], (Jerusalem: Dinor Center, 2005).

21. Ariel Picard, *HaPhilosofyia Shel Harav Ovadia Yosef BeIdan Shel Tmorot* [The Philosophy of Rabbi Ovadia Yosef in an Age of Transition] (Jerusalem: Hartman, 2007).

BIBLIOGRAPHY

Amar, Shlomo. *Shema Shlomo* [The Hearings of Shlomo]. Vol. 4. Bnei Brak: Shema Shlomo, 2001.

Arama, Yitzchak. *Akeydat Yitzchak* [The Binding of Issac]. Translated by Eliyahu Munk. New York: Lambda Publishers, 2001.

Brill, Alan. "Review of Benny Brown's Book on the Hazon Ish by Etkes." *The Book of Doctrines and Opinions*. June 26, 2012. https://kavvanah.wordpress.com/2012/06/26/review-of-benny-browns-book-on-the-hazon-ish-by-etkes/.

Brown, Benjamin. "Jewish Political Theology: The Doctrine of Daat Torah as a Case Study." *Harvard Theological Review* 107 (July 2014): 255–89.

Foucault, Michel. *The Archeology of Knowledge*. New York and London: Routledge, 2002.

Kaye, Alexander. "Eliezer Goldman and the Origins of Meta-Halacha." *Modern Judaism* 34, no. 3 (2014): 309–33.

Picard, Ariel. *Halacha Ba'olam Hadash* [Halacha in the New World]. Jerusalem: Hartman, 2012.

———. *HaPhilosofyia Shel Harav Ovadia Yosef BeIdan Shel Tmorot* [The Philosophy of Rabbi Ovadia Yosef in an Age of Transition]. Jerusalem: Hartman, 2007.

Rubin, Nissan. "Teoryut Sociologiyout-Antropologiyout KeMisgeret LeParshanut Textim" [Sociological and Anthropological Theories as a Framework for Textual Interpretation]. In *Halacha, Meta Halacha Ve'Philosofyia* [Halacha, Meta Halacha and Philosophy], 98–21. Jerusalem: Van Leer, 2001.

Samet, Moshe. *Hadash Asur Min HaTorah* [The New Is Forbidden by the Torah]. Jerusalem: Dinor Center, 2005.

Scholem, Gershom. "Mitoch Hirhurim al Chochmat Yisrael" [Contemplations on Wissenschaft des Judentums]. In *Dvarim Bego* [Selected Essays], 385–403. Tel Aviv: Am Oved, 1982.

Statman, Daniel. "Judaism and Democracy: The Current Debate." In *On Liberty: Jewish Perspectives*, edited by Daniel Frank, 129–49. London: Curzon, 1999.

Zunz, Leopold. *Ha'Drashut BeYisrael* [On the Sermons]. Jerusalem: Bialick, 1982.

Part II

Defining the Borders of Israel Studies

Chapter Four

Israel, Palestine, and Holy Land Studies in Post-Soviet Territory

Views, Trends, and Prospects

Dzmitry Shavialiou

For more than twenty-five years, Israel Studies has been enjoying academic legitimacy in post-Soviet territories. In the late 1980s and early 1990s Israel Studies was released from direct ideological control of the ruling Communist party. The discipline received everything that could be desired—wide access to information, the possibilities of academic trips to Israel, to the subject-matter, wide groups of students studying the issue, including students of Hebrew, and so forth. The situation was the same in a related field, Holy Land Studies, which also flourished after the dissolution of the Soviet Union. At the same time, another related sphere, Palestine Studies, had many scholars in the 1990–2000s but lacked cohesion of topics and ideas. In this chapter I try to focus on trends and prospects of Israel Studies, as well as two related fields—Palestine Studies and Holy Land Studies—in the post-Soviet states. Moreover, it is an attempt to sum up my personal observations.[1]

ISRAEL STUDIES: BACKGROUND AND CURRENT TRENDS

First and foremost, I would like to make a remark concerning the explanation of the term *Israel Studies*. There is not any precise definition of what Israel Studies is. Israel Studies is generally understood to include multidisciplinary scholarship which focuses on Israeli history, politics, economics, and culture—but the definitions vary, as well as which period of time should be analyzed.

One narrow definition covers the period from the foundation of the State of Israel, in 1948. A second definition includes an expanded period, from 1917 and the advent of the Balfour Declaration. Finally, a third periodization places a starting point for academic focus at the first Zionist *aliya* of the late nineteenth century. In this way the study of the *Yishuv*, both the Old and the New, covering the history of Zionism, is considered an aspect of Israel Studies. As for this author, I prefer to use the second definition, but for this paper, I concede the third broader periodization in order to enlarge the topic analyzed below.

One further remark concerns geographical scope. Speaking about post-Soviet Israel Studies, two countries could be considered centers of the discipline's development—Russia and Ukraine. Both countries have their own tradition of Oriental studies. But Russia has a strong colonial history, which naturally influenced knowledge about the Orient. Moreover, Russia has a tradition of Middle Eastern Studies, particularly the Moscow School of Oriental Studies—academics and research institutions which focus their research on the contemporary Middle East; whereas the Leningrad (Petersburg) Academic School concentrates on the ancient Near East.

Ukraine also has some tradition of Oriental research, although it is comparatively weak. The history of Oriental Studies in Ukraine is not a long one, going only so far back as the revolutionary period in 1918. Just as Orientalist (I mean academic, not philosophical) traditions began to take shape, the repressions of the 1920s–1930s annihilated all opportunities to create this sphere of studies. In 1991, the Ukrainian Institute of Oriental Studies—as a separate unit of the Ukrainian Academy of Science—was founded in Kiev. But its foundation was probably a political decision of the post-Soviet Ukrainian authorities—made as an homage to professor Omelyan Pritsak, an eminent scholar of Turkish Studies and medieval Ukrainian history, who at that time returned to Ukraine from the United States.[2] Meanwhile, both countries, Russia and Ukraine, have been centers of Jewish Studies since the early 1990s. This is another reason for Israel Studies' strong position in Ukraine.

During the Soviet period there was a narrow circle of academics involved in Israel and Middle Eastern studies. To varying degrees all of them reviled Israel and Zionism. In 1972 the Department of Israel Studies was founded in the Academy of Sciences of the USSR. While Moscow sought to comply with academic standards, on Soviet peripheries—for example, in Kiev and Minsk—academics concentrated on heavy criticism of the Bund and Zionism—it was an easy way to make a career.[3]

It is rather difficult to concentrate on a separate date or event which could be considered as a starting point for the development of Israel Studies as the academic discipline in the post-Soviet era. Contacts between Israeli and Soviet academics were established even before the fall of the Soviet Union. In January 1990, an Israeli delegation headed by Ezer Weizman, then the minister for science and technology, visited Moscow. Soviet academics and Israeli officials signed an agreement of cooperation which began official contacts between scholars.[4]

After the collapse of the Soviet Union, the Department of Israel Studies increased its contacts all over the world. In 1993 the Association of the Study of Israel was established on the initiative of the then head of the department Andrey Fedorchenko.[5]

As a result of the perestroika of the late 1980s and later the collapse of the Soviet Union in 1991, ideological obstacles broke down. The political situations in the world also promoted the development of Israel studies. On December 16, 1991 the UN revoked its resolution on "Zionism as a form of racism and race discrimination."[6] Together with this, Arab-Israel rapprochement was changing the region in the 1990s. Up to the late 1980s Soviet academics had criticized Israel and Zionism, but in the 1990s the same group changed their minds in the face of new circumstances—such as the fall of the Soviet Union and the establishment of contacts with Israeli partners. Some reorganized themselves as quickly as possible. At the same time, in the early 1990s the strong opponents of Zionism became marginalized or even disappeared from the academic environment. As Jewish Studies emerged in the 1990s, Israel Studies was considered to be part of it.

It is necessary to point out that the post-Soviet territories, and Russia above all, are not a center of Israel Studies as an academic discipline. I admit that they are one of the centers of Jewish Studies, but as for the study of Israel, the FSU countries are probably on the periphery of the academic discipline—they do not set any tendencies in the sphere.

I suppose that two features distinguished Israel Studies in the post-Soviet countries. First, it is the territory of the former Soviet Union with definite unified traditions of science, education, and, naturally, management of them, at first in the Russian Empire and then in Soviet Russia. Secondly, the Russian language functions as the *lingua franca* of academia in the FSU. There have been several attempts to use native languages for academic writing, but all of them have thus far failed. The reality is that all authors want their books and articles to be read. All (or almost all) academics across the former Soviet Union who are involved in Middle Eastern Studies read in Russian, but few of them read in the national languages of the USSR. (No one in Russia or in Ukraine will read a paper in the Kyrgyz language, for example; on the contrary, a paper written in Russian could be read in Ukraine, Belarus, Kyrgyzstan, etc.).

I could only assume that there are two reasons why scholars from any post-Soviet state outside Russia write in their indigenous language. One could have an extremely anti-Russian ideological point of view—resolving thus not to write in "the empire's language." This was rather popular in the 1990s. But now, generally, only Ukrainians prefer this, following the 2014 annexation of the Crimea by Russia. Most of them try to use English as the academic language of the world. One more reason exists. It is an open secret that in the 1990s–2000s, plagiarism was a rather common tendency of the post-Soviet humanities, and one has few chances to be caught doing this writing in an indigenous language, while it is a far riskier prospect when writing in Russian. Thus, two things distinguish post-Soviet academics from their colleagues in other regions—common history and traditions of academic life, as well as usage of Russian as the academic *lingua franca*.

Looking back to the Israel Studies of the early 1990s: I have mentioned that after the collapse of the Soviet Union, FSU academics found themselves in a strange situation. All of them previously had criticized Israel and Zionism, but at the moment their country disappeared, they faced a new situation as Russian-Israeli relations progressively developed. In this way, during the 1990s, two groups of academics were shaped. The first admitted another basis for their academic work wishing to stay in touch with Israel Studies. They changed their views on Israel and Zionist ideas and began to study Israeli politics, Soviet/Russian-Israel relations, and so forth. (I use the term "conformists" for them.) They established close contacts with Israeli academia.

Another group of scholars involved in the study of Arab-Israel relations and Middle East peace process are called "Arabists." Despite their understanding of Israel, they criticized Israeli policy toward Palestinians. Their key topic of research is Arab-Israeli affairs. According to my terminology, both groups are "old men of the Soviet Union," receiving education in Arab Studies mainly during the Soviet period (in the late Soviet period there were several groups of students educated in Middle Eastern affairs with Hebrew as a language of study).

A third group of scholars emerged through the activities of the Moscow Center for University Teaching of Jewish Civilization ("Sefer") in the 1990s–2000s. The idea behind its foundation appeared in the early 1990s and was authored by Nehemia Levtzion—an Israeli academic.[7] Through the combined efforts by Russian scholars and their Israeli and Western partners (among them Shaul Stampfer, Victoria Mochalova, Rashid Kaplanov, Leonid Matsikh, and John Klier), as well as several senior officers of the Russian Department of American Jewish Joint Distribution Committee (mainly, Ralph Goldman and Rabbi Jonathan Porath) in 1994, the Moscow Center of Jewish Studies was set up.[8] Frankly speaking, it has been the most successful academic project established in Russia in the post-Soviet period. To sum up the results of its work since 1994, I can say that for twenty-five years the center has established a generation of scholars intimately involved in Jewish Studies in the post-Soviet states. It is a very positive and impressive outcome of the center's activity.

From the very beginning, the Moscow Center has patronized Israel Studies. So far, the Center used the intellectual potential of Israeli academics for organizing conferences, schools (a sort of informal education), lectures, and internships. Thanks to the Moscow Center, the group of scholars involved in Israel Studies today has increased. They were starting from scratch, unburdened by Soviet preconceptions on Israel and Zionism. Moreover, some of the papers produced by these authors were very pro-Israeli and without any critical thinking. By the mid-2010s, this group was still small, with up to twenty persons, thirty to forty-five years old, engaged in Israel Studies due to efforts by the "Sefer" Center and its alumni—mainly from Russia, Belarus, and Ukraine. According to my terminology, these are the "mid-generation" scholars.

Now there are four centers (regional schools) of Israel Studies which have formed since the early 1990s. These are based around educational establishments, and the differences between them lie in a range of research topics.

First, the "Moscow School" of Israel Studies is the most productive center with its academic institutions and educational establishments—the Institute of Oriental Studies of the Russian Academy of Sciences, the Institute for the Study of Asian and African Countries with its Chair in Jewish Studies, and *MGIMO* University (formerly the Moscow State Institute of International Relations).[9] Two educational establishments—the Institute for the Study of Asian and African Countries and *MGIMO* University—have regular Hebrew classes with the additional learning of one European language, as well as internships in Israel, lectures in particular topics of Israeli politics, economics, and so forth. A circle of instructors absorbed scholars from the three groups of academics—"conformers," "Arabists," and "mid-generation." Andrey Fedorchenko, Alexander Krylov, Irina Zvyagelskaya, Dmitry Maryasis, Tatyana Nosenko, and many others are among the representatives of the "Moscow School."

Second, a group of scholars involved in Israel Studies (as a part of Middle Eastern Studies) was formed at the University of Nizhny Novgorod beginning in the early 1990s. Research themes here discussed the Arab-Israel conflict, Israel policy toward the post-Soviet states, and the U.S. policy toward the Middle East (Oleg Kolobov, Alexander Kornilov, Elizaveta Iakimova, among others are in that local group).

Third, there is a local center in Siberia—with Tomsk, Omsk, and several other universities, which have courses in the fields of Israel and Middle Eastern Studies. The range of their research topics include British policy in the Middle East and toward Palestine (Mikhail Agapov, Vladimir Rumyantsev, Mikhail Shapovalov, and others are among this group).

Fourth, in the 1990s to the early 2000s, a circle of researchers was developed at Odessa University and the Odessa branch of the National Institute of Strategic Studies of Ukraine. This group of scholars concentrates on Middle

Eastern affairs and Israel foreign policy (Marina Vorotnyuk, Alla Zakharchenko, and others work on those topics). The researchers shared an educational background from Odessa University, including Middle Eastern languages. It seems that this "regional school" was destroyed by the events of 2014 in Ukraine. The Odessa Branch of the Ukrainian National Institute of Strategic Studies was closed by the authorities in Kiev during 2015.[10] The official statement announcing the reason for the institute's shutdown spoke about cutting state expenditures. But another reason seemed to exist: the Ukrainian authorities mistrusted the Odessa region after 2014, as Odessa tried to resist the change of power in Kiev and gave strong support to Viktor Yanukovich.[11] As other scholars are solitary and scattered across the countries of the FSU, more regional schools and groups of academics focused on Israel Studies are unlikely to be formed in the near future.

Moreover, other Ukrainian scholars were not able to form a "regional school" of Israel Studies in Kiev, despite the rapid development of Jewish Studies in Ukraine since the late 1980s. Ukrainian researchers engaged in Israel Studies are following the same tendencies in the sphere of studies like other scholars of the post-Soviet territories. I wish to stress the point that this division of regional schools is overly rigid. The reality is much more fluid and ill-defined.

In detecting trends in Israel Studies in the FSU, first and foremost it is necessary to note that almost all papers are written in a descriptive manner; few have any deep analysis of the issues they address. It is essential to admit that a presence of academic debates is an indicator of a discipline's development. If there are academic debates in any branch of knowledge, it is good for that academic sphere. There is a lack of such disputes within Israel Studies in the post-Soviet period. I could list only three topics debated in special journals during twenty-five years of Israel Studies in the former Soviet Union: 1) the definition of Israel Studies and its achievements in post-Soviet countries,[12] 2) British-French rivalry for the Middle East during 1918–1923,[13] and 3) reasons behind the Balfour Declaration.[14] It is apparent there is almost no debate in the study of Israel within the FSU.

It is necessary to lay out the problems of the post-Soviet humanities which surely influenced the course of Jewish and Israel and Middle Eastern Studies. One issue concerns the existence of several authoritative academic clans which exclude outsiders. These clans usually have management positions in educational establishments and academic institutions, as well as leverage to advance decisions favorable for them. However, under these circumstances another group of scholars appeared, the "marginalized," who try to keep their distance from the quarrels of the academic clans.

Another characteristic of contemporary humanities within the FSU is the old age of most academics. In the late 1980s to 1990s the academic sphere rapidly declined: salaries fell, and many academics were forced to leave research or teaching to earn a living. Many found different places of work, while many escaped from the fallen Soviet Union to the West. Due to these circumstances, those of the younger generations reluctantly chose academic careers. This has been a model for the humanities and social studies for the last twenty-five years. The development of this model produced a one-generation gap in academia: there are old men who went into academia during the Soviet period, and there are youngsters who joined the academy in the 2000s during a period of relative economic stabilization among the post-Soviet states.

In addition, the declined post-Soviet educational system rarely produced scholars—it became the function of informal education (e.g., schools and seminars organized by the "Sefer" Center, etc., but not the classical system of higher educational establishments—graduate, postgraduate courses, MA programs, etc.). It is worthwhile to note that the old tradition of personal scientific schools which were spread during the period of the Russian Empire and the Soviet epoch almost disappeared. In that sense "school" is an academic tradition of transferring knowledge from "schoolmen" to their apprentices; it combined both a formal and informal method of education (for example, there is Klyuchevsky's school among historians, or Krachkovsky's school in Oriental Studies, etc.).[15] As a result, a real "schoolman" became a dying breed, and there is a lack of real teachers able to captivate students.

Moreover, Israel Studies in the post-Soviet states has two contradictory trends. On one hand, complete freedom of speech is observed in Israel Studies, so far as Israel is not a priority of these states' foreign policy. Moreover, some states held the inertia of Soviet policy toward Israel (e.g., Russia, as well as Belarus), because Israel also has no interests in strengthening contacts with them (except periods of Avigdor Lieberman's terms of office as minister for foreign affairs in 2009–2012 and 2013–2015).[16] Thus, a scholar can study any period or any topic—the post–Soviet authorities do not consider these topics or persons as a threat to their power. On the other hand, academics of the post-Soviet states are out of touch with world trends in Israel Studies. They rarely deliver lectures during international conferences, they are not members of professional associations, very few of them follow tendencies in the discipline (for instance, the struggle between the followers of the BDS movement and their opponents, debates between Israeli leftists and rightists, etc.). I will only note that all the problems become even more serious on the periphery of the former Soviet territory, outside Moscow and Saint Petersburg.

As the results indicate, there is stagnation in the sphere of Israel Studies in the post-Soviet states. On the one hand, students of Israel topics gained many opportunities for their development in the 1990s. From that period a few groups of scholars were formed: the "old men of the Soviet Union" ("conformists" and "Arabists"), as well as "mid-generation" scholars. Three regional schools also formed in Moscow, Nizhny Novgorod, and Odessa. On the other hand, there is a situation of stagnation brought on by several factors, despite intensive development in the 1990s. This includes the depression of the educational system, as well as a gap of one generation of scholars in the transfer of knowledge. This depression caused clannishness where one group of academics supports its members while abusing others regardless of academic background or achievement. Further, post-Soviet states have not placed Israel on the list of priorities in foreign policy—another factor which has contributed to the deterioration of Israel Studies.

PALESTINE STUDIES IN THE 1990s–2000s: ONE ISSUE FOR THE STUDY

Two terms are often considered to have the same meaning—"Palestine Studies" and "Holy Land Studies." The definition of "Palestine Studies" is often given as a full range of issues related to the study of Palestine since either the Muslim conquest of the Levant in the seventh century, or the Ottoman conquest of the land in the early sixteenth century: that range of issues includes inter-religious relations, relations between *milletler* and the power of the Ottoman Empire, as well as between the Port and the Great Powers.[17] Due to this broad definition, some academics combine the two concepts of "Palestine studies" and "Holy Land Studies." This was the trend of the 2000s. Thus, in 2002 the *Journal of Holy Land and Palestine Studies* was established and published by Edinburgh University Press. The journal brings together all topics related to "two nations and three faiths."

There is also a stricter meaning of the term "Palestine Studies" which dates back to the early 1960s: the Institute of Palestine Studies was established in 1963 in Beirut. It deals with the Palestine-Israel conflict, as well as the socioeconomic and political state of Palestinian society. This trend defined the term for a long period of time. For this chapter I will separate the two terms—"Palestine Studies" and "Holy Land Studies," following the stricter meaning of the term "Palestine Studies," as it conceptually relates to all issues regarding the Palestinians as ethnicity (ethnic entity) since the early twentieth century. "Holy Land Studies" is supposed to have religious (or confessional) components—relations between communities, Churches in the Holy Land, use of religious tools in the struggle between the Great Powers, and so on. I hasten to note that this difference is subtle.

The collapse of Soviet socialist ideology caused a decrease in academic interest on national liberation movements, including the cause of Palestine. Probably, the last work devoted to Palestinian resistance was a feature article on the issue authored by a group of the leading Soviet scholars of Middle Eastern affairs.[18]

In the late 1980s and early 1990s many academics from Arab Studies who previously had interests in the cause of Palestine from the late 1980s were involved in Israel Studies as a new and favorable growth sphere; at the same time, many academics were forced to escape to another profitable sphere—for example into diplomatic service—during the depressed epoch of the 1990s.

While men left the academic sphere, there were no diversity of views and ideas. Under such circumstances there was the only one principle topic upon which Palestine Studies focused: the peace process between Israel and the Palestinians and its prospects. In addition, few scholars continued their old tradition—research in Palestine topics (for instance, Vladimir Kisilyov, Yevgeny Pyrlin).[19]

Views on a Palestine-Israel peace settlement can be divided easily into two main groups: the first is the "optimists," those who believe that both sides are able to achieve comprehensive peace. "The future must be peaceful," as Yevgeny Pyrlin declared in one of his books.[20] He also argued: "It is essential for everyone who is interested in Middle Eastern affairs and goes into it completely to have the sense of 'historical optimism' about the inevitability of reconciliation among Israelis and Palestinians."[21]

The minority group of academics studying the Palestine-Israel conflicts, the "pessimists," did not believe in such a prospect. Their key arguments concentrate on two assertions. First, it is completely impossible to obliterate the strife which has accumulated for generations. Second, various actors—both external and internal—have sufficient interest in the conflict as to prevent its resolution. While the details of the views on Palestine-Israel peace prospects beg further elaboration, that it is not a purpose of this chapter. As for this author, I count myself among the smaller group of "pessimists" in respect to this issue. There is a majority of "optimists" among older-generation academics, while a majority of "pessimists" belong to the circle of "mid-" and "younger-generation" researchers. Notably, debates between "optimists" and "pessimists" is a sort of discourse between idealists and realists, respectively, on foreign policy issues.

A final area of controversy can be observed in the Palestine Studies of the post-Soviet epoch. It is discourse between "Arabists," those who support the Arab (Palestinian) point of view on the Middle East conflict, and those who follow Israeli opinion on the matter. This second group was numerous in the 1990s and early 2000s. Now, by the late 2010s, both groups are more or less equal, and few individuals express extreme support for either point of view. Many academics attempt to provide a balanced if not fully objective opinion.

To sum up, although Palestine Studies faced academic attrition, many works were devoted to mainly one topic of this sphere—the peace process between Israel and the Palestinians, which is to say that Palestine Studies within the FSU retains only one truly active area academic investigation.

HOLY LAND STUDIES: SURVEY OF POST-SOVIET HISTORIOGRAPHY

While selected reviews of publications in the fields of Israel and Palestine Studies were published from the 1990s to the 2010s, not one survey devoted to Holy Land Studies appeared during this period. This chapter stands as the first attempt to observe the state of this academic field.

To begin, it is necessary to note that Holy Land Studies has been the most successful among the three related fields discussed in this chapter. In the 1990s this area received state support, as well as interest from both academics and the wider public.

The current state of this academic field arose in 1992, when the key actor of up-to-date activity in dissemination of knowledge on the Holy Land was reformatted. In May 1992 the Presidium of the Supreme Council of Russia decided to remove the Palestine Society from the Academy of Science and restored to the Society its old title "The Imperial Orthodox Palestine Society." It is necessary to recall that from the 1920s into the 1980s the Palestine Society existed as an academic club in the system of the Academy of Science of the USSR.[22] In 1992, the Society ceased to be an academic institution and became a sort of public organization receiving support from both the state and the Russian Orthodox Church. The reorganized Society closely modeled the old "Imperial" organization from before 1917: it combined research and propaganda to be used as an implement of Russian influence in the Middle East. This intention was rather fruitful due to close links between activists of the "renewed" Palestine Society, the Orthodox Church, and the Ministry for Foreign Affairs.

Unlike the other disciplines under review in this chapter, Holy Land Studies demonstrates a variety of historiographical lines—each with its own specific features. This can be explained by the fact that state power encouraged interest toward the Russian imperial past, particularly after the collapse of the Soviet Union. By the late 1990s the Russian presence in the Middle East preceding the 1917 Revolution became a core issue among historical research topics. Moreover, interest toward the issue in the 2000s arose due to strengthening Russian influence in Middle Eastern affairs.

It is appropriate to recall, briefly, the situation in Russian foreign policy toward the Middle East in the 1990s and 2000s. Up to the mid-1990s Russia was not interested in the region beyond what little contact with the Gulf countries was necessary in the hopes of finding investments and agreements on arms sales. However, these attempts failed to produce tangible results. Attempts to strengthen contacts with Israel were abortive too.[23]

As conservative circles grew in power during the second half of the 1990s (there were two key state figures who represented conservatives—Yevgeny Primakov and Yury Luzhkov), Russia progressively turned attention toward the Middle East.[24] When Primakov took office as the Minister for Foreign Affairs in 1996, he drafted features of Russian foreign policy which included a declaration of multivectoral focus for foreign policy; its implementation without regard for Western partners' concerns; the promotion of cooperation between Russia, India, and China as a counterweight to U.S. demands; as well as intense interest in the Middle East. The region was considered a "traditional partner" of Russia since Soviet times. These features were the basis for the so-called Prymakov Doctrine, which supposedly is still being followed today.[25]

However, I can say with some certainty that in Moscow there has been no strategic vision of developing relations between Russia and Israel, or Russia and the Palestinians until now. I can also suggest that there was one key question of interest for the Russian political establishment in dealing with Palestinians (and Israel as well). This was the issue of Russian properties in Israel and the Palestinian-administrated territories since the 1990s. That, in fact, tended to turn to the Russian past in the Holy Land. As early as 1992, the Russian Ministry for Foreign Affairs published a compilation of documents prepared by the ministerial Historical and Documentary Department on this issue.[26] In addition to this set of documents, other materials were also published.[27]

It is necessary to stress the fact that all scholars involved in the study of the Holy Land are interested primarily in the time period before the 1917 Revolution, that is to say the epoch of a flourishing Russian presence in the Middle East. A few scholars study activities of the "White" and the "Red" in the Holy Land following the schism in the Russian Church after the 1917 October revolution, as well as the period after 1991—the fall of the Soviet Union.[28] Based on this, I can suppose that for researchers the Soviet period was irrelevant from a political perspective. Scholars who were involved in Holy Land Studies and in the activity of the renewed Imperial Orthodox Palestine Society after 1991 were sure that the October revolution, and the Soviet period in a whole, upset the natural course of history, and thus stopped the natural development of Russia. During this period Russians purchased nothing in Palestine, meaning that there was no political necessity to refer to the period after 1917. Thus, political necessity ordered research. In turn, Palestinian academic circles were fully aware of this situation in the political establishment and the academe in Moscow. As a result, papers on Russian-Palestinian ties appeared in the 1990s and early 2000s.[29] To gain the support of Russia, Palestinians handed over plots of land under Palestinian control to Russians. In 1997, the Palestinian Authority gave a Russian monastery in Hebron to the Moscow Patriarchate. There was some evidence that Palestinian police had dislodged priests of the Russian Orthodox Church Abroad from that monastery.[30] Palestinians also gave the plot of land with the Oak of Mamre to Moscow.[31] On January 15, 2000, the Palestinian Authority handed over one more plot of land to Moscow, the Metochion of St. John the Baptist.

Thus, political interests created research interests. A certain number of academic publications appeared. I will try to characterize these publications, which seem to be based on some historiographical models. Yet it must be noted that, above all, the papers of Russian academics are disputed in this chapter, because in the FSU countries only a handful of researchers are involved in the study of the Holy Land.[32] The main topics of investigation which interest Russian and post-Soviet researchers include two Russian ecclesiastical missions into the Holy Land (the first one headed by Porfiri Uspenski in 1847–1854, and the second one sent to Jerusalem after the Crimean War in 1854–1856); the life, activity, and writings of Antonin Kapustin; the activity of the Russian Orthodox Palestine Society; research done by Russian Orientalists in the Ottoman Empire; contacts and ties between Moscow and Jerusalem Patriarchates; Russian purchases in Palestine; Russian schools in Palestine before 1914; and the influence of Russian Orthodoxy on the Arab cause (Arab nationalism). In the post-Soviet historiography, all these topics are titled "Russian-Palestinian ties."[33]

Some models seem to have formed during the 1990s and 2000s in post-Soviet historiography of the Holy Land. The first is a descriptive model which has roots in the 1980s. When the rise of academic interests toward the Holy Land began, several Soviet scholars issued articles on the Palestine Society.[34] A series of books and articles devoted to the Russian presence in Palestine before 1917 was published at the beginning of the 2000s.[35] Probably the first published book, which covered the entire period of Russian ecclesiastical presence in Palestine, was written by Irina Vorobyova—*Russian Missions to the Holy Land in 1847–1917* (in Russian).

All the authors who follow this model try to depict the details of the topics mentioned above. They stress both old cultural ties between Russia and Palestine, as well as the considerable influence of the Russian Church and the Palestine Society on the indigenous people of the Holy Land. The most popular subjects are the scientific activity of the Palestine Society and the heads of the Russian Jerusalem Mission (Porfiri Uspenski and Antonin Kapustin) in the fields of history and archeology. Among works using the descriptive model are those which reconstruct the activities of local offices of the Imperial Orthodox Palestine Society up to 1917.[36] It is necessary to note that historians following the descriptive model try to avoid any conceptual frameworks or theoretical foundations.

This group of scholars is likely to have evolved in Saint Petersburg, working with the rich archival collections of Saint Petersburg.[37] A similar group was formed in Moscow, which publishes *Pravoslavnyj Palestinskij sbornik*.[38]

In the mid-2000s the second model, the neo-conservative one, appeared in the historiography of the Russian presence in the Middle East before 1917. The framework for Russian neoconservatism in Holy Land Studies was provided by Nikolay Lisovoy and Boris Yamilinets. Moreover, I can assume that the scholars of that model predicate their work on the stereotype of the "Official Nationality" doctrine proposed by Count Sergey Uvarov in 1833.[39] These scholars redesigned Uvarov's formula of "Orthodoxy, Autocracy, and Nationality." Neoconservatives accept these pillars as the only foundations for Russia's actions both in the past and today, and, at the same time, as the only basis for research in the history of the Holy Land, and, in broader context, the history of the Russian Church. This thesis on Orthodoxy as the methodological approach is continued in Lisovoy's 2006 book *Russian Ecclesiastical and Political Presence in the Holy Land and the Middle East in the 19th and early 20th centuries* (in Russian). Moreover, neoconservatives focus on the "Western hazard" as the core factor for Russian internal and external policy. I assume that it reflects the old opposition between pro-Western liberals (westernists, or *zapadniki*) and conservatives (Slavophiles).

This group of neoconservative authors tends to blame the West for all problems in the Holy Land, because of the religious rivalry there. From their point of view, it is Europe that destroyed Russian positions in the Middle East.

Neoconservatives argue that Russia was forced to enter the Holy Land. This was caused by struggle between Orthodox, Catholic, and Protestant Churches—therefore Russia was "the only Orthodox Empire, the successor of Byzantium in the post-Byzantine period."[40] Catholics were the main antagonists and foes of Orthodoxy in the Holy Land.[41] But not only religious rivalry compelled Russia to enter Palestine, but the struggle between the Great Powers as well.[42] Moreover, several authors pay special attention to rivalry between Russia and the West for "Russia is the geopolitical force and stand-alone system equidimensional to the total West."[43]

Neoconservatives avoid sweeping assessments as to Russian policy in the Middle East during the early twentieth century. They ignore the fact that Russia took part in the partition of the region during World War I. Moreover, Lisovoy denies any colonialist aims of Russia in Palestine.

Historians of the neoconservative model stress the particular role of the Arabs of Palestine in the history of Russian-Palestinian ties. Yamilinets even coins the term "the people of Palestine," which means, first and foremost, Christian Arabs, and then Muslims as well. In addition, neoconservatives invented the concept of "dual oppression of Christian Arabs"—from both the Greek clergy and Ottoman Muslims.

However, authors' visions differ on the details, such as those relating to reasons for Russian failures in the region. For example, quarrels between

Antonin Kapustin and some figures in the Palestine Committee in Saint Petersburg are given varied explanations. While Yamilinets accuses high-ranking officials of the Ministry for Foreign Affairs of their Western/ European orientation, and misunderstanding of the situation in Palestine, Lisovoy compliments Russian diplomats.[44] Be that as it may, there are only few disputed details; neoconservative theory is rather coherent, being finally formulated in 2006 with its current contours.[45]

The increasing influence of postcolonial theory in contemporary historiographical and media discourse has affected Russian historians as well—perhaps leading to the advent of a new postcolonial model in Holy Land Studies within Russia. So far, the only paper written in this potentially nascent model is authored by Dimitry Bratkin.[46] His paper employs the concepts of "the Self" and "the Other," concentrating on images of the Holy Land. Bratkin tries to compare Western (British) and Russian approaches in Holy Land Studies, but in some cases Bratkin's points of view on differences between British and Russian lines in the field of study are rather disputable. He is wrong to claim that the Palestine Society was not a private initiative.[47] Moreover, while Bratkin states that the Palestine Society immediately started to gather special books and manuscripts on the Holy Land, it is difficult to accept the relevance of this point because the British Palestine Exploration Fund did the same as well.[48] Without discussing the work in detail, I stress that in comparison with neoconservatives, the potentially nascent postcolonial model argues that Russia, as well as Britain, had their own imperial interests in the Middle East. However, the postcolonial model has only just begun to take shape, and it is still too early to consider the model established on its apparent use in one chapter.

CONCLUSION

This chapter has presented a survey of three related areas—Israel, Palestine, and Holy Land Studies, demonstrating that there are varied groups of researchers involved in the study of Israel. The "old-generation" group has two blocks: One is the "conformists," those who in the late 1980s to early 1990s understood advantages of a new undeveloped sphere of research (cooperation with Israeli partners, internships in Israel, etc.) and in return stopped their criticism of Zionism and "Israeli aggression." The other block, "Arabists," are nonconformists who preferred their previous attitudes. In this regard it is essential to present here the opinion of Yevgeny Pyrlin:

> At my age ... it is embarrassing to change my views and deny my creed. After all, illusions also have the right to exist, in particular if they are sincere and dictated by long-standing political belief.[49]

This block is small like other groups, but reputable both in the halls of power and in academic quarters.

Researchers of the "mid-generation" group began their academic careers in the 1990s. The Moscow Center "Sefer" (established in 1994) played a key role in their growth as scholars. "Youngsters" belong to another small group of persons who were captured by the sphere of Jewish studies in the 2000s. There are also four regional groups, or schools, of academics in the former Soviet Union states—in Moscow, Nizhny Novgorod, Siberia, and Odessa.

To sum up the reasons why, in the 1990s and 2000s, some researchers chose the spheres of Jewish and/or Israel Studies: it was a new undeveloped academic sphere in the FSU countries—and it was enticing to be involved in an emergent sphere of study; some who entered Jewish Studies in the 1990s had national sensitivities toward Israel—those feelings naturally caused the rise of that sphere in the 1990s.[50] Also, for a dozen of years or more, Jewish Studies gave several advantages other spheres could not offer—such as conferences, internships, travel grants, and so forth. Many academics who were engaged in Israel Studies took part in various projects of cooperation with Israeli and American colleagues, such as the *Eshnav* program of the Center "Sefer" and the Hebrew University of Jerusalem, the joint internship of *MGIMO* University and the Harry S. Truman Research Institute for the Advancement of Peace at the Hebrew University of Jerusalem, the Summer Institute for Israel Studies at Brandeis University, and so forth. Finally, for many academics of the "mid-generation" group, those summer school conferences were the only way to communicate with academia, persons with the same interests. It should be noted that there was the reverse process: as rich private individuals or Western donors decreased their support to Jewish institutions in the FSU countries during the second half of 2000s, the outflow of scholars involved in Jewish Studies began.

I would say that authorities of the FSU states have been beneficial to Israel Studies: they did not impede the efforts to develop the sphere of Israel Studies. I suppose that in time Israel Studies may become as common a discipline as other fields of Area Studies.

For the last dozen years, Palestine Studies became an academic field focusing on a single topic—the peace process in the Middle East in its various aspects. It remains the main issue of study up to now. This key topic is being taught in many universities across the FSU countries.

One further question was added to the list of priorities within Palestine Studies by Russian Arabist Grigory Kosach in the 2000s, the Communist movement in Palestine and the Middle East during the 1920s and 1930s. However, Kosach's research covers the entire region, and thus his work relates to Middle Eastern studies more broadly, rather than to the narrower sphere of Palestine Studies. There are also some works by Mikhail Agapov which investigate some details of the issue.[51]

This chapter has also presented a survey of Holy Land Studies in post-Soviet Russia. It is the most successful field of Area Studies in the post-Soviet period: during this time, various historiographical models have appeared, and classical writings of Russian scholars of Holy Land Studies were published (Alexey Dmitrievsky, Vasily Khitrovo, etc.). Relationships between authorities, academics, and Orthodox clerics were strengthened as well. Whereas post-Soviet Russia, like the other FSU countries, did not invest in Israel or Palestine Studies, the example of Holy Land Studies has clearly demonstrated that only active support from a state has been capable of enabling the gradual development of any field of Area Studies.[52]

NOTES

1. This chapter is written in the framework of the research project "Imagined Territories of Russian Identity: The Case of Palestine" (#18–78–10062) supported by the Russian Science Foundation.

2. Omeljan Pritsak (1919–2006) was a Ukrainian and American scholar who had special interests in medieval Ukrainian history. He was educated at Lviv University and the universities of Berlin and Göttingen. He obtained his doctorate in 1948 at the University of Göttingen. He spent 1960–1961 at Harvard University and returned there as professor of linguistics and turcology in 1964. He was a cofounder of Harvard's Ukrainian Research Institute, and a founder of the journal *Harvard Ukrainian Studies*. While he is considered to be Agafangel Krimski's apprentice with whom he met from late 1939 to early 1941, Pritsak's colleagues at Harvard University saw him as a structuralist, mainly because of the close contacts with eminent linguist Roman Jakobson. In 1989 professor Pritsak founded the Oriental Institute of the Ukrainian National Academy of Sciences and the Ukrainian journal of Oriental studies *Skhidnyj Svit*. He spent his last years in the United States. Agafangel Efimovich Krimsky (1871–1942) was a Russian, Soviet, and Ukrainian Orientalist, historian, and a literary scholar; he makes an important contribution to the study of Iran, Turkey and the Turkish language, Arabic literature, as well as the Crimean Tatars. He was one of the founders of the Ukrainian Academy of Sciences in 1918. In the 1920s Krimsky was involved in the creation of the literary Ukrainian language, a project designed by the Soviet power. From the late 1920s he suffered persecution as a "bourgeois nationalist" up to 1939. In 1941 he was arrested and exiled to Kazakhstan. A brief account of the development of Oriental studies in Ukraine is given in Ella Cigankova, *Shodoznavčì ustanovi v Ukraïnì (radâns'kij period)* [The Institutions of Oriental Studies of Ukraine in the Soviet Period] (Kiev: Kritika, 2007).

3. The Bund (also The Jewish Labour Bund, or The General Jewish Labour Bund in Lithuania, Poland, and Russia; in Yiddish: *Algemeyner Yidisher Arbeter Bund in Lite, Poylin un Rusland*) is a Jewish Socialist party founded in 1897.

4. Ezer Weizman (1924–2005) was an Israeli politician. In 1993–2003 he was the president of Israel; in 1989–1990 he held the post of minister for science and technologies.

5. Andrey Vasilyevich Fedorchenko, born in 1958, is a Russian economist. He was the head of the Department of Israel Studies at the Institute of Oriental Studies, Russian Academy of Sciences, in 1992–2004. See Andrey V. Fedorchenko, "Palestine and Israel Studies in Russia," in *Russian Orientalists to the 36th ICANAS* (Moscow: Institute of Oriental Studies of Russian Academy of Science, 2000), 61–67; about the history of the Department of Israel Studies of the Soviet/Russian Academy of Science see Tatyana Nosenko and Nina Semenchenko, *Naprasnaya vražda. Očerki sovetsko-izrail'skih otnošenij 1948–1991 gg.* [The Futile Enmity: Essays on the Soviet-Israeli Relations, 1948–1991] (Moscow: Institute of Oriental Studies of Russian Academy of Science, 2015), 233–37.

6. See A/RES/46/86, December 16, 1991. Elimination of racism and racial discrimination; This reversed previous resolution that Zionism was a "form of racism and racial discrimina-

tion." See A/RES/3379 (XXX), November 10, 1975. Elimination of all forms of racial discrimination.

7. Nehemia Levtzion (1935–2003) was an Israeli scholar in the fields of Islamic and African studies. In 1978–1981 he was the dean of the Faculty of Humanities at Hebrew University of Jerusalem. In 1982–1987 he was the director of the Ben-Zvi Institute. In 1992 he became the academic chairperson of the International Center for University Teaching of Jewish Civilization being involved in the development of Jewish studies in Russia. See Canadian Association of African Studies, "The Legacy of Nehemia Levtzion (1935–2003)," *Canadian Journal of African Studies/Revue Canadienne des Études Africaines* 42, no. 2/3 (2008): 230–49.

8. Professor Sha'ul Stampfer, born in 1948, is an Israeli and U.S. historian, specializing in East European Jewry in the early modern period and Jewish education. He was one of the founders of Jewish academic and educational institutions in the very late period of the Soviet Union. In 1991 he initiated the foundation of Jewish University in Moscow. In the 1990s–2000s he instructed many in the post-Soviet states. See Semyon Charny, "Evrejskij universitet v Moskve (1991–2009) [The Jewish University of Moscow]," *Materialy Šestnadcatoj ežegodnoj meždunarodnoj meždisciplinarnoj konferencii po iudaike* [The Proceedings of the 16th Moscow Conference on Jewish Studies]) 2 (2009): 490–522. Viktoria Valentinovna Mochalova, born in 1945, is a Soviet and Russian philologist, a specialist in the history of Polish literature. Since 1973 she has been a research assistant at the Institute of Slavic Studies of Russian Soviet/Russian Academy of Sciences. She is one of the founders of the "Sefer" Center. Rashid Muradovich Kaplanov (1949–2007) was a Soviet and Russian historian who specialized in the history of Portugal. Since the 1970s he had started his research in Jewish history. In the early 1980s he was actively involved in the work conducted by the semilegal Jewish Historical and Ethnographic Commission which connected official Soviet academic institutions and underground Jewish clubs. In 1994 Dr. Kaplanov was one of the founders of the "Sefer" Center and headed its Academic Council. In 2002–2006 he was elected president of the European Association of Jewish Studies. On Dr. Rashid Kaplanov see: SEFER Center for University Teaching of Jewish Civilization, *Rashid Muradovič Kaplanov: Trudy. Interv'û. Vospominaniâ* [Rashid Muradovich Kaplanov: Papers. Interviews. Memory] (Moscow: SEFER Center, 2011); see also Kaplanov's obituary in *The Times* on January 7, 2008. Igor Krupnik, "Problemy etnografičeskogo izučeniâ evreev v SSSR: vosem' let spustâ" [On Problems of Ethnographic Study of Jews in the USSR: Eight Years Later], in *Ističeskie sud'vy evreev v Rossii i SSSR: načalo dialoga* [Historical Destinies of Jews in Russia and the USSR: The Beginning of a Dialogue] (Moscow: Jewish Historical Society, 1992), 28–40 Igor Krupnik (ed.); also "Kak my zanimalis' istoriej . . . i etnografiej: K 35–letiû Evrejskoj istoriko-etnografičeskoj komissii, 1981–1990 gg" [About Us Studying History and Ethnography: To the 35th Anniversary of the Jewish Historical and Ethnographic Commission, 1981–1990], in *Sovetskaya iudaika: istoriâ, problematika, personalii* [Jewish Studies in the USSR: History, Problems, and Persons] (Jerusalem/Moscow: Gesharim, 2017), 286–360, Mark Kupovetsky (ed.). Leonid Aleksandrovich Matsikh (1954–2012) was a Jewish-Russian philosopher and theologist. In the early 1990s he was engaged in cooperation with the International Center for University Teaching of Jewish Civilization (Jerusalem). In the mid- and late 1990s he worked for the American Jewish Joint Distribution Committee in Moscow. John Doyle Klier (1944–2007) was a U.S. and British historian of East European Jewry and Russia. Being in Russia in the early 1990s, he contributed to the foundation of Jewish scholarship in post-Soviet Russia. Ralph Goldman (1915–2014) was a Jewish public figure. In the 1950s he was D. Ben-Gurion's advisor. From the mid-1970s he worked as a senior officer at the American Jewish Joint Distribution Committee (AJJDC). On Ralph Goldman, see Tom Shachtman, *I Seek My Brethren: Ralph Goldman and "The Joint". Rescue, Relief, and Reconstruction—The Work of the American Jewish Joint Distribution Committee* (New York: Newmarket Press, 2001). From 1988–2003 Rabbi Jonathan Porath was a senior officer of the Russian Department in "the Joint" Jerusalem office. He is a specialist in Jewish community building. He has served as an advisor of various Jewish communities' projects in the United States. He is considered a founder of the Hillel youth movement in Russia and the former Soviet Union countries.

9. The Institute of Oriental Studies of the Russian Academy of Sciences is one of the main Russian academic institutions for the study of Asia and Africa. It was established in 1818 as the Asiatic Museum. As it now stands, the Institute arose in 1930. The Institute for the Study of Asian and African Countries is a special department at Moscow State University which trains specialists in Oriental languages, history, economics, and politics. It was established in 1956. The Institute's chair in Jewish studies was created in 1998. Moscow State Institute of International Relations, now known as *MGIMO* University, is a higher educational establishment which trains diplomats and specialists in politics, international trade, international law, and so on. The University was founded in 1944. It has positioned itself as the elite educational establishment during the Soviet period, as well as during the post-Soviet one.

10. Alexander Garmatenko, "V Odesse rešili zakryt' strategičeskij institut" [The Strategic Institute Is Reported to Be Closed in Odessa], *Vesti*, March 3, 2015. https://vesti-ukr.com/odessa/91057-v-odesse-zakryvajut-strategicheskij-institut.

11. Viktor Fedorovych Yanukovych, born in 1950, is a Ukrainian politician. In 1997–2002 he served as the governor of Donetsk *Oblast'*. In 2002–2004 and 2006–2007 he held the post of the prime minister. In 2010 he was elected president. He was removed from his post by the Euromaidan Revolution in 2014 and finally escaped to Russia. Change of power in the Ukraine in 2014 caused internal unrest, separatist sentiments, increase in extremism, and, finally, Russian intervention into Ukrainian politics. Odessa was one of the Ukrainian regions which gave strong support to Viktor Yanukovych. In Odessa *Oblast'* during the second round of elections 74.14 percent voted for Yanukovich, while 19.52 percent voted for his key opponent Yulia Tymoshenko (according to results presented by the Central Election Commission of Ukraine). See Centralna viborča komisiâ Ukraïni. Pìdsumki golosuvannâ z viboriv Prezidenta Ukraïni 7 lûtogo 2010 roku [The Central Election Committee of Ukraine. The Results of the Presidential Election, February 7, 2010]. http://www.cvk.gov.ua/pls/vp2010/WP0011.

12. Alek D. Epstein, "Osnovnye napravleniâ i novye tendencii v razvitii izrailevedčeskih issledovanij v 80-90-e gody" [Main Areas and New Tendencies in the Development of Israel Studies in the 1980s–1990s], *Vostok (Oriens)* [The Orient] 1 (2001): 172–80; "Izučenie Izraila v Rossii (1991–2006): dostiženiâ i problemy" [The Study of Israel in Russia, 1991–2006], *Vostok (Oriens)* [The Orient] 2 (2007): 167–70; Dzmitry Shavialiou, "Izrailevedenie i palestinovedenie v sovremennoj Rossii (k voprosu o definiciâh i sostoânii otraslej" [Israel Studies and Palestine Studies in Contemporary Russia (On Definitions and Current State of Affairs)], *Vostok (Oriens)* [The Orient] 5 (2007): 216–20.

13. Alexander Fomin, *Vojna s prodolženiem. Veliokobritaniâ i Franciâ v bor'be za 'osmanskoe nasledstvo'* [The Continuing War. Great Britain and France in the Struggle for 'the Ottoman Legacy'] (Moscow: Universitet Dmitriâ Požarskogo, 2010); Dzmitry Shavialiou, "Review of: Fomin, Alexander. *Vojna s prodolženiem* [The Continuing War] (Moscow, 2010)]," *Vostok (Oriens)* [The Orient] 6 (2011): 177–79.

14. Dzmitry Shavialiou, "Deklaraciâ Bal'fura 2 noâbrâ 1917 g. i sionistskij proekt 18 iûlâ 1917 g.: semantičeskij analiz teksta" [The Balfour Declaration, November 2, 1917, and a Zionist Project, July 18, 1917: Semantic Analyses], *Belorusskij žurnal meždunarodnogo prava i meždunarodnyh otnošenij* [Belarusian Journal of International Law and International Relations] 1 (2000): 82–86; Anton Shandra, "Novye podhody k interpretacii deklaracii Balfura v sovremennoj otečestvennoj istoriografii" [The New Approaches to the Interpretation of the Balfour Declaration in Modern National Historiography], *Političeskaâ žizn' Zapadnoj Evropy: antičnost', srednie veka, novoe i novejšee vremâ* [Political Life in Western Europe: Antiquity, Middle Age, Modern and Recent History] 11 (2016): 116–20; Mikhail Shapovalov, "'Palestinskoe nasledstvo' v politike Vremennogo pravitelstva (mart-aprel' 1917)" [The 'Palestine Legacy' in the policy of the Provisional Government, March–April 1917)], *Novejšaâ istoriâ Rossii* [The Recent History of Russia] 2 (2017): 19–32; "Pričiny sozdaniâ Deklaracii Balfura: stoletnij dokument v rossijskoj intrerpretacii" [Reasons for the Balfour Declaration: 100 Years Old Document in Russian Interpretation], *Stanovlenie evrejskoj gosudarstvennosti v XX veke: klûčevye sobytiâ* [The Establishment of Jewish Statehood in the 20th Century: Key Events] 1 (2018): 172–81.

15. Vasily Osipovich Klyuchevsky (1841–1911) was an eminent Russian historian in the late imperial period. He studied at Moscow State University and learned from Sergey Solov-

yov, who is considered one of the founders of Russian historiography. V. O. Klyuchevsky wrote about Russian history, mainly the medieval period. His main book is based on a course in Russian history which he lectured at the University. There is an edition of Klyuchevsky's *A History of Russia* in English (London-New York, 1911–1926). Ignaty Yulianovich Krachkovsky (1883–1951) was an outstanding Russian Orientalist. He is considered one of the founders of Arabic scholarship in Soviet Russia. He studied at the University of Saint Petersburg. His last apprentice, Anna Arkadyevna Dolinina, wrote an academic biography of her teacher *Nevolnik dolga* (Saint Petersburg, 1994). Krachkovsky's writings were published in Russian in 1955–1960. Many of his works were translated into European languages and Arabic. He is the author of the literal and exact translation of the Quran into Russian.

16. Avigdor Lieberman, born in 1958, is an Israeli politician of Soviet origin. He started his political career in Israel in the early 1980s. He has been one of the founders of the Israeli 'Russian' party 'Yisra'el Beiteinu' for the 1999 election. Lieberman's party, 'Yisra'el Beiteinu,' is considered close to the Revisionist Zionism of Ze'ev Jabotinsky. In 2016 he filled the post of defense minister. On Lieberman's views on politics, economy, and the Arab question, see Avigdor Lieberman, *Ničego, krome pravdy* [Nothing but the Truth] (Tel-Aviv: Ivrus, 2005).

17. *Millet*, plural *milletler*, is a Turkish word that describes a system of laws for confessional communities in the Ottoman Empire. One of the classic books on early Palestine was written by a Russian diplomat in the Ottoman Porte. See Konstantin Bazili, *Siriâ i Palestina pod tureckim pravitel'stvom v istoričeskom i političeskom otnošeniâh* [Syria and Palestine under Turkish Rule in the Historical and Political Contexts] (Jerusalem/Moscow: Gesharim, 2007 [ca. 1860s]).

18. Evgeniy Dmitriev et al., "Palestinskoe dviženie soprotivleniâ" [The Palestine Resistance]. In *Novejšaâ istoriâ arabskih stran Azii 1917–1985* [The Recent History of the Arabic Countries of Asia, 1917–1985] (Moscow: Nauka Publishing House, 1988), 223–68.

19. Vladimir Ivanovich Kisilyov (1924–2008) was a Soviet and Russian historian and a journalist, specializing in Middle Eastern affairs. He headed the Department of Israel Studies at the Institute of Oriental Studies of the Soviet Academy of Sciences from its foundation in the early 1970s. Vladimir Kisilyov's academic interests were focused on the national liberation movement in Sudan and the Palestine question. Dr. Kisilyov was the academic advisor of Mahmoud Abbas, the then Palestinian political activist, during his study in Moscow. Yevgeny Dmitrievich Pyrlin (1932–2001) was a Soviet and Russian Orientalist and diplomat. His academic interests were focused on the Palestine problem. During the Soviet period he wrote under the pen name Yevgeny Dmitriev. He wrote his last two books under his real name. See Yevgeny Pyrlin, *100 let protivoborstva. Genezis, evoluciâ, sovremennoe sostoânie i perspektivy rešeniâ palestinskoj problemy* [100 Years of Confrontation: The Genesis, Evolution, Present State, and Prospects for Solving of the Palestine Problem] (Moscow: ROSSPEN Publishing House, 2001); see also *Trudnyj i dolgij put' k miru: vzglâd iz Moskvy na problem bliznevostočnogo uregulirivaniâ* [The Hard and Long Road to the Peace: A View from Moscow on the Middle East Settlement] (Moscow: ROSSPEN Publishing House, 2002). On Pyrlin's last books, see Dzmitry Shavialiou and Maryna Malakhvey, "Review of: Pyrlin, Yevgeny, *100 let protivoborstva. Genezis, evoluciâ, sovremennoe sostoânie i perspektivy rešeniâ palestinskoj problemy* [100 Years of Confrontation: The Genesis, Evolution, Present State, and Prospects for Solving of the Palestine Problem]. (Moscow, 2001) and Pyrlin, Yevgeny, Trudnyj i dolgij put' k miru: vzglâd iz Moskvy na problem bliznevostočnogo uregulirivaniâ [The Hard and Long Road to the Peace: A View from Moscow on the Middle East Settlement] (Moscow, 2002)," *Vostok (Oriens)* [The Orient] 6 (2003): 176–80.

20. Pyrlin, *100 let protivoborstva. Genezis, evoluciâ, sovremennoe sostoânie i perspektivy rešeniâ palestinskoj problemy*, 11.

21. Pyrlin, *100 let*, 19.

22. All the periods of activity of the Palestine Society could be divided into four stages. The first one is 1882–1917, "the imperial period" of Palestine Society, which is considered the most productive one. In that period the Society made the most of its significant scientific discoveries, maintained education in its own schools, and looked after Russian pilgrims in the Holy Land. The Society received support from state institutions—the Ministry for Foreign Affairs and the

Synod—as well as the Russian Orthodox Church, and enjoyed backing of the imperial family. On the Palestine Society of that period in English, see Derek Hopwood, *The Russian Presence in Syria and Palestine, 1843–1914. Church and Politics in the Near East* (Oxford: Clarendon Press. 1969), 99–158; in Russian, see also: Alexey A. Dmitrievsky, *Imperatorskoe Pravoslavnoe Palestinskoe Obŝestvo i ego deâtelnost' za istekshuû četvert' veka 1882–1907* [The Imperial Orthodox Palestine Society and Its Activity during the Last Quarter of a Century, 1882–1907] (Saint Petersburg: Oleg Abyshko Publishing House. 2008). For a short survey of the Society's archival documents in Saint Petersburg, see Alexander Grushevoy, "Imperatorskoe Palestinskoe obŝestvo (po peterburgskim arhivam)" [The Imperial Orthodox Palestine Society (According to Materials from Petersburg Archives], in *Arhivy russkih vizantinistov v Sankt-Peterburge* [Records of Russian Byzantinists in Saint Petersburg] (Saint Petersburg: Dmitrij Bulanin Publ. House, 1995), 134–56; for a survey of Society's history from 1882 up to the 2000s, see Nikolay Lisovoy, "Imperatorskoe Pravoslavnoe Palestinskoe Obŝestvo: 125 let služeniâ Cerkvi i Rossii" [The Imperial Orthodox Palestine Society: 125 Years in the Service of the Church and Russia], in *Dmitrievsky, Alexey. Imperatorskoe Pravoslavnoe Palestinskoe Obŝestvo i ego deâtelnost' za istekshuû četvert' veka 1882–1907* [Dmitrievsky, Alexey. The Imperial Orthodox Palestine Society and Its Activity during the Last Quarter of a Century, 1882–1907], Nikolay Lisovoy (ed.) (Saint Petersburg: Oleg Abyshko Publishing House, 2008), 371–432. The second stage applies to the period from 1917 to the mid-1930s, which witnessed the revolutionary period in Russia and the split in the Church and in the Palestine Society. Two Palestine Societies appeared, one which was related to the Russian émigré and the Russian Orthodox Church Abroad, and one remained in Soviet Russia. The Society in Russia was included in the Academy of Sciences and had such a status till 1992. During that period both Societies, the "White" and one which was in Soviet Russia, had litigation for properties abroad remaining from the prerevolutionary times. The Palestine Society in the Soviet Union was the most active during the 1920s. A. Grushevoy argued that the Society was officially closed from June 1923 to 1925 (see Grushevoy, 134). By the late 1930s the activity of the Society ceased. The third stage passes through the 1950s to the late 1980s. The activity of the Palestine Society in the Soviet Union was renewed in 1950 and was due to Soviet contacts with Israel and Moscow desire to penetrate to the Middle East. Meanwhile, activity of the Society focused on research and publishing. The Leningrad academicians revived the journal *Palestinskiy sbornik*. The first issue of *Sbornik* was published in 1954. In the 1950s to the 1980s the journal of the Society published many publications in the fields of Hebrew and Bible studies, as well as the Semitic languages and history of the ancient Near East, while in the Moscow office of the Society there were ideological activities against Zionism and Israel. There are some published letters concerning the revitalization of the Society's activity in 1930 and 1950 written by I. Krachkovsky ("Zapiski o deâtel'nosti Rossijskogo Palestinskogo obŝestva" [Papers on the Activity of the Russian Palestine Society], in *Neizvestnye stranicy otečestvennogo vostokovedeniâ* [Unknown Stories of Russian Oriental Studies] vol.1 [Moscow: Vostočnaâ literature Publishing House, 1997], 137–54). It was I. Krachkovsky who had proposed to revive the journal of the Palestine Society. The fourth period began in 1992 with the new status of the Society as a public institution.

23. On relations between Russia and Israel, see memoirs by the Russian ambassador to Israel in 1991–1997, Alexander Bovin (*Zapiski nenastoâŝego posla* [The Papers of a Fake Ambassador] [Moscow: Zakharov Publishing House, 2001]).

24. Yevgeny Maksimovich Primakov (1929–2015) was a Soviet and Russian scholar—a specialist in contemporary history of the Arab countries and Middle Eastern affairs. In 1956–1970 he served as a journalist, including his service as a Middle Eastern correspondent of a central Soviet newspaper *Pravda*. In 1977–1985 he was the director of the Institute of Oriental Studies of the USSR Academy of Sciences. In 1985–1989 he headed another academic institution—Institute for World Economy and International Relations. He was in the inner circle of the Soviet leader Mikhail Gorbachev in 1989–1991. In 1991–1996 he was the chief of the Russian intelligent service. He held the post of Foreign Minister in 1996–1998, and served as the Russian Prime Minister in 1998–1999. On his career and traveling across the Middle East, see Yevgeny M. Primakov, *Konfidencialno: Bližnij Vostok na scene i za kulisami (pervaâ polovina XX - načalo XXI veka)* [Classified: The Middle East in the Theatre and Beyond]

(Moscow: Rossijskaâ gazeta, 2006). Yury Mikhaylovich Luzhkov, born in 1936, is a Russian politician. During Soviet times he worked in the chemical industry. From the late 1970s he became a member of Moscow governing bodies. In 1992–2010 he was the mayor of Moscow.

25. The term "the Prymakov doctrine" was presumably coined by the current foreign minister of Russia Sergei Lavrov; see TASS, "Lavrov: v nedalëkom budušem istoriki sformuliruût takoe ponâtie, kak 'doktrina Primakova'" [Lavrov, In the Near Future Historians Will Formulate Such Term as the 'Primakov Doctrine'], *TACC*, October 28, 2014. https://tass.ru/politika/ 1537769. After that article the concept of the Prymakov doctrine appeared in academic and media discourse.

26. Vladimir N. Trutnev, "Russkaâ diplomatiâ i Rossijskoe Imperatorskoe Pravoslavnoe Palestinskoe obŝestvo (po materialam Arhiva Vnešnej Politiki Rossii)" [The Russian Diplomacy and the Russian Imperial Orthodox Palestine Society (According to Materials from the Archive of Foreign Policy of Russia)], in *Diplomatičeskij Ežegodnik 1992* [The Diplomatic Yearbook 1992] (Moscow: Publishing House "International Relations," 1992), 249–68.

27. Yuriy V. Suslikov, "Sud'ba rossijskoy sobstvennosti [The Fate of Russian Property] [part 1]," *Aziâ i Afrika segodnâ* [Asia and Africa Today] 6 (1995): 75–80; "Sud'ba rossijskoy sobstvennosti [The Fate of Russian Property] [part 2]," *Aziâ i Afrika segodnâ* [Asia and Africa Today] 7 (1995): 46–51.

28. On the period after 1917, see Oleg Budnitskii, *Rossijskie evrei meždu krasnymi i belymi [1917–1920]* [Russian Jews between the Reds and the Whites] (Moscow: ROSSPEN Publishing House, 2006), 413–17; Gabriel Zifroni, "Rusim ''adumim' ve–rusim 'levanim' be–Yerušalaim" ['Red Russians' and 'White Russians' in Jerusalem], *Katedra* 5 (1977): 162–95; Maryna Shavialiova, Khristina Vitiv, and Dzmitry Shavialiou, "Ob odnom episode iz istorii Russkoj dukhovnoj missii v Ierusalime (po materialam arhivnogo dela J15/2880 Cental'nogo sionistskogo arhiva Izrailâ)" [An Episode from the History of the Russian Ecclesiastical Mission in Jerusalem (According to the Archival File J15/2880 of the Central Zionist Archives of Israel], *Tsaytshrift/Časopis* [The Journal] 9, no. 4 (2014): 177–91; only one episode is excluded from that rule—it is so called "the Orange deal" (in Russian *Apelsinovaâ sdelka*), an agreement between the Soviet Union and Israel on October 17, 1964, according to which the Soviet Union sold twenty-two pieces of property to Israel.

29. Omar Makhamid, *Rossiâ i Palestina: dialog na rubeže XIX–XX vekov: Istoriko-literaturnye očerki* [Russia and Palestine: Dialogue at the Turn of the 19th–20th Centuries. Historical and Literary Profiles] (Saint Petersburg: Liki Rossii, 2002); The League of Arab States and the Embassy of the State of Palestine in the Russian Federation. Special Issue. *Palestina - Rossiâ: svâz' vremën* [Palestine and Russia—Historical Liaisons]. S.l., S.a.

30. Alexander Yanovitsky, "Prisutstvie i interesy Russkoj Pravoslavnoj Cerkvi v Zemle Izrailâ," [Presence and Interests of the Russian Orthodox Church in the Land of Israel], *Lekhaim* 8, no. 232 (2011). https://lechaim.ru/ARHIV/232/yanovitskiy.htm

31. The Oak of Mamre, also known as the Oak of Sibta, or the Oak of Abraham, is a site near old Mamre, now in Hebron. The tree refers to Genesis 18:1, 4 (King James Version). The plot of land with the Oak was given to Russia on July 5, 1997.

32. One of the most successful attempts to gather researchers from all the countries who study the Holy Land is *Ierusalimskij Pravoslavnyj Seminar* (the journal has been published in Russian since 2010).

33. Porfiri Uspenski (Konstantin Aleksandrovich Uspenski) (1804–1885) was a priest of the Russian Orthodox Church, a Russian theologian, traveler, and Orientalist. He initiated the foundation of the Russian ecclesiastical mission in Jerusalem in 1847. See Hopwood, *The Russian Presence*, 33–45. Antonin Kapustin (Andrey Ivanovich Kapustin) (1817–1894) was an Orientalist, theologian, and Byzantinist, he headed the Russian Ecclesiastical Mission in Jerusalem in 1865–1894. See Hopwood, *The Russian Presence*, 77–95.

34. A. F. Berednikov, "Rossijskoe Palestinskoe obŝestvo: K stoletiû so dnâ osnovaniâ" [The Russian Palestine Society (in Commemoration of the Centenary of Its Founding], *Narody Azii i Afriki* [The Peoples of Asia and Africa] 6 (1983): 88–92; Alexander V. Krylov, "Rossijskoe Palestinskoe obŝestvo i otečestvennoe vostokovedenie" [The Russian Palestine Society and Russian Oriental Studies], *Vestnik Moskovskogo universiteta. Seriâ 13* [The Bulletin of Moscow University. Series 13] 4 (1989): 16–33; Alexander Krylov and Nadezhda Sorokina, *Imper-*

atorskoe Pravoslavnoe Palestinskoe Obŝestvo i otečestvennoe vostokovedenie [The Russian Orthodox Palestine Society and Russian Oriental Studies] (Moscow: The Publishing House of MGIMO University, 2007).

35. Irina Vorobyova, *Russkie missii v Svâtoj zemle v 1847–1917 godah* [Russian Missions to the Holy Land, 1847–1917] (Moscow: Institute of Oriental Studies Publishing House, 2001); Makhamid, *Rossiâ i Palestina*; Boris Yamilinets, *Rossiâ i Palestina. Očerki političeskih i kulturno–religioznyh otnošenij (XI–načalo XX veka)* [Russia and Palestine. Essays on Political, Cultural and Religious Relations in the 19th–early 20th Centuries] (Moscow: Institute of Oriental Studies of Russian Academy of Science, and Saint Petersburg: Letnij Sad Publishing House, 2003); Nikolay Lisovoy, "Russkoe prisutstvie v Svâtoj zemle: učreždeniâ, lûdi, nasledie [Russian Presence in the Holy Land: Institutions, Persons, and Legacy] [part 1]," *Otečestvennaâ istoriâ* [The National History] 2 (2003): 19–36.

36. Kirill E. Baldin, "Sozdanie mestnyh organizacij Imperatorskogo Pravoslavnogo Palestinskogo Obŝestva (1890-e gg.)" [Establishing of Local Offices of the Imperial Orthodox Palestine Society during the 1890s], *Vestnik Ivanovskogo gosudarstvennogo universiteta. Seria "Gumanitarnye nauki"* [The Bulletin of Ivanovo University. Series of the Humanities] 4, no. 12 (2012): 8–16; Valery Cys' and Olga Cys', *Otdely Imperstorskogo Pravoslavnogo Palestinskogo obŝestva v Zapadnoj Sibiri v konce XIX - načale XX vv.: Osnovnye napravleniâ, soderžanie i rezultaty deâtelnosti* [Offices of the Imperial Orthodox Palestine Society in Western Siberia in the late 19th–early 20th centuries: Activity and Its Outcomes], (Nizhnevartovsk: The Publishing House of Nizhnevartovsk University, 2014); "Finansovye osnovy funkcionirovaniâ zapadno-sibirskih otdelov Imperstorskogo Pravoslavnogo Palestinskogo obŝestva v konce XIX - načale XX v." [The Financial Framework for West Siberian Offices of the Imperial Orthodox Palestine Society in the late 19th–early 20th centuries], *Vestnik Pravoslavnogo Svâto-Tihonovskogo gumanitarnogo universiteta* [The Bulletin of Saint Tikhon's University] *II*, 1.

37. Lora Gerd, "Arhimandrit Antonin Kapustin i ego naučnaâ deâtelnost' (po materialam peterbergskih arhivov)" [Archimandrite Antonin Kapustin and His Researches (According to Materials from Petersburg Archives)], in *Rukopisnoe nasledie russkih vizantinistov v arhivah Sankt-Peterburga* [Manuscripts of Russian Byzantinists in Archives of Saint Petersburg] (Saint Petersburg: The Archive of Russian Academy of Science in Saint Petersburg, 1995), 8–35; *Rossiâ i Pravoslavnyj Vostok. Konstantinopol'skij patriarhat v konce XIX v.: Pisma G.P.Begleri k prof. I.E.Troickomu 1878–1898 gg.* [Russia and the Orthodox East. The Patriarchate of Constantinople in the Late 19th Century: Letters by G. P.Beglery to Prof. I. E.Troitsky in 1878–1898] (Saint Petersburg: Oleg Abyshko Publishing House, 2003); *Konstantinopol' i Peterburg: Cerkovnaâ politika Rossii na Pravoslavnom Vostoke (1878–1898): Avtoreferat dissertacii... doktora istoričeskih nauk* [Constantinople and Petersburg: Russian Church Policy in the Orthodox East, 1878–1898. Abstract of Dissertation] (Saint Petersburg: The Institute of History in Saint Petersburg, 2006); Grushevoy, "Imperatorskoe Palestinskoe obŝestvo (po peterburgskim arhivam)."

38. See also the website of the Imperial Orthodox Palestine Society: http://www.ippo.ru.

39. Sergey Semionovich Uvarov (1786–1885) was a Russian statesman in the period of Nicholas I and a connoisseur of the antique world. He headed the Russian Academy of Science in 1818–1855. He invented the "Official Nationality" doctrine.

40. Nikolay Lisovoy, "Russkoe prisutstvie v Svâtoj zemle: učreždeniâ, lûdi, nasledie [Russian Presence in the Holy Land: Institutions, Persons, and Legacy] [part 1]," *Otečestvennaâ istoriâ* [The National History] 2(2003): 19–36, 22.

41. Yamilinets, *Rossiâ i Palestina.*

42. Lisovoy, "Russkoe prisutstvie v Svâtoj zemle: učreždeniâ, lûdi, nasledie [Russian Presence in the Holy Land: Institutions, Persons, and Legacy] [part 1]."

43. Natalya Narochnitskaya, "Staryj 'vostočnyj vopros' v novoj anglosaksonskoj politike" [The Old 'Eastern Question' in the New Anglo-Saxon Politics.], *Meždunarodnaâ žizn'* [International Affairs] 8 (2001): 75–89, 76.

44. Compare: Yamilinets, *Rossiâ i Palestina*, 103–17; Lisovoy, "Russkoe prisutstvie v Svâtoj zemle: učreždeniâ, lûdi, nasledie [Russian Presence in the Holy Land: Institutions, Persons, and Legacy] [part 1]," 22–31.

45. Nikolay Lisovoy, *Russkoe duhovnoe i političeskoe prisutstvie v Svâtoj zemle i na Bližnem Vostoke v XIX - načale XX v* [Russian Religious and Political Presence in the Holy Land and the Middle East] (Moscow: Indrik Publishing House, 2006).

46. Dmitry Bratkin, "Imperatorskoe Pravoslavnoe Palestinskoe obŝestvo na fone zapadnogo palestinovedeniâ" [The Imperial Orthodox Palestine Society against a Background of Western Palestine Studies], *Religiovedenie* [Religious Studies] 4 (2016): 122–29.

47. I. Vorobyova has proven that the Russian Palestine Society was modeled on the Palestine Exploration Fund (*Russkie missii v Svâtoj zemle v 1847–1917 godah*, 91).

48. On collections of PEF, see its website: https://www.pef.org.uk.

49. Pyrlin, *100 let protivoborstva. Genezis, evoluciâ, sovremennoe sostoânie i perspektivy rešeniâ palestinskoj problemy*, 10.

50. Several scholars had previously noted this. See David Fishman, "Thiyatam shel mada'ey ha–yahadut be–Rusya bi–shnot ha–tish'im [The Revival of Jewish Studies in Russia in the 1990s]," *Yehudey brit ha–mo'atsot be–ma'avar* [The Soviet Jews at a Crossroads] 4, no. 19 (2000): 250–60; Stephanie Hofman, "'Al pe'ilot merkaz 'Sefer' ba–brit ha–mo'atsot leshe'avar" [On the Activity of the 'Sefer' Center in the Former Soviet Union], *Yehudey brit ha–mo'atsot be–ma'avar* [The Soviet Jews at a Crossroads] 4, no. 19 (2000): 261–64.

51. Mikhail Agapov, *Istoki sovetsko–izrail'skih otnošenij: 'Evrejskij nacional'nyj očag' v politike SSSR v 1920–e–1930–e gg.* [The Origin of the Soviet-Israeli Relations: The Jewish National Home in the USSR policy in the 1920s–1930s] (Tumen': Vector–book, 2011); *Evrejsko–palestinskoe soobŝestvo v sovetskoj bližnevostočnoj politike v 1939–1948 gg.* [The Jewish-Palestinian Community in the Soviet Middle Eastern Policy, 1939–1948] (Tumen': Vector–book, 2012).

52. Alexey Afanasyevich Dmitrievsky (1856–1929) was a Russian scholar, historian of the Russian Church, Byzantinist, and theologian. Between 1907–1918 he was the secretary of the Imperial Orthodox Palestine Society. Vasili Nikolaevich Khitrovo (1834–1903) was a Russian statesman. He initiated the foundation of the Russian Palestine Society, which was established in 1882.

BIBLIOGRAPHY

A/RES/3379 (XXX). November 10, 1975. Elimination of all forms of racial discrimination.

A/RES/46/86 December 16, 1991. Elimination of racism and racial discrimination.

Agapov, Mikhail. *Istoki sovetsko–izrail'skih otnošenij: 'Evrejskij nacional'nyj očag' v politike SSSR v 1920–e–1930–e gg.* [The Origin of the Soviet-Israeli Relations: The Jewish National Home in the USSR policy in the 1920s–1930s]. Tumen': Vector-book, 2011.

———. *Evrejsko-palestinskoe soobŝestvo v sovetskoj bližnevostočnoj politike v 1939–1948 gg.* [The Jewish-Palestinian Community in the Soviet Middle Eastern Policy, 1939–1948]. Tumen': Vector-book, 2012.

Baldin, Kirill E. "Sozdanie mestnyh organizacij Imperatorskogo Pravoslavnogo Palestinskogo Obŝestva (1890–e gg.)" [Establishing of Local Offices of the Imperial Orthodox Palestine Society during the 1890s]. *Vestnik Ivanovskogo gosudarstvennogo universiteta. Seria "Gumanitarnye nauki"* [The Bulletin of Ivanovo University. Series of the Humanities] 4, no. 12 (2012): 8–16.

Bazili, Konstantin. *Siriâ i Palestina pod tureckim pravitel'stvom v istoričeskom i političeskom otnošeniâh* [Syria and Palestine under Turkish Rule in the Historical and Political Contexts]. Jerusalem/Moscow: Gesharim, 2007 [ca. 1860s].

Berednikov, A. F. "Rossijskoe Palestinskoe obŝestvo: K stoletiû so dnâ osnovaniâ" [The Russian Palestine Society (in Commemoration of the Centenary of Its Founding)]. *Narody Azii i Afriki* [The Peoples of Asia and Africa] 6 (1983): 88–92.

Bovin, Alexander. *Zapiski nenastoâŝego posla* [The Papers of a Fake Ambassador]. Moscow: Zakharov Publishing House, 2001.

Bratkin, Dmitry. "Imperatorskoe Pravoslavnoe Palestinskoe obŝestvo na fone zapadnogo palestinovedeniâ" [The Imperial Orthodox Palestine Society against a Background of Western Palestine Studies]. *Religiovedenie* [Religious Studies] 4 (2016): 122–29.

Budnitskii, Oleg. *Rossijskie evrei meždu krasnymi i belymi [1917–1920]* [Russian Jews between the Reds and the Whites]. Moscow: ROSSPEN Publishing House, 2006.

Canadian Association of African Studies. "The Legacy of Nehemia Levtzion (1935–2003)." *Canadian Journal of African Studies/Revue Canadienne des Études Africaines* 42, no. 2/3 (2008): 230–49.

Centralna viborča komisiâ Ukraïni. Pìdsumki golosuvannâ z viborìv Prezidenta Ukraïni 7 lûtogo 2010 roku [The Central Election Committee of Ukraine. The Results of the Presidential Election, February 7, 2010]. http://www.cvk.gov.ua/pls/vp2010/WP0011.

Charny, Semyon. "Evrejskij universitet v Moskve (1991–2009) [The Jewish University of Moscow]." *Materialy Šestnadcatoj ežegodnoj meždunarodnoj meždisciplinarnoj konferencii po iudaike* [The Proceedings of the 16th Moscow Conference on Jewish Studies]) 2 (2009): 490–522.

Cigankova, Ella. *Shodoznavčì ustanovi v Ukraïnì (radâns'kij period)* [The Institutions of Oriental Studies of Ukraine in the Soviet Period]. Kiev: Kritika, 2007.

Cys', Valery, and Olga Cys'. *Otdely Imperstorskogo Pravoslavnogo Palestinskogo obŝestva v Zapadnoj Sibiri v konce XIX—načale XX vv.: Osnovnye napravleniâ, soderžanie i rezultaty deâtelnosti* [Offices of the Imperial Orthodox Palestine Society in Western Siberia in the late 19th—early 20th centuries: Activity and Its Outcomes]. Nizhnevartovsk: The Publishing House of Nizhnevartovsk University, 2014.

———. "Finansovye osnovy funkcionirovaniâ zapadno-sibirskih otdelov Imperstorskogo Pravoslavnogo Palestinskogo obŝestva v konce XIX - načale XX v." [The Financial Framework for West Siberian Offices of the Imperial Orthodox Palestine Society in the late 19th–early 20th centuries] *Vestnik Pravoslavnogo Svâto—Tihonovskogo gumanitarnogo universiteta* [The Bulletin of Saint Tikhon's University] *II*, 1, no. 62 (2015): 112–24.

Dmitriev, Evgeniy, et al. "Palestinskoe dviženie soprotivleniâ" [The Palestine Resistance]. In *Novejšaâ istoriâ arabskih stran Azii 1917–1985* [The Recent History of the Arabic Countries of Asia, 1917–1985], 223–68. Moscow: Nauka Publishing House, 1988.

Dmitrievsky, Alexey A. *Imperatorskoe Pravoslavnoe Palestinskoe Obŝestvo i ego deâtelnost' za istekshuû četvert' veka 1882–1907* [The Imperial Orthodox Palestine Society and Its Activity during the Last Quarter of a Century, 1882–1907]. Saint Petersburg: Oleg Abyshko Publishing House. 2008.

Epstein, Alek D. "Osnovnye napravleniâ i novye tendencii v razvitii izrailevedčeskih issledovanij v 80–90–e gody" [Main Areas and New Tendencies in the Development of Israel Studies in the 1980s–1990s]. *Vostok (Oriens)* [The Orient] 1 (2001): 172–80.

———. "Izučenie Izrailâ v Rossii (1991–2006): dostiženiâ i problemy" [The Study of Israel in Russia, 1991–2006]. *Vostok (Oriens)* [The Orient] 2 (2007): 167–70.

Fedorchenko, Andrey V. "Palestine and Israel Studies in Russia." In *Russian Orientalists to the 36th ICANAS*, 61–67. Moscow: Institute of Oriental Studies of Russian Academy of Science, 2000.

Fishman, David. "Thiyatam shel mada'ey ha-yahadut be-Rusya bi-shnot ha-tish'im" [The Revival of Jewish Studies in Russia in the 1990s]. *Yehudey brit ha-mo'atsot be-ma'avar* [The Soviet Jews at a Crossroads] 4, no. 19 (2000): 250–60.

Fomin, Alexander. *Vojna s prodolženiem. Veliokobritaniâ i Franciâ v bor'be za 'osmanskoe nasledstvo'* [The Continuing War. Great Britain and France in the Struggle for 'the Ottoman Legacy']. Moscow: Universitet Dmitriâ Požarskogo, 2010.

Garmatenko, Alexander. "V Odesse rešili zakryt' strategičeskij institut" [The Strategic Institute Is Reported to Be Closed in Odessa]. *Vesti*. March 3, 2015. https://vesti-ukr.com/odessa/91057-v-odesse-zakryvajut-strategicheskij-institut.

Gerd, Lora. "Arhimandrit Antonin Kapustin i ego naučnaâ deâtelnost' (po materialam peterbergskih arhivov)" [Archimandrite Antonin Kapustin and His Researches (According to Materials from Petersburg Archives)]. In *Rukopisnoe nasledie russkih vizantinistov v arhivah Sankt-Peterburga* [Manuscripts of Russian Byzantinists in Archives of Saint Petersburg], 8–35. Saint Petersburg: The Archive of Russian Academy of Science in Saint Petersburg, 1995.

———. *Rossiâ i Pravoslavnyj Vostok. Konstantinopol'skij patriarhat v konce XIX v.: Pisma G. P. Begleri k prof. I. E. Troickomu 1878–1898 gg.* [Russia and the Orthodox East. The

Patriarchate of Constantinople in the Late 19th Century: Letters by G. P. Beglery to Prof. I. E. Troitsky in 1878–1898]. Saint Petersburg: Oleg Abyshko Publishing House, 2003.

———. *Konstantinopol' i Peterburg: Cerkovnaâ politika Rossii na Pravoslavnom Vostoke (1878–1898): Avtoreferat dissertacii... doktora istoričeskih nauk* [Constantinople and Petersburg: Russian Church Policy in the Orthodox East, 1878–1898. Abstract of Dissertation]. Saint Petersburg: The Institute of History in Saint Petersburg, 2006.

Grushevoy, Alexander. "Imperatorskoe Palestinskoe obŝestvo (po peterburgskim arhivam)" [The Imperial Orthodox Palestine Society (According to Materials from Petersburg Archives]. In *Arhivy russkih vizantinistov v Sankt-Peterburge* [Records of Russian Byzantinists in Saint Petersburg], 134–56. Saint Petersburg: Dmitrij Bulanin Publ. House, 1995.

Hofman, Stephanie. "'Al pe'ilot merkaz 'Sefer' ba-brit ha-mo'atsot leshe'avar" [On the Activity of the 'Sefer' Center in the Former Soviet Union]. *Yehudey brit ha-mo'atsot be-ma'avar* [The Soviet Jews at a Crossroads] 4, no. 19 (2000): 261–64.

Hopwood, Derek. *The Russian Presence in Syria and Palestine, 1843–1914. Church and Politics in the Near East*. Oxford: Clarendon Press. 1969.

Krachkovsky, Ignaty. "Zapiski o deâtel'nosti Rossijskogo Palestinskogo obŝestva" [Papers on the Activity of the Russian Palestine Society]. In *Neizvestnye stranicy otečestvennogo vostokovedeniâ* [Unknown Stories of Russian Oriental Studies], Vol. 1, 137–54. Moscow: Vostočnaâ literature Publishing House, 1997.

Krupnik, Igor. "Problemy etnografičeskogo izučeniâ evreev v SSSR: vosem'let spustâ" [On Problems of Ethnographic Study of Jews in the USSR: Eight Years Later]. In *Istoričeskie sud'vy evreev v Rossii i SSSR: načalo dialoga* [Historical Destinies of Jews in Russia and the USSR: The Beginning of a Dialogue], edited by Igor Krupnik, 28–40. Moscow: Jewish Historical Society, 1992.

———. "Kak my zanimalis' istoriej... i etnografiej: K 35–letiû Evrejskoj istoriko-etnografičeskoj komissii, 1981–1990 gg" [About Us Studying History and Ethnography: To the 35th Anniversary of the Jewish Historical and Ethnographic Commission, 1981–1990]. In *Sovetskaya iudaika: istoriâ, problematika, personalii* [Jewish Studies in the USSR: History, Problems, and Persons], edited by Mark Kupovetsky, 286–360. Jerusalem/Moscow: Gesharim, 2017.

Krylov, Alexander V. "Rossijskoe Palestinskoe obŝestvo i otečestvennoe vostokovedenie" [The Russian Palestine Society and Russian Oriental Studies]. *Vestnik Moskovskogo universiteta. Seriâ 13* [The Bulletin of Moscow University. Series 13] 4 (1989): 16–33.

Krylov, Alexander, and Nadezhda Sorokina. *Imperatorskoe Pravoslavnoe Palestinskoe Obŝestvo i otečestvennoe vostokovedenie* [The Russian Orthodox Palestine Society and Russian Oriental Studies]. Moscow: The Publishing House of MGIMO University, 2007.

The League of Arab States and the Embassy of the State of Palestine in the Russian Federation. Special Issue. *Palestina - Rossiâ: svâz' vremën* [Palestine and Russia—Historical Liaisons]. S.l., S.a.

Lieberman, Avigdor. *Ničego, krome pravdy* [Nothing but the Truth]. Tel-Aviv: Ivrus, 2005.

Lisovoy, Nikolay. "Russkoe prisutstvie v Svâtoj zemle: učreždeniâ, lûdi, nasledie [Russian Presence in the Holy Land: Institutions, Persons, and Legacy] [part 1]." *Otečestvennaâ istoriâ* [The National History] 2 (2003): 19–36.

———. "Russkoe prisutstvie v Svâtoj zemle: učreždeniâ, lûdi, nasledie [Russian Presence in the Holy Land: Institutions, Persons, and Legacy] [part 2]." *Otečestvennaâ istoriâ* [The National History] 3 (2003): 84–103.

———. *Russkoe duhovnoe i političeskoe prisutstvie v Svâtoj zemle i na Bližnem Vostoke v XIX - načale XX v* [Russian Religious and Political Presence in the Holy Land and the Middle East]. Moscow: Indrik Publishing House, 2006.

———. "Imperatorskoe Pravoslavnoe Palestinskoe Obŝestvo: 125 let služeniâ Cerkvi i Rossii" [The Imperial Orthodox Palestine Society: 125 Years in the Service of the Church and Russia]. In *Dmitrievsky, Alexey. Imperatorskoe Pravoslavnoe Palestinskoe Obŝestvo i ego deâtelnost' za istekšuû četvert' veka 1882–1907* [Dmitrievsky, Alexey. The Imperial Orthodox Palestine Society and Its Activity during the Last Quarter of a Century, 1882–1907], edited by Nikolay Lisovoy, 371–432. Saint Petersburg: Oleg Abyshko Publishing House, 2008.

Makhamid, Omar. *Rossiâ i Palestina: dialog na rubeže XIX - XX vekov: Istoriko-literaturnye očerki* [Russia and Palestine: Dialogue at the Turn of the 19th–20th Centuries. Historical and Literary Profiles]. Saint Petersburg: Liki Rossii, 2002.

Narochnitskaya, Natalya. "Staryj 'vostočnyj vopros' v novoj anglosaksonskoj politike" [The Old 'Eastern Question' in the New Anglo-Saxon Politics.] *Meždunarodnaâ žizn'* [International Affairs] 8 (2001): 75–89.

Nosenko, Tatyana, and Nina Semenchenko. *Naprasnaya vražda. Očerki sovetsko-izrail'skih otnošenij 1948–1991 gg.* [The Futile Enmity: Essays on the Soviet-Israeli Relations, 1948–1991]. Moscow: Institute of Oriental Studies of Russian Academy of Science, 2015.

Primakov, Yevgeny M. *Konfidencialno: Bližnij Vostok na scene i za kulisami (pervaâ polovina XX - načalo XXI veka)* [Classified: The Middle East in the Theatre and Beyond]. Moscow: Rossijskaâ gazeta, 2006.

Pyrlin, Yevgeny. *100 let protivoborstva. Genezis, evoluciâ, sovremennoe sostoânie i perspektivy rešeniâ palestinskoj problemy* [100 Years of Confrontation: The Genesis, Evolution, Present State, and Prospects for Solving of the Palestine Problem]. Moscow: ROSSPEN Publishing House, 2001.

———. *Trudnyj i dolgij put' k miru: vzglâd iz Moskvy na problem bližnevostočnogo uregulirivaniâ* [The Hard and Long Road to the Peace: A View from Moscow on the Middle East Settlement]. Moscow: ROSSPEN Publishing House, 2002.

SEFER Center for University Teaching of Jewish Civilization. *Rashid Muradovič Kaplanov: Trudy. Interv'û. Vospominaniâ* [Rashid Muradovich Kaplanov: Papers. Interviews. Memory]. Moscow: SEFER Center, 2011.

Shachtman, Tom. *I Seek My Brethren: Ralph Goldman and "The Joint". Rescue, Relief, and Reconstruction—the Work of the American Jewish Joint Distribution Committee.* New York: Newmarket Press, 2001.

Shandra, Anton."Novye podhody k interpretacii deklaracii Balfura v sovremennoj otečestvennoj istoriografii" [The New Approaches to the Interpretation of the Balfour Declaration in Modern National Historiography]. *Političeskaâ žizn' Zapadnoj Evropy: antičnost', srednie veka, novoe i novejšee vremâ* [Political Life in Western Europe: Antiquity, Middle Age, Modern and Recent History] 11 (2016): 116–20.

Shapovalov, Mikhail. "'Palestinskoe nasledstvo' v politike Vremennogo pravitelstva (mart-aprel' 1917)" [The 'Palestine Legacy' in the policy of the Provisional Government, March-April 1917)]. *Novejšaâ istoriâ Rossii* [The Recent History of Russia] 2 (2017): 19–32.

———. "Pričiny sozdaniâ Deklaracii Balfura: stoletnij dokument v rossijskoj intrerpretacii" [Reasons for the Balfour Declaration: 100 Years Old Document in Russian Interpretation]. *Stanovlenie evrejskoj gosudarstvennosti v XX veke: klûčevye sobytiâ* [The Establishment of Jewish Statehood in the 20th Century: Key Events] 1 (2018): 172–81.

Shavialiou, Dzmitry. "Deklaraciâ Bal'fura 2 noâbrâ 1917 g. i sionistskij proekt 18 iûlâ 1917 g.: semantičeskij analiz teksta" [The Balfour Declaration 2 Nov 1917 and a Zionist Project 18 Jul 1917: Semantic Analyses]. *Belorusskij žurnal meždunarodnogo prava i meždunarodnyh otnošenij* [Belarusian Journal of International Law and International Relations] 1 (2000): 82–86.

———. "Izrailevedenie i palestinovedenie v sovremennoj Rossii (k voprosu o definiciâh i sostoânii otraslej" [Israel Studies and Palestine Studies in Contemporary Russia (On Definitions and Current State of Affairs)]. *Vostok (Oriens)* [The Orient] 5 (2007): 216–20.

———. "Review of: Fomin, Alexander. *Vojna s prodolženiem* [The Continuing War] (Moscow, 2010)]." *Vostok (Oriens)* [The Orient] 6 (2011): 177–79.

———. "Ob izrailevedenii v postsovetskih gosudarstvah (pertečen' problemnyh voprosov)" [On Israel Studies in the Post-Soviet States (A List of Main Issues)]. In *Aktualnye problemy istorii, etnologii, filologii i prava evreev* [Topical Issues of Jewish History, Ethnology, Philology, and Law], 123–25. Chişinău: Judaica Institute (Moldova), 2013.

Shavialiou, Dzmitry, and Maryna Malakhvey. "Review of: Pyrlin, Yevgeny, *100 let protivoborstva. Genezis, evoluciâ, sovremennoe sostoânie i perspektivy rešeniâ palestinskoj problemy* [100 Years of Confrontation: The Genesis, Evolution, Present State, and Prospects for Solving of the Palestine Problem]. (Moscow, 2001) and Pyrlin, Yevgeny, Trudnyj i dolgij put' k miru: vzglâd iz Moskvy na problem bližnevostočnogo uregulirivaniâ [The Hard and Long Road to the Peace: A View from Moscow on the Middle East Settlement] (Moscow, 2002)." *Vostok (Oriens)* [The Orient] 6 (2003): 176–80.

Shavialiova, Maryna, Khristina Vitiv, and Dzmitry Shavialiou. "Ob odnom epizode iz istorii Russkoj dukhovnoj missii v Ierusalime (po materialam arhivnogo dela J15/2880 Cental'nogo sionistskogo arhiva Izrailâ)" [An Episode from the History of the Russian Ecclesiastical Mission in Jerusalem (According to the Archival File J15/2880 of the Central Zionist Archives of Israel]. *Tsaytshrift/Časopis* [The Journal] 9, no. 4 (2014): 177–91.

Suslikov, Yuriy V. "Sud'ba rossijskoy sobstvennosti [The Fate of Russian Property] [part 1]." *Aziâ i Afrika segodnâ* [Asia and Africa Today] 6 (1995): 75–80.

———. "Sud'ba rossijskoy sobstvennosti [The Fate of Russian Property] [part 2]." *Aziâ i Afrika segodnâ* [Asia and Africa Today] 7 (1995): 46–51.

TASS. "Lavrov: v nedalëkom budušem istoriki sformuliruût takoe ponâtie, kak 'doktrina Primakova'" [Lavrov, In the Near Future Historians Will Formulate Such Term as the 'Primakov Doctrine']. *TACC*, October 28, 2014. https://tass.ru/politika/1537769

Trutnev, Vladimir N. "Russkaâ diplomatiâ i Rossijskoe Imperatorskoe Pravoslavnoe Palestinskoe obŝestvo (po materialam Arhiva Vnešnej Politiki Rossii)" [The Russian Diplomacy and the Russian Imperial Orthodox Palestine Society (According to Materials from the Archive of Foreign Policy of Russia)]. In *Diplomatičeskij Ežegodnik 1992* [The Diplomatic Yearbook 1992], 249–68. Moscow: Publishing House "International Relations," 1992.

Vorobyova, Irina. *Russkie missii v Svâtoj zemle v 1847–1917 godah* [Russian Missions to the Holy Land, 1847–1917]. Moscow: Institute of Oriental Studies Publishing House, 2001.

Yamilinets, Boris. *Rossiâ i Palestina. Očerki političeskih i kulturno-religioznyh otnošenij (XIX - načalo XX veka)* [Russia and Palestine. Essays on Political, Cultural and Religious Relations in the 19th–early 20th Centuries]. Moscow: Institute of Oriental Studies of Russian Academy of Science, and Saint Petersburg: Letnij Sad Publishing House, 2003.

Yanovitsky, Alexander. "Prisutstvie i interesy Russkoj Pravoslavnoj Cerkvi v Zemle Izrailâ," [Presence and Interests of the Russian Orthodox Church in the Land of Israel]. *Lekhaim* 8, no. 232 (2011). https://lechaim.ru/ARHIV/232/yanovitskiy.htm

Zifroni, Gabriel. "Rusim ''adumim' ve–rusim 'levanim' be–Yerušalaim" ["Red Russians" and "White Russians" in Jerusalem]. *Katedra* 5 (1977): 162–95.

Chapter Five

Israel in the Mirror of Iran

An Iranian Approach to Jewish and Israeli Messianism

Amir Rezaeipanah

Judaism and the Jewish community are some of the most problematic topical categories in the contemporary history of Iran. On one side, as Judaism is the oldest of the Abrahamic religions, a kind of status and respect is felt among Muslims, especially the Shi'ites, toward Judaism. From this perspective, this religion is among the permanent and eternal religions of *al-Islam*.[1] In the Muslims' view, Judaism has a legitimate and true nature, and foundation, which gradually and due to distortion (*tahrif*) and innovation has deviated away from the right path. In countries like Iran, which since long in the past has had a significant and influential population of Jews having their prominent places (like their pilgrimage sites such as the Tomb of Esther and Mordechai in Hamadan or the Tomb of Daniel in Shush, the Tomb of Habakkuk in Tuyserkan and the Peighambariyeh mausoleum in Qazvin) and certain Jewish rituals, the social relations and acceptance of the followers of this religion have been normal and ordinary. However, on the other side, because of some differences and challenges between the Muslims and the Jews in nascent Islam, which has produced some anti-Jewish Qur'anic sayings, there is a kind of pessimism and doubt toward Jews in the Muslims collective unconscious.

The issue of fear and hope in relation to Jews in different eras, especially after the 1979 Islamic Revolution, has underlain many challenges and discussions in Iran. From the revolution onward, the manner of interaction with Judaism and the Jews has altered from the historico-religious and sociocultural frames of the past, taking on a political and theological shape. Although there had been challenges and protests over the Arab-Israeli Conflict and Palestine, from this date (1979) onward, the issue of confronting Israel and a distorted group of the people of Israel was outlined as one of the identity-giving bases of the Islamic Republic of Iran (IRI). Since this era, the duality of the Oppressed-Oppressor (*Mustazaf-Mustakber*) was highlighted as the basis of constructing the identity of the Islamic system.

The basic category of the process of the connection between the political and the religious, in both the IRI and Israel, is messianism. Messianism is a kind of problematic in the political logic, and especially the foreign policy, of Iran and Israel.[2] However, Israel, on one side, has been, besides the United States, the most prominent enemy and "other" of the Islamic Republic of Iran throughout its existence. In the words of ayatollah Khomeini, like a "cancerous tumor" (*Qode-ye Saratani*) never to be tolerated. On the other side, in the view of the heads of Israel, Iran as an Islamic-Shiite country, having an activist approach based on political activism, can be a source of many challenges and crises for the only Jewish nation-state of the world. In macro-scale, although Iran and Israel as non-Arab majority states could have many convergence and alliance lines within the Islamic-Arabic region of the Middle East, North Africa, and especially the Persian Gulf countries, however, their activist and antagonistic ideologies destroy most bases of communication. In fact, political Islam in Iran and Zionism in Israel feed from some sources, especially in ideology and political theology which, prior to making real convergence, pave the way for their divergence. The issue of supporting the Muslim lands and defending Palestine and Quds is one of the central subjects in Iran's Islamic revolution, and the slogan that "the Quds route, passes from Karbala" is a central motivation for Iran's warriors during the Iran-Iraq war. This subject has continued in the postwar era. For example, in the appearance of ISIS (Islamic neofundamentalism) and the intensification of the Syria crisis, the media elites and the heads of the IRI have talked about the emerging crisis as a "Western, Hebrew, Arabic" axis. They used the term "the martyred defenders of holy shrines" (*Shohada-ye Modafee Haram*) for those killed in this battle and what the IRI views as a holy war. These kinds of concepts present a Shiite apocalyptic view based on the existence of a global front of evil, which is now in front of the IRI and the West, centered on the United States, Jewishness represented by Israel, and Arabic ignorance, centered on Saudi Arabia, and some of the Arabic countries are the main axes of what the IRI sees as a satanic and outrageous alliance. However, the issue of Jewish citizens residing in Iran is raised in various parts of the country's constitution, as well as many of its main texts and laws—especially in the civil law entitled "the religious minorities" (articles like article 13, 14, 64, and 67 of the constitution). Although legislation differentiates between the citizens due to their religion, it has also tried, as far as possible, to guarantee Jews—and followers of other religions considered divine within Islam—civil rights, legal mechanisms, as well as social and political positions.

It seems that a set of politico-strategic, sociocultural, and, finally, religious-ideological factors underlie some positive and negative approaches in the field of "Jewish and Israel studies" during the era of the Islamic Republic of Iran. Accordingly, two different dimensions, one conservative and one radical, simultaneously observe this field of study in the Islamic Republic of Iran. The conservative field observes Jewish Studies, and the radical one involves Israel studies. This subject has been more indicative in messianism, as one of the most central debates in political theology. This study concentrates on the thought foundations and results of one of the main incompetencies and challenges observed within the theological study in the Middle East: looking at science through a window of politics. In other words, in Iran, and maybe to an extent in Israel, the investigation of certain dimensions of political theology, especially messianism, holds a taboo aspect; or, in more precise terms—this field is considered a proprietary one, and entering it has been generally viewed as a "bureaucratic" dimension; in other words, political theology, in a security-based bureaucratic and pragmatic order, is imagined as strengthening politics and the political order. In this sense, the religious in a general meaning and *Shariah* in a specific conception are interpreted as tools for the fixation of the existing bureaucratic structure and strengthening the power of the hegemon power. The bureaucratic conception of religion from the Safavids era in Iran and prior to it was theorized in the Sunnah world in the shade of the overcoming thought that says "might makes right" (*al-haqu leman qalaba/ taghalob*) and, as a result of an articulated hidden discourse, the authoritatives had the right to interpret some of the religious and legal limitations in line with their power extendance.

The main focus of this chapter is the methodological incompetency and challenges to political theology rooted in the epistemological, ontological, and sociological fields. Perhaps one of the reasons that the Iranian researchers and politicians, and probably mutually those in Israel, cannot deal with, absent any presuppositions or logically, the subjects of Jewish Studies, Israel Studies, Iranian Studies, Shi'ite Studies, and Islamic Studies, arises from a historic heritage and the accumulation of some of the misunderstandings in their collective mentality. Unless three circles—non-Jewish Iranian researchers, Iranian Jews, and Iranian politicians/elites—overcome this problematic challenge to find a reasonable solution, there is no possibility for the existence of properly rational iterations of Jewish Studies and Israel Studies as academic fields in Iran.

JEWISH IDENTITY IN THE SHADE OF ISLAMIC TRADITION

Muslims generally believe that the divergence and detachment circles toward Israel are more than the convergence bases. This subject has been repeatedly emphasized in the holy Quran, wherein is stated that the enmity of Jews toward Muslims equals that of the polytheists: "You shall certainly find the Jews and those who associate partners with Allah are the most vehement of the people in enmity against those who believe" (Al-Meada/ 82). It is also stated that, as a result of the conflicts between Muslims and Jews:

> You shall, certainly, be tried in your substance and lives and you shall certainly hear from those who were given the Scripture before you and from those who set up equals (to God) a good deal of hurtful abuse. But if you are patiently persevering and guard against evil, then this (attitude) is worth being followed with constancy and firm determination. (Al-Imran/ 186)

"Those who were given the Scripture" is a Quranic term referring to the Abrahamic religions, and here specifically refers to the Jews. The holy Quran says that after God blessed and favored the people of Israel, because of their intolerance and ingratitude, they went down to Egypt and they were smote with abasement and destitution. The holy Quran also accuses them with disbelief in the divine verses, and the prophets' murders, and so considers Jews as caught up in God's wrath and anger:

> "And when you said, 'Moses! (we are weary of one kind of food so) we will not at all remain content with one and the same food, pray, therefore, to your Lord for us that He may bring forth for us some of that which the earth produces, of its vegetables, of its cucumbers, its corn, its lentils and its onions.' He (- God) said, 'Would you take in exchange that which is inferior (—delicious food) for that which is superior (—the realization of the noble object of your life)? (If this is so) then go to some town and you will certainly have (there) all that you have demanded.' And lo! it so happened, they were smitten with abasement and destitution and they incurred the displeasure of Allah. That was because they denied the Messages of Allah and sought to kill His Prophets unjustly and that was because they disobeyed and had been transgressing. (Al-baqara/ 61).

In the holy Quran's words, the Israelites didn't even entirely abide Moses, where he complains:

> (Recall the time) when Moses said to his people, 'My people! why do you malign me when you know that I am certainly a Messenger from Allah to you.' But when they deviated from the right course, Allah let their hearts deviate (as they were), for Allah guides no transgressing people to success. (As-Saff/ 5)

In this verse, Israelites are referred to as the "transgressing people" which means those who emphasize on doing sin and disobedience. In this understanding, the Israelites break their covenant with God, and, as a result, they were cursed, and they are those who pervert the words of the Divine Book:

> So on account of their breaking their covenant We deprived them of Our blessings, and We let their hearts become hardened. Now they pervert the words from their proper context (of the Divine Book) and (in doing so) they have abandoned a good portion of what they were (reminded of and) exhorted with. And you will never cease to discover one dishonesty (or the other) on their part, with the exception of a few of them; so pardon them and pass (them) over. Verily, Allah loves the doers of good to others. (Al-ma'ida/ 13)

> Jews are people who have believed in "*al-jibt*" (idols) and "*al-taqut*" (devil), two high levels of disbelief, and have tried to exchange the right with wrong: Did you not see those who received a portion of the Book, that they believe in idols (*al-jibt*) and the devil (*al-taqut*), and say regarding the disbelievers that they are more rightly guided than the Muslims. (An-Nisa/ 51)

In the view of the holy Quran, it promises two instances of rebellion and corruption of the Jews, one of them is through the murder of Isaiah and the opposition of Jeremiah and the other is through the murder of Zechariah and Yahya:

> And We decreed for the Descendants of Israel in the Book that, "You will indeed create great turmoil in the earth twice, and you will surely become very proud." So when the first of those promises came, We sent upon you Our extremely militant bondmen—they therefore entered the cities pursuing you; and this was a promise that had to be fulfilled. (Al-Isra/ 4–5)

Muslims believe that many of the Jews' thoughts and rituals are distorted and invalid. For example, "And the Jews said, 'Allah's hand is tied'; may their hands be tied—and they are accursed for saying so! In fact, both His hands are free, He bestows upon whomever He wills." (Al-ma'ida/ 64)

There is a saying in Farsi, "*Irad-e Bani-Israeli*" ("The excuses of the children of Israel"), which is related to the Israelis "behavior"; this issue refers to some verses in the holy Quran. In these verses, the Quran—besides saying that God has blessed and favored the Jews and has excelled them over others "O Descendants of Israel! Remember the favor of Mine, which I bestowed upon you and gave you superiority over others of your time (by sending the Noble Messengers to your nation)" (Al-baqara/ 47)—presents a brief of their history and refers to their criticisms in relation to Moses's request to sacrifice a lamb. In some other parts of the Quran, there is knowledge and warnings about the negative features of the Jews, while the Christians are considered to be better friends to Muslims in comparison. In other surahs of the Quran, *al-aaraf* and *taha*, the story of "*ijil al-dhahab*" (or Golden calf) is referred to as one of the Jews' distortions in the absence of Moses.

Accordingly, an escape route should be found from these people and their religion's seditions and enmity. Although in many ways Islamic ontology, through its common roots with Judaism, is aligned with it, these two religions have many lines of differentiation and separation. Judaism and Islam are two religions having a strong law; the issue at hand is their detachment dimensions and points of difference and separation. In comparison with its relationship to Christianity, the Islamic tradition expresses a more serious and intense otherness toward Judaism.

Based on the Islamic texts, foretelling of the rise of prophet Mohammad is mentioned in the original texts of Judaism, especially the Hebrew bible. There is a quotation from Metatron (an archangel in Judaism and known in Judaism as the Recording Angel or the Chancellor of Heaven) which says God has chosen you [the Jews] to be prophets of the Ismaelites to save you from Edom.[3] In the Islamic view, some rabbis and movements like Sabbatai Sevi have distorted this and, in the shade of Zionism, turned it conversely. In the Islamic tradition there is a negative expression, *Israeliat*, which has been used by some like Ka'ab al-Ahbar, Abdullah ibn Salam, Wahb ibn Munabbih, and Ubaid ben Shadhia Jorhomi as a sign of efforts by Jews and other non-Muslims to distort the Islamic sources and texts.

However, as will be said, according to some scholars like Gershom Scholem, this other-making of Islam and Judaism is mainly rooted in the advent of Zionism. So, the issue of the advent of Zionism's activist and pragmatist ideas toward the Jewish religion paved the way for the withdrawal of the image of Jews from isolation and representing historical oppression, shifting the historical image of the homeless and oppressed Jews to Jews having land and state. This also strengthened anti-Israeli and anti-Jewish sentiment and activities and also led to the denial of the the the Holocaust.[4]

REVOLUTIONARY ELITE AND ISRAEL; ANTI-ZIONIST

Within the Islamic Republic of Iran is the concept that Iran contains the most important and prominent population of Muslims and Shi'ites in the world. The formal name for this concept is "*Umm Al-Qura-ye Jahan-e Islam*" (Iran as the Center of the Muslim World) and its leader is named "*vali-ye amr-e moslemin-e jahan*" (the commander of the world's Muslims). The IRI is the manifestation of the most serious and central interpretation of the political Islam and the jurisprudential Islamic ideology in the Shiite world (and in a general meaning in the Muslim world). On the other hand Israel, as the only political unit of Jews, in the shade of the hegemony of Zionist thought and through passing the "Jewish state" law, considers itself as the main trustee of planning the affairs of the Jewish people (as the best and chosen people of God) throughout the world.

Although during the revolutionary struggles to overthrow the Pahlavi regime, the issue of the Arab-Israeli conflict was a major subject, after the

Islamic revolution the issue of othering Israel and supporting Palestine became a basic and central factor in articulating the discourse of the Islamic revolution. The revolutionary elites of Iran defined one of their main responsibilities and duties as liberating and emancipating Palestine and Quds (Jerusalem) from Israel. In their viewpoint, the Palestinians are an oppressed people who have been captured by global imperialism, and the Islamic revolution of Iran has the duty of supporting, emancipating, and liberating them.

Through a three-fold division in Iran's foreign policy and post-revolutionary relations' structure, a better understanding of the IRI's other-making toward Israel can be articulated. Such a thing can, to some extent, be said about Israel, and thus talking about Iran doesn't mean a unidirectional subject matter.

The Ideological Level

Ideology observes the identity-based foundations. The Islamic system, in this part, recognizes its identity and others according to the Islamic and revolutionary patterns. Political Islam, based on the idea of *Velayat-e faqih* (Guardianship of the Islamic Jurist), and the pillars of *Jomhuriat* (Republic), and *Islamiat* (Islamism), articulates the center of this discourse. This level aims to recognize the "self" and "other" among other nation-states. The national identity pillars and categories are defined as a result of the interactions which observe this domain. On this level the concepts of *mellat* (nation) and *Ummah* (religious community) are blended together.

Two basic fields can be differentiated on this level. First is the abstract domain of ideology in which Israel is an "other," and in relation to the United States as a fundamental and *big* "other." Second is the pragmatic and practical ideology, which lacks the determinism of the abstract one. In this pragmatic reading, those countries are placed in the domain other-making strategies whose existence is not in the agonistic domain but in the antagonistic one:

> According to the IRI's constitution, Iranian foreign policy is crafted according to four fundamental principles: first, rejection of all forms of external domination; second, preservation of Iran's independence and territorial integrity; third, defence of the rights of all Muslims without allying with hegemonic powers; and, fourth, the maintenance of peaceful relations with all non-belligerent states.[5]

As a result, Iran's support of Palestine, Lebanon and Syria, and its opposition to Israel can be understood. In the international arena and in foreign policy, Iran has three important aims: the formation of a Shiite government; defending Muslims; and fighting what they view as the arrogance through which Israel and the United States (as the "global arrogance axes") threaten Iran's other aims.[6] In such a framework, the tensions between a tendency to export the revolution and moving toward greater convergence with the broader world is one of the most challenging aspects for the decision-makers of postrevolutionary Iran.[7]

The important point within the ideological aspect is that ideology has a flexible and fluid state in Iran (and in Israel, for that matter). Ideology is no longer a simplifying logic to deal with real-world complexities, shoring up presuppositions taken for granted, or presenting value-based judgments without external facts. Rather, Iran's (and again Israel's) ideological logic contains consistent pragmatic and security-based dimensions.[8] On this level, the Islamic republic seeks to build connections with nations instead of states.[9]

The Strategic Level

On the strategic level, the main axes of national power are national security and the national economy. Accordingly, if on the ideological level power software is talked about, on the strategic level the subject matter is the hardware that strengthens foreign policy and foreign relations. It can be said that Iran's best allies in the Middle East and the Persian Gulf can be countries with two features of being non-Muslim and non-Arab; however, in the historical moment, Iran's revolutionary elites decided to consider Israel and the United States in their antagonistic domain as Iran's main enemies and rivals. As a result, Israel is viewed as the enemy of Iran's national security, one that is destroying the economy and national development of the Islamic Republic of Iran. Israel's image in this area is as a potential and even actual enemy. On the strategic level, struggle with and other-making toward Israel in different layers like defending the oppressed and the resistant groups like Hamas, Hezbollah, Islamic Jihad, the progress of the nuclear program, and so on, are considered as the base of strengthening the presence and strategic depth of the Islamic Republic of Iran. Accordingly, although the IRI doesn't recognize Israel as a nation-state, studies concentrated on such a nation-state inevitably pass through a set of negative presuppositions and images which negate a realistic outlook or an analysis based on rationality.

In this regard, the security-based approach in most of the research on Israel is related to foreign policy, national and international security, the Palestine issue, the sociology of violence in Israel, and so forth.[10] There is generally an attempt to demonstrate Iran's pre-1979 revolution relations with Israel as relations full of deception, and as having a military and unstable nature; consistent elements of this scholarship also include elements of apartheid, nationalism, and nostalgia that have been attended to about Israel.[11] Notably, there are detractors from these foci, contending that Israel and Judaism are not questions for Iran's scholars and that there should not be such strict other-making.[12]

The Diplomatic Level

Iran's nodal point and concept on the diplomatic level is national interest. Diplomacy's many types—formal diplomacy, general diplomacy, media diplomacy, religious diplomacy, cultural diplomacy, tourism diplomacy, and personal diplomacy—are tools for advancing national interests. It seems that Iran's diplomacy, at least on the obvious level, seeks to minimize Israel's power and influence in the region and within the international system. A main part of Iran's alliances and ties, especially on three levels—the Muslim world, the nonalignment movement, and the global front of anti-imperialism—consider this objective.

THE RELIGIOUS, THE POLITICAL, AND THE SOCIAL

One of the main parameters and components in comprehending the process of Iran's (and Israel's) politics and policy-making (as a base for analyzing the Iranian approach to Jewish and Israel studies) is understanding and explaining how the political is related to the religious. On a more macro level, how they are related with the social and the discursive. The notional and meditative structure dominating these two players is affected by the historical heritage and the accumulation of the myths and their semantic systems throughout history. Political Islam in the IRI, and Zionism as ideology in Israel, are the symbols of theoretical and practical ties between the religious, the discursive, the political, and the social, from which prominent theoretical and objective consequences have issued especially in the field of mutual studies in political theology and messianism.

The basic point and category in the process of how the political and the religious are related in these two lands is messianism. Messianism is a kind of problematic and complex issue in the political logic, and especially the foreign policy, of Iran and Israel. This problematic essentially enters the notion of seeking a lost era or reaching a bright future, belief in the duality of good and evil and their historical and permanent confrontation, the negation of oppression and cruelty, deontology, activism, as well as internationalist beliefs and so forth. in the political culture of a territory. Shiite and Jewish messianism have been realized in a widespread base from idealism and normativism to realism and pragmatism, and have articulated the circles of the political creation, especially in foreign policy, in the shade of an idealized realism.

The result of the relation between the different mentioned fields has been the highlighting of certain approaches based on political mysticism, fatalism, mission-orientation, acceptance of holy suffering, martyrdom and sacrifice, an ideological-pragmatic conception of events and processes, and a mixture of national and transnational beliefs, and so on. Studies concerning the fields of Jews and Israel also have a positive or a negative approach toward their self and other discourses.

AN ALTERNATIVE AS *MAHDAVIAT*

Besides the negative and divergent bases of the Islamic tradition and the other-making relations and discourse of the Islamic revolution's discourses, the native experience of Shiite-Islamic messianism articulates a third factor of misunderstanding in the case of Iranian scholarship on Jewish and Israeli political theology, concentrating on messianism. The manner that elites, politicians, and researchers, especially Iranian Jews (who have secondhand knowledge about Jewish languages, culture, and law), comprehend Jewish and Israeli political theology, especially its messianism, is affected by Shiite-Islamic messianism or the native thought of *Mahdaviat*. In fact, there is a kind of simulation and tautology in Iranian thought about this issue.

Probably, in some dimensions and fields, the same meaning, identity, nature, and function are imagined for the Jewish apocalyptic messiah (Mashiach) that are imagined for *Mahdi*. In this way, Mashiach is understood through the context of *Mahdi*. The common dimension of this simulation can be recognized by three categories: "justice," "emancipation or salvation," and "a messianic global empire."[13]

In genealogy and historical analysis, from the ancient times, Iranians were familiar with subjects like messianism, salvation, emancipation, redemption, justice, and so on in the frame of waiting for the advent of *Saoshyant* (*Saoshyans*). Messianism in the pre-Islamic thought of Iran, especially in the Zoroastrian era, was represented in the fundamental confrontation of *Ahura* (good) and *Ahriman* (evil), and in accepting periods of hardship and suffering before the advent of *Saoshyant*.[14] Messiah is a superman possessing *farrah-e Izadi* (divine grace) and charisma, like the apostles has innate ascetic, richness, and independence has ultranatural and ultramaterial power; is well-known as virtuous and honest; and fights the dominant and devilish beliefs and religions.[15] The objective and practical result of the politics and tradition of *iranshahri* (Iranianship) thought is the emergence of *Saoshyant* and the idealistic sovereign, and the subsequent *farshookart* and renewal and revival of the world. In this era, *asha* (*aša/arta*) (truth) is objectively represented and *druj* (deceit, falsehood) withdraws. *Saoshyant* is the enemy of ignorance and darkness and is the executer of justice, liberation, and emancipation principles. Fire is the symbol of the Zoroastrian religion, and Mazdayasna is the symbol of purity and light of the messiah's advent era.[16]

Messianism became more highlighted in the Islamic era, and after presenting an Iranian-Shiite reading in the framework of *Mahdaviat* thinking and discourse. Shiite messianism, which is presented in Mahdi, the apocalyptic savior, is a dynamic element in the Shiites' social and individual lives. *Intizar* (awaiting) is based on counting down and patience full of holy suffering along with the *zohor* (advent) of a holy and innocent ultrahuman from the family of the last divine prophet, Muhammad, during the apocalypse. The promised Mahdi comes to make the world full of *idalat* (justice) after it was filled with *zolm* (oppression): "Through him, Allah will fill the earth with fairness and justice as if it had been filled with oppression and cruelty."[17]

In Islamic messianic thought, the Shiites', Muslims', and finally humanity's emancipation, salvation, and redemption are based on the acceptance and realization of the historical mission and duty of the followers and establishing an ideal Islamic political-religious community, a nation based on the element of belief.[18] Mahdi is a perfect human who is both guided and guiding; a level even higher than the transcendental level of Islamic mysticism.[19] Mahdi (in the Sunni Islam "renewer or *mujaddid* of the era"[20]) is at the center of the dynamism of the theoreticians and scientists, especially the Islamic millennialists, and different interpretations by Shiites and Sunnis of the "last hour" viewpoint, and the nearness of the end of the world, resurrection, and apocalypse (documented by some verses of the Quran like "the [promised] Hour may be near at hand" [Ash-Shura/17], "the Hour is about to come" [Ghafir/59], and so on).[21] Shiite Islam developed a kind of belief in divine justice based on holy suffering which was to some extent lost in the historically more dominant Sunni Islam. The theory of emancipation is fed by the element of martyrdom in Shi'ism, an element that is based on Imam Hussein's unique martyrdom.[22]

Mahdaviat is considered as the continuity of *Imamat* and *Velayat* principles in Shi'ism. Throughout the history of Shi'ism there was generally a kind of passive and nonactivist waiting. In this kind of waiting, the main element is *Taqiya* (a precautionary dissimulation or denial of religious belief and practice in the face of persecution). According to this principle, Shiites should not and cannot utter their beliefs especially in relation to the apocalypse era or Armageddon or act toward it. Any activist effort is rejected or even *haram* (forbidden). In this regard *Isalate Tahrim* (authenticity of the forbidden) was slightly moderated with the advent of the Safavid dynasty and the leadership of Shah Ismail, one of the grandchildren of Safi-ad-din Ardabili, son-in-law and successor of Zahed Gilani. The Safavid movement rose in the power vacuum, political instability, social turmoil, and anomy which followed the Mongol attack led by Hulagu Khan into the heart of the Middle East and the Muslim world, including Baghdad, the Abbasid capital.[23] The Safavids and *ahle Khanghah* upon the sufi and semimessianic currents like Naqshbandi, Noorbakshia, Shadhili, Qadiriyya, Mevleviya, Teyforiyya, Rafaeiyya, Bektashi, ahle Fotowat and Okhowat, the followers of Shah Nimatullah Wali, and so on have represented themselves as people of idea, power, and action.[24]

From the Safavid era and with the manifestation and consolidation of the Shiite-Iranian government of the Shiite, *Dhi Shokat and Dhi Eghtedar Sultan* (the king who is both Shiite and powerful) messianism and *Mahdaviat* thought was reformulated with two positive (observing Shiite-Iranian identity) and negative (applying agonism "controversy" and antagonism against discursive others, generally the Sunnis) dimensions; its Iranian-Shiite identity was affected and the position of the *Dhi Shokat and Dhi Eghtedar Sultan* was upgraded to the rank of the deputy of the absent imam.[25] The Safavids, from the beginning, had apocalyptic claims and approaches.[26] Sufism, Shi'ism, *Iranshahri* and interpreting Islamic caliphate and kingship tradition articulated the components of the Safavids semimessianic government.[27]

Iranian-Shiite messianism continued its gradual process in different shapes until the Islamic revolution and the formation of the Islamic republic system (such as the notion of *tamadon-e bozorg* "Great civilization" of Mohammad Reza Shah); with the advent of Political Islam and a jurisprudential Islam with *Velayat-e faqih* as the nodal point, messianism developed a different color. The principles of *Velayat* and *Idalat* acted as the strengthening base of this issue. After the Islamic revolution, *esalate ibahe* (authenticity of permission and authorization) and an active awaiting replaced the previous passive one. Based on the formal reading and the main stream, *Velayat-e faqih* is the logical continuum of the *imamat* and *Velayat* principles. In imam Khomeini's thought, the *Veliy-e faqih* has the authority of the infallible Imam, albeit on a lower level. In fact, *Velayat-e faqih* is the Shiites *imamat* and *Velayat*, minus the *Ismat* (infallibility) element. *Imamat* and virtue are manifested in the existence of the twelve imams who are the descendants of imam Ali and the prophet's daughter, Hazrate Fatemeh. The twelfth imam, named Mahdi, is absent and the apocalyptic savior of the Shiites. In his absence, according to the *Velayat-e faqih* notion, the *faqih* takes his place.[28] According to the fifth article of the constitution "During the occultation of the Wali al-'Asr (may God hasten his reappearance), the leadership of the *Ummah* devolves upon the just and pious person, who is fully aware of the circumstances of his age, courageous, resourceful, and possessed of administrative ability, will assume the responsibilities of this office in accordance with Article 107." The revolutionary elites called ayatollah Khomeini "Imam," and many of them considered him as the only activist and fighter who, during *asre Qeybate Kobra* (the Major Occultation era), can pave the way for imam Mahdi's just and global government.[29] This issue led to some people calling themselves the awaited Imam.[30] The theoretical bases of messianism, in the light of the principle of *Velayat-e faqih,* formulated the meaning, identity, and legitimating bases of postrevolutionary Iran. These were based on Islamic religious categories and the practical consequences of these categories.[31] This led to the isolation of any unideological conception of Jewish Studies, and especially of Israel Studies.

IRANIAN JEWISHNESS (*KALIMIS*)

The Iranian Jews, who have been present for about three thousand years, are generally called *Kalimi*. *Kalimi* is a name given to Prophet Moses as indicated in the Quran, a man who spoke to God. Iranian Jews, numbering about fifteen thousand people, have always been among the most effective sociopolitical and economic groups of people in Iran.[32] This issue, especially after the constitutional era, has been significant, and two of the Jewish and Christian minorities have had an effective presence in the modernist processes based on new technologies; they even brought about some of these new tools, technologies, and concepts.

This Jewish and Christian pioneership in some cases underlies some of the negative trends of the Ulama and the traditional groups, and sometimes led to their *tahrim* and *takfir*. In the mentality and collective memory of some Iranians, especially the religious groups, the Jews are imagined as abnormal and sometimes destructive citizens of the sociocultural system and structure. In comparison to *Kalimi* and *Mousavi*, which have a positive denotation, *Johud* is a negative expression which sometimes is used to address Jews. Also, in some cases and categories, a kind of self-alienation can be recognized among Iranian Jews. Although some, like Michael Meyer, believe that the experience of enlightenment, antisemitism, and Zionism are the three forces which have formulated Jewish identity more than anything else—Asian and African Jews, especially those in Iran, have experienced different forces, among which colonialism and Islam are most important.[33]

Of course, this lack of complete sociability, particularly in the era of Islamist governance, doesn't mean the rejection or absolute negativity of the Iranian Jews or the *Kalimian*. Most of the Iranian Jewish personalities have high face and prestige, and have important roles in the political, social, and economic realms. Despite some of the existing inadequacies and discrimination, the Jews in Iran live their social lives freely and in special fields are preeminent. In Iran's system of religious democracy, although being Muslim is of the parameters and standards of having high ranks, in the social eras and the existing public structures, the Jews generally have an appropriate rank and position. Synagogues and religious places like the Tomb of Daniel in Shush, the Jews' religious, educational, clinical, welfare, cultural, and social centers are highly respected, and there are strong social relationships between this religion and other Iranian citizens. However, it seems that there are few research-based activities and field studies on the life of the Jews' communities. *Anjoman-e kalimian-e Tehran* (Tehran Jewish Committee) is the most important religious association of the Iranian Jews.[34] While during the presidency of Mahmood Ahmadinejad, there were pressures resulting from his messianic populist approaches and his rejection of the Holocaust, this has changed during the presidency of Hassan Rouhani. He and his foreign minister, Mohammad Javad Zarif, have congratulated the advent of the Jewish New Year to Jews globally, and particularly to Iranian Jews, wishing them a very happy New Year.

TWO PARADIGMS: CONSERVATISM AND RADICALISM

According to the Islamic negative and divergent heritage, the existing political other-makings and the mentality of the *Mahdaviat* notion, two different and even opposite paradigms in relation to messianism have formed in Iran toward Jewish Studies and Israel Studies. The conservative paradigm generally contains Jewish Studies, and the radical one is defined in relation to Israel Studies. In this context, Jewish theology and particularly messianism have been conservative and ultimately positive, while Israel Studies has been radical and consequently negative. Iranians accept anything they reach in Jewish Studies and consider the status quo equivalent to their conception. Even though in studying Israeli theology, especially messianism, the first option is rejection. Accordingly, it is believed that Israeli messianism should be rejected. In fact, balance in the Jewish and Israeli political theology has generally been a missing and defective factor. The approach in the field of Jewish Studies, especially Jewish theology and political mysticism, and the Kabbalah movement, is conservative. On the other side, in Israel Studies the approach is critical and radical. Negation and rejection is the central principle. Israel Studies in Iran has generally been focused on self-positive foregrounding in relation to Zionism. In other words, these works represent a kind of verbal violence and negative associations. In most instances, scholars do not see because it exists, they see because they want to see.

CATEGORIES AND PROBLEMS

One of the prominent features of Jewish political theology, like Shiite Islam, is the activeness of messianism and waiting for the emergence of a savior during the apocalypse. In this sense, Messiah is a historical and religious phenomenon that has been referred to in the Hebrew Bible and Jewish interpretations, but messianism is a social-discursive construct which is articulated in the bidirectional relations between political structures and social contextures and in the interaction with time and history (like Mahdi and *Mahdaviat* in Shi'ism). Messianism is the process of producing and reproducing semantic and meaning systems and coding and decoding from collective memory and minds of Jews on Mashiach in the shade of extant hidden and evident power throughout Jewish history. A significant portion of the texts and literatures produced in the Jews' sociopolitical thought and action proves this subject. Mashiach, or the Jews promised man, is who will fulfill the desires and wishes of the people of Israel. Through the emergence of Zionist thought, the manner of awaiting for the emergence of this messiah has been significantly and revolutionarily transformed.

So great is this transformation that Jewish messianism can be divided into pre- and post-Zionism eras (as it was mentioned, two conservative and radical approaches were formed in relation to Israel Studies and Jewish Studies, especially political theology and messianism). The serious difference in relation to these conceptions is mainly related to certain issues: first, the function of Messiah and his movement's ideology and discourse; second, the duties and missions of the believers and the Jews' in relation to the messianic movement in the Armageddon and its activeness or passiveness; third, the nature and functions of the state or essentially the necessity of constructing a Jewish nation-state or rejecting such an existence; fourth, the issue of the holy land and the obligation or lack of justifiability for the Jews returning to the land; fifth, the amount of attention to the issues of emancipation (besides redemption and salvation) and resistance; sixth, sacred or holy suffering and the acceptance of hardship and suffering toward the realization of messianic aims and desires. This chapter tries to critically analyze the existing texts in each of these areas and describe the micro- or macrodifferences and changes in the thought of Jewish theoreticians and policymakers toward messianism, before and after the emergence of the Israeli state. This is effective in analyzing identity and otherness, and the borders of justifying actionism and even violent acts (verbally and physically).

THE FUNCTIONS OF MESSIAH AND HIS MOVEMENT

In stimulating the Iranian perspective with messianism, the nodal point in relation to Jewish messianism is the concept of justice. In this approach, the main function of the apocalyptic Messiah is the realization of justice. The savior comes to fill the world with justice and welfare, after it was filled with injustices and oppressions. Mashiach comes to revive the lost status of his followers, the Jews, the logical system of the world and humanity; he comes to rearticulate the chain of equivalence of the religious apocalyptic ideology in relation to others. According to Younes Hamami Lalehzar:

> Among the necessary signs to recognize the identity of Mashiach, rebuilding the Temple in Jerusalem is enough. Mashiach gathers all the diaspora; he guides the world in a way which all will worship God seamlessly. This will be the era of peace and conciliation; in the era of Geula there will be no sin.[35]

The issue of the chosen people in Judaism was mainly spoken about in the pre-Christian and pre-Islamic eras when Judaism was against paganism; so Mashiach comes to realize the supremacy of belief and faith. The radical view is that Mashiach is a Jew and comes to the Jews, and his main aim is the people of Israel and Jerusalem; as a result, those who see this fact will accept the Jewish faith. However, what is mostly accepted is that in such a day all will worship God, and according to the holy Bible, they will even use the same name for God.[36]

Most of Iranian academic and nonacademic elites and researchers in studying Israeli messianism find that this kind of messianism is like a tool for confronting *Mahdi-e Moeud* (the awaited Mahdi). In the Iranian view, Zionist ideology thus sanctions any kind of confrontation for preventing the advent of *Mahdi*. The base of the middle east and the Persian Gulf oppositions can be understood as a reference to the perception of Zionists and the Israeli state's apocalyptic planning. By such a logic, Israeli messianism equals conspiracy against any true understanding of messianism, namely, Islamic and Shiite messianism. The Israeli messiah and his functions are not based on a true conception of the Hebrew bible and history, in this framework, but are a consequence of the interests of the leading governments.

Iranians conceive of Jewish messianism as a passive one, like the traditional Shiite's approach. After the emergence of Zionist ideology and the codification of Israeli political theology and messianism, Mashiach's function and his movement change to an active one. Zionists are activists, and some of them violent and radical people who give a radical and antagonistic reading of the awaited Mashiach. Zionism has merged traditional messianism with modern politics and has prompted the diaspora with a strengthened feeling of nationalism and the revival of the glory of ancient Israel. Zionism has interpreted messianism in a political context in an attempt to establish a political system based on the idea of emancipation and relate it to modern nationalism.[37] Iranian researchers consider justice to be a concept of Judaism that was lost through its distortion in Zionism. In the context of the dominant figures of Israel, the function of Mashiach is not the establishment of justice but guaranteeing Israel's security-based equations.

In Iranian scholarly assessments, during the emergence of Zionism, messianism was distorted from its principal form and turned into an instrumental concept by means of which the leaders of the "Zionist Regime" (a name the Islamic Republic of Iran gives to Israel) legitimate their functions.[38] The announcement of Jerusalem as Israel's capital is aligned to apocalyptic war and moving the borders of opposition and enmity into the holy places: Jerusalem or *Quds* or *Beit-ol-Moqaddas*, the Muslim's favorite city, and *Al-Aqsa* Mosque, the Muslim's first *qiblah*.

THE DUTIES AND MISSIONS OF THE BELIEVERS AND THE JEWS

It is a challenging issue to say what the duties of a Jew and the Jewish community are toward Mashiach and the apocalyptic movement. John Ashton classifies the messianic idea on a grid with four coordinates: "1. Time: when will the redemption take place? 2. Scene: where does redemptive action take place? 3. Agency: who performs redemptive acts? And 4. Scope: what will be redeemed?"[39] When the belief in messianic determinism is strong, and emancipation in a special way imminent, when emancipation is behind the door, logic dictates passive waiting in addition to trust in God and the realization of the will of the holy ruler. On the other side, when "there is affinity between messianism and violence," people lose control and actively function.[40] This is the pragmatic dimension of theology and the political act arising from messianism. A process, which has passed from mere reading and finding texts, has assessed messianism and the awaited savior in the social frame and activism.

According to the Iranian approach, the main difference between the Jewish and Israeli conceptions of Maschiach's followers' duties is the centrality of the traditional Jewish texts, and the activism of social actions and practices and the collective actions in Israeli messianism. In this approach the passive and historical wait is replaced by an active and socialized one. Based on Jewish teachings, a Jewish person should pass all the borders in front of him until all get unified and remain as a solid ethnicity.[41] Israeli messianism is an activist and violent process, which asks for an act toward the Zionist messianic ideology especially in relation to the resistant front (including the Islamic Republic of Iran and all the countries and movements which are opposing the United States, Israel, and the "arrogant system"). As Hamami Lalehzar says:

> Moses ben Maimon speaks very nice about this issue, our enthusiasm for Mashiach's era is not aimed to dominate on the world or the nations; it's for the emancipation from the oppressors' power of hegemony which prevents us from doing our divinely duties. Our passion for such a day is because in that time all the honest and righteous people gather and logic and truth dominate the world.[42]

THE NATURE AND FUNCTIONS OF THE STATE

Certain issues are discussed a great deal, such as the state's nature, nation, Israeli nationalism and Jewish internationalism, Hebrew as the Jewish national language, and establishing a Jewish state. Here, the difference and opposition between the native (national) and universal and also the macro-dimensions in Iran and Israel have been generally talked about. So, this is an important issue to understand the borders between the internal and external dimensions and the national and transnational interests and duties. As a result, determining the limits of citizenship and commitment to the Jewish believers is of importance. These may be discussed in relation to traditional and (post)modern messianism. Negar Partow describes this thus: "In Israel after the foundation of the state, Revolutionary Messianism remained concentrated on an institutionally based narrative."[43] Revolutionary messianism is against the traditional and classical approach, understands Jewish messianism in the base of a Jewish nation-state, and puts the state in the position of the messianic era agent. In fact, Israeli messianism is a kind of semiotics rise and conceptual redefinition and revisionism in methods, ways, and values.

The enactment of the Jewish land law and the formal change of the secularist nature of the Israeli state can also be interpreted in this regard, and in relation to the duality of nationalism and internationalism:

> Following the creation of the state of Israel in 1948, some idealists of the left of the Zionist movement believed that Israeli leaders might seriously consider the prophetic image of the state that was "a light unto the nation," basing its policies on the principle of justice and right.[44]

Many scholars, like Yosef Salmon, Michael Brenner, and Jakob Klatzkin, have studied the relation between religion, nationalism, and the nature of Judaism.[45] In most of these studies, the exile period and the Israelis' hardships are the main factors of the rise and continuance of the state of Israel. Although "the notion of centrality, or the direct impact of Israel on a peripheral Jewish population, has three distinct frames of reference: the state of Israel, the Jewish people and the Hebrew religion," Iranian scholarship views Zionist ideology as a deviant one which has seized the people of Israel and the Hebrew religion for the interests of Israeli leaders and *Istekbar-e Jahani* (the global arrogance); moreover, "the contemporary state of Israel is not a religious one and in most cases it is anti-religion."[46] Following the foundation of Israel, the diaspora turned into a national community and messianism was no longer an abstract and internationalist idea but a subcategory of nationalism. The Jews made a way through history and had different responsibilities: the responsibility of other-making.[47]

In this reading, messianism (theoretically and practically) is focused on all humanity, and the Jews as the "chosen people" have the responsibility of enacting it. This can be investigated in relation to the governing ideology of Israel (the Zionist idea), and this is one of the serious issues in Israel's foreign policy and international relations. Zionist ideology in many cases, like immigration to Israel and emigration from Israel, uses the terminology of Jewish messianic literature (Aliya/Yerida).

Probably, the most important simulation and distortion in this field of the Iranian studies of political theology and Israeli messianism is related to the Shiite-Islamic theory of *Umm Al-Qura*. According to this theory, the IRI is the main land of righteousness and goodness fighting many others and enemies, and the conservation of this land is the most important function of all the believers and people. Political researchers and agents have generally expressed such simulation and tautology toward Israel as a state built by a group considering themselves the best group and the destined victors of the apocalyptic war.

THE HOLY LAND

"In January 1990 Prime Minister Shamir had made his 'big Israel' speech, taken to mean that he intended to fill the OTs [Occupied Territories] with Soviet Jews, saying 'Big immigration requires Israel to be big as well' [. . .]."[48] Shamir stated that "big immigration requires Israel to be big as well... we must have the Land of Israel and we have to fight for it, struggle for it." He added that "just when many among us were saying that time is working against us, time has brought us this aliyah and has solved everything."[49]

Some post-Zionist scholars and Zionist critics, like Israel Shahak, who are highly attended to by the Iranian elites, state that:

> In a famous talmudic passage in *Tractate Ketubot*, page 111, which is echoed in other parts of the Talmud, God is said to have imposed three oaths on the Jews. Two of these oaths that clearly contradict Zionist tenets are: 1) Jews should not rebel against non-Jews, and 2) as a group should not massively emigrate to Palestine before the coming of the Messiah. (The third oath, not discussed here, enjoins the Jews not to pray too strongly for the coming of the Messiah, so as not to bring him before his appointed time.) During the course of post-Talmudic Jewish history, rabbis extensively discussed the three oaths.[50]

In the Iranian approach, one of the manifestations of Jewishness is the wish for returning to the promised and holy land. This is Jewish messianism full of activism and violence. According to some Israeli Jews, hardline Christian Zionists walked a wrong road because the establishment of "Greater Israel" and the displacement of the Palestinians through any means, especially violence, is incompatible with Christ's message of love and affection. The foundation and expansion of Israel and moving toward the promised land is something in line with the superpowers' interests, especially the United States.[51]

As David Ben-Gurion said in a meeting of Israeli ambassadors July 17, 1950:

> So long as there exists a Jewish Diaspora . . . Israel cannot behave as other states do and take into account only its own geographic and geopolitical situation or limit its concerns to its own citizens and nationals only. Despite the fact that the Jews living abroad are in no legal way part and parcel of Israel, the whole Jewish people, wherever it resides, is the business of the State of Israel, its first and determining business. To this Israel cannot be neutral: such a neutrality would mean renouncing our links with the Jewish people.[52]

Accordingly, in studying Israel's political theology, most Iranians consider the Jews as violent people who are willing to seize the Promised Land at any cost. The Islamic republic views Israel as a dictatorship and even an apartheidist "ethnic democracy" based on Israeli nationalism, and as a result its messianism is also based on its ethnic supremacy. Walter Eytan, an Israeli diplomat, says: "The messianism latent in the Jewish soul, stimulated by the miracle of Israel's return, was ready to embrace the entire world. With the fulfillment of biblical prophecy, a new era of peace and good will could be dawning for all men."[53]

EMANCIPATION, REDEMPTION, AND SALVATION

Galut (exile), Israelis' holy suffering, and a need to compensate for the Jews' difficult eras are some bases in the analysis of emancipation, redemption, and salvation in Judaism. Jewish messianism can be described as such: "Judaism, in all its forms and manifestations has always manifested a concept of redemption as an event which takes place publicly, on the stage of history and within the community."[54] Emancipation and salvation are categories related to faith and mysticism.[55] One of the most promising elements is passing from the era of advent, horrors, turmoil, wars, hopes and fears, and expectations, reaching the era of the establishment of the "awaited" which the Jews call Geula, and have many questions on what will happen in this era: how will human life change?; whether God's orders change or not?; and so on.[56]

> Expressions like "rebirth," "the dawn of redemption," "the lost generation of slavery and first of redemption" reoccurred in the writings and speeches of the [Zionist] pioneers, and many believed that they were "building the Third Temple" in the political sense. As the negation of diasporic history, Zionist redemption was viewed as a renewal of the Jewish or Israelite history of Antiquity.[57]

In the words of Joskowicz and Katz: "Modern political Zionism, the second type of messianism without Messiah, refers to a quasi-messianic return of the

Jewish people to their ancient lands without waiting for, and without need of, a messianic figure."[58] Iranian scholars believe that the unreligious Zionism, at its inception, used Jewish messianism as a tool for the realization of the promised redemption and salvation. From this perspective, like the Western scholars, even religious Zionism moved toward a pragmatic approach and broke from the history of the notion of redemption, emancipation, and salvation. This was a result of the necessity of articulating a secure life in the land of Palestine.

Messianism is a prompting structure which has unified the diaspora (the chain of equivalence) and manifested them as people out of global history (logic of difference). This unique messianism outlines the Jews as the chosen ethnicity and challenges contemporary global history. In mainstream Judaism, this subject underlies the foregrounding of some elements like martyrdom, and in Zionism is a consequence of seeking supremacy and invasion. So, seeking emancipation in Judaism and Zionism has resulted in two opposing results: resistance and the activism of a holy belief, and invasion and destructive actionism. In the Iranian view, Zionists are unbelievers who are claiming belief in the historical apocalypse, so, the opponents and the rival discourses of the Zionist and especially post-Zionism and new Zionist political theology, emancipation, and salvation are highly attended to.

According to Israel's mainstream, Zionism has its name from the prophetic and messianic expression of "Zion," which denotes the redemption of the people and the land. It should be noted that even for Ben-Gurion and other Jewish secular nationalists, the Hebrew bible is the spiritual, historical, and cultural touchstone of Jewish identity and the Jews' ties with the land of Israel.[59]

In Scholem's words:

> There is revolution where there is an attempt to create a messianic kingdom without Torah. In the last analysis, there can be no revolution for the Jews. The Jewish Revolution is exclusively the reattachment to Torah.[60]

In the Iranian view, while Zionism and Israeli ideology have actually changed to anti-Bible and anti-Zion, Judaism has its originality despite the distortions; but Zionist political theology lacks any originality and legitimacy.

SACRED OR HOLY SUFFERING AND THE ACCEPTANCE OF HARDSHIP

Judaism is the religion of secrets. In this Abrahamic religion, concepts are expressed through secretive and complex signs and symbols. This is beyond the essence of religion as a transmaterial and multilayered issue. Probably one of the main reasons of this subject, in relation to martyrdom and the holy suffering attributed to messianism, is the unique evolution of the Jews and the people of Israel and the unconventional relation it has with other religions, groups, ideologies, thoughts, and even historical people and political unites. Furthermore, Zoroastrianism can be one of the main sources of belief in the apocalyptic savior, the redemptive Messiah, millennialism, and the re-advent of chiliasm.[61]

There is a belief in fate and mission in Judaism. Messiah ben Joseph and Messiah ben David will come at a determined time, and the fate of humanity will change through the centrality of the Jews as the chosen people. However, some rabbis have equated the messianic era to the rising of the sun; this happens step by step and gradually. The darkest period of Judaism, the Shoah, brought about many messianic movements which have a redemptive nature in their foundation, and each emphasizes that emancipation should now take place and cannot wait passively.[62] "Pre-nationalist historians used this 'holy scripture . . . not really accessible to the mind' to narrate a secular history of the 'Jewish nation,'" as seasoned Israeli cultural critic Moshe Machover concisely explains in his review of Shlomo Sand's book *The Invention of the Jewish People*:

> Jews already "knew" that they were all direct descendants of the Patriarchs Abraham, Isaac, and Jacob who was renamed "Israel" by God. Thus they were all "literally" Bnei Yisrael (Sons of Israel). Their God-promised and God-given homeland was Eretz Yisrael (Land of Israel). . . . Eventually—to cut a long story short—the Jews were punished "for their sins" and were exiled from their homeland by the Romans. But at the End of Days God will send his Mashiach ben-David (anointed scion of David), who will ingather the exiled Jews and return them to their homeland, the Land of Zion. All that remained for Zionist ideology to do was to secularize this sacred narrative. The eschatological bit, the "return" to Zion, was converted into a political colonizing project—hence its very name: "Zionism"—with the impressively bearded Theodor Herzl as secular messiah or his herald.[63]

That some like Hertzberg use the term "secular messianism" to define the spiritual essence of the Zionist enterprise may sound like an oxymoron, or at least a paradox (which, on some level, it is).[64]

CONCLUSION

The process of finding and understanding scientific subjects must generally exist under the shade of unscientific categories. In other words, you understand something which for its conception you have experienced specialized and nonspecialized training directly and indirectly; and, the more the deficiency in that field, the more lack of accuracy you face.

In relation to Jewish Studies and Israel Studies in Iran, with a concentration on political theology and especially messianism, attending to the extant and unique context and perspective is of importance. There is a local approach which is not necessarily based on scientific rules and parameters. About the Jewish people and the political theology in messianism, we should accept a number of narratives which pass some categorizations like Ashkenazi and Sephardi; local approaches which have been affected by the historical heritage and existing abstract realities.

In the structure of Islamic identity, Judaism has always been considered a moderate "other." This process of other-making has been tenser and more serious in Islamic lands, especially in postrevolutionary Iran, with the rise of Israel and Zionist ideology. Thus, this process has moved from agonism to antagonism and even verbal and physical violence. By attending to the duality of good and evil, the oppressed and the oppressor, this subject has had its impact on scholarship in the fields of Jewish Studies and Israel Studies and formulated a special duality. The centrality of survival and the pragmatic trend, besides the technical defects and lack of familiarity with Jewish culture and the Hebrew language, underlies the raw and immature studies of Judaism and Israel within Iran. Messianic action contains a pragmatic metaphysics and dimensions of messianic populism; and, from messianic image to action, Judaism and Israel are articulated as imagined, not necessarily as they are. The apocalyptic events and processes, like the Holocaust, are in a static field based on their relationship with the self and the other identity, and the processes of inclusion and exclusion, are accepted or rejected.

NOTES

1. "Indeed, the religion in the sight of Allah is Islam" (Ali-'Imran/ 19)
2. Amir Rezaeipanah, *Analyzing the Bases of the Genesis of the Messianic Thought in the Foreign Policy of the I. R. of Iran and Israel*, PhD Thesis, (Tehran: Shahid Beheshti University, 2019).
3. Markus Bockmuehl and James Carleton Paget, *Redemption and Resistance: The Messianic Hopes of Jews and Christians in Antiquity* (London: T&T Clark, 2007), 296.
4. Adam Chalom, *Jews and the Muslim World: Solving the Puzzle* (Michigan: International Institute for Secular Humanistic Judaism, 2010), 20–21.
5. Anoushiravan Ehteshami and Mahjoob Zweiri, *Iran's Foreign Policy from Khatami to Ahmadinejad* (Ithaca, NY: Ithaca Press, 2008), xiii.
6. Mahmood Sariolghalam, "The Foreign Policy of the Islamic Republic of Iran; Theoretical Critic and the Coalition Plan," *Majlis & Rahbord, Majlis Research Centre* 9, no. 35 (2002), 67.
7. Said Amir Arjomand, *After Khomeini: Iran under His Successors* (Oxford: Oxford University Press, 2009), 133.
8. Hossein Bashiriyeh, *Revolution and Political Mobilization* (Tehran: Tehran University Press, 1992), 81.
9. Ray Takeyh, *Guardians of the Revolution: Iran and the World in the Age of the Ayatollahs* (Oxford: Oxford University Press, 2009), 58–63.

10. Amir Mohammad Haji-Yousefi, Masoumeh Sani Joshaghani, and Masoumeh Talebi, "The State of the Art on Israel Studies in Iran," *Research Letter of Political Science* 6, no. 2 (2011): 99–138, 125–26.

11. See Ahmad Gol Mohammadi, "Iran and Israel Relationship Narrated Documents Prime Minister (1357–1327)," *Public Law* 4, no. 6 (2002): 79–109; Naser Hadian, "The Uncivilized Nature of the State of Israel," *Middle East Journal* 4 (1995); Shojae Ahmadvand, "Israeli Political Ideological Zionism," *Public Law* 6, no. 12 (2004): 15–45.

12. Mohammad Ghouchani, "The Jewish Question Is Not Our Problem," *Baztabe Andishe* 72 (2006).

13. Yehoiakin Ben Ya'Ocov, *Concepts of Messiah: A Study of the Messianic Concepts of Islam, Judaism, Messianic Judaism and Christianity* (Bloomington: WestBow Press, 2012), xi–xii.

14. Josef W. Meri and Jere L. Bacharach (eds.), *Medieval Islamic Civilization: L-Z, index; an Encyclopedia* (London/ New York: Routledge, 2006), 500.

15. Catalin Negru, *History of the Apocalypse* (North Carolina: Lulu Press, 2015).

16. Reza Najafzadeh, "Messianism in Iranians' Political Theology," *Jostarha-ye Siyasi-ye Moaser* [Contemporary Political Studies] 2, no. 1 (2011): 137–63, 148.

17. Mohammad-Baqer Majlesi [Allama Majlisi], *Bihar Al-Anwar*, 110 Volumes, Committee of Shi'a Jurists (eds.) (Beirut: Dar Ihya Turath al Arabi, 2000), vol. 51, 156.

18. Abdulaziz Sachedina, *Islamic Messianism: The Idea of the Mahdi in Twelver, Shi'ism* (Albany: State University of New York Press, 1981), 2.

19. Sarah Harvey and Suzanne Newcombe, *Prophecy in the New Millennium: When Prophecies Persist* (Farnham: Ashgate Publishing Limited, 2013), 90–91.

20. By reference to a hadith attributed to the prophet Muhammad (pbuh) "Verily Allah sends to this *Ummah* at the head of every one hundred years someone who will renew the *Deen* for it."

21. Jean-Pierre Filiu, *Apocalypse in Islam* (California: University of California Press, 2011), 49.

22. Saïd Amir Arjomand, *Sociology of Shi'ite Islam: Collected Essays* (Leiden: Brill, 2016), 5.

23. Nikki R. Keddie, *Modern Iran: Roots and Results of Revolution* (New Haven, CT: Yale University Press, 2006); Ira Lapidus, *Islamic Societies to the Nineteenth Century: A Global History* (Cambridge University Press, 2012).

24. Amir Rezaeipanah and Somaye Shokati Moqarab (eds. trans.), *Identity, Discourse and Elections in Iran* (Tehran: Neveeseh, 2016), 34

25. Asghar Montazer Saheb (ed.), *Alam-ara-ye Shah Esmaeil* (Tehran: Elmi va Farhangi, 2005), 220; See also Iskandar Beg Munshi, *Tarikh-I alam-ara-yi Abbsi* (Tehran: Amir Kabir, 2003); Mahmoud ibn Hidayatu'llah Afvashteh, *Naqavat Al-asar*. By effort of Hussein Eshraqi (Tehran: Scientific and Cultural Publication, 1994).

26. Catherine Wessinger (ed.), *The Oxford Handbook of Millennialism* (Oxford: Oxford University Press, 2011), 278.

27. Amir Mohammad Haji-Yousefi and Amir Rezaeipanah, "Explaining the Evolution of the Pragmatic Aspect of Messianism Discourse in the Jewish-Israel Political Theology (Jewish Messianism as a Social Construction)," *Quarterly Journal of Political Research in Islamic World* 8, no. 1 (2018): 125–57; Zahra Khoshkjan and Amir Rezaeipanah, "An Analysis of the Principles and Functions of the Concepts of Emancipation and Messianism in Jewish Pragmatic Theology," *Ensanpajoohi-e Dini* [Religious Anthropology] 14, no. 37 (2017): 45–66.

28. Arjomand, *Sociology of Shi'ite Islam*; Nikki R. Keddie, *Iran: Religion, Politics and Society: Collected Essays* (London/New York: Routledge, 1981).

29. Abbas Amanat, *Apocalyptic Islam and Iranian Shi'ism* (London: IB Taurus, 2009), 193.

30. Patrick H. O'Neil, "A Messianic State? Ideology, Rationality and Eschatology in Iranian Politics," 2013, 13.

31. Mehdi Khalaji, "Apocalyptic Politics: On the Rationality of Iranian Policy," *Washington Institute for Near East Policy: Policy Focus* 79 (2008); Arshin Adib-Moghaddam (ed.), *A Critical Introduction to Khomeini* (Cambridge: Cambridge University Press, 2014).

32. Homayoun Samieh, "Interview with the leader of the Tehran Jewish Association," *Entekhab*, December 24, 2017. http://www.entekhab.ir/fa/news/384984.
33. See Michael Meyer, *Jewish Identity in the Modern World* (Seattle: University of Washington Press, 1990); Daniel J. Schroeter, "A Different Road to Modernity: Jewish Identity in the Arab World," in *Diasporas and Exiles: Varieties of Jewish Identity*. Howard Wettstein (ed.) (London: University of California Press, 2002), 151.
34. Samieh, "Interview with the leader of the Tehran Jewish Association."
35. Younes Hamami Lalehzar, "Messianic Era in Judaism Perspective," *Bina* 45 (2017).
36. Arash Abaei, "The Manner and Features of Jewish Messianism," *Bina* 32 (2006).
37. Negar Partow, *Divine Sovereignty and State Authority in Israel and Iran*. Doctoral Thesis for PhD in Religious Studies. Victoria University of Wellington. 2011, 47.
38. Ahmad Zeidabadi, *Religion and Government in Israel* (Tehran: Rooz-negar Publications, 2002), 168.
39. John Ashton, *Revealed Wisdom: Studies in Apocalyptic in Honour of Christopher Rowland* (Leiden: Brill, 2014), 57.
40. Mark Juergensmeyer, Margo Kitts, and Michael Jerryson, *The Oxford Handbook of Religion and Violence* (Oxford: Oxford University Press, 2012), 94.
41. Omid Shayan Mehr, "Pasah, Eid of Freedom," *Bina* 44 (2017).
42. Hamami Lalehzar, "Messianic Era in Judaism Perspective."
43. Partow, *Divine Sovereignty and State Authority in Israel and Iran*, 19.
44. Jalil Roshandel and Nathan Chapman Lean, *Iran, Israel, and the United States: Regime Security vs. Political Legitimacy* (Oxford: Praeger, 2011), 35.
45. See Yaacov Yadgar, *Sovereign Jews: Israel, Zionism, and Judaism* (Albany: State University of New York, 2017).
46. See Ernest Krausz and Gitta Tulea (eds.), *Jewish Survival: The Identity Problem at the Close of the Twentieth Century* (New Jersey: Transaction Publishers, 1998); Abaei, "The Manner and Features of Jewish Messianism."
47. Daniela Flesler, Tabea Alexa Linhard, and Adrián Pérez Melgosa. *Revisiting Jewish Spain in the Modern Era* (New York: Routledge, 2013), 117–18.
48. Edgar O'Ballance, *The Palestinian Intifada* (New York: St. Martin's Press, 1998), 79.
49. Clive Jones, *Soviet Jewish Aliyah, 1989–1992: Impact and Implications for Israel and the Middle East* (London: FRANK CASS, 1996), 57.
50. Israel Shahak and Norton Mezvinsky, *Jewish Fundamentalism in Israel* (New Edition. London: Pluto Press, 2004), 18.
51. John J. Mearsheimer and Stephen M. Walt, *The Israel Lobby and U.S. Foreign Policy* (New York: Farrar, Straus and Giroux, 2007).
52. Dov Waxman, *The Pursuit of Peace and the Crisis of Israeli Identity: Defending/Defining the Nation*. (Hampshire: Palgrave Macmillan, 2006), 46.
53. Uri Bialer, *Between East and West: Israel's Foreign Policy Orientation 1948–1956* (Cambridge: Cambridge University Press, 1990), 2.
54. Yehuda Liebes, *Studies in Jewish Myth and Messianism* (New York: State University of New York Press, 1993), 94.
55. Ramin Lalehpour, "The Days from Pasah and Shavuot 'Heralding the Real Freedom,'" *Bina* 44 (2014).
56. Hamami Lalehzar, "Messianic Era in Judaism Perspective."
57. Stephen Sharot, "Judaism in Israel: Public Religion, Neo-Traditionalism, Messianism, and Ethno-Religious Conflict," in *The SAGE Handbook of the Sociology of Religion*. James A. Beckford and Jay Demerath (eds.) (London: SAGE, 2007), 675.
58. Ari Joskowicz and Ethan B. Katz (eds.), *Secularism in Question: Jews and Judaism in Modern Times* (Pennsylvania: University of Pennsylvania Press, 2015), 83.
59. Joel Peters and David Newman (eds.), *The Routledge Handbook on the Israeli–Palestinian Conflict* (London/New York: Routledge, 2013), 163.
60. Jack Lester Jacobs, *Jews and Leftist Politics; Judaism, Israel, Antisemitism, and Gender* (Cambridge: Cambridge University Press, 2017), 235.
61. Laura Knight-Jadczyk, *The Secret History of the World and How to Get Out Alive* (Red Pill Press, 2005), 328.

62. Avraham Weiss, *Principles of Spiritual Activism* (Hoboken: KTAV Publishing House, 2002), 195.

63. Katie Attwell, *Jewish-Israeli National Identity and Dissidence; The Contradictions of Zionism and Resistance* (New York: Palgrave Macmillan, 2015), 43; Shlomo Sand, *The Invention of the Jewish People*, Y. Lotan (trans.), English Paperback Ed. (London: Verso Books, 2009), 75.

64. Peters and Newman (eds.), *The Routledge Handbook on the Israeli–Palestinian Conflict*, 163–64.

BIBLIOGRAPHY

Abaei, Arash. "The Manner and Features of Jewish Messianism." *Bina* 32 (2006).
Adib-Moghaddam, Arshin (ed.). *A Critical Introduction to Khomeini*. Cambridge: Cambridge University Press, 2014.
Afvashteh, Mahmoud ibn Hidayatu'llah. *Naqavat Al-asar*. By effort of Hussein Eshraqi. Tehran: Scientific and Cultural Publication, 1994.
Ahmadvand, Shojae. "Israeli Political Ideological Zionism." *Public Law* 6, no. 12 (2004): 15–45.
Amanat, Abbas. *Apocalyptic Islam and Iranian Shi'ism*. London: IB Taurus, 2009.
Amir Arjomand, Saïd. *After Khomeini: Iran under His Successors*. Oxford: Oxford University Press, 2009.
———. *Sociology of Shi'ite Islam: Collected Essays*. Leiden: Brill, 2016.
Ashton, John. *Revealed Wisdom: Studies in Apocalyptic in Honour of Christopher Rowland*. Leiden: Brill, 2014.
Attwell, Katie. *Jewish-Israeli National Identity and Dissidence; The Contradictions of Zionism and Resistance*. New York: Palgrave Macmillan, 2015.
Bashiriyeh, Hossein. *Revolution and Political Mobilization*. Tehran: Tehran University Press, 1992.
Ben Ya'Ocov, Yehoiakin. *Concepts of Messiah: A Study of the Messianic Concepts of Islam, Judaism, Messianic Judaism and Christianity*. Bloomington: WestBow Press, 2012.
Bialer, Uri. *Between East and West: Israel's Foreign Policy Orientation 1948–1956*. Cambridge: Cambridge University Press, 1990.
The Bible, the Book of Isaiah. http://biblescripture.net/Isaiah.html.
Bockmuehl, Markus, and James Carleton Paget. *Redemption and Resistance: The Messianic Hopes of Jews and Christians in Antiquity*. London: T&T Clark, 2007.
Chalom, Adam. *Jews and the Muslim World: Solving the Puzzle*. Michigan: International Institute for Secular Humanistic Judaism, 2010.
Ehteshami, Anoushiravan, and Mahjoob Zweiri. *Iran's Foreign Policy from Khatami to Ahmadinejad*. Ithaca, NY: Ithaca Press, 2008.
Filiu, Jean-Pierre. *Apocalypse in Islam*. California: University of California Press, 2011.
Flesler, Daniela, Tabea Alexa Linhard, and Adrián Pérez Melgosa. *Revisiting Jewish Spain in the Modern Era*. New York: Routledge, 2013.
Ghouchani, Mohammad. "The Jewish Question Is Not Our Problem." *Baztabe Andishe* 72 (2006).
Gol Mohammadi, Ahmad. "Iran and Israel Relationship Narrated Documents Prime Minister (1357–1327)." *Public Law* 4, no. 6 (2002): 79–109.
Hadian, Naser. "The Uncivilized Nature of the State of Israel." *Middle East Journal* 4 (1995).
Haji-Yousefi, Amir Mohammad, Masoumeh Sani Joshaghani, and Masoumeh Talebi. "The State of the Art on Israel Studies in Iran." *Research Letter of Political Science* 6, no. 2 (2011): 99–138.
Haji-Yousefi, Amir Mohammad, and Amir Rezaeipanah. "Explaining the Evolution of the Pragmatic Aspect of Messianism Discourse in the Jewish-Israel Political Theology (Jewish Messianism as a Social Construction)." *Quarterly Journal of Political Research in Islamic World* 8, no. 1 (2018): 125–57.
Hamami Lalehzar, Younes. "Messianic Era in Judaism Perspective." *Bina* 45 (2017).

Harvey, Sarah, and Suzanne Newcombe. *Prophecy in the New Millennium: When Prophecies Persist*. Farnham: Ashgate Publishing Limited, 2013.
Jacobs, Jack Lester. *Jews and Leftist Politics; Judaism, Israel, Antisemitism, and Gender*. Cambridge: Cambridge University Press, 2017.
Jones, Clive. *Soviet Jewish Aliyah, 1989–1992: Impact and Implications for Israel and the Middle East*. London: FRANK CASS, 1996.
Joskowicz, Ari, and Ethan B. Katz (eds.). *Secularism in Question: Jews and Judaism in Modern Times*. Pennsylvania: University of Pennsylvania Press, 2015.
Juergensmeyer, Mark, Margo Kitts, and Michael Jerryson. *The Oxford Handbook of Religion and Violence*. Oxford: Oxford University Press, 2012.
Keddie, Nikki R. *Iran: Religion, Politics and Society: Collected Essays*. London/New York: Routledge, 1981.
———. *Modern Iran: Roots and Results of Revolution*. New Haven, CT: Yale University Press, 2006.
Khalaji, Mehdi. "Apocalyptic Politics; On the Rationality of Iranian Policy." *Washington Institute for Near East Policy: Policy Focus* 79 (2008).
Khoshkjan, Zahra, and Amir Rezaeipanah. "An Analysis of the Principles and Functions of the Concepts of Emancipation and Messianism in Jewish Pragmatic Theology." *Ensanpajoohi-e Dini* [Religious Anthropology] 14, no. 37 (2017): 45–66.
Knight-Jadczyk, Laura. *The Secret History of the World and How to Get Out Alive*. Red Pill Press, 2005.
Krausz, Ernest, and Gitta Tulea (eds.). *Jewish Survival: The Identity Problem at the Close of the Twentieth Century*. New Jersey: Transaction Publishers, 1998.
Lalehpour, Ramin. "The Days from Pasah and Shavuot 'Heralding the Real Freedom.'" *Bina* 44 (2014).
Lapidus, Ira. *Islamic Societies to the Nineteenth Century: A Global History*. Cambridge University Press, 2012.
Liebes, Yehuda. *Studies in Jewish Myth and Messianism*. New York: State University of New York Press, 1993.
Majlesi, Mohammad-Baqer [Allama Majlisi]. *Bihar Al-Anwar*. 110 Volumes. Committee of Shi'a Jurists (eds.). Beirut: Dar Ihya Turath al Arabi, 2000.
Mearsheimer, John J., and Stephen M. Walt. *The Israel Lobby and U.S. Foreign Policy*. New York: Farrar, Straus and Giroux, 2007.
Meri, Josef W., and Jere L. Bacharach (eds.). *Medieval Islamic Civilization: L-Z, index; an Encyclopedia*. London/ New York: Routledge, 2006.
Meyer, Michael. *Jewish Identity in the Modern World*. Seattle: University of Washington Press, 1990.
Munshi, Iskandar Beg. *Tarikh-I alam-ara-yi Abbsi*. Tehran: AmirKabir, 2003.
Najafzadeh, Reza. "Messianism in Iranians' Political Theology." *Jostarha-ye Siyasi-ye Moaser* [Contemporary Political Studies] 2, no. 1 (2011): 137–63.
Negru, Catalin. *History of the Apocalypse*. North Carolina: Lulu Press, 2015.
The Noble Quran. Amatul Rahman Omar (trans.) http://www.qurandislam.com.
O'Ballance, Edgar. *The Palestinian Intifada*. New York: St. Martin's Press, 1998.
O'Neil, Patrick H. "A Messianic State? Ideology, Rationality and Eschatology in Iranian Politics." 2013. https://ssrn.com/abstract=2316288 or http://dx.doi.org/10.2139/ssrn.2316288.
Partow, Negar. *Divine Sovereignty and State Authority in Israel and Iran*. Doctoral Thesis for PhD in Religious Studies. Victoria University of Wellington. 2011.
Peters, Joel, and David Newman (eds.). *The Routledge Handbook on the Israeli–Palestinian Conflict*. London/New York: Routledge, 2013.
Rezaeipanah, Amir. *Analyzing the Bases of the Genesis of the Messianic Thought in the Foreign Policy of the I. R. of Iran and Israel*. PhD Thesis, Shahid Beheshti University, 2019.
Rezaeipanah, Amir, and Somaye Shokati Moqarab (eds. trans.) *Identity, Discourse and Elections in Iran*. Tehran: Neveeseh, 2016.
Roshandel, Jalil, and Nathan Chapman Lean. *Iran, Israel, and the United States: Regime Security vs. Political Legitimacy*. Oxford: Praeger, 2011.

Sachedina, Abdulaziz. *Islamic Messianism: The Idea of the Mahdi in Twelver, Shi'ism*. Albany: State University of New York Press, 1981.
Saheb, Asghar Montazer (ed.). *Alam-ara-ye Shah Esmaeil*. Tehran: Elmi va Farhangi, 2005.
Samieh, Homayoun. "Interview with the leader of the Tehran Jewish Association." *Entekhab*. December 24, 2017. http://www.entekhab.ir/fa/news/384984.
Sand, Shlomo. *The Invention of the Jewish People*. Y. Lotan (trans.). English Paperback Ed. London: Verso Books, 2009.
Sariolghalam, Mahmood. "The Foreign Policy of the Islamic Republic of Iran; Theoretical Critic and the Coalition Plan." *Majlis & Rahbord, Majlis Research Centre* 9, no. 35 (2002).
Schroeter, Daniel J. "A Different Road to Modernity: Jewish Identity in the Arab World." In *Diasporas and Exiles: Varieties of Jewish Identity*, edited by Howard Wettstein, 150–63. London: University of California Press, 2002.
Shahak, Israel, and Norton Mezvinsky. *Jewish Fundamentalism in Israel*. New Edition. London: Pluto Press, 2004.
Sharot, Stephen. "Judaism in Israel: Public Religion, Neo-Traditionalism, Messianism, and Ethno-Religious Conflict." In *The SAGE Handbook of the Sociology of Religion*, edited by James A. Beckford and Jay Demerath. London: SAGE, 2007.
Shayan Mehr, Omid. "Pasah, Eid of Freedom." *Bina* 44 (2017).
Takeyh, Ray. *Guardians of the Revolution: Iran and the World in the Age of the Ayatollahs*. Oxford: Oxford University Press, 2009.
Waxman, Dov. *The Pursuit of Peace and the Crisis of Israeli Identity: Defending/Defining the Nation*. Hampshire: Palgrave Macmillan, 2006.
Weiss, Avraham. *Principles of Spiritual Activism*. Hoboken: KTAV Publishing House, 2002.
Wessinger, Catherine (ed.). *The Oxford Handbook of Millennialism*. Oxford: Oxford University Press, 2011.
Yadgar, Yaacov. *Sovereign Jews: Israel, Zionism, and Judaism*. Albany: State University of New York, 2017.
Zeidabadi, Ahmad. *Religion and Government in Israel*. Tehran: Rooz-negar Publications, 2002.

Chapter Six

Turkish Jews' Perspectives on Israel

Özgür Kaymak

Jews were one of the most populous non-Muslim minority groups of Istanbul during the years in which the Turkish Republic was founded, and historically had constituted a very important part of the city's culture, daily life, and class structure. Today, there is a Jewish population of approximately fifteen thousand in Turkey.[1] More than 95 percent of this population lives in Istanbul. Turkish Jews have lost the largest part of their population due to the large-scale immigration to Israel after its establishment in 1948. The Jewish community continued to shrink demographically as a result of continued immigration spread over the years due to the pressure and discrimination Jews suffered as a minority, and due to economic or individual reasons.[2] The community is 96 percent Sephardi. Turkey's Jewish community has been shrinking steadily in Istanbul's urban spaces in recent years because of a decrease in the number of births, aging demographics, mixed marriages, and also migration to various parts of the world—but primarily to Israel—due to the political, social, and economic crises the country has endured through in the last four years. From January 2018 until June 2018, the Istanbul Jewish community experienced seventy deaths, but only ten births. As of 2014, the average age in the community is forty-nine years. In 2017, the number of people who migrated to Israel was four hundred.[3] More have moved to the United States and other countries. Turkey's Jewish community's population is estimated to be only five thousand people by 2040.[4]

Considering this brief discussion, this study examines Turkish Jews' attitudes toward Israel, their perception of Israel, and the kind of symbolic and social capital that they build therewith. It mainly focuses on Turkish Jews' personal attachments to Israel, such as having an emotional bond with Israel; being proud of, excited about; being or feeling ambivalent toward Israel; loyal to and/or trusting in Israel; and depending on Israel for feeling secure.

As I mentioned earlier, immigration to Israel has gained momentum in recent years. Thus, this chapter also assesses whether having an emotional bond with Israel is an important factor for migrating there, and whether Israel is a "future destination" for young Jews. Only through the answers to these questions, I believe, can one have a general understanding of Jewish perspectives in contemporary Turkey. To that end, this study uses the oral history and in-depth interview narratives based on a large-scale field study I conducted during work on my doctoral dissertation between 2013 and 2017, and a field study conducted in Istanbul between January and May 2018—focusing on Turkish Jews of various ages, socioeconomic classes, and genders.

Although it is not possible to achieve a "perfect" profile of the Jews based in Istanbul—nor does this chapter promise to offer one—the profile developed in this chapter makes a significant contribution to our knowledge of Jews of Istanbul, their citizenship practices through a detailed analysis of their relationships, and the kind of symbolic capital they have built with Israel—an understudied area in the Jewish and Israel Studies literature within Turkish academia. Although there has been a remarkable increase in research on non-Muslim minorities in recent years, scholarly works focusing on the sociology of daily life of non-Muslims are limited. Much of the extant research concerning political engagement in Turkey centers on general understandings of the opinions and behaviors of the broader Turkish population. However, these studies have largely ignored the legal, social, and economic barriers that directly influence the structures and realities of ethnic and racial minority citizenship practices. Considering that gap in the literature, this chapter questions the relationship of Turkish Jews with Israel.

The fact that being Jewish is often equated with being Israeli by the majority, and that Jews are viewed as "foreigners" or "guests" by the broader society, Jews have been obliged to mask their real thoughts and feelings about—and connections to—Israel in the public sphere in order not to be stigmatized as "the enemy within." This is a matter that deeply affects the everyday life practices and citizenship/identity perceptions of Turkish Jews. Not being able to share thoughts and feelings about Israel with the wider society is perhaps the most sensitive element of their ethnoreligious identity—in other words, their red line. Investigating these factors, this chapter contributes to the identity and citizenship literature. This analysis does not purport to be an exhaustive one, but rather it is intended as a substantial beginning and as an invitation to other scholars to further advance this avenue of research. I see my results as a perspective rather than as a truth-claim.

The rest of the chapter proceeds as follows: I will first detail the current state of the literature on Jewish-Israel Studies in Turkish academia from a critical perspective. Secondly, I will outline the methodology of the study which will be followed by a statement of the main issue of this research and an analytical assessment based on the conceptual and theoretical background discussed above.

LITERATURE REVIEW ON JEWISH-ISRAEL STUDIES IN TURKISH ACADEMIA

This section summarizes Jewish-Israel Studies produced in recent years by Turkish academia and analyzes critically the reasons for the lack of "Jewish-Israel Studies" at universities in Turkey.[5] Although there is invaluable scholarship in this discipline produced outside of Turkey, such scholarship is outside the scope of this chapter.

Within academic and political literature, the number of studies on non-Muslim minorities[6] have increased since the end of the 1990s and especially in the mid-2000s. Academic works on minorities produced in Turkey have mainly focused on the inequalities produced in conjunction with the founding of the Turkish nation-state and on the citizenship-state relationship from a legal, historical, and political framework. Many of these works contributed to the development of discussion about the historical attempt at creating a homogeneous national identity out of a disparate population of many ethnic minorities, and brought Turkey's official historical thesis into question. There are very few qualitative studies in the academic field analyzing non-Muslims' social construction processes through their daily lives in a comparative perspective, and moreover studies focusing on Turkish Jews and Israel and their relationality are almost nonexistent. This chapter may be one of the first steps in the effort to eliminate this gap. Oral history studies have become an interdisciplinary paradigm for history, political science, medicine, psychology, psychoanalysis, women's studies, cultural anthropology, and literature. Among the increasing number of oral history and memory studies of the last fifteen years, only a few academic works have been associated with non-Muslim minorities living in Turkey. The studies of Leyla Neyzi and Rıfat N. Bali are seminal works in the literature. Neyzi conducted oral history studies, especially on Jews and Armenians, and examined problems of self and belonging among minority individuals.[7] Libra Publishing, founded by Rıfat N. Bali, produces a large portion of the academic and semiacademic publications on Turkey's Jewish community in the fields of history, culture, literature, architecture, and politics.[8] Besides academic studies, there are also semiacademic popular works about the Jewish community in Turkey, addressing their everyday life and neighborhood practices.[9]

Since the mid-2000s, there has been an increase in the number of studies completed in master's and doctoral programs at universities in Turkey, both in Turkish and English, which have developed counternarratives to the official historical thesis. In the last ten years, a few works of oral history and in-depth interviews have been conducted examining the daily life experiences of non-Muslim minorities. The distribution of the thesis topics which study Turkish Jews and Israel can be summarized as follows: When we do a search on the thesis database of the Council of Higher Education (YÖK)[10] using the key words "Musevi," "Yahudi,"[11] "İsrail [Israel]," "Holokost [Holocaust]," and "Siyonizm [Zionism]," the results reveal a list of theses completed mostly in departments of music, architecture, religion, history, philosophy, public administration, international relations, English and American language, and literature. Although still few in number, starting in the 2000s, field studies have been conducted in the fields of sociology, anthropology, and international relations, which mostly focus on the perception of Jewish identity and the relation between citizenship and minority identity.[12] A search with the keyword "Musevi" reveals nine doctoral dissertations and master theses.[13] One of these theses belongs to the sociology department; others are written in history, music, architecture, religion, and political science departments. A search with the keyword "Yahudi" results in a list of 103 theses, five in the field of sociology and one in anthropology. Other theses are written in the departments of history, religion, international relations, journalism, architecture, philosophy, music, communication, American and English language, and literature. No theses are listed based on the search for the keyword "Holocaust."[14] There are five dissertations that include the keyword "Zionism"; these theses were written in the departments of religion, international relations, history, and political science. Finally, there are 198 theses that contain the keyword "Israel." Almost all have been completed in the departments of political science and international relations. They are primarily on topics of security, Israel-Turkey relations, strategic cooperation between the two countries, as well as Israel and Turkey's foreign policies. There were no sociological studies addressing the Jewish community in Turkey.

Despite the rise in recent years of the number of theses written on Turkish Jews and Israel, theses and monographs aiming to transform the voices of the subaltern into public information, giving space to the perception of ordinary minority individuals, examining the perceptions of Turkish Jews on Israel, and developing counternarratives to the official history thesis still do not occupy their deserved space in the Turkish academic literature.[15]

The lack of "Jewish-Israeli Studies" as a discipline in Turkish academia was mentioned above. The establishment of *Yahudi Çalışmaları Topluluğu* (YATOÇ—Community of Jewish Studies) in May 2015 as part of *Türkiye Kültürleri Araştırma ve Uygulama Merkezi* (TÜKAM—Research and Application Center of Turkey's Cultures) was the most recent attempt. However, the center, which was planned to be established within Istanbul Bilgi University, was not approved by YÖK. In the past two years, several talks and panels have been organized in order to increase public awareness about the Holocaust and the Turkish Jewish community in Turkey. Examples of these activities include a panel titled "Discussing the Holocaust in Turkey: Memory, Awareness and Education," organized by Bilkent University in Ankara in April 2016 and another Holocaust-themed panel in December 2016 with Dr. Cory Guttstadt (Bali, 2017b). I gave a talk myself titled "Being Jewish in Istanbul" at Bilgi University in December 2017 based on my doctoral dissertation research.

METHODOLOGY OF THE STUDY

The focus of the study is based on oral history and in-depth interviews I conducted with Jews living in Istanbul of different generations, social classes, and genders between 2013 and 2017 as part of my doctoral dissertation—and for an ongoing study focusing on the Jewish community. The universe of this study consisted of a total of sixty individuals: thirty-four women and twenty-six men. I sought to achieve a gender balance among the interviewees. In terms of age, interviewers are divided into three age groups: 25–43, 45–60, 65–93. Most of the interviewees are in the middle and upper-middle social classes.[16] In terms of their professional distribution, there is a wide range of specialization: middle- and high-level manager in the corporate sector, painter, teacher, life coach, tennis instructor, advertiser, translator, dentist, lawyer, businessman, travel agent. Most of the men over the age of sixty-five are retired, and almost all women within this age group are housewives. Most interviewees over the age of forty are married. The snowball sampling method was used to reach the interviewees. Due to the sensitivity of the subject, the names of the interviewees were not explicitly used. A coding system indicating age and gender (for example, M / W, 35) was used. The data of the study is composed of the profiles of the participants, the transcription of the interviews, and the field notes. Because of the confidentiality principle, I have personally transcribed the conversations that I recorded.

This study does not claim to present a representative sample regarding Jews living in Istanbul. It is based on a sample of sixty people out of a population of approximately fifteen thousand. However, I believe the data collected gives us important structural information regarding the community. The qualitative approach I employed reveals the Jewish experiences through the voices of the community members and enables me to convey the informants' subjective interpretations and experiences.

ON THE SYMBOLIC BOND
TURKISH JEWS CONSTRUCT WITH ISRAEL

There are two primary factors behind the symbolic bond which Turkish Jews construct with Israel. The first is that there are relatives and friends who have emigrated from Istanbul who live there. The family elders of some of the interviewees from the Jewish community in Istanbul migrated to Mandate Palestine in the 1930s for idealistic purposes in order to establish the State of Israel. In the following years, this migration wave continued due to economic reasons, discriminatory practices in Turkey, and individual reasons. Almost every interviewer has a close relative, friend, and an acquaintance living in Israel today. Due to the proximity of Israel to Turkey, and especially because of their devotion to Istanbul, it was observed that Jews who have migrated come to visit frequently during summer holidays. Today, they maintain their connections with family, relatives, and friends in Istanbul through social media.

The other phenomenon that constitutes the emotional connection of Turkish Jews to Israel and which makes them uniquely distinguished from other congregations (compared to *Rum* Orthodox and Armenian communities) is the Holocaust. According to Moshe and Segev, the Holocaust and the State of Israel were the two most formative events of the twentieth century for the Jewish people and Jewish identity. Even though the Jews who were interviewed did not lose a close relative in the Holocaust, for them, the history of exile and genocide and having awareness and consciousness of the past are memories to never forget and to pass down from generation to generation. Thus, in this respect Jewish collective identity has precedence over all manner of individual identity. Therefore, Israel occupies a very special place for Turkish Jews.[17] The fact that there is a state that overlaps with their ethno-religious identities creates a sense of confidence. As an interviewee stated, as a nation living with the consciousness of "it is in our codes, we can be expelled at any moment," the State of Israel is seen as a guarantee. The establishment of the State of Israel for Jews of the first generation was only a dream and utopia until 1948. In this context, I observed that the Jews of the first generation had a stronger emotional connection with Israel than the youth.

> You can take my money after this, but you can't take my life. Israel is the reason I stand proud and upright. (M, 69)

I observed that all the interviewees consider Istanbul as their homeland, but at the same time they have developed a strong relationship with Israel based on security, especially for the reasons mentioned above, and they see Israel as a kind of "insurance policy."

> For me, Israel represents my honor and my pride. You know what Israel means? Although we adopt every country we go to as our own, we are always reminded that "you are not from here". Here is a society that has been downtrodden and killed at will throughout the world until Israel is established in 1948. There is a society that is crushed and killed in all parts of the world. Once Israel is established, there is a sense that "no one can oppress me anymore." Be certain that even a Jew in America feels that way. Israel is a great support for Jews. (W, 44)

> As I grew older, as I learned about politics, I no longer have any emotional attachment to Israel, but every human being wants security. Because I know that if the state of Israel had not existed, they would have smashed me like a cigarette but in many parts of the world. I didn't dream of going to Israel, but may God perpetuate the existence of Israel. (W, 34)

> The Jews have a sympathy for Israel. If a bomb hits there, it is different for you and me. Because it is always in danger, always has an enemy. Everybody's trying to destroy it. So you understand, there is such a feeling, because of these emotions. (M, 65)

Turkish Jews state that living in Israel is not an attractive choice for them because of the very harsh and difficult living conditions due to Israel being a country constantly at war, and its people being more selfish for this reason, the extremely competitive lifestyle, unfavorable climatic conditions, language difficulties, and very different cultural habitus from what they are used to in Turkey. However, they also describe Israel as a "special country" built with great sacrifice, where more civilized, educated, and free people live than in Turkey, which fulfills requirements of a democratic and welfare state, and where feelings of unity and togetherness is very strong. It was mentioned earlier that the first generation of Jews formed a stronger bond with Israel than the younger generation. For the former, the painful memory of discriminatory citizenship practices that have been applied against the non-Muslim minorities since the establishment of the Republic (such as the 1934 Thrace Pogrom, 1942 Wealth Tax, September 1955 Pogrom)[18] is still very strong and they do not believe that they will be accepted as equal citizens. These factors—in other words, what is sometimes referred to as "minority psychology" that is shared with and observed in the other non-Muslim communities in Turkey—play an important role in the bond developed with Israel and the trust felt toward it by the first generation.

> I have a deep affection for Israel. Everyone has a relative there definitely, it is impossible to remain indifferent. (W, 84)

> That's an interesting country. You view the soldier, the police there differently. I saw how they were organized during the war, they are smart people. There's no way for Turkey to understand this. They immediately write on

social media "God damn Israel." Of course, Israelis have this sense of "we know it best" in everything. Maybe this psychology comes from the fact that they grow up fast without a childhood. It's a special country, it's easy to talk from the outside, without experiencing it. (W, 61)

For me, it's not a country to live in. Here is my homeland. Can you tell me what I'm going to do there even if Israel sends a plane and takes me there? I do not know the language, the way of life, I do not know their customs, what would I do in that country? I'm used to the air and water here. But if my grandson says "Things are bad, I want to leave," I would say "It's your choice," but I would not say "Definitely go to Israel." It's not the world's best, most beautiful, most comfortable country to live in. Everything is very difficult there. Can you afford the luxury you're used to here? (W, 74)

For me, it is the last exit door. If they kick me out and I cannot do anything else, it is the only place that will take me. I never want to go unless I have to. There are many relatives there. Most of them left for economic reasons. All of my first cousins are there. . . . It has a lot to do with the age you leave as well. They are having difficulty adapting to their culture there. Israel is a very difficult country. You have to have a warrior character; not for me at all. (M, 26)

A large majority of Turkish Jews interviewed in the scope of this study said that they went to Israel at least once in their lives. However, except for a few, all interviewees in the young and middle-age groups have said that until the last two or three years, they had not considered going and living in Israel unless they were in a very difficult situation, which meant either an economic difficulty and/or feeling insecure because of their Jewish identity. The number of Turkish Jews who made *Aliyah* has increased in the last three years.[19] The profile of those who are migrating has also changed. Migrants in the last few years are mostly between the ages of twenty-five and forty, graduates of Istanbul's leading universities, and middle- or high-level managers at international firms. In other words, more young Jews with high levels of sociocultural capital and skills are leaving. This contrasts with those who made *Aliyah* after the establishment of Israel in 1948, who were from mostly lower-middle-class Jews. In the early 2000s, following the economic crisis in the country, Turkish Jews whose social welfare levels fell, preferred to go to Israel and live. Whereas in recent years, starting from 2010, some Turkish Jews made *Aliyah* mainly to get away from the political and social crises in Turkey. The change in the sociodemographic profiles of the immigrants also begs the following question: Is Israel becoming a future destination for young Turkish Jews? Although it is not possible to answer this question for the moment, this is a social issue that occupies the top place on the agenda of the Turkish Jewish Community and has caused unease and sadness due to their declining population.[20]

> For me, that is a holiday resort, a place where I go to see my cousins. I hope it remains that way, I would not go one day because I am forced to. But if you see me leave now, just know that I am escaping, because I am afraid of something. Lots of my friends made Aliyah in the last two years. The ones that migrated before were mainly from lower socio-economic class. But now the qualified young ones are planning to go. That's sad. (W, 26)

Israel is a country of last resort, where they will go "when push comes to shove." On the other hand, those who have contemplated going there in recent years have stated, sadly, that it is a "choice out of necessity" because they view the rising anti-Semitism, conservatism, Islamization of the education system under the JDP government, and the increasing authoritarian and repressive practices after July 15, 2016,[21] as threatening the future of their children and because they think life in Israel or another country would be more free. Israel is advantageous compared to other European countries because of the existence of friends and relatives who can provide support and the social security benefits provided by the state. In addition, among the interviewees who planned to migrate to Israel, some had a more pious life style and developed a stronger emotional connection with Israel. For more religious Jews, making *Aliyah* is a step toward finding authenticity and an imagined perfect Jewish life, which is impossible to attain in Turkey.

> You are free there (Israel). My brother is going next year for education. He is going to a Jewish High School now in Istanbul. All his friends are going to Israel. He is going to be left alone. It is a choice brought about by necessity. Otherwise, I would never go to live there if there was no reason. Because I love here physically more. However, that is the place that will raise the least amount of difficulties. (M, 22).

The interviewees stated that after the coup attempt of July 15, 2016, they were particularly uncomfortable with the news that appeared in the conservative media stating "Fetullah Gülen is a Jew." Young interviewees emphasized that the idea of "leaving" was always in the back of their minds, but it was strengthened after July 15, that it was increasingly difficult to live as a Jewish individual in the country with the burdens of collective and individual memory,[22] the rise of anti-Israeli and anti-Zionist sentiments in society in recent years, the entrenchment of anti-Semitism, and the discriminatory practices that they experienced in their daily lives. Israel thus has come to be viewed as a haven for young Jews in the context of the political, economic, and social crises that Turkey has endured in recent years, a country where they will not be discriminated against because of their Jewish identity and deem their own and their children's future to be safe.

> We would continue to live here, of course, but we would also be looking for a way to escape. (M, 37)

> My uncles say, "I prefer to go to Greece and live there"; my mother's side says, "I prefer to go to Izmir if I leave Istanbul"; my father's side says, "Maybe it would be better if we went to the Netherlands." Everyone is talking about leaving. In fact, dissatisfaction level about the general state of affairs was very high. July 15 was like rubbing salt on the wound. There was always the idea of leaving, it's only getting stronger. If you want to establish a connection between July 15 and Jewish identity, you can establish it in this way: There was always the idea of leaving, July 15 strengthened it. (M, 33)

Another reason behind the preferences of young people to go to Israel is that they want to marry a Jew. A few of the young people who have recently thought of migrating to Israel have stated that it is very difficult to find a partner with whom they can connect emotionally and share worldviews in the narrow community of Istanbul.

> I do not see the future good here, there is a very religious government and it seems to me that it is getting worse. And it is now very difficult to marry someone from within the community here, I want to marry a "Jew," you have more chances in Israel. There are acquaintances, relatives. That's where I'm safe. But my childhood is here (Istanbul), my family is here, my memories are here, nothing can delete that. (W, 33)

RISING ANTI-SEMITISM AND ITS EFFECT ON MIGRATION OF TURKISH JEWS

One of the most significant problems threatening Turkish Jews, and an important factor in the bond they construct with Israel and their decision to migrate, is the rising anti-Semitism in society. According to the Anti-Defamation League's (ADL) world ranking of the most anti-Semitic countries, Turkey ranks first with 69 percent. Iran is in second place with 56 percent.[23] After the *Mavi Marmara* incident in 2010,[24] Israeli-Turkish relations have come almost to a standstill, and the situation had caused great uneasiness and trepidation among the Jews of Turkey.

I observed that the first and second generations of non-Muslim individuals' anxiety, fear, and distrust caused by the discriminatory citizenship practices they encountered in the past have not disappeared completely. So, they had reservations in all their interactions with the state and believed that in case of a change in political context and straining of the relationship between Israel and Turkey, a repeat of previous events might will occur. For these reasons, they have little belief that they will ever be seen as equal citizens.

Likewise, the anti-Israel and anti-Jewish rhetoric used by the political leaders with vote concerns prior to elections, during the clashes between Israel and Palestine in the summer of 2014, headlines containing hate speech appearing in the right-wing media, equating Jews living in Turkey with being

Israeli, claiming a connection between Jews and Israel and the Gezi Park Protests, the association of FETÖ with the Jews after the July 15 coup attempt, and the restriction of freedom in social life as citizens have directly affected the lives of Jewish citizens and caused them to feel great insecurity in their own country.

The most significant basis for discrimination of Jews in Turkey is to equate being Jewish to being an Israeli. Thus, they are positioned as "the other" not only on the basis of religion, but also on the assumption that "all Jews are Israeli." They are further alienated because of the negative and enemy image of Israel in Turkey. Israel is positioned as the "Other" in terms of religion, and religious differences serve to increase prejudice and anti-Semitism. When I conducted my PhD fieldwork I noted that during periods of increased tension between Turkey and Israel, the Jewish community began to fear and worry due to the nativist and belligerent rhetoric of political elites, and the anti-Semitic rhetoric of nationalist conservative news media outlets.

> I feel I belong here. But I thought about leaving lately. Among my circle of friends there are some who left. The reason for their departure is not loyalty to Israel, but Recep Tayyip Erdoğan's politics, the trend of the country, there is terrible anti-Semitism; we have never experienced this until today. In the last 2–3 years, I cannot believe it. . . . I cannot believe that our neighbors have become this way. . . . We talked to a lot of people from our age group, we talked a lot during the Gaza events about leaving. My parents cannot leave, where they will go after this age. . . . (M, 33)

> In every prayer we have, the phrase "next year in Jerusalem" is uttered, but I have never thought of living there. It's (Israel) a very difficult country. To go there, either you must have experienced a very traumatic event, or be a strong Zionist. I thought about going lately. Some within my circle have gone, from among my friends. The reason for their departure is the AKP's policies, the trend of the country, there is terrible anti-Semitism. (M, 36)

While on the one hand, there are many Jews, especially among the older generations, who have developed a strong relationship of trust/connection with Israel, there are exceptions to this feeling of closeness. The differences in political views is a decisive factor in the relationship with Israel. The Jews, which are politically closer to the left, harshly criticize Israel's Palestinian policy and emphasize that just because they are Jewish doesn't mean they would try to legitimize Israeli policy. They say they would not choose Israel as a first choice even if they thought of immigration. However, Jews who advocate the left-wing view and speak it in the public sphere are a minority within the community. In a previous study, I discovered that the community has an apolitical structure in general. Jews were used as a trump card or hostage in Turkey's foreign policy for years. The uneasiness and the pressures they experience during political crises with Israel and their non-acceptance as nationals and treatment as foreigners in their own country provides a broad basis for explaining their lack of participation in local and national politics, staying apolitical as a political choice.[25]

> I have nothing to do with Israel. In addition, I view the policy it pursues very fascist. America's got your back, a man kills your two soldiers, and you go and bomb the mosque. You don't have to go and have the mosque bombed and kill 100 people no matter what. You're using a disproportionate amount of force, and you're throwing bombs and missiles into the heart of the city. And then you say, "We warned, but they didn't evacuate." War takes place between soldiers and not between the public and the military. (M, 47)

SPANISH AND PORTUGUESE CITIZENSHIP

Apart from migration to Israel, over the past two to three years, Canada, the United Kingdom, Spain (Barcelona, Valencia), and Portugal are the new migration destinations for many upper-middle-class Turkish Jews. Due to the political developments culminating in a disputed vote to expand President Erdogan's already substantial executive powers, many Turkish Jews applied for or received passports from Spain and Portugal. While the common cause is fear, practical reasons such as E.U. residence permits and visa-free travel in Europe provided by Spanish or Portuguese citizenship have also been influential in this choice. Jews display heightened anxiety about the possibility of future political developments eroding the legitimacy of their symbolic capital. Turkey no longer has favorable living conditions for young Jews. According to the fieldwork conducted by Balta and Altan-Olcay, which analyzes the new classes in Turkey mobilizing their resources so that they receive U.S. citizenship at birth, this anxiety results in a desire to institutionalize their distinctions by acquiring citizenship at least for their children. This finding is also relevant for middle- and upper-middle-class Turkish Jews. On the other hand, the interviewees (almost all of them) who have applied and/or received Spanish or Portuguese citizenship do not consider becoming an Israeli citizen. They do not prefer this for a variety of reasons, such as the negative image of Israel in the world and the distress brought on by living in a country that is in constant conflict. Thus, apart from the symbolic bond Turkish Jews have constructed with Israel, they display pragmatic behavior when it comes to acquiring Israeli citizenship.

CONCLUDING REMARKS

Studies regarding non-Muslim minorities in Turkey have mainly focused on the discriminatory citizenship practices they faced from historical, legal, and political perspectives. Thanks to this literature, many subjects that were not included in the official history have been introduced to Turkish historiography in the late 1990s and the beginning of the 2000s for the first time from a critical perspective. These studies are mainly concentrated on topics of citizenship and nationalism. There has been an increase in recent years of studies focusing on the daily life practices of Jews, one of the non-Muslim communities in Turkey that historically constituted an important element of the urban culture, daily life, and social structure. However, there is still much more work to be done in this field. This study, which focuses on the bonds Turkish Jews have established with Israel within the framework of their citizenship practices, can be included in this line of inquiry.

Analyzing Turkish Jews' personal attachment to Israel, based on the interviews conducted with individuals from all three generations, one of the main findings of this study is that the common feeling within the community toward Israel is pride and confidence, and a sense of security through the presence of the Israeli state. Israel serves as a psychological insurance policy. However, the first generation's emotional bond with Israel is stronger than that of young people. In this respect, generational factors are one clear criterion determining the level of identification with Israel. Moreover, the community is not monolithic. Overall, Turkish Jews, like all other social groups, have contested identities. There are and always will be layers of identity. For some, religious and cultural aspects of their Jewish identity are dominant. For others, non-Jewish universal factors take primacy in their sense of identity. Differences in political leanings among the Turkish Jews also operate as a factor in the relations established with Israel. The Jews, who are politically closer to the left, are harshly critical of Israel's Palestinian policy and stress that they have not had any emotional connection with Israel.

Although immigration to Israel has been rising among the Turkish Jews, I found that the emotional ties with Israel have not played a primary role in this process. Rather, the most important reasons why young people decide to make *Aliyah* are the perceived threat with regard to their family's future from the JDP government that has adopted political Islam, rising anti-Semitism, conservatism, and the authoritarian and repressive character of the regime after July 15, 2016. Israel is a destination that is advantageous mainly because of the existence of friends and relatives who can provide support, and the social security provided by the state. In other words, young Jews' preference to go to Israel in recent years reflects a way to escape the political, social, and economic conflict in Turkey even though they regard Istanbul as their homeland—and have developed a very strong emotional bond. They experience a serious dilemma between staying and "leaving out of necessity." In addition, other personal reasons behind immigration to Israel include nationalistic goals, increasing religiosity, building a freer life, seeking adventure, and marrying a Jew.

Considering these findings, it should be noted that this study does not claim to present a complete picture of the Jewish community living in Istanbul. It was carried out with the middle- and upper-middle-class Jews living in Istanbul. As noted previously, with the establishment of the State of Israel in 1948, the Jews of the lower-middle-class, especially those living in Hasköy and Balat, migrated to this country. In my discussions within the scope of my doctoral thesis, it was emphasized that there was significant poverty within the community as a result of the economic crises during the 2000s. In this context, the class structure of the community is currently constituted mainly by the middle-class. In the future, a field study that will be carried out with qualitative methods among the lower-middle-class members of the Jewish community would be useful in understanding the heterogeneous, layered socioeconomic class structure of the community. Another variable of the study, other than the generation and social class, was gender. No gender differences were observed in the perceptions of Jews in Istanbul regarding Israel.

Scarcity of interdisciplinary studies of Turkish Jews using qualitative methods has led to the need to base this study's theoretical framework on the fieldwork. Through its focus on the everyday life of an important ethnoreligious minority in Turkey, and analysis of their bonds with Israel and the causes of rising migration rate in recent years in the community, the study aims to contribute to citizenship and minority literature.

NOTES

1. The size of the Jewish population in Turkey according to the country's first census of 1927 was 82,000 out of a total population of 13,500,000. During the time between the Second World War and the establishment of the State of Israel 40 percent of the Jewish population in Turkey immigrated to Israel. See Esther Benbassa and Aron Rodrigue, *Türkiye ve Balkan Yahudileri Tarihi* [The History of Turkish and Balkan Jews], translated by Ayşe Atasoy, 3rd ed. (İstanbul: İletişim Yayınları, 2010), 45. According to the official census of 1945, the Jewish population was 76,965 and by 1955 it was 45,995. See Fuat Dündar, *Türkiye Nüfus Sayımlarında Azınlıklar* [Minorities in the Turkish Population Census], 2nd ed. (İstanbul: Çiviyazıları, 2010), 168–69.

2. Turkish citizenship is firmly tied to Turkish national identity, which has predominantly excluded non-Muslims; because the identity component of citizenship was superior to its legal meaning. Since the founding of the Republic (1923), Turkish Jews experienced many traumas and were viewed as scapegoats and leverage, but not as equal citizens. Among the discriminatory citizenship practices and examples of trauma that have deeply affected Jews of Turkey since the founding of the Republic are the 1934 Thrace Pogrom and the 1942 Wealth Tax. See N. Rıfat Bali, *Cumhuriyet Yıllarında Türkiye Yahudileri: Bir Türkleştirme Serüveni (1923–1945)* [Turkish Jews during the Republican Period: The Adventure of Turkification (1923–1945)], 7th ed. (İstanbul: İletişim Yayınları, 2005), 69; see also Ayhan Aktar, *Varlık Vergisi ve Türkleştirme Politikaları* [Wealth Tax and Turkification Policies], 11th ed. (İstanbul: İletişim Yayınları, 2012); Avner Levi, *Türkiye Cumhuriyeti'nde Yahudiler* [Jews in the Republic of Turkey], 3rd ed. (İstanbul: İletişim Yayınları, 2010); Benbassa, *Türkiye ve Balkan Yahudileri Tarihi*. Jews were compelled to confront a growing rise of anti-Semitism in the last ten years under the JDP (Justice and Development Party) rule. According to the Survey on Social

and Political Trends in Turkey conducted by Kadir Has University's Center for Turkish Studies, announced on January 31, 2018, 37 percent of the respondents stated they did not want to have a Jewish neighbor. See Eli Haligua, "Toplumun %31,7'si Musevi komşu istemiyor" [31.7 percent of the society do not want a Jewish neighbor], *Avlaremoz*, February 2, 2018. According to the Istanbul-based Hrant Dink Foundation's Media Watch on Hate Speech Report (January–April 2018), after Armenians, Jews are the most frequently targeted ethnic group in Turkish media. See Hrant Dink Foundation, "Medyada Nefret Söylemi İzleme Raporu, Ocak-Nisan 2018" [The Hate Speech Monitoring Report in the Media, January–April 2018] (Şişli/İstanbul: ASULIS, 2018). Rising anti-Semitism in Turkey is a dominant factor, if not the number one, for migration to Israel as well as to other countries.

3. More details will be provided later in the chapter on the issue of immigration to Israel.

4. This information was obtained from an interview with one of the leaders of the Jewish community in Turkey in June 2018. Here I would like to point out that this "data" is an estimated number. It is observed that the Rabbinate has developed a set of practical rules for enrolling children born of mixed marriages (especially if the father is Jewish and the mother is Muslim) to the community, and old rigid rules have started to relax compared to the past. But what is important here is whether the children of what we can call the 4th generation—that is, the children from mixed marriages—will be considered as within or outside the community. It is very difficult to predict that from today even if we consider the declining population of the community. As will be discussed later in the chapter, in the last three to four years, upper-middle-class families have been encouraging their children to study abroad because of Turkey's political and social crisis and the inadequacy of the education system. There is a question of whether any of those children who study abroad (especially in the United States, Britain, and Canada) will return to Turkey. In addition, it was observed that some emigrants to Israel, the United States, Canada, the UK (London), Spain, and Portugal have returned to Turkey after a certain period of time for a variety of reasons. Therefore, it is becoming increasingly difficult to estimate what the population of the Jewish community of Turkey will be in the coming years. This study provides a current profile of the social structure of the community. I would like to thank Karel Valansi for her valuable contributions on this point.

5. Over the past forty years, Jewish studies has blossomed into a vibrant and sophisticated academic field. According to the Association for Jewish Studies (AJS) there are more than 250 endowed professorships in Jewish Studies at eighty-five colleges and universities in North America. In 2012, Israel Studies was being thought in twelve centers and institutes, eleven in the United States and one in Canada; in nine programs, seven of which are in the Unites States; and two MA programs in the United Kingdom. See Dean Phillip Bell (ed.), *The Bloomsbery Companion to Jewish Studies* (London, New York: Bloomsbury, 2015), 23.

6. In this study, the term "non-Muslim minorities" refers to the *Rum* Orthodox, Jewish, and Armenian communities in Turkey. The author acknowledges the interchangeable use of *Rum*, Greek, Hellen, Byzantine, and Grec. *Rum* Orthodox is used here in differentiation with the Greek Orthodox (denoting those who belong to Greek nationality) to refer to those who stayed in the Ottoman Empire after 1821 and then automatically became, first, Ottoman subjects and then citizens of the Turkish Republic in 1923.

7. See Leyla Neyzi, *"Ben Kimim?" Türkiye'de Sözlü Tarih, Kimlik ve Öznellik* ["Who Am I?" Oral History, Identity and Subjectivity in Turkey], 5th ed. (İstanbul: İletişim Yayınları, 2013); "Strong as Steel Fragile As a Rose: A Turkish Jewish Witness to the Twentieth Century," *Jewish Social Studies* 12, no.1 (2005): 167–89; *İstanbul'da Hatırlamak ve Unutmak: birey, bellek ve aidiyet* [Remembering and Forgetting in Istanbul: Individual, Memory and Belonging] (İstanbul: Tarih Vakfı Yurt Yayınları, 1999).

8. For current studies on Jews of Turkey published by Libra Press, see N. Rıfat Bali, *1934 Trakya Olayları* [1934 Thrace Events] (İstanbul: Libra Kitap, 2012); N. Rıfat Bali (ed.), *"Aliya" Türk Yahudilerinin İsrail'e Göç Hikayeleri* ["Aliya": The Stories of Turkish Jews Migration to Israel] (İstanbul: Libra Kitap, 2018); N. Rıfat Bali, *Antisemitism and Conspiracy Theories in Turkey.* (İstanbul: Libra Kitap, 2013); N. Rıfat Bali (ed.), *"Genciz, Türk'üz, Yahudiyiz, Yerli Yabancı Değiliz"-Türk Yahudi Gençleri Anlatıyor* ["We Are Young, Turkish, Jewish, We Are Not Foreigners"- Young Turkish Jews Are Telling] (İstanbul: Libra Kitap, 2017); N. Rıfat Bali, *İsrail Başkonsolosu Ephraim Elrom'un İnfazı- "Çok Cesur Bir Adamdı, Sonuna*

Kadar Direndi" [The Execution of Ephraim Elrom, the Consulate of Israel- "He was a very brave man, he resisted until the end"] (İstanbul: Libra Kitap, 2016); N. Rıfat Bali, *Safehaven: İkinci Dünya Savaşı Sonrasında Türkiye'deki Nazi Varlıkları Meselesi)* [Safehaven: The Issue of Nazi Assets after the Second World War] (İstanbul: Libra Kitap, 2018); N. Rıfat Bali, *The Silent Minority in Turkey: Turkish Jews* (İstanbul: Libra Kitap, 2013); N. Rıfat Bali (ed.), *This Is My New Homeland, Life Stories of Turkish Jewish Immigrants* (İstanbul: Libra Kitap, 2018); N. Rıfat Bali, *Türkiye'de Holokost Tüketimi (1989–2017)* [Holocaust Consumption in Turkey (1989–2017)] (İstanbul: Libra Kitap, 2017); Özgür Kaymak, *İstanbul'da Az(ınlık) Olmak: Gündelik Hayatta Rumlar, Yahudiler, Ermeniler* [Being a Minority in Istanbul: Rums, Jews and Armenians in the Daily Life] (İstanbul: Libra Kitap, 2017); C. Mehmet Kösemen, *A Karakaş Speaks: Interviews with a Member of Turkey's Crypto-Judaic "Dönme" Community* (İstanbul: Libra Kitap, 2018); Belçim Taşçıoğlu, *Nation and State Building in Israel (1948–1967) and Turkey (1923–1946): A Comparative Assessment* (İstanbul: Libra Kitap, 2018). Outside academic literature, in recent years, we have been witnessing a dramatic increase in developments in the cultural sphere. Founded in 1993, Aras Publishing publishes both Turkish and Armenian works in the literature, history, and cultural fields of Armenian writers. ISTOS, founded in 2012, is the youngest publishing house to offer Greek and Turkish publications on the history, culture, and life of the *Rums* of Istanbul and the memory of this geography.

9. For a few examples see Roni Marguiles, *Ailem ve Diğer Yahudiler* [My Family and the Other Jews] (İstanbul: Everest Yayınları, 2018); Aaron Kohen, *Ortaköy ve Museviler, Zaman Tünelinden Bir Bakış* [Ortaköy and Jews, A View from the Time Tunnel] (İstanbul: Kapı Yayınları, 2011); Viktor Albukrek, *Bir Zamanlar Büyükada 1931–1961 anıları* [Once upon a Time Büyükada Memories of 1931–1961], 2nd ed. (İstanbul: Adalı Yayınları, 2013); Rita Ender, *Aile Yadigarları* [Family Trophies] (İstanbul: İletişim Yayınları, 2018); Rita Ender, *İsmiyle Yaşamak* [Living with a Name], 2nd ed. (İstanbul: İletişim Yayınları, 2016); Raşel Meseri and Aylin Kuryel, *Türkiye'de Yahudi Olmak, Bir Deneyim Sözlüğü* [Being a Jew in Turkey, A Dictionary of Experience], 2nd ed. (İstanbul: İletişim Yayınları, 2017); Yahya Koçoğlu, *Azınlık Gençleri Anlatıyor* [Young Minorities are Telling], 3rd ed. (İstanbul: Metis Yayınları, 2004); Eli Şaul, *Balat'tan Bat-Yam'a* [From Balat to Bat-Yam], 2nd ed. (İstanbul: İletişim Yayınları, 2010).

10. The Council of Higher Education (YÖK) was established with Law No. 2547 dated November 6, 1981. This law has commenced a restructuring process of academic, institutional, and administrative aspects in higher education. With this law, all higher education institutions in Turkey have gathered under the roof of YÖK; academies, universities, educational institutions have been transformed into the faculties of education, and conservatories and vocational higher schools (VHS) have been affiliated to universities. See YÖK, "Tez Tarama" [Scanning Theses], Accessed August 30, 2018. https://tez.yok.gov.tr/UlusalTezMerkezi/tarama.jsp.

11. Since the word "Yahudi" [Jew/Jewish] is generally used in a negative and alienating sense by the society at large in Turkey, the community members mostly use the word "Musevi" which has the same meaning. The word "Musevi" refers to the religion of Judaism and the person who believes in this religion; it refers to the followers of Moses. No definite information is available in the literature on how and when the word "Musevi" was built.

12. For one of the first PhD dissertations written in this field, see Şule Toktaş, "Citizenship, Minorities and Immigrants: A Comparison of Turkey's Jewish Minority and Turkish-Jewish Immigrants in Israel," PhD diss., Bilkent Üniversitesi Public Administration and Political Science, 2004, 69.

13. Theses written both in Turkish and English are included in this research. The data was obtained from the Council of Higher Education (YÖK) on August 30, 2018.

14. I mentioned above that since the beginning of 2000s, there has been studies in response to the official history thesis in Turkey. When the term "genocide" is used in Turkish academia, what is meant is the Armenian Deportation/Genocide of 1915. The terms "Armenian" and "genocide" were taboo concepts until the end of the 1990s. In 2015, since that year marked the one hundreth anniversary of 1915, many valuable studies, mostly from abroad, contributed to the field. Also, at universities in Turkey, international conferences and panels were organized for the first time by the NGOs. However, since the Holocaust was not experienced in these lands, it has not drawn much attention from academia and is a neglected subject in Turkey. See

Corry Guttstadt, *Türkiye, Yahudiler ve Holokost* [Turkey, Jews and Holocaust], 2nd ed., translated by Atilla Dirim (İstanbul: İletişim Yayınları, 2016). In addition, the scarcity of academics in the field of genocide studies in Turkey, the difficulty in reaching the very few archives, language barrier, and budget shortages are also factors that constitute the biggest obstacles for the lack of studies in the field of Holocaust studies.

15. For a few examples of monographs based on doctoral and master's theses conducted in this field, see Kaymak, *İstanbul'da Az(ınlık) Olmak*; Karel Valansi, *The Crescent Moon and The Magen David* (Lanham: Hamilton Books, 2018).

16. More details will be provided later in the chapter on the social class structure of the community.

17. The strength and nature of the connection with Israel is often used as an indicator of Jewish identity among Diaspora Jews. JPR collected data on Jewish identity—from eight countries including the UK—and it published its findings in April 2018. According to the report, support for Israel is a stronger feature of Jewish identity among European Jewry than American Jewry. See Simon Rocker, "Is There Any Such Thing as European Jewish Identity?" *The Jewish Chronicle*, May 11, 2018. According to a study published by the Cohen Center for Modern Jewish Studies, the increasing percentage of young Jewish adults who participate in Israel experience programs, in particular, Taglit-Birthright Israel, suggests a strong possibility that American Jewish ties to Israel may be stronger in the future. See Theodore Sasson, Benjamin Phillips, Charles Kadushin, and Leonard Saxe, *Still Connected: American Jewish Attitudes towards Israel* (Waltham MA: Brandeis University Cohen Center for Modern Jewish Studies, 2010): Travel to Israel is an important factor in attachment to Israel. The author did not reveal any data regarding the importance of visits to Israel within the scope of this study.

18. The 1934 Pogroms which occurred in the Thrace region, considered to be the first anti-Semitic incident in the Turkish Republic, stand as a primary and striking example. In June 1934, Jewish houses and workplaces were physically assaulted, the intense violence and ravishment resulted in the forced emigration from the territory. The cornerstone of the discriminatory practices against non-Muslims was the capital tax implemented in 1942 (Wealth Tax). Considering that the non-Muslims paid 87 percent of this special tax to cover the expenses of the Turkish government during the Second World War, it would not be wrong to argue that this tax fell heavily on non-Muslims. Depicting the non-Muslim citizens as "black marketeers," the media also served as a strong propaganda apparatus in this period. September 6–7 Pogroms in 1955 targeted notably the Istanbul *Rum* Orthodox Community as well as other non-Muslim communities. Trauma experienced by non-Muslims in the 1955 Pogroms have hardly vanished even today and prevented the hope of non-Muslims to be considered as equal citizens after the shift to the multiparty system. As a result of these Turkification policies, by 1955 the non-Muslims of Turkey dropped below 1 percent of the population at large—in other words, non-Muslims were actually removed from Turkish society.

19. Following the *Mavi Marmara* incident in 2010, 155 Turkish Jews migrated to Israel. Average numbers for migrations between 2011 and 2016 was around 100 people. Following the coup attempt on July 15, 2016, the number of migrants reached 248 people. According to Bali ("*Aliya*") the number of people who migrated to Israel in July 2017 is 378 people. According to the Jewish Agency Report 2016, 17,398 people made *Aliyah* from the Middle East and Turkey. See The Jewish Agency for Israel, "2016–2017 Performance Report" (New York: The Jewish Agency for Israel, 2018).

20. This subject has also frequently been mentioned in popular culture in recent years. See Mois Gabay, "Türk Yahudileri Gidiyor mu?" [Are Turkish Jews Leaving?], *Şalom*, December 10 2014.

21. On July 15, 2016, a group within the Turkish Armed Forces, who belong to the organization referred to as *Fetullahçı Terrör Örgütü* (FETÖ- Gülenist Terrorist Organization) led by Fethullah Gülen tried to carry out a coup d'état, attacking state buildings and killing over two hundred citizens.

22. The traumas in personal and the collective memory of families (1934 Thrace pogrom, 1942 Wealth Tax, 1955 Pogrom, synagogue bombings) are conveyed to subsequent generations through a variety of strategies. Although they did not experience these events, their bitter memories constitute a burden for young Jews. See Özgür Kaymak, "İstanbullu Yahudilerin

Kolektif Travmatik Bellekteki Ses(sizlik)leri" [Voices-Silence of Istanbul Jews in the Collective Traumatic Memory], *MSFAU Journal of Social Sciences* 2, no. 17 (2018): 148–63.

23. Karel Valansi, "Ira Forman: "Yükselen Antisemitizmden Endişeliyiz" [Ira Forman: We are Worried about Rising Anti-Semitism], *Şalom*, June 11 2014; Ivo Molinas, "Yahudi Karşıtlığı" ["Anti-Semitism"], *Şalom*, May 28, 2014.

24. On May 31, 2010, Israeli forces boarded the Turkish ship, the *Mavi Marmara*, which was part of a flotilla carrying supplies to Gaza. Nine people on the ship were killed in the ensuing violence. According to a 2010 survey conducted in the United States, 70 percent of respondents did not believe the incident had any effect on their attachment to Israel. Of those who believed that it did have an effect, two-thirds believed it made them feel more attached to Israel. See Sasson, *Still Connected*.

25. Özgür Kaymak, "Political Participation of Turkish Jews in Istanbul: A Comparison between Generations," *Turkish-Jewish Entanglements, Resilience, Migration and New Diasporas, International Symposium*, University of Graz, June 18–19, 2018.

BIBLIOGRAPHY

Aktar, Ayhan. *Varlık Vergisi ve Türkleştirme Politikaları* [Wealth Tax and Turkification Policies]. 11th ed. İstanbul: İletişim Yayınları, 2012.

Albukrek, Viktor. *Bir Zamanlar Büyükada 1931–1961 anıları* [Once upon a time Büyükada Memories of 1931–1961]. 2nd ed. İstanbul: Adalı Yayınları, 2013.

Bali, N. Rıfat. *1934 Trakya Olayları* [1934 Thrace Events]. İstanbul: Libra Kitap, 2012.

———. (ed.). *"Aliya" Türk Yahudilerinin İsrail'e Göç Hikayeleri* ["Aliya": The Stories of Turkish Jews Migration to Israel]. İstanbul: Libra Kitap, 2018.

———. *Antisemitism and Conspiracy Theories in Turkey*. İstanbul: Libra Kitap, 2013.

———. *Cumhuriyet Yıllarında Türkiye Yahudileri: Bir Türkleştirme Serüveni (1923–1945)* [Turkish Jews during the Republican Period: The Adventure of Turkification (1923–1945)]. 7th ed. İstanbul: İletişim Yayınları, 2005.

———. *Devlet'in Yahudileri ve "Öteki" Yahudi* [The Jews of the "State" and the "Other" Jew]. İstanbul: İletişim Yayınları, 2004.

———. (ed.). *"Genciz, Türk'üz, Yahudiyiz, Yerli Yabancı Değiliz"—Türk Yahudi Gençleri Anlatıyor* ["We Are Young, Turkish, Jewish, We Are Not Foreigners"—Young Turkish Jews Are Telling]. İstanbul: Libra Kitap, 2017.

———. *İsrail Başkonsolosu Ephraim Elrom'un İnfazı—"Çok Cesur Bir Adamdı, Sonuna Kadar Direndi"* [The Execution of Ephraim Elrom, the Consulate of Israel—"He was a very brave man, he resisted until the end"]. İstanbul: Libra Kitap, 2016.

———. *Safehaven: İkinci Dünya Savaşı Sonrasında Türkiye'deki Nazi Varlıkları Meselesi)* [Safehaven: The Issue of Nazi Assets after the Second World War]. İstanbul: Libra Kitap, 2018.

———. *A Scapegoat for All Seasons: The Donmes or Crypto-Jews of Turkey*. İstanbul: Isis Press, 2008.

———. *The Silent Minority in Turkey: Turkish Jews*. İstanbul: Libra Kitap, 2013.

———. (ed.). *This Is My New Homeland, Life Stories of Turkish Jewish Immigrants*. İstanbul: Libra Kitap, 2018.

———. *Türkiye'de Holokost Tüketimi (1989–2017)* [Holocaust Consumption in Turkey (1989–2017)]. İstanbul: Libra Kitap, 2017.

———. *Türkiye'de Yayınlanmış Yahudilikle İlgili Kitap, Tez ve Makaleler Bibliyografisi (1923–2003)* [A Bibliography of Books, Theses and Articles Published in Turkey Concerning Judaism 1923-2003]. İstanbul: Turkuaz Yayıncılık, 2004.

Balta, Evren, and Altan-Olcay Özlem. "Class and Passports: Transnational Strategies of Distinction in Turkey." *Sage* 50 (2016): 1106–22.

Benbassa, Esther, and Aron Rodrigue. *Türkiye ve Balkan Yahudileri Tarihi* [The History of Turkish and Balkan Jews]. 3rd ed. Translated by Ayşe Atasoy. İstanbul: İletişim Yayınları, 2010.

Bell, Dean Phillip. (ed.). *The Bloomsbery Companion to Jewish Studies*. London, New York: Bloomsbury, 2015.
Ben-Moshe, and Zohar Segev. *Israel, the Diaspora and Jewish Identity*. Canada: Sussex Academic Press, 2010.
Dündar, Fuat. *Türkiye Nüfus Sayımlarında Azınlıklar* [Minorities in the Turkish Population Census]. 2nd ed. İstanbul: Çiviyazıları, 2010.
Ender, Rita. *Aile Yadigarları* [Family Trophies]. İstanbul: İletişim Yayınları, 2018.
———. *İsmiyle Yaşamak* [Living with a Name]. 2nd ed. İstanbul: İletişim Yayınları, 2016.
Gabay, Mois. "Türk Yahudileri Gidiyor mu?" [Are Turkish Jews Leaving?]. *Şalom*. December 10, 2014. http://www.salom.com.tr/haber-93320-turk_yahudileri__gidiyor_mu__.html
Guttstadt, Corry. *Türkiye, Yahudiler ve Holokost* [Turkey, Jews and Holocaust]. 2nd ed. Translated by Atilla Dirim. İstanbul: İletişim Yayınları, 2016.
Haligua, Eli. "Toplumun %31,7'si Musevi komşu istemiyor" [31.7 Percent of the Society Do Not Want a Jewish Neighbor]. *Avlaremoz*. February 2, 2018. http://www.avlaremoz.com/2018/02/02/toplumun-17si-musevi-komsu-istemiyor-2/
Hrant Dink Foundation. "Medyada Nefret Söylemi İzleme Raporu, Ocak-Nisan 2018" [The Hate Speech Monitoring Report in the Media, January–April 2018]. Şişli/İstanbul: ASULIS, 2018. https://hrantdink.org/attachments/article/1356/Medyada%20Nefret%20Söylemi%20İzleme%20Raporu%20Ocak-Nisan%202018.pdf
The Jewish Agency for Israel. "2016-2017 Performance Report." New York: The Jewish Agency for Israel, 2018. http://www.jewishagency.org/sites/default/files/Performance_Report_2016-17.pdf
Kaymak, Özgür. *İstanbul'da Az(ınlık) Olmak: Gündelik Hayatta Rumlar, Yahudiler, Ermeniler* [Being a Minority in Istanbul: Rums, Jews and Armenians in the Daily Life]. İstanbul: Libra Kitap, 2017.
———. "İstanbul'da Rum, Yahudi ve Ermeni Cemaatlerinin Sosyo-Mekansal İnşası" [The Socio-Spatial Contruction of Rum, Jewish and Armenian Communities] PhD diss., İstanbul Üniversitesi Public Administration and Political Science Department, 2016.
———. "İstanbullu Yahudilerin Kolektif Travmatik Bellekteki Ses(sizlik)leri" [Voices-Silence of Istanbul Jews in the Collective Traumatic Memory]. *MSFAU Journal of Social Sciences* 2, no. 17 (2018): 148–63.
———. "Political Participation of Turkish Jews in Istanbul: A Comparison between Generations." *Turkish-Jewish Entanglements, Resilience, Migration and New Diasporas, International Symposium*. June 18–19, 2018. University of Graz.
Koçoğlu, Yahya. *Azınlık Gençleri Anlatıyor* [Young Minorities Are Telling]. 3rd ed. İstanbul: Metis Yayınları, 2004.
Kohen, Aaron. *Ortaköy ve Museviler, Zaman Tünelinden Bir Bakış* [Ortaköy and Jews, A View from the Time Tunnel]. İstanbul: Kapı Yayınları, 2011.
Kösemen, C. Mehmet. *A Karakaş Speaks: Interviews with a Member of Turkey's Crypto-Judaic "Dönme" Community*. İstanbul: Libra Kitap, 2018.
Levi, Avner. *Türkiye Cumhuriyeti'nde Yahudiler* [Jewish in the Republic of Turkey]. 3rd ed. İstanbul: İletişim Yayınları, 2010.
Marguiles, Roni. *Ailem ve Diğer Yahudiler* [My Family and the Other Jews]. İstanbul: Everest Yayınları, 2018.
Meseri, Raşel, and Aylin Kuryel. *Türkiye'de Yahudi Olmak, Bir Deneyim Sözlüğü* [Being a Jew in Turkey, A Dictionary of Experience]. 2nd ed. İstanbul: İletişim Yayınları, 2017.
Molinas, Ivo. "Yahudi Karşıtlığı" ["Anti-Semitism"]. *Şalom*. May 28, 2014. http://www.salom.com.tr/haber-91224-yahudi_karsitligi_.html
Neyzi, Leyla. *"Ben Kimim?" Türkiye'de Sözlü Tarih, Kimlik ve Öznellik* ["Who Am I?" Oral History, Identity and Subjectivity in Turkey]. 5th ed. İstanbul: İletişim Yayınları, 2013.
———. *İstanbul'da Hatırlamak ve Unutmak: birey, bellek ve aidiyet* [Remembering and Forgetting in Istanbul: Individual, Memory and Belonging]. İstanbul: Tarih Vakfı Yurt Yayınları, 1999.
———. "Strong as Steel Fragile as a Rose: A Turkish Jewish Witness to the Twentieth Century." *Jewish Social Studies* 12, no.1 (2005): 167–89.

Rocker, Simon. "Is There Any Such Thing as European Jewish Identity?" *The Jewish Chronicle*. May 11, 2018. https://www.thejc.com/judaism/features/is-there-any-such-thing-as-european-jewish-identity-1.464027.

Sasson, Theodore, Benjamin Phillips, Charles Kadushin, and Leonard Saxe. *Still Connected: American Jewish Attitudes towards Israel*. Waltham MA: Brandeis University Cohen Center for Modern Jewish Studies, 2010.

Şaul, Eli. *Balat'tan Bat-Yam'a* [From Balat to Bat-Yam]. 2nd ed. İstanbul: İletişim Yayınları, 2010.

Taşçıoğlu, Belçim. *Nation and State Building in Israel (1948–1967) and Turkey (1923–1946): A Comparative Assessment*. İstanbul: Libra Kitap, 2018.

Toktaş, Şule. "Citizenship, Minorities and Immigrants: A Comparison of Turkey's Jewish Minority and Turkish-Jewish Immigrants in Israel." PhD diss., Bilkent Üniversitesi Public Administration and Political Science, 2004.

"Türk Yahudiler Gidiyor mu?" [Are Turkish Jews Leaving?]. *Milliyet*. June 2, 2018. http://www.milliyet.com.tr/turk-yahudiler-gidiyor-mu--gundem-2604507/

Valansi, Karel. *The Crescent Moon and The Magen David*. Lanham: Hamilton Books, 2018.

Valansi, Karel. "Ira Forman: "Yükselen Antisemitizmden Endişeliyiz" [Ira Forman: We Are Worried about Rising Anti-Semitism]. *Şalom*. June 11 2014. http://www.salom.com.tr/arsiv/haber-91384-ira_forman__yukselen_antisemitizmden_endiseliyiz_.html

YÖK. "Tez Tarama." [Scanning Theses]. Accessed August 30, 2018. https://tez.yok.gov.tr/UlusalTezMerkezi/tarama.jsp

Chapter Seven

Israel Studies, the Jewish Challenge

Yakov M. Rabkin and Yaacov Yadgar

Editor's Note: The following chapter is the edited transcription of a lunch discussion panel between Professors Yaacov Yadgar, from the University of Oxford, and Yakov M. Rabkin, from the Université of Montréal. The focus of the discussion addressed many other relevant aspects regarding the conference topic "Intersections between Jewish Studies and Israel Studies in the 21st Century" as well. Please note: The discussion took place on May 23, 2018, which means the law "Israel as the nation-state of the Jewish people" from July 18, 2018, was not yet a reality.

THE LUNCH DISCUSSION

YAACOV YADGAR. Having been invited to reflect on the intersection on Jewish Studies and Israel Studies, we thought that a dialogue between the two of us would serve the purpose better than two separate chapters. We have both dealt extensively with matters pertaining to the various intersections between Zionist ideology, Israeli nation-statehood, and Jewish traditions which preceded them and continue to live alongside them. Our aim in this dialogue was thus to build on this background to highlight some of the challenges that define the encounter between Israel Studies and Jewish Studies, hoping that this will be read not as a definitive conclusion but as an invitation to expand and continue the conversation. We begin by raising some of the issues that touch directly upon the main concerns of the symposium.

The intersection between Jewish studies and Israel studies can be approached from various angles: disciplinary, historical, essentialist, and so forth. Being a student of political sociology interested in contemporary Israel, I would suggest that one of the angles from which to approach this issue is to look at the influence on the State of Israel and Zionist ideology on our understanding (or, I would suggest: misunderstanding) of Judaism or Jewishness. This would necessarily also apply to how we understand the very notion of a "Jewish State."

So, let me put my argument forward in very general terms: One of Israel's greatest successes as a polity has been its ability to position itself in the center of Jewish life throughout the world. It is quite hard to find nowadays Jews inside or outside of Israel who do not define their Jewishness vis-à-vis a strong presence of the State, one way or another. This is true not only in the case of Jews who have positive views of Zionism and the State of Israel. It seems to me that among anti-Zionist Jews, too, the centrality of the State of Israel in defining their Jewishness (in this case, by way negative reflection) is apparent.

Yet, at the same time, Israel has never managed to fully articulate—if it ever genuinely tried to do so—the very meaning of *Jewish* politics. It left open the question of Jewish identity, or the meaning of Jewishness, read in the framework of the Jewish state.

To put it differently: What does it mean for Israel to be a Jewish State? I would argue that tackling this issue could be a fruitful gateway to careful consideration of the intersection of Jewish studies and Israel studies. Simply put, the State of Israel influences what we understand to be Jewish, specifically the notions of a Jewish State and of Jewish politics. We sometimes feel very comfortable talking about the "status quo" on matters of "religion" in Israel, on religion and politics, and so forth, without realizing that there is a depth of questions—of a historical, political, and conceptual nature—that are left unanswered. Tackling these questions, I would argue, is a necessary first step that we often seem to ignore, carrying with us a severe gap as we move forward.

YAKOV RABKIN. In order to fill such a gap, the two fields may intersect. The impact of the establishment of the Zionist state in Palestine had an immediate and radical impact on Jewish communities in the Arab countries. As my distinguished colleague and namesake said just a few minutes ago, the State of Israel has imposed its centrality on Jewish communities and has affected the evolution of Jewish identities around the world.

Teaching the centrality of Israel, a policy that has been applied in most non-ultra-Orthodox Jewish schools for decades, has borne fruit. As a result, many Jews would find it difficult to separate Zionism from Jewish identity as it has been taught to them. Their identity is often centered on political support for the State of Israel, and they see advocacy for Israel—a special course in the curriculum of many private Jewish schools—as a key part of being Jewish. In most non-Haredi synagogues, support for Israel has entered liturgy. The congregants' enthusiasm is palpable when they chant the blessing for the State of Israel and its armed forces, enthusiasm that seems often missing in the traditionally central parts of the communal service such as the silent *amida* prayer. Many Jews have simply not noticed that their traditional religious and ethnic identity has morphed into a new political one. They support Israel financially, attend concerts by Israeli singers, and some go as far as to encourage their children to serve in the Israeli army. The existence of a state with a flag, a powerful army, and a prosperous economy confers pride and a sense of involvement in something bigger than private life. This evolution reflects both Israel's policies and the nature of Jewish identities, and it would therefore offer a case of intersection of Jewish and Israel Studies.

YADGAR. I would reply by stating the obvious, which you alluded to but still needs to be clearly articulated, since it complicates things. This has to do with the necessity to clearly distinguish between Israel Studies and Jewish Studies: If we only learn Israel through the Jewish perspective, we would be doing great injustices to the multivocality of the society in Israel, as well as to the multiethnicity of this society. We would be ignoring the fact that Israel has a large minority of non-Jews who should necessarily be part of our political, intellectual, and academic interest in Israel.

This, again, is obvious. It may be that among certain audiences it does not require mentioning at all. However, I think that when we study the way Israel understands—or, again misunderstands and misinterprets—the notion of its own Jewishness, we can see that the conflation of Israeliness and Jewishness, has exactly to do with the exclusion of non-Jews from the framework of Israeli statehood. I would argue that this exclusion is at the heart of this Israeli construction of Jewishness.

Let me explain: Among other things (and this is most convincingly articulated in Rabkin's book, *What Is Modern Israel*), Zionism transforms Judaism—or rather Jews—from a community of people who observe or aim to observe or to live their life according to a certain ethical doctrine, law, or worldview, into an "ethno-national" group, defined "objectively" by its supposed common biological origin. It transforms the definition of Jewish identity from being understood by what Jews do to being defined by what Jews "are." This point of view is external to Judaism. It is an adaptation or adoption of an East-European notion of "organic" (as opposed to civic) nationalism, by which one's national identity is considered a "biological" matter of one's "blood."

Zionist ideologues kept on asking themselves "what makes us Jewish?"—but they never came to a collectively agreed answer. Instead, they preferred to see their Jewishness as something that is intrinsic to their "essence." (Hence, it cannot be clearly defined.) Ahad Ha'am would famously address this by calling: "Ask the sun why it shines!" The essentialist answer he alludes to—the sun shines because it is the sun; a Jew is a Jew because his essence if "Jewish"—manifest a mythological, nonrational, and rather apolitical understanding. Similarly, H. Y. Brenner poses the question "How can we become not us?"; like his fellow Socialist-Zionist ideologues, he, too, sees his main challenge as the release from Judaism. He seeks to cease being Jewish (in the negative, "exilic" notion of this), while reclaiming Jewish nationhood, and moreover, envisaging confrontation with the natives of Palestine in the name of this nationhood. His ultimate answer? "Workers' colonies!" That is, he is saying, "Don't ask me this question regarding the meaning of my, our Jewishness. It is too difficult to answer. Let us focus instead on establishing the socialist communes," the creation of which is motivated exactly by our claim to Jewishness. Translated into the politics of the State, this was ultimately understood to imply a very crude nationalistic arithmetic of a majority of "Jews" against a minority of non-Jewish Palestinian Arabs. Nevertheless, the State must have a measure by which to identify (or define) this majority as Jewish. Tellingly, it has none.

The State does not have a definition of its own, and instead it gives the rabbis the role of gatekeepers. The rabbis, for their part, perform their rabbinical understanding of Jewish Law. We may say that they think about their decisions on matters of "Who is a Jew?" primarily in theological or "religious" terms, and only secondly, if ever, in "political" terms. But they are clearly expected to perform the role of national gatekeepers, and this results in a problematic partial adoption of rabbinic reasoning into a general non-rabbinic notion of what Jewishness is. This leads to a focus on the Jewish "mother" or "blood" as the most important element in one's Jewishness. As far as I know, Jewish traditions have not been satisfied with a Jewish ancestry alone to make one meaningfully Jewish. Instead, these traditions focused on certain ways of life as the "essence" of Jewishness.

RABKIN. Returning to the relationship between the two academic fields, one must be aware of the defiantly antireligious tenor of the Zionist founding fathers. Our colleague Amnon Raz-Krakozkin of Ben-Gurion University reflected, with both precision and concision, the paradox of the position held by the founders of Zionism: "God does not exist, and he has promised us this land." As my colleague already mentioned, Jewishness has traditionally been defined in the framework of a relationship with God. The words spoken by the celebrated Arab philosopher and Rabbi Saadia Gaon (882–942) more than one thousand years ago—"Our nation exists only within the Torah"—have not only a normative, but also an empirical meaning. According to the prominent Israeli intellectual Yeshayahu Leibowitz (1903–1994), "they testified to a historical reality whose power could be felt up until the nineteenth century. It was then that the fracture, which has not ceased to widen with time, first occurred: the fissure between Jewishness and Judaism. The majority of Jews—while sincerely conscious of their Jewishness—not only does not accept Judaism, but abhors it." While many may find illogical the mainstream Israeli definition of Jewishness, the point here is not to debate it but, rather, focus on examining it, however inconsistent it may be. This is why it is so important that the scholarly approach remain independent of the self-definition of the object.

Coming from the History of Science, I'm particularly sensitive to this issue. For example, a certain method of analysis and separation, nowadays commonly known as chromotography, was used in chemistry, physics, and biology. But within each discipline it used to be called differently. It is only by breaking out of the disciplinary framework imposed by the object of study that we realize that its self-definition blocks our vision. This is what I meant when I said that references to Polish nationalism may be more useful for understanding Zionism than quotes from Judaic sources. This detachment is just as important in examining relations between Jewish and Israel Studies lest we become distracted by otherwise laudable attempts to change the definition of Jewishness.

YADGAR. I'm not talking about affecting change. I believe study should focus on the construction of the very meaning of Jewishness. The construction of the meaning of Israel being a Jewish state is not an ideological exercise. I am being attentive to the consequences of this identification. As critics have pointed out, if you consider what Israel does along the demographic considerations of a Jewish majority versus a non-Jewish (Palestinian-Arab) minority, its self-identification as Jewish may very well be seen as only a euphemism for a racial way of thinking along national lines. You come to understand that "a Jewish state" might very well mean "simply" a non-Arab state.

In this regard, I think, again, that the interface—or the problematic interactions—between the study of Israel and the study of the Jewish world is the way by which this Israeli construction along some seventy years of statehood encouraged the creation of a historically new, political, and nation-statist meaning of Jewishness.

To put it differently: part of the history that we are considering now is a history of the (successful) nationalization of Judaism. Moreover: it seems, currently, to be the most successful trend in the Jewish world: the nationalization of Jews or Jewishness or Judaism is not limited to the state that is identified the State of Jews, or the Nation-State of the Jewish People, as the new "Nation-State" bill would have it.[1]

Consider, for example, the heated debate surrounding this proposed Basic Law that would "anchor" Israeli's identity as the nation-state of the Jewish People. The latter would constitutionalize Israel's identity as Jewish state. But the very meaning of this remains rather vague in the bill itself—

beyond, that is, the preference of Jews over non-Jews, as collectives, if not as individuals.

This cannot possibly be limited to Israel Studies: it is an issue pertaining to the Jewish world as a whole. Israeli Jewishness projects itself on the wider Jewish world.

RABKIN. I would agree with that, but I would add that it is just as important to understand how the evolution of Jewish identities in Eastern and Central Europe engendered Zionism and the entire national project. In other words, what happened in the shtetls of the Pale of Settlement starting from the mid-nineteenth century is crucial for understanding today's Israel.

The Political Zionism of Vienna and Basel needed Jews who would actually settle in Palestine and embody the new ideology on the ground. Herzl and his friends were like generals without an army. The army, so to speak, came mostly from the shtetls of the Russian Empire. Just like urbanized Jews in the rest of the world, Jews of Russia's urban centers were indifferent or even hostile to the Zionist idea. Vladimir Jabotinsky may be the only Zionist leader to be born in a major Russian city (Odessa), even then his influence in the Zionist settlements of Palestine was modest at best.

The emergence of the secular Jew in the Russian empire is the cornerstone of the Zionist project. It didn't emerge in Iran, nor in America. Moreover, Russian Jews spread the Zionist idea to other Jewish communities. For example, even in Morocco the first Zionist cell was established by Russian Jews. The impact of this revolutionary reformulation of Jewishness by Russian Jews remains fundamental in today's Israel. This is illustrated by the unprecedented ease of the political integration of Soviet immigrants and the fact that all of Israel's prime ministers were either born in the Russian Empire or their parents were born there.

As to the centrality of Israel that has been reshaping many Jewish identities, it is an instance of Zionist cultural policy and could be approached from both angles, that of Jewish Studies and Israel Studies. But not right away. One must recall that scholarship cannot react to changing situations with the speed of the media, and that it manifests a good degree of inertia. Thus, the emergence of secular Jewish identity in Eastern and Central Europe also took a while to be understood in scholarly, rather than programmatic terms. And in many parts of the world, such as Morocco where I have been invited to lecture, the concept of "secular Jew" sounds as nonsensical as that of "secular Muslim" because both terms are Christian and therefore largely alien to indigenous Moroccans, whether Jews or Muslims.

YADGAR. You raise very important questions, and I guess if I answer all of them it will take over the whole discussion. I'll try to be maybe too telegrammic. First, regarding this latest exchange whether they are secular or not secular, the problem starts with our use of a Christian-embodied, historically situated concept of religion, secularity in state politics, whatever.

It is wrong to think they apply to all the history of all humanity. There are no secular Jews because secular is, or speculum of the church, has never been translated to the Jewish world. There are now Jews that define themselves as secular, it would be simply stupid of my side to say there are no secular Jews because they identify themselves as secular, and it is important to them. But to think that we have this category of secularism which we see as supposedly wholly embodied in, I don't know let's say in Ireland—they don't go to church anymore—can somehow translated haphazardly in Tel Aviv is wrong, as it's simply wrong to say that there are secular Muslims or to assume that secularism would easily translate.

This may also be a good place to talk about the "nationalization of religion," that is: political uses of what we would usually call "the religious" for the promotion of the state and its ideology. Both apologists and detractors of this phenomenon agree that the split between "religious" and "secular" as applied to Jewish experience was a novelty introduced around the mid-nineteenth century. Thus, it preceded the Zionist project—which adopted it and instrumentalized the concept of the secular Jew. The apologetical way would simply say that that's how the world works now; that nowadays people in the world identify as secular or religious, that religion is that something that belongs to the church, it is individual and nonpolitical, while politics is ideally purely secular. Zionism emerges within the Christian world, both conceptually and geographically, and it redefines Jewish politics as secular. For the apologists, the problem with non-European Jews is that they still haven't caught up with this development. For the detractors, these Christian concepts pervert Jewishness and Judaism and constitute an imposition of an external conceptual ideological framework that leads to destructive results.

Nationalization of Judaism is an important object of scholarly inquiry for Jewish Studies. In contradistinction to Israel Studies, Jewish Studies can focus on non-Zionist Jewish political thought and its relationship with nationalism and statism.

RABKIN. I would just add that in light of what we both said about the Christianization of our understanding of the Jews—scholars need not use categories such as "secular" even when the people they study define themselves as secular. Scholars are expected to take a step back and define the reality they observe in ways that could be applicable to—and understandable by—both European and non-European Jews. In this sense, it is potentially fruitful that Jewish studies develop outside the Western world, for example, in China, India, Japan, and Korea. Non-Western scholars may actually develop different concepts and approaches that will enrich the work of all of us.

YADGAR. Indeed, it is important to problematize the very conceptual framework, which is what we are both trying to do. We see that the State of Israel is defined primarily as a state of Jews, and only secondarily as a Jewish state. And we see this as a central distinction that brings to life the state's problem of defining Jewishness.

The Rabbis haven't dealt much with this politicized understanding of Jewishness because it was never a central matter of concern for them. The problem is a problem only in the framework of nationalism and the nationalization of Jewish history. The nation-state defines itself as the state of the Jews and falls into the problems of the arithmetic of Jews versus non-Jews. Israel is probably the only country in the world which makes it its own business to define one's Jewishness.

We can, quite easily, think together about the many diverse ways in which a state or political body would be meaningfully defined as Jewish via a constitution that manifests Jewish ideas. There is an endless multiplicity of meanings of Jewishness and many constituting frameworks may manifest these, while being at the same time completely indifferent to the racial make-up of its population: as long as the constitution remains in place and respected, we would identify the political body constituted by it as Jewish, without defining individuals as Jewish or not.

RABKIN. To sum up, Israel Studies and Jewish Studies are structurally different. Jewish Studies is a conglomerate of diverse fields and approaches, which does not possess intellectual coherence. For example, it may include biblical exegesis, the philosophy of Hannah Arendt, and the history of Yiddish theater. One need not know the other two to deal with any one of the three. To study Yiddish theater, one must understand the history of Russian theater. Similarly, to explore the thought of Hannah Arendt one must be familiar with German philosophy. Biblical exegesis would be of little use in either of these fields. Jewish Studies can be characterized by a significantly higher degree of intellectual dispersion than Israel Studies. Intellectual links between the two may be real and productive, for example, in the study of the evolution of Israel's varieties of Judaism. But in order to study Israel's army it is obviously more important to be familiar with British, German, and American military doctrines than to delve into the biblical accounts of King David's campaigns.

Unlike social history, for example, the field of Jewish Studies exists largely thanks to external circumstances rather than as an outgrowth of an intellectual endeavour. Jewish Studies is an eclectic area that emerged largely after the Second World War under the impetus of private sponsors and foundations who wanted something Jewish to be taught and researched at the university of their choice. Precursors of Jewish Studies can be found in the nineteenth century in the *Wissenschaft des Judentums* in Germany, the *Soci-*

été d'études juives in France, and the *Jewish Quarterly Review* in England. In the 1920s, a group of Italian Jewish scholars initiated the publication of *La Rassegna mensile di Israel*. These precursors were intellectually consistent in that their main focus was the religion of Judaism. Concerned about their integration in the ambient society, most of these scholars conceptualized Judaism as a religion and Jews as a confession. Nowadays, their scholarly interests would be termed Judaic Studies.

Israel Studies is by definition a newer field as it focuses on a more recent reality, the Zionist movement and the state it engendered in 1948. Moreover, it has a degree of disciplinary consistency because it deals with various aspects (e.g., anthropological, political, or sociological) of the same circumscribed object. But in this case too, external circumstances have played an important role as Zionist donors and pro-Israel foundations have stimulated the development of centers of Israel Studies around the world. This is quite common in Area Studies in general, even though it is usually state institutions that support studies of the respective country abroad, rather than their fans abroad.

While there exist attempts to show that the Zionist movement stems from within the Jewish continuity, familiarity with ethnic nationalism in Europe in the nineteenth century is at least as important for our understanding of Zionism as delving into medieval Jewish history. Knowledge of the origins of such modern states as Greece, Poland, or Rumania sheds crucially important light on the ideological roots of the State of Israel. It is also important to understand various protestant movements, which had actively promoted "the ingathering of the Hebrews" by human initiative well before the emergence of the Zionist movement.

NOTE

1. At the time of the symposium, the bill has yet to pass the legislative process. It has cleared all hurdles as of July 2018.

Part III

The Place of Israel Studies Contested?

Chapter Eight

Israel Studies, Intersectonality, and the Changing American College Scene

Aharon Klieman

Not since the height of the anti-Vietnam War protests in the 1970s has the American college campus served so readily as a mirror for a worrisome national drift toward polarization, as well as being itself the catalytic agent for student activism and political radicalization. As of academic year 2018–2019, leading educational centers from Columbia University on the east coast to the University of Michigan in the Midwest and Berkeley on the west coast find themselves resembling a veritable zone of conflict and confrontation rather than the gated intellectual communities of reflection and study they were and still are meant to be. It is particularly distressing to find the State of Israel and, by extension, Israel Studies at the center of controversy and mounting student strife at these and a number of other accredited institutions of learning.

The impact of this escalating battle over the Jewish state's legitimacy—as well as the academic standing of Israel-related programs in the humanities and in the social sciences—is almost uniformly negative. In the first instance, supporters of both find themselves under relentless attack, thrust on the defensive and divided over exactly how to respond. In the second instance, the very nature of college life is being adversely affected, with students, faculty, and university administrators alike deflected from their true calling and from what are believed to be the main goals of higher education—to facilitate contemplative, rational inquiry in the quest for knowledge and objectivity; to provide an open forum for civilized debate and a free exchange of ideas by assuring a respectful hearing for diverse viewpoints; and, at a minimum, to safeguard the civil rights of students to a safe learning environment.

When the Swarthmore "Students for Justice in Palestine" organization tables a petition accusing their college of being an "accessory to the occupation of Palestine" by allowing the sale of Israeli-brand Sabra *hummus* on campus—calling it "morally unacceptable"—it is clear that the environment on campus is no longer conducive to serious learning and scholarship.[1] With each passing semester, as outspokenness among undergraduate students displaces enlightenment in peer esteem, fewer and fewer North American colleges remain immune to what has now become a nationwide campaign aimed at defaming Israel. Nor are they assured of being able to continue providing the cloistered setting and "safe spaces" conducive to serious teaching, research, and debate.

OUT OF THE CLASSROOM

What the storm over Israel and Zionism does more than anything else is to remove these subjects from the classroom and library, where they belong, and onto the campus green, with all this implies for academic standards and behavioral codes. Ideally, a student ought to be encouraged to concentrate on formal studies: course syllabi and weekly homework reading assignments, in-class discussion and copious note-taking, sharpening writing skills in independent research papers and, not least, cramming for mid-term and final exams. Similarly, academia prizes logic and reasoning, critical thinking, thoughtful and civil discourse, marshaling factual evidence, and honing one's powers of artful persuasion.

How American universities are attempting and, for the most part, failing to grapple at present with the contentious subject of Israel threatens, however, to contravene even these essential accepted rules and norms for scholarly engagement. Once aggressive militants and agitators defy academic conventions and seize the quad, the entire nature of the debate changes; indeed, it ceases to be a debate but rather an adversarial clash—a clash marked by emotionalism, intolerance, and other such singularly unacademic and irrational traits as polemics and dogmatism accompanied by stridency and militancy, shaming, verbal violence, labeling, and intimidation of those holding opposing views. Hence, the descent into sloganeering and the irresponsible bandying about of such simplistic yet charged terms in reference to Israel as "occupation," "war crimes," "racism," "colonialist imperialism," "apartheid regime," "dispossession," "ethnic cleansing," or "genocide."

When taking sides becomes more important than taking notes, the net result is to poison student and student-faculty relationships while dragging the university away from purely scholarly pursuits into a latter-day battlefield. A battlefield pitting a hostile coalition of combative anti-Israel, pro-Palestinian advocates against pro-Israel supporters locked in a fierce ideological and political war of words. To such an extent that the American academy has now joined the United Nations and other international forums, the Gaza Strip, and Israel's borders with Syria and Lebanon as a yet another front line in the encompassing Arab-Israeli conflict. In such a supercharged atmosphere, all those concerned—from university presidents, deans and professorial colleagues, alumni and trustees to campus security police—are understandably hard-pressed to preserve a semblance of academic excellence; of business as usual.

What might have begun modestly two decades ago as isolated local college incidents provoked by the Students for Justice in Palestine (SJP) and the Boycott, Divestment and Sanctions (BDS) movements has long since assumed the dimensions of a nationwide college pandemic.[2] Indicative of the nature of the spreading warfare being waged on a global scale to isolate and delegitimize Israel—including under the guise of constitutionally protected and university-sanctioned extracurricular activity—are a number of relatively recent incidents in the course of the 2017–2018 school year:

- On February 22, 2018, campus police at the University of Virginia had to restore order at the Brody Jewish Center-Hillel when an open panel discussion including reservists from the Israel Defense Forces was shouted down by student and nonstudent protesters chanting anti-Israel slogans.[3]
- March found a Palestinian professor of Ethnic Studies/Race and Resistance Studies at San Francisco State University condemned by sixty faith-based and higher education organizations for "highly inflammatory" statements and "incitement to violence" by calling admission of pro-Israel students a "declaration of war" against Arabs and Muslims.[4]
- That same month, the University of Illinois at Champaign-Urbana experienced unrest that only quieted down after students by a nearly 2–1 margin voted against yet another fiercely contested BDS motion aimed at divestment from companies dealing with Israel.[5]
- The State of New York's otherwise peaceful Stony Brook campus witnessed an ugly scene in May when its SJP chapter accused the university's Muslim chaplain, Sanaa Nadim, of a "heinous level of betrayal to the Palestinian people" by urging tolerance, accompanied by shouts of "We want Zionism off this campus."[6]
- In April, members of the SJP held an anti-Israel counterdemonstration at Columbia University near a booth marking Holocaust Remembrance Day, chanting slogans like "From the [Jordan] river to the [Mediterranean] sea, Palestine will be free."[7]
- Also in April, at neighboring Barnard College a group called Columbia University Apartheid Divest successfully lobbied for a referendum in which nearly two-thirds of the student body cast ballots approving divestment from Caterpillar, Boeing, Hewlett Packard, and five other American

companies doing business with Israel. Some three thousand Barnard alumnae promptly responded with a petition against its implementation, condemning the action on both educational and procedural grounds.[8]
- On April 23, a similar scenario played itself out at George Washington University in Washington, D.C. There, the pendulum swung from defeat of a divestment resolution in 2017 to its adoption (18–6) by the Student Association, only to be dismissed by GW's president Thomas LeBlanc as unrepresentative of the university's views, "and the university will not implement such a proposal."[9]
- Following the opening of the 2018–2019 academic year, Students for Justice in Palestine, largest of the pro-Palestinian movements in North America, brought some five hundred people from across the country to its annual conference on November 16–18. Although held on the Westwood campus of UCLA, pledged to academic freedom, SJP sessions and workshops were closed to the public and to nonregistered students.
- Later that month, the anti-Israel offensive invaded the otherwise laidback campus of California's small Pitzer College when its faculty voted to suspend the College's existing study abroad program with the University of Haifa, putting teachers at loggerheads with students who responded in turn by accusing their professors of restricting student learning opportunities.[10]
- In still another landmark, on December 6 the Student Government Assembly at New York University overwhelmingly adopted a resolution—supported by over sixty student organizations and thirty faculty members—insisting the university divest from companies that "play an active role in funding and perpetuating Israel's illegal occupation and its violation of human rights, making NYU complicit in these crimes."[11]

Adding to this list of campus "hot spots" in 2018 are two top-ranked schools, the University of Michigan in Ann Arbor and the University of California at Los Angeles (UCLA):

- The former was thrust into the national spotlight by a series of news reports. First, in the aftermath of a BDS resolution late in 2017 in favor of divestment passed for the first time in the Central Student Government (after ten previous attempts since 2002), only to then be opposed by six of eight Board of Regents members committed to "shield[ing] the endowment from political pressures." Second, when an associate professor of American and digital studies was disciplined for refusing to honor his initial consent to write a letter of reference for a student upon learning of her wish to study at Tel-Aviv University; for using class time in two courses to discuss personal opinions on behalf of boycotting Israeli institutions; and for misrepresenting university policy as sanctioning the anti-

Israel boycott. Again, when a fellow faculty member in the School of Art and Design displayed a picture of Prime Minister Binyamin Netanyahu next to Adolph Hitler, with the words "Guilty of Genocide."[12]
- Reluctantly sharing the national spotlight, UCLA's ongoing low intensity campus war over the Middle East conflict flared anew in May during a meeting of Israel supporters disrupted by protesters shouting: "We don't want two states. We want 1948!," and escalated further in September at news that the Westwood campus would be the November venue for an upcoming eighth annual National Students for Justice in Palestine Conference.[13]

Whatever else, these are anything but theatrical or postadolescent, sophomoric skirmishes.

Nor does there appear to be any prospect of their abating or deconflicting, as hinted at by news reports upon the opening of a nascent 2018–2019 academic year at Tufts University and registration for a fall course titled "Colonizing Palestine."[14] With a syllabus built around "path-breaking writers, filmmakers and thinkers" in the anti-Israel movement, this type of one-sided course, and the BDS crusade against Israel as a whole, poses a battery of discomforting questions. For university authorities: Do such course offerings qualify as education or political indoctrination? For social scientists: What accounts for a distant Middle East dispute insinuating itself into the American academic community? For those of us who insist there is ample justification for analyzing Israel, warts and all—including when and where criticism is warranted—Why is the BDS-led censure of Israel so extreme and so intemperate?

Although there can be many explanations, most of them valid and in fact complementary, this chapter underscores the salience of "intersectionality" reinforced by insights from coalition theory as a useful starting point.

INTERSECTIONALITY AND TARGETING ISRAEL

The "phoniest academic doctrine I have encountered in 53 years" is how one outspoken social commentator has seen fit to dismiss the notion of "intersectionality."[15] Yet from the standpoint of present-day academic politics and Israel Studies, its influence dare not be underestimated. For it happens to serve as the justification for an unholy alliance of seemingly disparate groups, inspired by the precedent of South Africa and leagued together in their determination to defame Zionism, demonize Israel, and ultimately to eliminate it as a sovereign geopolitical entity.

For our purposes, intersectionality is the collective response of previously isolated, disadvantaged elements of society uniting against the existing elite power structure and its cynical strategy of divide and rule. When applied in the narrower context of Israel, intersectionality and the BDS movement have given rise to a broad coalition notable for its diversity, determination, and disregard for civility by violating accepted standards of decorum inside and outside the classroom. By definition, social groups and organizations with intersecting identities and *ad hoc* interests are the clearest manifestation of this phenomenon; nevertheless, again in specific reference to Israel, the constellation of participating actors is pyramidal, allowing for the role, on the one hand, of individuals—agents provocateurs and true believers of a sort—and, on the other hand, established academic centers.

With respect to the former, there are a number of instances where a solitary figure at a particular school or department has used his or her academic credentials to offer a pro-Palestinian presence on campus and to wage a dedicated anti-Israel campaign under the guise of the twin principles of free speech and academic freedom. Among such scholar-activist enablers, one can cite the late Edward Said at Columbia as a role model for a younger generation of far more outspoken crusaders such as Sunaina Maira (University of California, Davis), Rabab Abdulhadi (San Francisco State University), George P. Smith (University of Missouri), and Jasbir Puar (Rutgers). Not least, Marc Lamont Hill (Temple University) recanted his witless yet televised endorsement at a United Nations forum for "a free Palestine from the river to the sea" while glossing over his far more revealing boast at having assiduously abstained from drinking even a drop of Israeli bottled water throughout his study mission to the region.[16]

As for academic centers, certain college departments afford an institutional base of operations for propagating the Palestinian narrative by sponsoring courses, programs, and events downplaying Israel—better still, by inviting Israeli or American Jewish speakers known for presenting Israel and its policies in an unfavorable light. Most hospitable for this purpose appear to be degree-granting programs in ethnic and multicultural studies, gender studies, and Middle East studies. A case in point is the Colonialism Studies and Women's Gender and Sexuality Studies departments at Tufts University, whose Fall 2018 course listings included the above-mentioned "Colonizing Palestine" (CST 0094-04). Taught by an avowed anti-Israel activist, Thomas Abowd, the course description prepares enrollees in advance for treating Israel as a country "which illegally occupies Palestine"[17]—not parts of Palestine, mind you, but Palestine in its entirety.

Without gainsaying the role of individuals and recognized, permanent, college units, spearheading the move to roll back Israel Studies in America is the broad-based student-led BDS movement. Whereas intersectionality originally might have been limited to "all self-professed victim minorities,"[18] when it comes to demonstrating against the Jewish and Zionist state, the umbrella now encompasses a loose and diffuse Left-Right network of remarkable diversity whose members—from socialists to racists and America Firsters—share a single common cause: enmity toward Israel and, oftentimes, by extension, to Jews.

Merely to illustrate here this conglomeration's extreme range, it is enough to cite some of its major constituent parts. First, in terms of ideology: anti-racist liberals condemning Israeli policies in the name of human rights aligned with Arab Americans and Muslims enlisted in the fight for Palestinian self-determination, whether in place of Israel or more moderately in fidelity to the so-called "two-state" solution. Similarly, progressive international leftists opposed to nationalism in general and Jewish nationalism in particular. Located at the opposite end of the spectrum is the Alt-Right segment of the white supremacist movement whose racism extends to Jews and to all things Jewish, to include Israel as well. Thus, one morning, greeting passersby and students near the Duke University campus were signs reading "Greedy Jews" and "End Zionist Oppression."[19]

Second, in organizational terms, a partial list includes fringe as well as mainstream groups. Most prominent are the hard-core organizations dedicated to warring against Israel and Israeli policies: Students for Justice in Palestine; Democratic Socialists of America; Palestine Solidarity Alliance; the Boycott, Divestment and Sanctions Movement. So, too, does the sprawling protest and boycott movement frequently benefit from four identifiably Jewish groups: IfNotNow; J Street U; Jewish Voice for Peace; and All That's Left—whose motivation is "unequivocal opposition to the occupation and our focus on the diaspora angle of resistance to the occupation rooted in the notion that all people(s) are equal."[20]

Depending upon the demographic makeup of each university's student body, campus politics and the need for coalition-building, additional voice and support often comes from secondary special interest groups. For example, among the sixty student groups at NYU petitioning to blacklist Israel and its supporters could be found the African Student Union, the Black Students Union, College Libertarians, the Mexican Student Association, NYU Slam! Poetry Club, NYU Students Against Gentrification and Expansion, and SHADES: For LGBTQ Students of Color and Allies at NYU.[21]

Largely motivated by a sense of solidarity, the theme of Palestinian victimization also tends to resonate with them. What their participation suggests, however, is (a) low awareness of the Arab-Israeli-Palestinian conflict's true complexity; (b) one-sided identification with the Palestinian narrative and total deafness toward Israel's; (c) selective outrage, to the point of obsession toward Israel contrasted by studied silence over glaring injustices in the world, whether in Turkey, Syria, Myanmar, or elsewhere.

Unnuanced, categorical condemnation of Israel is thus a distinguishing characteristic, with BDSers and their fellow travelers denying Israel any benefit of the doubt and for whom there are no shades of gray in the Arab-

Israel conflict. As the rhetoric heats up, and with it the pressure to adopt a principled stand—either for or against—fundamental distinctions are too easily lost in what has fast become a strident and polarizing student debate. For instance, the profound difference between advocating in favor of the Palestinians and their claim to statehood; opposing West Bank settlements and business enterprises; and categorically disqualifying Israel as a sovereign and Jewish state.

The above accounts for the third hallmark of the intersectional coalition's diversity: its tactical versatility in getting its message across—inside the classroom but especially outside, off-campus, within the local community and in the media, as well as on campus. Characteristic of the anti-Israel protest movement in general is its tendency to employ a blend of the conventional—such as collegiate debate, posters, orderly demonstrations, handing out leaflets and fliers—with the flagrant and the provocative. The latter includes abuse and intimidation of fellow students by equating Zionism with Judaism; by circulating exaggerated and even false material on the blogosphere. Most flagrant, from the standpoint of norms of civility, is the disruptive tactic of interrupting talks, heckling, and shouting down invited Israeli guest speakers, even those known to hold moderate views on peacemaking and for being public critics of specific Israeli domestic or foreign policies.[22] This, while, at the same time, defending their own behavior and tactics in the name of First Amendment freedoms of speech and assembly.

Aggressive tactics like these are now the new normal in American campus politics, signaling the spread of the adversarial conflict over Israel-Palestine to the United States, thereby posing a challenge of great magnitude for all parties concerned with higher education. Not least for Jewish students and, in turn, for serious, scholarly, in-depth study of Israel. Failure to recognize in time the seriousness of the threat presented by regressive groups masquerading as progressives, and to mount an effective, concerted counter, could mean nothing less than losing not only the campus war now raging but the longer-term, vital identification with Israel of the emerging generation of American leaders, scholars, and opinion-makers.

RETAKING THE CAMPUS

Every challenge calls for a response. In this instance, however, once student activists are prized over student scholars, Jewish undergraduates and those arguing the case for Israel Studies may be largely unprepared. To begin with, Jewish history and political culture have taught that the best defense is a good defense. As a diaspora and a minority people, Jews traditionally have been less inclined toward combativeness, relying instead upon moderation, dialogue, and compromise.

Unfortunately, reasoning together is proving wholly inappropriate against a determined opponent operating under few if any restraints. Caught off guard by the ferocity of the attack, and somewhat mortified at finding themselves in the eye of the campus storm, Jewish students and faculty—too often uninformed, outmatched, outnumbered, outshouted—have been slow to react. Still worse, provocations have caused divisiveness in their ranks over which of three responses is the wisest for contending with the annual campus wars: passive resistance, counterattacking, defection.

The first school of thought argues for moderation. For them, being dragged into ugly confrontations are antithetical to Jewish values, and they find descending to such levels of unacademic behavior unacceptable. Instead, this school of thought feels it is best to keep a low profile and to exercise restraint. To remain silent even in the face of provocations—as uncomfortable as this may be—until the storm passes and the BDS-led intersectionality coalition either loses credibility or dissolves, is the modus operandi of this school of thought.

In the interim, and in an effort to hasten the process, Jewish students of this persuasion are inclined, as one spokesperson expressed it, to "welcome discussion" and to "believe that dialogue with those who disagree with us is the key to reconciliation and understanding."[23] Others go beyond the quest for dialogue, placing their trust in university authorities to take remedial administrative action in the name of civil liberties and free speech, whereas still others, such as the Lawfare Project, go a step further by taking legal action to protect the civil rights of the Jewish and pro-Israel community on college campuses nationwide.

A second school takes a much stronger tack: steadfastness in fighting fire with fire by standing up and pushing back in Israel's defense. This school endeavors to make certain that an Israeli voice is heard and an Israeli presence felt on their campus—by proudly staging Israel Week as a counter to Apartheid Week, by proudly standing up for Israel and against BDS resolutions at student council meetings, and by demanding that university and city officials take immediate steps to guarantee free speech and freedom of assembly, in short, a call for a full-scale war against BDS. This school sees itself engaged in a struggle against campus bigotry, spearheaded by the Canary Mission since its founding in 2015, in the firm belief that "we all have the right to know if an individual has been affiliated with movements that routinely engage in anti-Semitic rhetoric and actions, promote hatred of Jews and seek the destruction of Israel."[24] However, in profiling both pro-Palestinian activist organizations and individuals as guilty of promoting hatred of the United States, Israel, and Jews on North American college campuses, Canary Mission has itself come under heavy criticism for witch-hunting and labeling.

Adopting a similar, yet distinctly more forceful, course of action in accepting zero tolerance toward Israel's enemies in academia is the Maccabee Task Force, also founded in 2015 and sworn to be "laser focused on one core mission—to ensure that those who seek to delegitimize Israel and demonize the Jewish people are *confronted*, *combatted* and *defeated*" (emphasis added).[25]

Yet a third school of thought has gained purchase, as witnessed by Jewish staff and students who opt to defect by lending their voice to the chorus of anti-Israelism. The motivation for such strong action obviously varies, although one theory gaining currency is that for many "twentysomethings" in the social justice movement turned off by Jewish ritual, their Judaism is condensed to the master concept of *"tikkun olam,"* of repairing the world.[26] For some it is simply to deny any personal or emotional link to Israel, disavowing the Zionist idea of Jewish national self-determination, and the very notion of Jews being anything other than a culture and a religion. From there, ideationally, it is only a short distance to insisting that Palestinian nationalism and right to self-determination is the more valid and compelling of the two parties contesting the right to sovereignty in and over the Holy Land. For others, formerly self-confessed Zionists, their justification for switching loyalties faults contemporary Israel for betraying theirs and their parents' image of an enlightened, liberal, democratic, and international law-abiding country.

Still others profess their deep and abiding concern for Israel's welfare, security, and longer-term survival, and that indeed it is precisely this fidelity that now forces them to join the protest movement in order to save Israel from itself, and from the evils of occupying and dispossessing another people. Surely one of the most embarrassing moments exposing the serious disconnect within the Jewish fold must have been when some thirty Jewish activists of the anti-occupation IfNotNow group gathered in midtown New York to recite *"kaddish"* (the Jewish mourning prayer) for Palestinians killed near the Gaza Strip border fence with Israel, among them confirmed *Hamas* militants.[27]

Silence is ill-advised; ignorance is deplorable yet remediable; acquiescence is shocking and disgraceful in equal measure. Whatever their motivation, whether a matter of conscience or convenience, this latter phenomenon of a younger generation of American Jews who disavow the legal and historical claims for a Jewish nation-state and cross the lines to side with Israel's critics and enemies, apart from its other implications, adds to the BDS coalition's empowerment by lending the latter coveted credibility. It also underlines intersectionality's negative "ripple effect," by exposing the growing rift within the broader American Jewish community and its college-aged population.

What we are seeing is an inability on the part of Jewish students as a whole to form a united front in facing the dual threat to their own secure position on the American campus and to that of Israel in American higher education. Instead, individual registered Jewish students find themselves at a loss for how to respond. Either that, or they and their representative student organizations are pitted against each other over strategy and tactics. To wit, toward the close of 2018, in what may portend things to come, more than a hundred pro-Israel student activists at seven universities publicly accused the previously cited Canary Mission with being not only "morally reprehensible," but also "counterproductive" because of its intimidating and overly aggressive monitoring of blacklisted BDS supporters.[28]

In effect, and by way of an interim summary, the changing North American college scene points to what one student leader rightly refers to as the "toxic normalization"[29] of the BDS academic war against Israel. This declared war offers no sign of abating. On the contrary, it is gaining both traction and momentum, now having escalated beyond proscribing the serious study of Israel in the United States into boycotting study abroad programs at Israeli academic institutions. Champions of Israel and of its legitimate place in American higher education should be under no illusions, for they, and we, are up against a resolute foe that has yet to reach its full potential in vindictiveness. This adversary has already demonstrated a capacity to divert students from the scholarly path, and to divert the energies of Jewish students and all those with an interest in Israel as a dynamic, multiethnic, and pluralistic society; as a Middle Eastern and global actor; as an imperfect but evolving democratic and Jewish state.

Besides going against its professed claim to be nonviolent by becoming increasingly militant, the movement is professionalizing, with funding and heavy backing from external advisers. Moreover, this war has also metastasized, taking the fight cross-country to campuses previously uninfected, and by infiltrating international as well as national professional scholarly associations, with the Asian American Studies Association in April 2013 being the first to adopt BDS.

This war has fed, in turn, two further disquieting trends, one of them being, as noted, the alienation of Jewish millennials and their seniors[30] to the extent of adopting the Palestinian narrative and tropes, and consequently joining the ranks of Israel's detractors in not insignificant numbers. Mindful of the limitations of public opinion surveys, nonetheless, polls do find support for Israel declining at an alarming rate. According to a reputable Pew Research Center finding, a full 42 percent of Jews aged eighteen to twenty-nine do not support Israel more than the Palestinians.[31]

The other trend, fraught with far-reaching implications for American society and American Jewry alike, is a blurring of the line between holding anti-Israel and anti-Zionist views and anti-Semitism. It is worth pausing to note that the campus wars are being waged against a larger nationwide backdrop of, on the one hand, anti-Jewish sentiment once again injecting itself into the American mainstream, and, on the other hand, declining identification with as well as support for Israel, especially among liberal Democrats and today's younger generation of college-bound or college-graduate Jews.

Here, the aggregate statistical data is incontrovertible: while varying in notoriety or in frequency across campuses, there is a progressive rise in incidents directed not just at boycotting Israel but at harassing individual Jewish students.[32] This extends as well to ostracizing Jewish organizations, with slogans like "We want Zionism off this campus, so we want Hillel off this campus" only going to further corroborate this lethal linkage.[33] Leaving one observer to entitle his study of the subject, "From 'intersectionality' to the exclusion of Jewish students: BDS makes a worrying turn on US campuses."[34]

If campus wars over Israel, Jewish disunity, and converting anti-Israelism into anti-Semitism are three negative trends in American academia, then there may be slight comfort in one positive and at least potentially constructive outgrowth from Israel-centered intersectionality. Targeting Israel has at least the potential to force a rethinking on teaching Israel. A reassessment of Israel Studies in America could even result in a basic restructuring aimed at bridging the gap between Jewish Studies and Israel Studies, and bringing them closer together. To appreciate the crucial importance of such a move, however, requires both background and perspective.

RECONCILING ISRAEL STUDIES WITH JEWISH STUDIES

When we recall how ethnic and regional studies came to acquire academic standing in the United States during the last quarter of the twentieth century, individual course offerings and then degree programs built around modern Israel were a late entry. Their introduction therefore posed the immediate problem of precisely where to insert them within any given university's map of pre-existing disciplines and established programs, the two most logical candidates being either cognate Judaic Studies or, alternatively, Middle East studies.

Each proposal, however, ran up against a wall of resistance. Given their pro-Arab leanings and crucial petrodollar funding by Saudi Arabia and other oil-rich Arab countries, Middle East studies faculty and staff members expressed extreme resistance at serving as the home for Israel-centric research or seminars. Clearly, this would run counter to the Arab World's declared goal of portraying Israel as an artificial Zionist entity, and insistence upon denying it any recognition or regional standing whatsoever, neither symbolic nor academic.

When judged strictly in political and financial terms, this stance may have been readily understandable, whereas strenuous objections raised at the time against incorporating modern Israel into traditional Jewish Studies might seem rather surprising. Until we bear in mind that prominent Jewish scholars in the United States, many of them classicists by academic training and inclination as well as fully assimilated into America by choice, expressed at best lukewarm support for the imperative of a Jewish nation-state. Hence, their preference, likewise, for keeping Israel studies at a safe distance. More surprising still, rather than taking offense, their Israeli peers readily agreed to the separation, proving that academics, too, can make for strange bedfellows. For them, a key tenet of mainstream Zionism was the need for consciously breaking with the Jewish past and what Salon Baron famously termed the "lachrymose conception of Jewish history."

Given the entrenched positions of the established Middle East centers and Judaic Studies programs respectively, for lack of a consensual or better option a number of universities pioneering in Israel-related courses decided to integrate these course offerings within consenting political science and international relations departments. Or else to grant Israel Studies independent status as a unit apart, on the same level as Chinese, Russian, or Canadian studies programs. Hence the Faustian compromise whereby Israel Studies found themselves neither part of the Middle East nor an integral part of *Wissenschaft des Judentums*, the Science of Judaism.

Whatever the idiosyncratic university blueprint and *modus operandi* adopted years ago, the point is that with the passage of time and the accumulation of vested interests these original degrees of separation have long since become institutionalized, and thus not readily subject to change.

Except that BDS excesses—insisting Israel's crime lies in its being not only a rogue state, a terrorist state and an apartheid state but . . . a *Jewish* state—ironically threaten to act as the unintended agent for change. Due primarily to conflating Israel and Zionism with Jews and Judaism, this common threat is serving to underline what so many specialists in the study of these two fields and accustomed to being pigeonholed may have forgotten or chosen to forget: their shared foundations, their intersecting scholarly domains and, above all, their shared fate.

Even to entertain here the proposition of more closely integrating Israel Studies with Jewish Studies is to challenge accepted conventions, with the likely first line of opposition voiced by separatists in both respective domains who cling to the *status quo* and are adamant in preserving their insularity within the existing academic boundary lines. Not where the two areas of specialization might intersect but where they deviate. Ancient Israel versus modern Israel; the classics, history, and text versus politics, power, and policy; the humanities versus the social sciences. Two communities of scholars, so the traditional argument goes; two distinctly different methodologies (qualitative and quantitative); two seemingly unrelated disciplines.

While such logic is not lacking in cogency, nevertheless, there are overriding considerations at present that argue for greater synergy. Like any crisis, human, societal, or international, the BDS-precipitated U.S. campus crisis poses both a danger and an opportunity. Should the campus wars intensify as, realistically and soberly, there is every reason to expect, in light of the shared looming crisis working together more closely offers lobbyists for Jewish Studies and for Israel Studies a win-win situation. Truth be told, competitiveness and duplication best epitomize relations between the two scholarly communities: in enlarging student enrollment and tuition fees; in securing additional faculty positions from college deans; in applying to foundations for research grants and to private Jewish benefactors and federal government agencies for coveted funding.

Let me be clear: the call is not for merging the two fields or for erasing the disciplinary and administrative lines of separation so much as it is for rationing limited resources and harnessing unlimited interdisciplinary talents.

Contrary to those who would subscribe to gross misreadings by naysayers—like the Palestinian Authority's Mahmoud Abbas, who professes Israel to be "a colonial project that has nothing to do with Judaism"[35]—Jewish peoplehood, Judaism, and Israel are *chad hu*; for better or worse, indivisible and complementary. Therefore, this initiative deserves to be weighed in terms of the opening it provides for: (a) making the best of a distasteful and imposed situation, (b) mutual enrichment. Emphasizing the positive means:

- Recognition by Jewish Studies personnel that they can no longer in good conscience stand aside and watch colleagues in Israel Studies singled out for vilification on the assumption that they will remain immune to the anti-Israel campaigns being waged around them.
- Acknowledging that compartmentalization no longer works and that interdisciplinary teaching and research is the more promising pathway.
- Reframing into a seamless whole the contemporary state of Israel's deepest roots and place in the life, annals, experience, and thought of the Jewish people by ascribing its emergence not to expiation by the United Nations in 1947 for the Holocaust but as Zionism's linear evolution from within the wider panorama of Jewish history.
- Reenergizing the investigation of modern-day Judaism and of modern-day Zionism by inspiring collaborative scholarly research on unexplored and fertile subjects like "Comparative Jewish politics and forms of governance"; "A typology of leadership from biblical Israel to 21st century Israel"; "Jewish political economy"; "Is there a Jewish theory of international relations and conflict resolution?"

- Making each artificially dichotomous field of study that much more intelligible, more meaningful, more challenging, more relevant—and therefore more appealing—for university students.

Aside from this cluster of prospective and positive outcomes triggered by BDS, there is a fourth-side potential benefit for Israel Studies *per se* in the United States.

It is the possibility, ironically furnished by those most hostile to it, to prevent the academic study of Israel from becoming commonplace and from sliding into mediocrity. When observed closely, it is possible to discern that whereas only a few years ago Israel Studies may have enjoyed a growth spurt, the field may presently be experiencing a loss of momentum.[36] Hard-fought programs on Israel are undergoing—largely unobserved—a slow and gradual process of thinning out that ought to be of crucial concern for its direct relevance to the campus wars. Unless addressed in time, this drift, in and of itself, could very well play into the hands of those who would delight in seeing such programs rolled back, and Israel-centered courses deleted from university catalogues.

What are these cautionary signs of attrition? For this author, two indicators in particular stand out. Who teaches on Israel, and what courses are they teaching?

With reference to the first, there is a changing of the guard in representations of Israel. Reminiscent of the initial post-1945 start-up stages of Middle East affairs at American universities, courses about Israel have had to rely largely on Israeli scholars, both tenured and expert VIPs (visiting Israeli professors) on temporary appointments, until a younger cohort of American-born, American-trained postgraduate students would emerge to fill the vacuum and assume permanent positions. That transition has now taken place, resulting in a mixed faculty of non-Israelis, VIPs and Israeli expatriates permanently residing in the United States.

Reversing the order, the subgroup of former Israelis consists of not a few who for no fault of their own were unable to find their place professionally in Israeli academia due to the limited number of tenure-track positions, or to find their place ideologically in an Israeli society no longer to their liking. Some of their personal disappointment and disaffection as well as cosmopolitan leftist-secular political leanings thus find their way into classroom and seminar presentations.[37] So can this same tendency to become outspoken critics when abroad, especially of Netanyahu's four terms as prime minister, apply to Israelis on shorter-term appointments, many of them self-identified as iconoclastic new historians and revisionist sociologists.

To their credit, however, they do bring to the classroom firsthand personal experience—good or bad—in the army, society, and politics of Israel as well as complete mastery over Hebrew-language sources. Unfortunately, the same cannot be said for all those in the second subgroup of American-trained faculty with claims to expertise on one aspect or another of Israeli life and policy. Suggestive of the drawbacks in studying and commenting about Israel remotely, not only are many of them a step removed from direct participation, but their approach to Israeli issues is inevitably colored by their particular slant—namely, a distinctly American perspective, value system, and worldview. None of which are necessarily compatible with Israel's own self-definition as a Jewish nation-state or form of democracy. With Israel's threat environment, or how Israelis perceive and deal with their unique security dilemmas.

Moreover, shockingly, it is not uncommon to find journal articles and even entire monographs authored by respected commentators on Israel who are nonconversant in the reading of Hebrew documentation and forced therefore to rely exclusively upon English sources; for example, the daily English edition of *Ha'aretz*, with its own editorial agenda. Coupled with professors in the United States who are judgmental in observing Israel from the safe distance of eight thousand miles, this language deficiency raises grave methodological questions about the validity of what is taught, and opinions formed in the minds of impressionable students. When a professor of Israel Studies categorically expresses his opinion that "Israel has *always* assumed that driving its adversaries into the dirt, i.e., *humiliating* them, is an essential part of convincing them they could not win"[38]—imparting humiliation as the aim rather than deterrence—one has every right to be concerned. With written criticism like this from within the fold of Israel Studies, Palestinians and their allies on campus can rest easy, knowing their work is being done by others.

While on the subject of publications, there are grounds for suspicion that academic publishing houses, hypersensitive about catering to public and scholarly reading tastes—what will sell—are more inclined in recent years to accept marketable books critical of Israel. Rather than manuscripts complimentary of Israel, or even carefully balanced, for instance, in daring to assign to the Palestinians equal if not greater blame for the impasse in peacemaking and for past missed opportunities.

Lastly, there is the quiet revision in the character of the course offerings in Israel Studies now being favored and their direct connection to the BDS campus wars. The central argument here is that too many programs are downsizing, offering watered-down programs of study, or both. This is not because of a shortage of qualified instructors, or due to a drop in either student registration or student interest. Rather, this is primarily happening in order to avoid controversy and, if so, represents an invidious form of self-censorship.

Under the circumstances extant today on so many U.S. college and university campuses, Israel Studies program planners are inclined to shy away from courses likely to draw attention or singled out for criticism as too political—as too pro-Israel—and to favor instead those guaranteed to be less sensitive and yet geared to the current fashions of American undergraduates. Reflected in one catalogue after another, this silent displacement of core subjects is resulting in fewer and fewer courses on contemporary Israeli politics, on Israeli foreign affairs and security policy, on the Arab-Israeli conflict and peace process. In their stead, the emphasis is now on Israeli literature, music, and the arts, multiculturalism in contemporary Israeli cinema and television, Israeli society through Hebrew song and video, the political economy of Israel, Israeli feminism, and the like.

Without gainsaying the validity of such "soft" topics and their contribution to showcasing Israel's vibrant cultural landscape, if these electives are substitutes *for* rather than supplemental *to* courses addressing admittedly the most politically sensitive issues at the heart of present-day Israeli discourse in a responsible and scholarly way, then this imbalance threatens to neuter Israel studies programs. If widespread, this will eventually expose such diluted programs to criticism from within the academic community and disqualification on strictly academic grounds, thereby handing Israel's enemies the very victory they seek.

What is the true extent of this watering down of Israel Studies? Similarly, how many programs are affected by it? Short of a systematic mapping of all Israel Studies institutes and bachelor, masters, and PhD programs by the computerized number of permanent research and teaching positions, visiting professorships, yearly course catalogues, student registration, calendars of events, scientific publications, degrees awarded, and sources of funding, there are no authoritative answers. Still, the problem of sustaining balanced academic programs of the highest caliber in the face of external scrutiny does exist, needs to be faced, and is certainly worthy of further investigation and discussion. Just because courses and programs have come into existence is no guarantee of their sustainability.

One source of encouragement is the innovative role played since 2012 by the Washington-based Israel Institute in sustaining a vibrant, multifaceted field of Israel Studies in the United States in close partnership with universities and think tanks. Another is the Association for Israel Studies, formed in 1985 and devoted to the academic and professional study of Israel. Yet a third positive force deserves mention: the Charles and Lynn Schusterman Family Foundation whose philanthropic efforts mandate "broadening and deepening the quality of formal and informal Israel education at universities across the U.S."

With specific reference to the wisdom of more closely pairing Israel Studies with the established and reputable field of Jewish Studies, here, too, there is room for guarded optimism. Representative of the first generation of integrated programs is the Schusterman Center for Judaic and Israel Studies at the University of Oklahoma, upgraded from a progrm in 2014. More practiced still is the Institute for Israel and Jewish Studies, upgraded in 2016 from a Center founded in 1950, and thus a fixture at Columbia University.

Suggestive of more recent efforts now under way in this desired direction and the untapped potential for fruitful collaboration at the same time as safeguarding the recognized professional status of both academic pursuits is the Michael and Elaine Serling Institute for Jewish Studies and Modern Israel at Michigan State University, launched in 2018. Reconstituted from an original Jewish Studies Program and with an expanded mandate, it is designed to "enhance classroom experiences and research" and to "encompass the historical and geographic breadth of Jewish experiences." The Institute serves to coordinate the work of five core faculty and 25 affiliated faculty drawn from ten different departments and colleges.[39] Appropriately enough, its inaugural public event in September 2018 was a conference devoted to "Israel at 70: Community, Challenge and Creativity."

To conclude: Israel Studies as an accredited academic field is under siege on American college campuses—part of persistent and mounting efforts at the longer-term delegitimization of Israel as the state of the Jewish people. Aided and abetted by Israel's enemies through the use, and abuse, of intersectionality, these campus wars are in all likelihood going to be protracted, ugly, and oftentimes unacademic. The specific incidents cited here will fade with time and doubtless be superseded well into the 2020s by fresh on-campus encounters and outrages expanding upon the central theme posed in this chapter of intersectionality's negative impact upon the academic study of Israel in the United States.

In the face of such an onslaught, ivory tower complacency is simply not an option. Fighting back therefore requires (a) acknowledging this reality, (b) correctly gauging the nature and full extent of the threat, (c) demonstrating sufficient staying power to resist and prevail in eventually lifting the siege, and (d) to do so by calibrating the range of responses appropriate for each campus and type of provocation, whether in class or on the campus green.

One set of responses to avoid is either underestimating or exaggerating the nature of the challenge. This puts a premium on carefully navigating between standing by helplessly in the face of provocation and, at the other pole, succumbing to patently unbecoming, unworthy, and unacademic practices like stereotyping, closed mindedness, expressing uniformed opinion, name-calling, verbal violence, and worse.

One strategic response, as prescribed here, is to insist upon the highest standards in staffing and in course offerings, and to strive for nothing short of academic excellence in all aspects of the study of Israel, from lecturing to symposia to publications. Affirmative action includes, in the second instance, highlighting the (pardon the expression) intersectionality of "Jewish" and "Israeli." If anything good might yet emerge from the BDS campus struggle, translating Israel Studies and Jewish Studies intersections into innovative programs could be the first step in the historic diplomatic process of incorporating Israel into the Middle East . . . and, academically, into Middle East regional studies.

NOTES

1. "US college offers alternative hummus for anti-Israel students," *Times of Israel*, May 3, 2018. https://www.timesofisrael.com/us-college-offers-alternative-hummus-for-anti-israel-students/. Challenges to Sabra hummus—exclusively manufactured in the United States, in factories in Queens, New York, and Richmond, Virginia—being sold in college cafeterias were first reported at Princeton and De Paul Universities already in 2010. Tamar Lewin, "New Subject of Debate on Mideast: Hummus," *New York Times*, December 3, 2010.

2. Useful background reading on the origins, evolution, and spread of the anti-Israel movement in the United States can be found in Andrew Pessin and Doron S. Ben-Atar, *Anti-Zionism on Campus: The University, Free Speech and BDS* (Bloomington: Indiana University Press, 2018). See also *The Limits of Hostility: Students Report on Antisemitism and Anti-Israel Sentiment at Four US Universities* (Waltham, MA: Brandeis University, Steinhardt Social Research Institute, 2017); "The 40 Worst Colleges. The Algemeiner's 1st Annual List of the US and Canada's Worst Campuses for Jewish Students," *The Algemeiner*. https://www.algemeiner.com/the-40-worst-colleges-for-jewish-students-2016/.

3. Joe Heim, "Protestors disrupt Jewish student meeting at University of Virginia," *Washington Post*, February 23, 2018. https://www.washingtonpost.com/news/grade-point/wp/2018/02/23/protesters-disrupt-jewish-student-meeting-at-university-of-virginia/?utm_term=.23715fec48be.

4. "California professor calls university's acceptance of Zionists 'declaration of war,'" *Jewish News Syndicate*, March 22, 2018. https://www.jns.org/california-professor-calls-universitys-acceptance-of-zionists-declaration-of-war/.

5. Paul Miller, "BDS gets handed a devastating defeat at the University of Illinois," *Jewish News Syndicate*, March 15, 2018. https://www.jns.org/opinion/bds-gets-handed-a-devastating-defeat-at-the-university-of-illinois/.

6. "Pro-Palestinian US students slam Muslim chaplain for defending campus Hillel," *Times of Israel*, May 9, 2018. https://www.timesofisrael.com/pro-palestinian-us-students-slam-muslim-chaplain-for-defending-campus-hillel/.

7. Ben Sales, "Columbia students hold anti-Israel demonstration opposite Holocaust commemoration booth," *Jewish Telegraphic Agency (JTA)*, April 12, 2018. https://www.jta.org/2018/04/12/top-headlines/columbia-students-hold-anti-israel-demonstration-opposite-holocaust-commemoration-booth; see also Leila Beckwith and Tammi Rossman-Benjamin, "Anti-Israel bias reigns at Columbia," *New York Daily News*, December 28, 2017. http://www.nydailynews.com/opinion/anti-israel-bias-reigns-columbia-article-1.3723222.

8. Sara Hanau, "BDS vote passes at Barnard, sparking backlash from pro-Israel alums," *The New York Jewish Week*, April 25, 2018. https://jewishweek.timesofisrael.com/bds-vote-passes-at-barnard-sparking-backlash-from-pro-israel-alums/.

9. Abigail Marone, "GW refuses to implement BDS resolution passed by secret vote," April 26, 2018. https://www.campusreform.org/?ID=10822. The brief statement by the university's president can be found here: "Message from President LeBlanc on Student Association Resolution," *GWToday*, April 24, 2018. https://gwtoday.gwu.edu/message-president-leblanc-student-association-resolution.

10. Jackson Richman, "Pitzer College faculty votes to end study abroad in Israel, student government resists," *Jewish News Syndicate*, November 27, 2018. https://www.jns.org/pitzer-college-faculty-votes-to-end-study-abroad-in-israel-student-government-resists/; also, Elizabeth Redden, "Faculty vote to end Israel study abroad," *Inside Higher Ed*, November 28, 2018. https://www.insidehighered.com/news/2018/11/28/pitzer-faculty-vote-suspend-study-abroad-program-israel.

11. The resolution passed thirty-five in favor and fourteen abstentions, with only fourteen voting against. Taly Krupkin, "NYU Student Government passes Israeli-authored BDS resolution," *Ha'aretz,* December 8, 2018. https://www.haaretz.com/us-news/.premium-nyu-student-body-passes-israeli-authored-bds-resolution-1.6724640.

12. Material chronicling the series of events at the University of Michigan includes: Seffi Kogen, "Extremists on left, right empowering BDS on U.S. college campuses," *Ha'aretz,* November 29, 2017; Martin Slagter, "University of Michigan regents won't divest; oppose Israel sanctions," *MLive,* December 14, 2017. https://www.mlive.com/news/ann-arbor/index.ssf/2017/12/um_regents_decline_to_form_com.html; Jonathan Marks, "The Unprincipled Boycott of Israel," *Commentary,* September 20, 2018. https://www.commentarymagazine.com/foreign-policy/middle-east/israel/bds-principled-boycott-israel/; "58 groups call on U of Michigan to sanction professors who promote BDS," *The Times of Israel,* September 22, 2018. https://www.timesofisrael.com/58-groups-call-on-u-of-michigan-to-sanction-professors-who-promote-bds/; Kim Kozlowski, "UM disciplines prof over Israel letter controversy," *The Detroit News,* October 10, 2018. https://www.detroitnews.com/story/news/ local/michigan/2018/10/09/university-michigan-disciplines-professor-over-israel-letter-controversy/1580969002/; Jeremy Sharon, "Bennett slams University of Michigan for Netanyahu-Hitler comparison," *Jerusalem Post,* October 9, 2018. https://www.jpost.com/Israel-News/Bennett-slams-Michigan-U-for-Netanyahu-Hitler-comparison-569001.

13. For the two UCLA incidents, see Jonathan Marks, "How Campus Bullies Pulled Off the Anti-Israel BDS Movement," *Minding the Campus,* June 14, 2018. https://www.mindingthecampus.org/2018/06/14/how-campus-bullies-pulled-off-the-anti-israel-bds-movement/; Oren Peleg, "UCLA students speak out against upcoming National Students for Justice in Palestine conference," *Jewish News Syndicate (JNS),* September 30, 2018. https://www.jns.org/students-speak-out-against-upcoming-national-students-for-justice-in-palestine-conference-at-ucla/.

14. The local controversy over "Colonizing Palestine" at Tufts and its larger implications can be found in Jackson Richman, "New course at Tufts University advances Palestinian narrative, while shelving the Jews," *Jewish News Syndicate (JNS),* August 15, 2018. https://www.jns.org/new-course-at-tufts-university-advances-palestinian-narrative-while-shelving-the-jews/; and "'Colonizing Palestine' course at Tufts University draws criticism for 'one-sided narrative' on Israel," *Ha'aretz,* September 2, 2018.

15. Arguing against criticism of Israel by intersectional movements, Harvard law professor Alan Dershowitz is quoted by Rachel Frommer in "Alan Dershowitz derides theory of intersectionality in Columbia lecture, " *The Washington Free Beacon,* September 28, 2017. https://freebeacon.com/culture/alan-dershowitz-derides-theory-intersectionality-columbia-lecture/.

16. Kenrya Rankin, "Watch the UN speech that got Marc Lamont Hill fired from CNN," *Colorlines,* November 30, 2018. https://www.colorlines.com/articles/watch-un-speech-got-marc-lamont-hill-fired-cnn.

17. The course description is available on the Tufts University website, at https://as.tufts.edu/colonialismstudies/documents/coursesFall2018.pdf.

18. Ruth Wisse, "The Functions of Anti-Semitism," *National Affairs,* Number 33 (Fall 2017). https://nationalaffairs.com/publications/detail/the-functions-of-anti-semitism.

19. "Anti-Semitic and white supremacist posters hung near Duke campus," *Jewish Telegraphic Agency (JTA),* May 2, 2018. https://www.jta.org/2018/05/02/news-opinion/anti-semitic-white-supremacist-posters-hung-downtown-durham-north-carolina.

20. https://www.facebook.com/pg/AllThatsLeftCollective/about/?ref=page_internal.

21. The full listing of participating boycotters is found at https://bdsmovement.net/news/50-nyu-student-groups-endorse-boycott-divestment-and-sanctions-movement-palestinian-human.

22. A listing of such instances is found in a report by Scott Jaschik, "Who Gets Shouted Down on Campus?" *Inside Higher Ed,* February 26, 2018. https://www.insidehighered.com/news/2018/02/26/event-sponsored-jewish-and-pro-israel-groups-university-virginia-disrupted-and.

23. The quote is by Rebecca Stern, co-president of TorchPAC, a pro-Israel student organization, in an article penned by Yonah Jeremy Bob, "Standwithus demands that NYU punish students boycotting Israel," *Jerusalem Post*, April 27, 2018. https://www.jpost.com/Diaspora/StandWithUs-demands-that-NYU-punish-students-boycotting-Israel-Jews-552856.

24. As of September 2018 its homepage contained an extensive catalogue of 1,801 individuals, 555 professors, and 23 organizations charged with promoting hatred of the United States, Israel, and Jews on North American college campuses. https://canarymission.org/.

25. This mission statement appears on the Maccabee Task Force's website at https://www.maccabeetaskforce.org/. The organization's target for 2018–2019 is to double its footprint from forty to eighty campuses wherever a serious BDS and delegitimization of Israel challenge presents itself.

26. Jonathan Neumann, *To Heal the World? How the New Left Corrupts Judaism and Endangers Israel* (New York: St. Martin's Press, 2018).

27. Taly Krupkin, "Jewish activists arrested after protest over Gaza at U.S. Sen. Schumer's office," *Ha'aretz*, April 11, 2018.

28. The full text of the public statement plus the names of the student groups appear here: Andrew Silow-Carroll, "Jewish students: A blacklist of BDS supporters is hurting our efforts to defend Israel on campus," *Jewish Telegraph Agency (TGA)*, March 23, 2018. https://www.jta.org/2018/04/23/news-opinion/jewish-students-blacklist-bds-supporters-hurting-efforts-defend-israel-campus.

29. The term is used by GW for Israel president Tali Edid, quoted by Abigail Marone in reporting an April 2018 skirmish on George Washington University's Washington, DC, campus. https://www.campusreform.org/?ID=10822.

30. Upon taking the BDS cause national and turning to readers of the influential *New York Times* in an op-ed piece posing the rhetorical question "Is boycotting Israel considered 'hate'?," Joseph Levine, a professor of philosophy at the University of Massachusetts, Amherst and a member of the Jewish Voice for Peace Academic Advisory Council, in applying "public reason" baldly charged *opponents* of the Boycott, Divestment and Sanctions movement with involvement in "a dishonest branding campaign." *The New York Times International Edition*, September 5, 2018.

31. The Pew findings are reported in the following article: Amir Tabon, "Americans more divided over Israel 'than at any point' in recent history, study finds," *Ha'aretz*, January 23, 2018; see also Dov Waxman, *Trouble in the Tribe: The American Jewish Conflict over Israel* (Princeton: Princeton University Press, 2018).

32. It is instructive to compare an April 2017 quantitative account by the AMCHA Initiative on anti-Semitic activity throughout 2016 at U.S. colleges with the largest Jewish undergraduate populations (when incidents increased by 40 percent from 2015 to 2016) with a December 2017 study compiled by the Steinhardt Social Research Institute at Brandeis University (which reported that students at Brandeis, Harvard, the University of Pennsylvania, and the University of Michigan rarely found themselves exposed to anti-Semitism). By late 2018 this was no longer the case at either Brandeis or the University of Michigan. The AMCHA findings, "Antisemitism: At the Epicenter of Campus Intolerance" (April 2017) are at https://www.amchainitiative.org/wp-content/uploads/2017/04/Antisemitism_At-the-Epicenter-of-Campus-Intolerance_Report-2016.pdf; those of the Brandeis University report are at https://www.brandeis.edu/ssri/noteworthy/fourcampuses.html.

33. Hillel is the largest Jewish campus organization, connecting with students at more than 550 colleges and universities worldwide, but with most of them in the United States. The call for expelling the Hillel branch at Stony Brook University is cited in "Pro-Palestinian US students slam Muslim chaplain for defending campus Hillel," *Times of Israel*, May 9, 2018. https://www.timesofisrael.com/pro-palestinian-us-students-slam-muslim-chaplain-for-defending-campus-hillel/.

34. The author of the July 2018 study published in the *Fathom* journal sponsored by BITCOM (Britain Israel Communications and Research Centre) is Kenneth Waltzer, himself the executive director of the Academic Engagement Network, a national U.S. faculty organization committed to countering BDS. http://fathomjournal.org/from-intersectionality-to-the-exclusion-of-jewish-students-bds-makes-a-worrying-turn-on-us-campuses/.

35. The Palestinian Authority chairman's digression into Jewish history and libelous remark first came in a speech on January 14, 2018 and, despite being denounced, was repeated for a second time on April 30. Widely reported, his remarks are quoted in David Horovitz, "Abbas couldn't make peace with the Jews; he believes his own lies about us," *Times of Israel*, January 16, 2018. https://www.timesofisrael.com/abbas-couldnt-make-peace-with-the-jews-he-believes-his-own-lies-about-us/; and Alastair Thomas, "Foreign Office expresses concern over Abbas Shoah slur," *JC, The Jewish Chronicle*, May 1, 2018. https://www.thejc.com/news/uk-news/foreign-office-expresses-concern-over-abbas-shoah-slur-1.463592; longer translated excerpts from Abbas's April speech are available in an analysis by Itamar Marcus, "Jews' usury caused Antisemitism—speech by Mahmoud Abbas," *PMW, Palestinian Media Watch*, Bulletin, May 2, 2018. http://www.palwatch.org/main.aspx?fi=157&doc_id=25581.

36. Professor David Newman of Ben-Gurion University, writing in 2013, offered his impression of a "major growth"—both in America and Europe—in Israel Studies and of independently funded Chairs of Israel Studies. David Newman, "Borderline Views: Studying Israel in Los Angeles," *Jerusalem Post*, June 25, 2013. Firstly, however, a distinction needs to be made between "Israel Studies" and "chairs." What might be true of individual appointments does not necessarily extend to full programs or departments. In addition to which, the trajectory appears to have reversed itself downward in the interval since 2013.

37. This problématique is raised and analyzed in an important study by Miriam Shenkar, *The Politicization of Israel Studies* (Beersheba: Ben-Gurion University of the Negev Press, 2012.

38. Italics added. This particular generalization, putting Israel in a negative light—and in this instance, lacking any real substantive evidence—is confidently put forward by Paul Scham, a professor of Israel Studies at the University of Maryland, in his Opinion piece, "The Palestinians Won the 2017 Battle for Temple Mount. That's Good for Israel," which appeared in the *Ha'aretz* edition of August 2, 2017.

39. Transmitted to the author in a personal communication. Additional information about the Institute can be accessed at http://jsp.msu.edu/.

BIBLIOGRAPHY

"58 groups call on U of Michigan to sanction professors who promote BDS." *The Times of Israel*. September 22, 2018. https://www.timesofisrael.com/58-groups-call-on-u-of-michigan-to-sanction-professors-who-promote-bds/.

"Anti-Semitic and white supremacist posters hung near Duke campus." *Jewish Telegraphic Agency (JTA)*. May 2, 2018. https://www.jta.org/2018/05/02/news-opinion/anti-semitic-white-supremacist-posters-hung-downtown-durham-north-carolina.

Beckwith, Leila, and Tammi Rossman-Benjamin. "Anti-Israel bias reigns at Columbia." *New York Daily News*. December 28, 2017. http://www.nydailynews.com/opinion/anti-israel-bias-reigns-columbia-article-1.3723222.

Bob, Yonah Jeremy. "Standwithus demands that NYU punish students boycotting Israel." *Jerusalem Post*. April 27, 2018. https://www.jpost.com/Diaspora/StandWithUs-demands-that-NYU-punish-students-boycotting-Israel-Jews-552856.

"California professor calls university's acceptance of Zionists 'declaration of war.'" *Jewish News Syndicate*. March 22, 2018. https://www.jns.org/california-professor-calls-universitys-acceptance-of-zionists-declaration-of-war/.

"'Colonizing Palestine' course at Tufts University draws criticism for 'one-sided narrative' on Israel." *Ha'aretz*. September 2, 2018.

Dolsten, Joseph. "51 NYU student groups pledge to boycott Israel and its backers." *Times of Israel*. April 13, 2018. https://www.timesofisrael.com/51-nyu-student-groups-pledge-to-boycott-israel-and-its-backers/.

Frommer, Rachael. "Alan Dershowitz derides theory of intersectionality in Columbia lecture. " *The Washington Free Beacon*. September 28, 2017. https://freebeacon.com/culture/alan-dershowitz-derides-theory-intersectionality-columbia-lecture/.

Hanau, Sara. "BDS vote passes at Barnard, sparking backlash from pro-Israel alums." *The New York Jewish Week*. April 25, 2018. https://jewishweek.timesofisrael.com/bds-vote-passes-at-barnard-sparking-backlash-from-pro-israel-alums/.

Heim, Joe. "Protestors disrupt Jewish student meeting at University of Virginia." *Washington Post*. February 23, 2018. https://www.washingtonpost.com/news/grade-point/wp/2018/02/23/protesters-disrupt-jewish-student-meeting-at-university-of-virginia/?utm_term=.23715fec48be.

Horovitz, David. "Abbas couldn't make peace with the Jews; he believes his own lies about us." *Times of Israel*. January 16, 2018. https://www.timesofisrael.com/abbas-couldnt-make-peace-with-the-jews-he-believes-his-own-lies-about-us/.

Jaschik, Scott. "Who Gets Shouted Down on Campus?" *Inside Higher Ed*. February 26, 2018. https://www.insidehighered.com/news/2018/02/26/event-sponsored-jewish-and-pro-israel-groups-university-virginia-disrupted-and.

Kogen, Seffi. "Extremists on left, right empowering BDS on U.S. college campuses." *Ha'aretz*. November 29, 2017.

Kozlowski, Kim. "UM disciplines prof over Israel letter controversy." *The Detroit News*. October 10, 2018. https://www.detroitnews.com/story/news/local/michigan/2018/10/09/university-michigan-disciplines-professor-over-israel-letter-controversy/1580969002/.

Krupkin, Taly. "Jewish activists arrested after protest over Gaza at U.S. Sen. Schumer's office." *Ha'aretz*. April 11, 2018.

———. "NYU Student Government passes Israeli-authored BDS resolution." *Ha'aretz*. December 8, 2018. https://www.haaretz.com/us-news/.premium-nyu-student-body-passes-israeli-authored-bds-resolution-1.6724640.

Lewin, Tamar. "New subject of debate on Mideast: Hummus." *New York Times*. December 3, 2010.

Marcus, Itamar. "Jews' usury caused Antisemitism—speech by Mahmoud Abbas." *PMW, Palestinian Media Watch*. Bulletin. May 2, 2018. http://www.palwatch.org/main.aspx?fi=157&doc_id=25581.

Marks, Jonathan. "How Campus Bullies Pulled Off the Anti-Israel BDS Movement." *Minding the Campus*. June 14, 2018. https://www.mindingthecampus.org/2018/06/14/how-campus-bullies-pulled-off-the-anti-israel-bds-movement/.

———. "The Unprincipled Boycott of Israel." *Commentary*. September 20, 2018. https://www.commentarymagazine.com/foreign-policy/middle-east/israel/bds-principled-boycott-israel/.

Marone, Abigail. "GW refuses to implement BDS resolution passed by secret vote." April 26, 2018. https://www.campusreform.org/?ID=10822.

"Message from President LeBlanc on Student Association Resolution." *GWToday*. April 24, 2018. https://gwtoday.gwu.edu/message-president-leblanc-student-association-resolution.

Miller, Paul. "BDS gets handed a devastating defeat at the University of Illinois." *Jewish News Syndicate*. March 15, 2018. https://www.jns.org/opinion/bds-gets-handed-a-devastating-defeat-at-the-university-of-illinois/.

Neumann, Jonathan. *To Heal the World? How the New Left Corrupts Judaism and Endangers Israel*. New York: St. Martin's Press, 2018.

Newman, David. "Borderline Views: Studying Israel in Los Angeles." *Jerusalem Post*. June 25, 2013.

Peleg, Oren. "UCLA students speak out against upcoming National Students for Justice in Palestine conference." *Jewish News Syndicate (JNS)*. September 30, 2018. https://www.jns.org/students-speak-out-against-upcoming-national-students-for-justice-in-palestine-conference-at-ucla/.

Pessin, Andrew, and Doron S. Ben-Atar. *Anti-Zionism on Campus: The University, Free Speech and BDS*. Bloomington: Indiana University Press, 2018.

"Pro-Palestinian US students slam Muslim chaplain for defending campus Hillel." *Times of Israel*. May 9, 2018. https://www.timesofisrael.com/pro-palestinian-us-students-slam-muslim-chaplain-for-defending-campus-hillel/.

Rankin, Kenrya. "Watch the UN speech that got Marc Lamont Hill fired from CNN." *Colorlines*. November 30, 2018. https://www.colorlines.com/articles/watch-un-speech-got

-marc-lamont-hill-fired-cnn.

Redden, Elizabeth. "Faculty vote to end Israel study abroad." *Inside Higher Ed*. November 28, 2018. https://www.insidehighered.com/news/2018/11/28/pitzer-faculty-vote-suspend-study-abroad-program-israel.

Richman, Jackson. "New course at Tufts University advances Palestinian narrative, while shelving the Jews." *Jewish News Syndicate (JNS)*. August 15, 2018. https://www.jns.org/new-course-at-tufts-university-advances-palestinian-narrative-while-shelving-the-jews/.

———. "Pitzer College faculty votes to end study abroad in Israel, student government resists." *Jewish News Syndicate*. November 27, 2018. https://www.jns.org/pitzer-college-faculty-votes-to-end-study-abroad-in-israel-student-government-resists/.

Sales, Ben. "Columbia students hold anti-Israel demonstration opposite Holocaust commemoration booth." *Jewish Telegraphic Agency (JTA)*. April 12, 2018. https://www.jta.org/2018/04/12/top-headlines/columbia-students-hold-anti-israel-demonstration-opposite-holocaust-commemoration-booth.

Scham, Paul. "The Palestinians Won the 2017 Battle for Temple Mount. That's Good for Israel." *Ha'aretz*. August 2, 2017.

Sharon, Jeremy. "Bennett slams University of Michigan for Netanyahu-Hitler comparison." *Jerusalem Post*. October 9, 2018. https://www.jpost.com/Israel-News/Bennett-slams-Michigan-U-for-Netanyahu-Hitler-comparison-569001.

Shenkar, Miriam. *The Politicization of Israel Studies*. Beersheba: Ben-Gurion University of the Negev Press, 2012.

Silow-Carroll, Andrew. "Jewish students: A blacklist of BDS supporters is hurting our efforts to defend Israel on campus." *Jewish Telegraph Agency (TGA)*. March 23, 2018. https://www.jta.org/2018/04/23/news-opinion/jewish-students-blacklist-bds-supporters-hurting-efforts-defend-israel-campus.

Slagter, Martin. "University of Michigan regents won't divest; oppose Israel sanctions." *MLive*. December 14, 2017. https://www.mlive.com/news/ann-arbor/index.ssf/2017/12/um_regents_decline_to_form_com.html.

Tabon, Amir. "Americans more divided over Israel 'than at any point' in recent history, study finds." *Ha'aretz*. January 23, 2018.

"The 40 Worst Colleges. The Algemeiner's 1st Annual List of the US and Canada's Worst Campuses for Jewish Students." *The Algemeiner*. https://www.algemeiner.com/the-40-worst-colleges-for-jewish-students-2016/.

The Limits of Hostility: Students Report on Antisemitism and Anti-Israel Sentiment at Four US Universities. Waltham, MA: Brandeis University, Steinhardt Social Research Institute, 2017.

Thomas, Alastair. "Foreign Office expresses concern over Abbas Shoah slur." *JC, The Jewish Chronicle*. May 1, 2018. https://www.thejc.com/news/uk-news/foreign-office-expresses-concern-over-abbas-shoah-slur-1.463592.

"US college offers alternative hummus for anti-Israel students" *Times of Israel*. May 3, 2018. https://www.timesofisrael.com/us-college-offers-alternative-hummus-for-anti-israel-students/.

Waxman, Dov. *Trouble in the Tribe: The American Jewish Conflict over Israel*. Princeton: Princeton University Press, 2018.

Wisse, Ruth. "The Functions of Anti-Semitism." *National Affairs* 33 (2017). https://nationalaffairs.com/publications/detail/the-functions-of-anti-semitism.

Chapter Nine

Intersections between Israel Studies and Israel Education

Language-Use and Educational Programming

Shlomit Attias

The purpose of the word is to convey ideas.
When the ideas are grasped, the words are forgotten.

—Chuang Tzu

Titles can convey important information, express ideas, and construct concepts in one or two words. Their condensed language often stimulates interest in their deeper meaning and wider context—inviting inquiries regarding their message and role in framing perceptions. The title "Intersections between Jewish Studies and Israel Studies in the 21st Century,"[1] for example, triggers such interest and questions. The term "intersections" posits Jewish and Israel Studies as distinct fields dealing with different entities that only intersect at a certain time and/or place. Does such a depiction accurately portray the inherently interrelated study of Israeli and Jewish historical, cultural, and political, past and present, experiences? Although they are organized, situated, and named separately, can these fields and their subject matter be fully portrayed in terms of "intersections" rather than, for example, in terms of "interconnections?" What can this word choice say about the language-use in Israel Studies and its role in conceptualizing the field and defining the dynamics with its twin field of Jewish Studies?

Similar questions surfaced following my encounter with the name "Israel Education" in American Jewish discourse, and led me to a long-term and multisited ethnographic journey that followed the use of this new label in

Diaspora Jewish education discourse and programing.[2] Based on this study, the chapter discusses the naming and labeling of Israel-related programs in American Jewish education and the sociocultural and political contexts of this process—highlighting the circular dynamics between political and sociocultural perceptions, conflicts, crisis, and school programing. To that end, it reviews the historical and educational name distinctions of "Jewish" and "Israel"; outlines various names and naming approaches to Israel Education; and points to the naming and dividing of education programs and fields as a means for communicating ideas and shaping perceptions relating but not limited to the classroom environment.[3]

Despite their different realms of operation—Israel Education in Jewish schools and Israel Studies within universities—both fields emerged outside Israel and against the background of Israel-related sociocultural and political conflicts.[4] I argue that in certain perspectives and to some degree (1) their discourse exhibits similar meaning-making processes and involves identity politics; and (2) the complex dynamics between the twin fields of Israel Education and Jewish Education mirrors the complex dynamics between the twin fields of Israel Studies and Jewish Studies. Therefore, I propose looking at Israel Education naming processes and language-use as a way to expand the understanding of Israel Studies' multifaceted language dynamics.

SPLITTING A KINGDOM, DIVIDING A NAME, BIRTHING A NEW CONCEPT

The name distinction between "Israel" and "Jewish" is neither new nor unique to the academic or the educational fields. It is rooted in historical political conflicts and fractions. Following the split of the United Kingdom of Israel into the Kingdom of Judah and the Kingdom of Israel, the terms "Jewish" and "Judaism," both derived from the name "Judah," emerged as distinct from the name "Israel." Though generally referring to one people with one history, both names evolved in modern social, cultural, and political discourse as labels for differentiating between, among other things, religious and secular life and identities.

With European secularization and nationalism, and the subsequent partial emancipation of Jews into these societies at the end of the eighteenth century, conceptions of innate Jewish nationhood and religious unity were challenged and contested by ideologies and actions of new Jewish movements such as the *Haskalah* and later political and social Zionism.[5] As their historical religious-national identity began uncoupling, new national movements and religious denominations emerged, and different Jewish affiliations were formed, European Jewish communities faced their own religious-national crisis—a sociocultural and political revolution with continued impacts on the Jewish world today.[6] The attempts to differentiate between the religious and national aspects of Jewish existence versus the desire to preserve their unity have been at the core of debates identified and labeled as "the old Jew versus the new Jew," "Zionists versus anti-Zionists," "religious versus secular," "the Land of Israel versus the State of Israel," and lately, "Diaspora Jews versus Israeli Jews." I submit that the twin issues and names of Israel Studies versus Jewish Studies and Israel Education versus Jewish Education emerge as an extension of these disputes and discourse.

POLITICAL CRISES AND EDUCATIONAL PROGRAMMING

With the establishment of the State of Israel and the formation of its religious and general public-school systems, pedagogies of traditional and modern texts such as Bible and Hebrew literature, for example, were generally identified as religious and Hebrew studies.[7] Likewise, the pedagogy of modern Israel in Diaspora schools, albeit limited in scope and depth, remained largely part of Jewish and Hebrew studies.[8] The use of the terms "Jewish" and "Israel" to denote different programs in both education systems appears in connection to the discovery of major knowledge deficiencies of traditional studies among Jewish students in Israeli nonreligious schools and of modern Israel studies among American Jewish students. Debates regarding such deficiencies and their proper educational treatment reveal strong ties between these educational awakenings, the presence of sociocultural conflicts and political crises, and the development and naming of new school programs. For example, attention to the inadequate Jewish Studies in Israeli general public schools intensified as the status quo between religious and secular Israeli Jews changed and sociopolitical conflicts increased during the 1980s.[9] Attempts to resolve the knowledge deficiencies found in such schools led to a series of institutional actions such as the 1994 Shenhar Committee Report,[10] the opening of the Shenhar Headquarter in 1999 for implementing the committee's recommendations,[11] the development and naming of special Jewish curriculum for nonreligious schools and teacher training programs to enhance Jewish Studies pedagogy.[12] Yet, a wider and more intense interest in traditional Jewish Studies gained momentum in both the education system and the general public after the assassination of Prime Minister Yitzhak Rabin in 1995.[13]

The inadequate modern Israel pedagogy in American Jewish schools, though known to the education establishment, has been widely recognized and addressed especially in times of political crises. For example, following the 2000 Intifada in Israel, the 2001 UN World Conference Against Racism in Durban, South Africa, and the 9-11 terror attacks in the United States, Israel was blamed for the Intifada, Zionism was equated with racism, and

Jews were accused of being behind the 9-11 terror attacks.[14] These devastating events and their anti-Jewish outcomes throughout the United States, particularly the spread of belligerent anti-Israel protests and anti-Jewish expressions on campuses, shook the American Jewish communities and brought to the fore the status of their Jewish school education.[15] According to informants in my ethnographic study, the intensified anti-Jewish and anti-Israel demonstrations and their personal nature, as they often included personal assaults directed at Jewish students, placed the students in a defensive and reactive mode. In their efforts to respond to anti-Israel accusations, they realized they knew little to nothing about Zionism and modern Israeli history. This discovery, and the need to help them cope with their new hostile environment, brought their families, communities, and various American Jewish organizations to urgently develop informative programs on the Arab-Israel conflicts in order to prepare them to constructively respond to anti-Israel accusations. These early responsive programs were titled Israel Advocacy and served both college and high school Jewish students.[16] However, the growing professional and community debates regarding the educational goals and values of such programs led to their modification and renaming as Israel Education. This modified program soon evolved into a full-scale new pedagogic field named Israel Education.[17] The name and program distinction between Israel and Jewish education appeared for the first time in Diaspora schools.[18] Although the new field intended to address students' weakness in modern Israel Studies and provide a more cohesive Jewish education, the process of developing, naming, organizing, and teaching modern Israel content separately from Jewish curriculum involved dividing rather than consolidating Jewish education in Diaspora schools and polarizing rather than unifying its related professional and community discourse.[19]

Being rooted in educational crisis management and identity politics, the new field of Israel Education has been involved, from its inception, in meaning-making processes. Its naming practices, content development, professional discourses, community debates, and support received from various funding organizations—all illuminate the complex place and shifting role of Israel in American Jewish life and identity, stress the growing cultural-political distinction between "Jewish" and "Israel," raise questions about American Jews' relations with Israel, and reveal changes in these areas that extend beyond school confines.[20]

The development of a special curriculum as a means for coping and responding to local crises underlines the interrelation between sociopolitical conflicts and school programming. In his analysis of ideologies and educational processes, Michael Apple discusses the political background and media coverage of the 9-11 terror attacks and their role in the politicization process of American schools.[21] Following his arguments in this context, I claim that understanding the impacts of sociopolitical conflicts and crises on the developing and naming of Israel Education as a new pedagogic field cannot be achieved "without an understanding of the ways in which the global is dynamically linked to the local," or realized without analyzing the reaction and approach of its developers and practitioners to such situations, since their response "may create dynamics that have long-lasting consequences" on this field and its educational contents and messages.[22]

CONSTRUCTING NAMES, FORMING PERCEPTIONS, DEFINING IDENTITIES

Giving a distinctive name to a crisis-response program or field emphasizes the importance of naming in communicating both educational and political messages. Inquiries into the relationships between titles and their messages, or between naming processes and educational practices, afford insights into the broader sociocultural and political realities.[23] Ethnographic observations of language-use in schools and communities point to naming practices as a mode of highlighting, promoting, and communicating sociocultural and educational behavior and ideas.[24] According to scholars in Culture and Communication Studies, even the "construction of our own identities and the identities of others are closely tied with the naming and the labeling process."[25] In addition to shaping social concepts and articulating personal ideas, culture and communication scholars further stress that naming and names provide "insights both into patterns of cultural practice and into processes of cultural change," and "convey a great deal of information" about socio-cultural realities.[26] The following observation illustrates the use of program names and naming as a banner of school program and policy changes.

When presenting the newly restructured library website to the school faculty, the school librarian pointed out that the tab named Jewish Studies had been renamed Judaic Studies. With a baffled look the non-Jewish librarian noted: "I have been working here many years, it was always Jewish Studies. . . . I don't know what [Judaic Studies] means."[27] When I later inquired about this name change, the new Jewish Studies coordinator explained it as such: "[the name/title] Jewish Studies is more informal, and Judaic Studies has more of an academic tone," and added: "We [Jewish Studies teachers] wanted to make Jewish Studies more academic so we gave it an academic name . . . Judaic Studies."[28] The coordinator noted that the new curriculum was still in its developing stages and far from being complete but emphasized that it was not significantly different in its content than the previous Jewish Studies course. Apparently, since no drastic changes were planned for the course, the process of giving it a new name and announcing it to the school community before completing its modification was intended to express the school's new approach to Jewish Studies, change the "old image" of the department, and construct its "new image" as an academic field. By saying, "We wanted to make Jewish Studies more academic so we gave it an academic name," the coordinator underlined the centrality of the new name in formulating the changes they wanted to introduce, first to themselves and then to others. In other words, Jewish Studies teachers initiated a name change as a tool for shaping and communicating their department's new direction not only to the school faculty but also, if not primarily, to themselves. Accordingly, this renaming process appears to have had a dual function: (1) helping teachers shape their own view of the department's new identity; and (2) guiding others in grasping the new identity and direction of the old field.

A similar name-change process as a means for informing the teachers of a new policy was practiced again in the same school later that year. During the end-of-year faculty meeting, the principal announced in a more direct and clear fashion: "Next year we are changing the titles of our heads of faculties because we want to change [their] role. We are going to call [them] 'Department Leaders' because we are expecting them to lead the teachers in their professional needs."[29] Here, too, titles and names were selected and introduced as a means for communicating and constructing the school's new policies. In both cases, the school invested the names with the power to lead the efforts in structuring the substance and defining the meaning of the new programs, and in shaping their educational perceptions and framing their professional and general discourse.

Naming appears as a multidimensional process functioning simultaneously on several levels and serving a number of functions. It enables those creating and using the names, titles, and labels to internally and externally express, construct, and transform ideas, identities, and contents. According to Ting-Toomey, this process acts in a reciprocal way. In the process of developing personal identity, for example, she observes that "individuals construct their identities through 'naming,' and in turn their naming and labeling process shapes how they view themselves and others."[30] In this sense, naming educational programs and academic fields can shape and be shaped by the personal and professional approaches of both their developers and their practitioners, by their sociocultural and political realities and understanding, and by the program development process itself. This process is best exemplified by Israel Education naming and name transformation as I observed in my fieldwork and was expressed by Jewish educators involved in its pedagogy and in making and promoting it as a field.

Israel Advocacy

In their early form, Israel Education programs were viewed, functioned, and named as Israel Advocacy activities. As the boundaries between education and advocacy became blurry, and criticism about mixing these activities grew, their names and contents became critical in the decision-making of several American Jewish organizations invested in these programs. A representative of one such organization explained that following the experience of a family member with Anti-Israel activities, and in response to the rapidly growing anti-Israel activism on American campuses, they got involved in the developing and funding of Israel Advocacy programs in order to "prepare Jewish students to defend Israel." However, when the students appeared illiterate with regard to modern Israeli history and society during Israel Advocacy activities, and their Jewish identity and connection to Israel seemed weak, the organization decided to develop a new program to address these aspects. It named the program Israel Education. Yet, my informant explained that even though the new program dealt with modern Israeli history and society, its main purpose was to "acculturate . . . Jewish young people with the understanding that Israel is a key part of their Jewish identity." In other words, once it shifted its educational efforts from defending Israel to bolstering American Jewish identity, the organization found the name Israel Advocacy irrelevant for communicating its program changes and for transforming its new goals. Accordingly, the program development process led to a name change in order to: (1) express the organization's new plan to focus on Jewish identity formation and strengthening Jewish-Israel connection, and (2) distinguish it from its continued advocacy activities on the campuses. The organization used names to distinguish between the various Israel projects and as a way to express their different goals and to define their target audience: Israel Advocacy indicates its political "defense" programs for Jewish college students; Israel Education names its educational efforts in cultivating Jewish identity and connection with Israel among high school students; finally Israel Studies labels its support of contemporary Israel academic research.

Israel Engagement

For Adam, a veteran Jewish educator who has been involved in multiple Israel Education initiatives in various agencies, titles and name-choices of educational programs hold a key for understanding and expressing broader issues. Therefore, he claims that understanding the name "Israel Education" is critical for understanding the larger American Jewish education discourse. In his view, the use of both labels, "Israel Education" and "Jewish Education," fail to describe what he believes the education of Israel and Judaism ought to be—an experiential endeavor embodying Jewish identity, Jewish connection with Israel, and strong relationships between Israeli Jews and American Jews. Instead he suggests the name "Israel Engagement" and explains that his name choice as such: "means getting more intimate with Israel through trips, learning and experiences . . . [it offers] additional levels of engagement that education itself would not do." Adam understands the word "education" to mean school-confined academic work. Thus, he finds "Israel Education" an inadequate name for expressing, shaping, or actualizing Jewish identity or stimulating relations with Israel in a significant way. Since he attributes to names and titles the important role of expressing ideas and framing conceptions, he uses "Israel Engagement" as a more suitable name for his Israel-related programming and activities. "Israel Engagement" became the label of predominantly informal Israel programming.

Israel Peoplehood

A representative of another organization involved in the funding and developing of Israel-related programs informed me that they no longer use the name "Israel Education" in their Israel programs. Apparently, their field experience during Israel Education programming brought to the fore the need to strengthen Jewish identity and led the organization to re-evaluate and reframe its goals for Israel school programs. In this process, they found that the name "Israel Education" no longer expressed how they view their Israel programming, what they do or want to do in this field. Therefore, they renamed their Israel Education project "Jewish Peoplehood." The representative explained that rather than "just [to the] teaching about Israel," as they understand the name Israel Education to imply, this new name intends to reflect the organization's revised approach and promote a worldwide Jewish identity education. To that end they find Jewish peoplehood a more suitable name for highlighting their educational conception and practice vis-à-vis Israel.

The term "Jewish Peoplehood," introduced by Mordechai Kaplan, an American Rabbi and founder of the Reconstructionist Movement, as an alternative term for Jewish nationalism, has been used in a broad range of cultural, educational, and political discussions relating to topics such as Zionism, Jewish religion versus nationhood, and Israel-Diaspora relations.[31] However, since its revival in Jewish discourse, particularly in connection with and as an alternative to the title "Israel Education," this name has evolved, as did "Israel Education," into a new title for discussing and shaping Jewish education, identity, continuity, and relationships. The invigorated "Jewish Peoplehood" debates and wave of studies,[32] aided by philanthropic support and the opening of new centers under this name,[33] helped further disseminate and develop this concept. In this process, Jewish Peoplehood Education serves as a newly termed field bridging Jewish Education and Israel Education.[34] As an outgrowth of the Israel Education project and Jewish identity debates, Jewish Peoplehood Education adds another dimension to the understanding of Israel Education, naming, language-use, and dynamics.

The naming and labeling processes of Israel Education empower Jewish educators to construct, express, and classify their Israel pedagogy approaches and practices and at the same time help them shape their personal views of Israel. The reciprocity between naming, name developers, and name users, serves as a framework through which to examine the ways discipline and program naming and labeling influence and are influenced by professional and personal conceptions.

LANGUAGE CREATES SUBSTANCE— NAMING DEFINES SUBSTANCE

Despite past debates regarding the place of modern Israel in Diaspora Jewish schools, Israel pedagogy in such schools has remained largely part of Jewish education departments and is still entrenched in the teaching of Jewish history and culture. Yet, education discourses regarding global anti-Israel activism and its impact on Jewish sociopolitical local reality, critique of Israeli policies in academia and the media, and the rise of local and global anti-Semitic expressions, appear to generate either a decline or a revival of the role of Israel in Diaspora Jewish education systems.

The processes of naming, packaging, branding, and marketing Israel pedagogy as Israel Education help to set Israel Education apart from Jewish Education and turn it into an exclusive new discipline that is not an intrinsic part of Jewish Education.[35] Debbie, a Jewish high-school teacher heading the Israel Education program in her school, articulated this conceptual shift during our interview regarding Israel Education and its place in her teaching. When speaking of Israel Education programs in her school, Debbie focused entirely on Middle East politics and its role in this program. She explained that she views Israel Education as Israel Studies and emphasized the changes she implemented accordingly in this field. Debbie explained her motives for reorganizing and renaming the school's Israel Education program as follows:

> History of Israel is not a Jewish thing. Everybody thinks [it] is a Jewish subject, but it is not. . . . Israel is not necessarily a Jewish subject, even though it is important to us. . . . Israel history does not need to be part of Judaic [studies] . . . , moving this class to the History Department is my major achievement.[36]

As we use words to create substance and names to shape conceptual frames, in practice our language-use, naming, labeling, and titling express how we view and define the value of the object we name. In that way, we "create the phenomena that we name, [and] imperceptibly shap[e] . . . the experiences we recall."[37] The various name choices and transformation of Israel Education embody this reciprocal process in three ways: firstly, by reflecting the political changes in the American Jewish environment, then by reshaping their cultural and educational orientations toward Israel, and, lastly, by reframing their perception of Jewish identity. In that, the name/title of Israel Education becomes not only an expression of change but also an active agent of change. As a discursive process, during which "meanings change as we think about them; statements. . . events . . . and interpretations can mean different things to different people at different times," Israel Education programming and naming continue to develop and adjust according to local sociopolitical realities, cultural values, personal needs, and Israel-Diaspora relational dynamics.[38] Indeed, since its early appearance in the American Jewish Education system, this socially, culturally, and politically sensitive field has been constantly changing and being changed by Jewish policy makers, program developers, and practitioners, all of whom are observers and active participants in the broader Jewish and global sociopolitical changing realities.

The naming and renaming of Israel Education as I observed it in the American and Australian Jewish education systems affords a wider view of the context behind the emergence of this discipline and the shifts in it over time. One can glean certain narratives from the names and the changes they underwent. Regardless of the variations in the naming practices, the names of Israel Education tell the evolutionary story of this field, as it evolves from a local American Jewish instructional program to an acculturating project, and finally to a new global Jewish education field. As its focus moved from advocating for Israel to strengthening Diaspora Jewish identity, and then to promoting universal Jewish Peoplehood, Israel Education embodies the transformation of Diaspora Jewish pedagogy of Israel, its relationships with the Jewish state, and its Jewish self-perception and identity. In this shift, words, actions, and a sense of reality are inseparable in shaping this discourse. I argue that the manner in which Israel Education naming has unfolded is not arbitrary—it is symbolic and reflective of Diaspora Jewish realities and conflicts in and outside the school environment. In the words of Abe, a veteran Jewish educator and director of various Jewish and Israel programming: "Israel Education is actually a new fantasy of the American Jewish community [which is] constantly dealing with and trying to address the Israel question."[39] Abe uses the phrase "the Israel question," to echo the infamous phrase "the Jewish question" and proposes that the new Israel Education project, designed by and for the American Jewish community, serves as an attempted solution to its ongoing debates regarding the cultural and political place of Israel in Diaspora Jewish community life. His view of Israel Education illustrates yet another understanding of this program and presents a wider spectrum upon which this term rests in the American Jewish collective. Indeed, as my study demonstrates, the emergence and circulation of Israel Education naming and programming reflect the context of Jewish sociocultural and political shared experiences across time and space.[40]

CONCLUSIONS

Naming processes and the actual names and titles of programs, disciplines, and departments serve as windows through which to view the development and function of such organizations. In their role as program administrators responsible also for naming programs and centers, Armstrong and Fontaine observed that "as we use language to name, order, and codify the world, we both alter and create perceptions."[41] Accordingly, they assert that "the actual impact of our acts of naming may be much greater than we have imagined."[42]

My interest in the emerging new name of Israel Education, and my subsequent ethnographic inquiry of its meaning, use, and role, took me to multiple Diaspora Jewish schools, professional workshops, academic conferences, and community gatherings—where I observed and spoke with teachers, program directors, curriculum writers, school principals, community leaders, and representatives of various organizations. Their stories, experiences, views and conceptions of this name and program made it clear that "Israel Education" is more than a label or a program; it holds a key for revealing the wider sociopolitical reality of Diaspora Jewish life and for understanding the nuanced cultural layers of Israel-Diaspora relations. Tracing Israel Education language-use and naming helped find and understand the ties between cultural conflicts and sociopolitical crises and their role as catalysts for education reevaluation and program development. The development of Israel Education as a distinct field apart from Jewish and Hebrew studies in American Jewish schools involves identity politics and points to the shifting place of Israel in this Jewish society and its education systems.

I argue that the contemporary name distinctions and field divisions between Jewish and Israel Studies—are rooted in political crises, are shaped by political decisions, and serve Diaspora Jews as a mechanism for coping with internal, external, local, and global sociopolitical and cultural conflicts.[43] In his article titled "Anti-Semitism and the Birth of Jewish Studies," Robert Rockaway tells the story of the emergence of Israel Studies in the United States. He describes internal Jewish identity conflicts and claims that anti-Semitism gave birth to this field.[44] The emergence of Israel Studies in American universities also appears to be rooted in politicization processes of academia and in Jewish cultural and identity shifts: "the conceptualization of an educational space for Israel Studies is connected to shifting identities."[45]

Once expressed, words have an independent power not only to reflect on realities but also to form understandings and shape perceptions. As such we may ask, what does the term "intersections" want us to understand or think of Israel and Jewish Studies? An analysis of the language-use in these fields can illuminate their complex dynamic and clarify some of the differences and similarities with respect not only to their academic activities but also to their wider political-cultural discourse. Such an academic exploration may position the term "intersections" in a sharper perspective with regard to the establishment of Israel Studies as a distinct academic discipline apart from Jewish Studies; and the growing discourse that sees the Jewish and the Israeli as separated entities.

NOTES

1. The title of the conference at Gratz University, June 2018, upon which the present volume is based.
2. The fieldwork includes nearly five hundred hours of observations in the United States, Australia, and Israel, over forty hours of interviews, and thirty-nine questionnaires of Israel Education workshop participants.
3. Parts of this chapter appeared in my article within the *Journal of Jewish Education* in 2015.
4. See Miriam Shenkar, *The Politicization of Israel Studies* (Israel: Ben-Gurion University of the Negev Press, 2012); Shlomit Attias, "What's in a Name? In Pursuit of Israel Eduction," *Journal of Jewish Education* 81, no. 2 (2015): 101–35.
5. Jacob Katz, *Out of the Ghetto: The Social Background of Jewish Emancipation, 1770–1870* (Syracuse, Syracuse University Press, 1973); Shmuel Ettinger, "The Modern Period," in *A History of the Jewish People*, vol. 6. H. H. Ben-Sasson (ed.) (Cambridge: Harvard University Press, 1976), 727–1074.
6. See Oz Almog, *The Sabra—A Profile* (Tel Aviv: Am Oved Publishers Ltd., 2001); Eva Etzioni-Halevy, *The Divided People: Can Israel's Breakup Be Stopped?* (Lanham: Lexington Books, 2002); Alan Zuckerman and Calvin Goldscheider, *The Transformation of the Jews* (Chicago: University of Chicago Press, 1985); Yoram Hazony, *The Jewish State: The Struggle for Israel's Soul* (New York, Basic Books, 2000); David Hartman, *Israelis and the Jewish Tradition, An Ancient People Debating Its Future* (New Haven: Yale University Press, 2002); Simon Herman, *Israelis and Jews: The Continuity of an Identity* (New York: Random House, 1970); Ehud Luz, *Parallels Meet: Religion and Nationalism in the Early Zionist Movement (1882–1904)* (Philadelphia: Jewish Publication Society, 1988); R. Rosenthal (ed.), *The Inner Split: Judaism Here and Now* (Tel Aviv: Miskal, 2001); Robert Seltzer, *Jewish People, Jewish Thought: The Jewish Experience in History* (New York: Macmillan, 1980).
7. Tzvi Tzameret, *Alei Gesher Tzar (Across a Narrow Bridge: Shaping the Educational System during the Great Aliya)* (Beer-Sheva, 1997) [Hebrew]; *Yisrael Ba'asor Hrishon (Israel in the First Decade: The Development of the Education System)* (Tel-Aviv: The Open University Publishing, 2003).
8. Walter Ackerman, "Israel in American Jewish Education," in *Envisioning Israel*, G. Alon (ed.), (Jerusalem: Magnes, 1996), 173–90; Samuel Blumenfield, "Israel and Jewish Education in the Diaspora," *Journal of Jewish Education* 38, no. 4: (1968): 25–30; Barry Chazan, "Israel in American Jewish Schools in the Mid-70s," *Journal of Jewish Education* 52, no. 4 (1984): 9–12.
9. With the increase of ultraorthodox political representations in the Knesset (the Israeli parliament) and the rising number of releases from Army duties issued to religious men, conflicts between religious and secular Israeli Jews intensified and sharpened the disputes over Jewish identity. These developments also enhanced interest in Jewish education and led to the increase in Jewish programming in the school system and the general public.

10. A special committee convened by the Ministry of Education and chaired by Professor Aliza Shenhar studied the problems of Jewish education in public schools. Their report revealed that knowledge of Jewish laws and tradition among Jewish students attending secular schools was either minimal or nonexistent.

11. Report on the status of Jewish Studies in Israeli nonreligious schools, the Department of Education [Hebrew]. https://www.knesset.gov.il/mmm/data/pdf/m02465.pdf.

12. In 1996 the Shalom Hartman Institute created the Israeli Teacher Training Program (ITT). It aims at influencing the implementation of Judaic Studies at all levels of Israeli public schools through teachers' education. See their website: www.hartmaninstitue.com.

13. A. Gov, "Hiloni Ka-halachah" [A Secular Jew], *Anu Hayehudim Ha-hilonyeem* [We Secular Jews], Dedi Zucker (ed.) (Tel Aviv: Miscal Publishing, 1999), 43.

14. Such accusations were not limited to the Arab media. European, and some American news agencies, repeatedly made such references either directly or by reporting on those making such claims. Among the myriad of media and web references see Hillel Halkin, "The Return to Antisemitism," *Wall Street Journal*, February 5, 2002, www.opinionjournal.com/extra; also Andrew Sullivan, "Spreading the Greater Lie about Israel," *The London Times*, December 23, 2001, www.likud.nl/press122.html. On the issue of Zionism-Racism, see www.ngo-monitor.org; www.inminds.com/durban-conference.html; www.christianactionforisrael.org/un/durban.html. On 9-11, see www.whatreallyhappend.com/spying.html; www.whatreallyhappend.com/9-11BasicQuestions; www.rense.com/general44/those.html.

15. A media watch organization, HonestReporting, was launched during that time in order to fight media misrepresentation and fake news relating to the Middle East conflicts and other Jewish and Israel issues. See www.honestreporting.com. See for instance, "Israel did it again," October 15, 2002, a response to an article accusing Israel of being behind the sniper killing in the Washington, DC area. The Simon Wiesenthal Center, an international Jewish human rights organization, provides a regular report on anti-Semitic acts. These updates include also information about the Center's educational and political activism around the world against anti-Semitism. See the Simon Wiesenthal Center website www.wiesenthal.com.

16. R. Neuwirth and C. Suvall, "IKAR: Israel Knowledge, Advocacy and Responsibility," *Agenda: Jewish Education Israel Education* 18 (2004): 39–40.

17. See Karen A. Gerber and Aliza Mazor, "Mapping Israel Education: An Overview of Trends and Issues in North America (Research)," Gilo Family Foundation (2003); Bethamie Horowitz, "Defining Israel education. (Research paper)," *iCenter* (2012); Attias, "What's in a Name?"

18. The earliest mention of the term Israel Education is found in the title of a booklet written in 1997 by Elan Ezrachi and Barbara Sutnick, *Israel Education through Encounters with Israelis*, which was part of the project "Israel in Our Life."

19. Attias, "What's in a Name?"

20. Yonatan Ariel, "Building Community Momentum for Israel Education" *Makom: Renewing Israel Engagement* (2006); "Agenda: Jewish Education," *Israel Education* (2004): 18; Lisa D. Grant, "A Vision for Israel Education," paper presented at the Network for Research in Jewish Education Conference, June 2008; Lisa D. Grant, "Sacred Vision, Complex Reality: Navigating the Tensions in Israel Education," Jewish Educational Leadership. Lookstein Center for Jewish Education (2008): 1–13; Lisa D. Grant, Daniel Marom, and Yehudit Werchow, "Israel Education for What? An Investigation of the Purposes and Possible Outcomes of Israel Education," *Israel Education Research Briefs* (2012); A. Pompson and Daniel Held, "Why Israel? Re-viewing Israel Education through the Lenses of Civic and Political Engagement," *Journal of Jewish Education* 78, no. 2 (2012): 97–113.

21. Michael W. Apple, *Ideology and Curriculum*, 3rd ed. (New York: RoutledgeFalmer, 2004).

22. Apple, *Ideology*, 170.

23. S. Weitman, "Personal Names as Cultural Indicators: Trends in the National Identities of Israelis, 1882–1980," in *Perspectives on Culture and Society in Israel*, N. Gertz (ed.) (Tel Aviv: The Open University, 1988), 141–51, [Hebrew]; J. Gerhards, *The Name Game: Cultural Modernization and First Names* (New Brunswick, NJ: Transaction, 2005).

24. Shirley Brice Heath, *Ways with Words* (New York: Cambridge University Press, 1983).

25. Stella Ting-Toomey, *Communicating across Cultures* (New York: Guilford, 1999), 92.

26. Shoshana Blum-Kulka and Tamar Katriel, "Nicknaming practices in families," in *Cross-Cultural Interpersonal Communication*, S. Ting-Toomey and F. Korzenny (eds.) (Thousand Oaks, CA: Sage, 1991), 59–60.

27. Field notes, January 31, 2013.

28. Field notes, February 1, 2013.

29. Field notes, November 4, 2013.

30. Ting-Toomey, *Communicating across cultures*, 92.

31. On Kaplan, see Aryeh Cohen, "Jewish Peoplehood: Why?" *The Peoplehood Papers* 5 (2010): 5–7; see also Peter Y. Medding, "A Contemporary Paradox: Israel and Jewish Peoplehood," *Forum: On the Jewish People, Zionism, and Israel. World Zionist Organization* (1977): 5–16; Arthur I. Waskow, "The Future of Jewish Peoplehood," *Forum: On the Jewish People, Zionism, and Israel. World Zionist Organization* (1978): 109–24; Gary Rubin, *Peoplehood and Pluralism: Relations between American Jews and Israel* (New York: American Jewish Committee, 1988); Leonard Fein, "Notes on Re-imagining Jewish Peoplehood, June 7, 1993." http://www.bjpa.org/Publications/details.cfm?PublicationID=16165.

32. A search of the title Jewish Peoplehood in the BJPA website yields a veritable sea of articles published since 2007.

33. Such as, the Koret-Taube Peoplehood initiative and the Center for Jewish Peoplehood and Education in Jerusalem. See http://www.koretfoundation.org/publications/pdf/catalyst_winter_10.pdf; see also http://jpeoplehood.org/contact-us/.

34. See Elan Ezrachi, "Jerusalem as a Metaphor for Jewish Peoplehood," *The Peoplehood Papers* 3 (2008): 14–15; Barry Chazan, Richard Juran, and Michael B. Soberman, "The Connection of Israel Education to Jewish Peoplehood," *Israel Education Research Briefs*. (2013).

35. See "Mapping the Landscape: The Emerging Field of Israel Education. (Research paper)." *iCenter for Israel Education*. (2011); Horowitz, "Defining Israel Education. (Research paper)."

36. Field notes, February 1, 2011.

37. Cherryl Armstrong and Sheryl Fontaine, "The Power of Naming: Names That Create and Define the Discipline," *WPA: Writing Program Administration* 13, no. 1–2 (1989): 5–14, 8.

38. Ann E. Berthhoff, *The Making of Meaning* (Montclair, NJ: Boynton/Cook, 1981), 71.

39. Field notes, book #2, March 3, 2008.

40. G. Marcus, "Ethnography in/of World System: The Emergence of Multi-sited Ethnography," *Annual Review of Anthropology* 24 (1995): 95–117.

41. Armstrong and Fontaine, "The Power of Naming," 7.

42. Armstrong and Fontaine, "The Power of Naming," 5.

43. See Attias, "What's in a Name?"

44. Robert Rockaway, "Anti-Semetism and the Birth of Jewish Studies," *Tablet*, October 18, 2018.

45. Shenkar, *The Politicization of Israel Studies*, 16.

BIBLIOGRAPHY

Ackerman, Walter. "Israel in American Jewish Education." In *Envisioning Israel*, edited by G. Alon, 173–90. Jerusalem: Magnes, 1996.

"Agenda: Jewish Education." *Israel Education* (2004): 18.

Almog, Oz. *The Sabra—A Profile*. Tel Aviv: Am Oved Publishers Ltd., 2001.

Apple, Michael W. *Ideology and Curriculum*. 3rd ed. New York: RoutledgeFalmer, 2004.

Ariel, Yonatan. "Building Community Momentum for Israel Education." *Makom: Renewing Israel Engagement*. (2006). http://www.bjpa.org/Publications/details.cfm?PublicationID=6096.

Ariel, Yonatan. "Educating about Israel and Jewish Peoplehood: Murmurings on a Field in Formation." *The Peoplehood Papers* 5 (2010): 40–41. http://www.bjpa.org/Publications/details.cfm?PublicationID=11792

Armstrong, Cherryl, and Sheryl Fontaine. " The Power of Naming: Names That Create and Define the Discipline." *WPA: Writing Program Administration* 13, no. 1–2 (1989): 5–14. http://wpacouncil.org/archives/13n1-2/13n1-2armstrong.pdf
Attias, Shlomit. "What's In A Name? In Pursuit of Israel Eduction." *Journal of Jewish Education* 81, no. 2 (2015): 101–35.
Berthhoff, Ann E. *The Making of Meaning*. Montclair, NJ: Boynton/Cook, 1981.
Blumenfield, Samuel. "Israel and Jewish Education in the Diaspora." *Journal of Jewish Education* 38, no. 4: (1968): 25–30.
Blum-Kulka, Shoshana, and Tamar Katriel. "Nicknaming Practices in Families." In *Cross-Cultural Interpersonal Communication*, edited by S. Ting-Toomey and F. Korzenny, 58–76. Thousand Oaks, CA: Sage, 1991.
Brice Heath, Shirley. *Ways with Words*. New York: Cambridge University Press, 1983.
Chazan, Barry. "Israel in American Jewish Schools in the Mid-70s." *Journal of Jewish Education* 52, no. 4 (1984): 9–12.
Chazan, Barry, Richard Juran, and Michael B. Soberman. "The Connection of Israel Education to Jewish Peoplehood." *Israel Education Research Briefs*. (2013). http://www.bjpa.org/Publications/details.cfm?PublicationID=20975.
Cohen, Aryeh. "Jewish Peoplehood: Why?" *The Peoplehood Papers* 5 (2010): 5–7. http://www.bjpa.org/Publications/details.cfm?PublicationID=11788.
Cohen, Shari. "Naming and Framing." *CLAL Politics and Policy Archive*. (2001). http://www.bjpa.org/Publications/details.cfm?PublicationID=2425.
Elboim-Dror, Rachel. *Hebrew Education in Palestine 1914–1920*. Vol. 2. Jerusalem: Yad Izhak Ben-Zvi, 1990. [Hebrew]
Ettinger, Shmuel. "The Modern Period." In *A History of the Jewish People*, Vol. 6, edited by H. H. Ben-Sasson, 727–1074. Cambridge: Harvard University Press, 1976.
Etzioni-Halevy, Eva. *The Divided People*. Tel Aviv: Aryeh Nir Publishers Ltd., 2000.
Etzioni-Halevy, Eva. *The Divided People: Can Israel's Breakup be Stopped?* Lanham: Lexington Books, 2002.
Ezrachi, Elan. "Jerusalem as a Metaphor for Jewish Peoplehood." *The Peoplehood Papers* 3 (2008): 14–15. http://www.bjpa.org/Publications/details.cfm?PublicationID=11738.
Fein, Leonard. "Notes on Re-imagining Jewish Peoplehood, June 7, 1993." http://www.bjpa.org/Publications/details.cfm?PublicationID=16165.
Gerber, Karen A., and Aliza Mazor. "Mapping Israel Education: An Overview of Trends and Issues in North America, (Research)." Gilo Family Foundation (2003). http://www.bjpa.org/Publications/details.cfm?PublicationID=5982.
Gerhards, J. The Name Game: Cultural Modernization and First Names. New Brunswick, NJ: Transaction, 2005.
Gov, A. "Hiloni Ka-halachah" [A Secular Jew]. *Anu Hayehudim Ha-hilonyeem* [We Secular Jews], edited by Dedi Zucker, 40–46. Tel Aviv: Miscal Publishing, 1999.
Grant, Lisa D. "Sacred Vision, Complex Reality: Navigating the Tensions in Israel Education." *Jewish Educational Leadership*. Lookstein Center for Jewish Education (2008): 1–13. http://www.bjpa.org/Publications/details.cfm?PublicationID=4808.
Grant, Lisa D. (2009). A Vision for Israel Education. Paper Presented at the Network for Research in Jewish Education Conference, June 2008. http://www.bjpa.org/Publications/details.cfm?PublicationID=20968.
Grant, Lisa D., Daniel Marom, and Yehudit Werchow. "Israel Education for What? An Investigation of the Purposes and Possible Outcomes of Israel Education." *Israel Education Research Briefs* (2012). http://www.bjpa.org/Publications/details.cfm?PublicationID=20971.
Halkin, Hillel. "The Return to Antisemitism." *Wall Street Journal*. February 5, 2002.
Hartman, David. *Israelis and the Jewish Tradition, An Ancient People Debating Its Future*. New Haven: Yale University Press, 2002.
Hazony, Yoram. *The Jewish State: The Struggle for Israel's Soul*. New York, Basic Books, 2000.
Herman, Simon. *Israelis and Jews: The Continuity of an Identity*. New York: Random House, 1970.

Horowitz, Bethamie. "Defining Israel Education (Research paper)." iCenter (2012). http://jimjosephfoundation.org/wp-content/uploads/2012/01/iCenter_Bethamie.pdf.
Katz, Jacob. *Out of the Ghetto: The Social Background of Jewish Emancipation, 1770–1870*. Syracuse, Syracuse University Press, 1973.
Luz, Ehud. *Parallels Meet: Religion and Nationalism in the Early Zionist Movement (1882–1904)*. Philadelphia, Jewish Publication Society, 1988.
"Mapping the Landscape: The Emerging Field of Israel Education. (Research paper)." *Center for Israel Education*. (2011). http://www.theicenter.org/sites/default/files/Mapping%20the%20Field%20of%20Israel%20Education.pdf.
Marcus, G. "Ethnography in/of World System: The Emergence of Multi-sited Ethnography." *Annual Review of Anthropology* 24 (1995): 95–117.
Medding, Peter Y. "A Contemporary Paradox: Israel and Jewish Peoplehood." *Forum: On the Jewish People, Zionism, and Israel*. World Zionist Organization (1977): 5–16. http://www.bjpa.org/Publications/details.cfm?PublicationID=14035.
Neuwirth, R., and C. Suvall "IKAR: Israel Knowledge, Advocacy and Responsibility." *Agenda: Jewish Education Israel Education* 18 (2004): 39–40.
Pompson, A., and Daniel Held. "Why Israel? Re-viewing Israel Education through the Lenses of Civic and Political Engagement." *Journal of Jewish Education* 78, no. 2 (2012): 97–113.
Rockaway, Robert. "Anti-Semetism and the Birth of Jewish Studies." *Tablet*. October 18, 2018. https://www.tabletmag.com/jewish-arts-and-culture/272687/anti-semitism-jewish-studies-1960s.
Rosenthal, R. (ed.) *The Inner Split: Judaism Here and Now*. Tel Aviv: Miskal, 2001.
Rubin, Gary. *Peoplehood and Pluralism: Relations between American Jews and Israel*. New York: American Jewish Committee, 1988. http://www.bjpa.org/Publications/details.cfm?PublicationID=13952.
Seltzer, Robert. *Jewish People, Jewish Thought: The Jewish Experience in History*. New York, Macmillan, 1980.
Shapira, Anita. Ed. *A State in the Making—Israeli Society in the First Decades*. Jerusalem: The Zalman Shazar Center for Jewish History, 2001.
Shenkar, Miriam. *The Politicization of Israel Studies*. Israel: Ben-Gurion University of the Negev Press, 2012.
Sullivan, Andrew. "Spreading the Greater Lie about Israel." *The London Times*. December 23, 2001.
Ting-Toomey, Stella. *Communicating across Cultures*. New York: Guilford, 1999.
Tzameret, Tzvi. *Alei Gesher Tzar (Across a Narrow Bridge: Shaping the Educational System during the Great Aliya)*. Beer-Sheva, 1997. [Hebrew]
Tzameret, Tzvi. *Yisrael Ba'asor Hrishon (Israel in the First Decade: The Development of the Education System)*. Tel-Aviv: The Open University Publishing, 2003.
Waskow, Arthur I. "The Future of Jewish Peoplehood." *Forum: On the Jewish People, Zionism, and Israel*. World Zionist Organization (1978): 109–24. http://www.bjpa.org/Publications/details.cfm?PublicationID=14056
Weitman, S. "Personal Names as Cultural Indicators: Trends in the National Identities of Israelis, 1882–1980." In *Perspectives on Culture and Society in Israel*, edited by N. Gertz, 141–51). Tel Aviv: The Open University, 1988. [Hebrew]
Zuckerman, Alan, and Calvin Goldscheider. *The Transformation of the Jews*. Chicago: University of Chicago Press, 1985.

Part IV

The Middle Eastern Angle

Chapter Ten

Jewish Studies as Transdisciplinary Middle East Studies

Notes from Tunisia

Achim Rohde

This chapter joins the debate on the intersections between Jewish and Israel Studies from the perspective of a neighboring discipline—that is, Middle East Studies, or Islamic Studies. The conceptualization of a disciplinary field such as Jewish Studies, Israel Studies, or Middle East Studies involves defining their core and their margins, a process that is embedded in institutionalized settings and political contexts that have evolved over periods of time. My argument focuses on German-speaking academia and invites readers to look back briefly at the evolution of Oriental Studies—suggesting that parts of the nineteenth-century tradition of German Oriental Studies may inform an inclusive approach to Middle East Studies today. I would like to address all the above-mentioned disciplines as subgenres of a field of knowledge production that might be termed "Transdisciplinary Middle East Area Studies." To illustrate this approach, the chapter presents the results of an ongoing study by the author in the Tunisian-Jewish context.

CONVERGENT COGNATES: THE GERMAN ORIENTAL STUDIES TRADITION

As in the rest of Europe, both Jewish and Arabic or Islamic Studies were long united in German-speaking academia under the umbrella of Oriental Studies. Modern Oriental Studies evolved during the late eighteenth and early nineteenth centuries, growing out of early modern Christian Hebraic Studies.

Christian Hebraism included the study of Biblical texts in their original Hebrew or Aramaic versions, and the study of related languages, based on the belief that the correct meaning of Biblical texts could only be deciphered with recourse to other similar languages, such as Arabic. In the process, the Biblical texts were increasingly addressed in the geographic context in which they originated, thus reinforcing the association of Jews with "the Orient" in Christian thought.[1] This is where the groundwork was laid for the comparative philology which became the trademark of Oriental Studies in Germany during the nineteenth and early twentieth centuries.[2]

As the earlier humanist theological tradition declined—during the turn from the eighteenth to the nineteenth century—links between Judaism and Christianity, or between European modernity and its perceived Oriental heritage, were played down or negated, mirroring the Eurocentric and colonialist dark side of Enlightenment thought.[3] The association of Judaism and Islam as closely related and erroneous belief systems, and the depiction of Jews as Orientals, is a long-established trope in the German context—often with an anti-Jewish or anti-Semitic agenda directed against Germany's "inner Orient."[4] Some Christian-German Orientalists played an unsavory role in this regard.[5]

But at the same time, numerous Jewish scholars, most of them practitioners of or influenced by the *Wissenschaft des Judentums,* pursued Islamic and Jewish Studies simultaneously as part of the same disciplinary field. Jewish scholars were prominent in shaping the highly productive Arabic and Islamic Studies tradition in German academia all throughout the nineteenth and twentieth centuries into the Weimar period.[6] Through their work they also negotiated the status of Jews in German society as an Orientalized minority seeking recognition and acceptance.[7] In 1933, some 25 percent of all chairs of Oriental Studies in German universities were held by scholars who were defined as Jewish within the Nuremberg Laws.[8]

DISTANT RELATIVES

This common institutional and scholarly framework fell apart during the course of the Nazi period, due to the emigration or murder of Jewish scholars, while their non-Jewish colleagues largely stopped dealing with Jewish topics.[9] With notable exceptions, this tradition was not revived after 1945.[10] After the Holocaust, Orientalizing and thereby "Othering" Judaism on the part of German majority society was viewed as a component of modern anti-Semitism, and thus rejected. Instead, the post-1945 invention of a "Judeo-Christian civilization" necessitated the suppression of this Orientalist heritage and implied an occidentalization of German Jews.[11]

The fragmentation of the German Oriental Studies tradition was completed when, in the 1960s, Jewish Studies evolved into its own separate field in West Germany, relatively well-funded in comparison to other small disciplines, but also somehow isolated from more systematic disciplines like history, sociology, or anthropology—as well as from Arabic/Islamic Studies or Middle East Studies.[12] Apart from ancient Jewish history and theology, contemporary Jewish Studies in Germany mostly focus on Ashkenazi Jewish history. Israel Studies is a relative newcomer in this context, and has grown into a discipline of its own, often strongly linked to Jewish Studies. This corresponds to the image of Israel as a Jewish nation-state which forms a Westernized enclave within the region.

Some German universities today retain the historical structure of the old Oriental Studies tradition—placing Jewish Studies departments under one institutional roof along with Islamic or Arabic Studies, though there is not much interaction between them (e.g., Freiburg, Bamberg). Some universities (München, Halle-Wittenberg) have started to revive the old framework by offering study programs that combine Arabic/Islamic Studies and Jewish Studies.[13] The *Jüdische Hochschule* in Heidelberg has established a position for a junior professor dedicated to *Israel and Middle East Studies* (see the contribution by Johannes Becke in this volume). But there is no Middle East Area Studies center, like in Oxford, SOAS, Leiden, or Boston and Brandeis in the United States, where the study of Jewish or Israeli topics form an integral part of the setup. The Israel Studies Center in Munich is firmly rooted within the department of Jewish Studies.[14] At the other end of this scale is Marburg University's Centre for Near and Middle East Studies (CNMS), with seven chairs it is the single largest institution for Middle East and North Africa (MENA) Area Studies at a German university, where the study of Israel or Jewish topics are notable by their absence.[15]

The following section argues for a reversal of this disentanglement by presenting the case for a (re-)integration of Jewish and Israeli topics into the broader field of Middle East Area Studies, which would not replace disciplinary specializations but offer a kind of big roof to facilitate transdisciplinary and transregional or translocal research which combines various disciplinary perspectives.

JEWISH STUDIES WITHIN MIDDLE EAST AREA STUDIES

Much has been said regarding the Cold War legacy of Area Studies and its inbuilt tendency to otherize non-European or non-Western societies—at times reiterating old colonialist discourses. The spatial turn has added a new layer to this debate: along these lines, contemporary Area Studies should not look at any perceived region (or nation-state) in isolation. They should also move beyond a mere comparative approach of different world regions, because such an approach tends to leave the notion of areas or nation states as more or less separate spatial units with their own independent agency intact. Foucauldian historians emphasize the contingency of any given spatial entity as a mobile effect of regimes of governmentalities.[16] Old spatial concepts are superseded by new ones, but structures like demographic or linguistic patterns survive and marginalized political and societal discourses may regain strength, or in other words: older spatial layers or "shadow spaces" may resurface under altered circumstances, like a weakening or erosion of dominant governmental regimes.[17] "Post-Area Studies" or "Critical Area Studies" aim at

> [. . .] rethinking area studies epistemologically to avoid thinking in container entities such as "nation states" or, for that matter, "regions" and to focus instead on the mobility patterns and communicative processes of human interaction.[18]

One crucial characteristic of the contemporary world relevant for any critical understanding of Area Studies is that "there is no longer a tight coherence between physical and cultural space."[19] For instance, what is the object of knowledge for Iranian Studies, Turkish Studies, Israel Studies, Arabic Studies, or Islamic Studies, and so on, when all these people live among us in the globalized metropolitan? Consequently, scholars started to "move human action and interaction and its role in communicatively constructing space into the center of attention."[20] We are facing a multiplicity of interconnected and fluid cultural spaces existing alongside one another and sometimes in conflict with one another in various local environments across regions. This implies a multiscalar perspective of translocal, transnational, and transregional spaces of interaction. Space is understood here as a historically manufactured product based on collectively shared representations (descriptions, symbols, etc.). Instead of a supposedly geographically restricted area, space can be extremely diverse and more appropriately defined as interwoven "arenas" of dense social relations.[21]

Yet, vast differences exist between different kinds of mobility within and beyond the MENA region. Rigid border regimes are currently being (re-)installed between specific countries and whole regions in multiple parts of the world, calling into question the assumption of an increasingly integrated world system.[22] We therefore need to investigate how the current transformations in MENA countries are part of a contradictory process of blurring and transcending boundaries on the one hand, while at the same time reasserting them violently on the other. In this sense, Arjun Appadurai distinguishes circulation of forms and forms of circulation in order to explain junctures and differences in global cultural flows. He argues that "different [cultural] forms circulate through different trajectories, generate diverse interpretations, and yield different and uneven geographies."[23] In order to grasp such figurations, our analysis should incorporate a center-periphery perspective, which is conscious of power relations existing between various players. If the study of contemporary Israel or Jewish topics should form part of a broader Middle East Area Studies, these conceptual ideas are crucial starting points. They refer to uneven and contradictory patterns of social, cultural, and political change which need to be considered more systematically if we want to arrive at something that adequately conceptualizes the modern and contemporary Middle East in its complexity and interconnectedness. Along this line of thought, it would make more sense to speak of Israel-Palestine Studies, rather than Israel Studies in isolation.[24] Comparative studies focusing on specific aspects in Israel and other MENA countries would also be a promising venue.[25]

Within the Anglo-Saxon academia, which had absorbed numerous German-Jewish emigrants in the 1930s, Jewish and Middle East Studies remain more closely related than in contemporary German academia. Beyond polarized debates between proponents of Arab-Jewish nostalgia and Dhimmitude-polemicists, scholarship on the Middle East and North Africa increasingly addresses Jewish topics as an integral aspect of this field, particularly in the United States.[26] This scholarship is a useful counterweight to homogenizing images of the Middle East as a purely Muslim cultural space. It moves away from framing Jewish history in Muslim majority countries of the Middle East and North Africa (MENA) in communal terms isolated from the broader social context. Rather, Jews (and other marginal groups) are addressed as part of diverse local and (trans-) regional communities, power struggles, theological or political debates. The focus is on interaction, be it inclusive and accommodating, or polarizing and repressive.[27] More generally, this trend reflects the growing awareness among practitioners of Middle Eastern Studies of the historical and contemporary diversity of Middle Eastern societies, in this case its Jewish component, which is also becoming a topic in those countries themselves.

Recent years have seen the emergence of memorial practices and cultures of remembrance regarding Jewish communities that have ceased to exist in most MENA countries. Some are rediscovering the Jewish dimension within their history, and smaller Jewish communities persevere in countries such as Iran, Morocco, Turkey, and Tunisia. These developments bear witness to the renegotiating of historical narratives in post–Arab Spring MENA countries, both on the level of state-sponsored narratives (history education, truth commissions, etc.) and on the level of civil society activism (including online activism), resulting in a growing visibility of the margins and a weakening of homogenizing identity discourses that were so characteristic of postcolonial MENA nation-states.

"JEWISH TUNISIA" AS A CASE STUDY

Related developments can be observed in Tunisia, where the Arab Spring began, and where a multifaceted political and societal transformation is still in process today. This section presents results from the author's ongoing research in the Tunisian context, and situates the project conceptually within Middle East Area Studies. To what extent, then, do post–Arab Spring Tunisian politics and public discourse take into consideration the country's Jewish population and its Jewish diaspora? How do changes in this context relate to the broader political and social transformation of Tunisia? Can we detect changes in the Jewish community's own self-perception in the "new" Tunisia? What forms of interaction and transnational collectivity have developed between Jewish Tunisians and Jewish communities in other countries such as Israel and France? What are the voids, tensions, and contradictions in this discursive and relational setting?

The following case study pursues a two-pronged research strategy, which analyzes contemporary reconfigurations of Tunisian politics and society from the perspective of a marginal group—that is, Jews—while simultaneously investigating the emergence of a "Jewish Tunisia" as an imaginative cultural space inhabited by Tunisian Jewry and its diaspora that interacts with contemporary Tunisian society and politics, or with their respective countries of residence, in particular Israel and France.

Theoretically speaking, this study addresses what Deleuze and Guattari first described as a process of de-/re-territorializing collective identities in globalized and diverse societies.[28] Such processes also occur in the context of profound changes in the political order of a given country, such as happened in Tunisia during the Arab Spring. For example, the post-2011 Tunisian government has installed a transitional justice process and initiated reforms for history education in schools.[29] Patton emphasized the spatial dimension of identities, not in a geographically determined sense, but in a culturally symbolic sense.[30] A deterritorialized conception of space encompasses Bhaba's postnational "intermediate place," "transition space," or "third space" of cultural memory and production.[31] Accordingly, a territory can be "a system of any kind, conceptual, linguistic, social, or affective."[32] Processes of deterritorialization necessitate a simultaneous reterritorialization; in other words, a reclassification under altered conditions, eventually resulting in symbolic "cultural sites," which function as points of orientation for reconfigured collective identities.[33]

Jews have lived in the territory of modern-day Tunisia for millennia.[34] The area became a place of refuge for exiled Andalusian Jews during the late Middle Ages.[35] Along with other immigrant communities, European Jews played an important role in the formation of Tunisia as a "Mediterranean crossroads" during the seventeenth to nineteenth centuries.[36] A large segment of the Jewish-Tunisian population immigrated to other countries in recent centuries, mostly to France, Canada, Italy, and Israel. During the Second Word War the Jewish population was briefly persecuted and interned.[37] However, the majority did not leave the country until the 1960s.[38] Tunisia is one of the few Arab countries in which a small Jewish community still exists, mostly on the island of Jerba, with smaller pockets in Tunis and single families in other cities.[39] Although Tunisia was never at the forefront of the Arab struggle against Israel, deteriorating relations between the two countries during the 1980s put the remaining Tunisian Jews in an awkward position.[40] The officially sanctioned Tunisian Arab nationalism pasted over the deeply rooted diversity of Tunisian society, thus rendering Jews largely invisible.[41] Still, through all the years of Bourghiba's and Ben Ali's reign, Jews were always officially considered legitimate members of the Tunisian nation. At times, the Tunisian government tacitly approved the spread of knowledge regarding the diversity of Tunisian society as an instrument to curb the influence of Islamism, which Ben Ali considered the gravest threat to his rule. Hence, as part of the reforms of higher education in the early 1990s, several universities introduced Hebrew language programs and sent students abroad to pursue Jewish Studies.[42] Jewish emigration from Tunisia was a slow and gradual process, unlike in Libya, Egypt, or Algeria, where emigration was the result of sudden upheaval or expulsion. Further, the Tunisian-Jewish diaspora maintains personal and economic relations in Tunisia.[43] Despite the gradual degradation of the physical remnants of Tunisia's Jewish history, many synagogues and cemeteries are still maintained and taken care of.[44] The affirmation, however ambivalent, of cultural diversity in postcolonial national discourse set Tunisia apart from other Arab-nationalist ruled countries of the MENA region and served to legitimize the *ançien régime* in the international arena.[45]

In contemporary Tunisia, like in any Arab country, people tend to react emotionally toward the Israel-Palestine conflict and identify with the Palestinian plight for freedom from oppression. Unfortunately, public discourse surrounding Jewish issues in Tunisia often conflates Jews in general and Jewish Tunisians on the one hand with Israeli policies toward Palestinians on the other.[46] In January 2018 one of the twelve synagogues located on Jerba was vandalized in an apparent antisemitic attack.[47] When in November 2018 a Tunisian branch of the French NGO LICRA (Ligue internationale contre le Racisme et l'Antisémitisme) was opened in Tunis, protests erupted scandalizing alleged ties between the Tunisian and the French LICRA branches.[48] The latter is being criticized for its pro-Israel policies, and consequently, the Tunisian LICRA branch was denounced as working toward the "normalization" of "the Zionist entity."[49] But Tunisian LICRA activists and sympathizers were adamant in claiming theirs was a purely Tunisian organization with a local Tunisian agenda of defending minority rights.

Yet, at the same time, there is an increasing awareness and acceptance among the Tunisian public of the Jewish component to the country's history, and Jews are considered legitimate members of the Tunisian nation by most Tunisians. A rediscovery of Jewish heritage within the MENA region is apparent in the form of novels, academic books, and film productions in postrevolutionary Tunisia—as it has in other Arab countries in recent years.[50] In 2017 the Tunisian government announced its plan to open a Jewish Museum in the capital Tunis, both in order to revive tourism and to raise consciousness concerning the diversity of Tunisian society past and present, as a kind of antidote against Salafist tendencies.[51] The pledge was repeated by Prime Minister Yousef Chahed when he visited the Ghriba compound in May 2018.[52] A former Jewish children's home in central Tunis was selected as the site for the future museum. In 2018, "International Association for the Safeguarding of the Cultural Heritage of the Jews of Tunisia" was formed in Paris, in order to promote the idea of such a museum among the Tunisian-Jewish diaspora in France, and to begin collecting artifacts and raise money—which the Tunisian government is chronically short of.[53]

As part of the reshuffling of the Tunisian government in November 2018, Prime Minister Chahed nominated René Trabelsi as minister of tourism; he was approved by parliament with a majority of 127 out of 160.[54] Trabelsi owns a travel agency in Paris and is the scion of a Tunisian-Jewish family; his father is the longtime head of the civil association that organizes the annual Ghriba pilgrimage on the island of Jerba.[55] His nomination was met with opposition in Arab nationalist and leftist circles. Yassine Aayari, an activist blogger during the revolution of 2011 turned member of parliament as an independent with Islamist leanings,[56] filed a complaint at court which was subsequently rejected—wherein he pointed to article 74 of the Tunisian constitution (stating that only Muslims can hold government offices) and claimed that Trabelsi faces a conflict of interests as minister of tourism, being himself a businessman in the tourism sector.[57] Despite such examples of enmity toward Jews in the Tunisian public sphere, and despite the usual social media vitriol surrounding events that involve Jews or raise Jewish topics in contemporary Tunisia, commentators from quality media outlets defended the nomination of Trabelsi as legitimate and suggested his professional background made him well suited to remold the Tunisian tourism sector in the twenty-first century. Trabelsi is the third Jew nominated for a ministerial post in postindependence Tunisia, and the first since the mid-1950s, at a time when the Tunisian Jewish community was still numerically strong compared to today. Tunisia is currently the only Arab country with a Jewish minister. Skeptical voices will argue that Trabelsi was chosen for purely opportunistic reasons and with an eye toward international donors and tourists. Still, this sends an encouraging message also to other marginal groups in Tunisian society who struggle for recognition and acceptance, such as Amazigh, people of color, or LGBTQ people.[58]

Even the Islamist an-Nahda party, in a symbolic gesture designed to broaden its electoral appeal, in the February 2018's municipal elections nominated a Jewish candidate, Simon Slama, on its list in the city of Monastir. Of course, this was largely a PR stunt and a symbolic gesture designed to broaden its electoral appeal in the hometown of modern Tunisia's founding President Habib Bourghiba, where the party's main secular rival Nidaa Tunis holds solid majorities.[59] When the French comedian of Tunisian-Jewish origins, Michel Boujenah, who left his native Tunis at the age of ten in the 1960s, performed at the Festival Carthage in July 2017, scandal and protests erupted over his political views regarding Israel/Palestine while playing down his attachment to Tunisia; however, the performance was sold out and well received by the audience.[60]

Indeed, many links still exist between Tunisia and its Jewish diaspora living in France, Israel, or elsewhere. Cultural memorial activities, like those of the *Société d'Histoire des Juifs de Tunisie*, established in Paris in 1997, illustrate lasting ties between the Diaspora and the country of origin.[61] Nostalgia for Tunisia is recognizable in the literature and culture of diaspora Jews.[62] The website *harissa.com* has evolved from a nostalgic platform of remembrance into a virtual space of encounter and discussion that also includes a news section and caters to anyone with an interest in Jewish topics and Tunisia living in France, Israel, or Tunisia itself.[63] In Israel, emigrants from Tunisia have been largely prevented from interacting directly with their country of origin for decades, and they have experienced a devaluation of their cultural roots in a country that fashions itself as an icon of Western modernity within the Middle East. Still, Jews of Tunisian origin as well as others who migrated to Israel from Arab or Muslim majority countries have established "ethnic-religious communities of memory"—illustrating a lasting attachment to their countries of origin. Thus, during the 1990s, a spiritual center catering to Tunisian Jews was established in Moshav Eitan (in southern Israel), a town which itself had been founded by emigrants from the island of Jerba in 1955.[64] Exceptional biographies like that of Jerba-born artist Rafram Hadad, who grew up in Jerusalem, left Israel in 2004, and lives in Tunis today, indicate the parameters of the imaginable if circumstances allow.[65]

THE GHRIBA PILGRIMAGE AS LIMINAL SPACE

This section summarizes the author's experiences during field trips to Jerba in 2017 and 2018. The annual Ghriba pilgrimage on the Tunisian island of Jerba attracts Jewish pilgrims and visitors on the occasion of Lag BaOmer

(18 Iyar on the Jewish calendar).⁶⁶ It is a boisterous festival lasting three days and serves as a meeting place for the local Jewish community and other Tunisian Jews. Israelis and French people of Tunisian-Jewish origin visit the country on this occasion in increasing numbers. Under the *ançien régime*, the Ghriba was an annual gathering of the declining Jewish community and attracted Jewish tourists from abroad but remained walled off and largely unknown to the wider Tunisian public. Since 2011, the Ghriba has become a highly visible event in Tunisia—leading politicians, diplomats, scholars, journalists, and public figures pay visits. A range of cultural activities and public events are staged around the traditional pilgrimage.⁶⁷ The rituals themselves are not particularly Jewish; rather, they resemble traditional folk culture and a spirituality that combines various elements, some of whom are shared by Jews as well as Muslims.⁶⁸ The Ghriba is a venue where senses of belonging and identity are experienced and renegotiated, on individual, communal, cultural, and national levels, by Jews from many different places, including even Chabad activists.

The ageing Tunisian tourism infrastructure is geared toward mass tourism.⁶⁹ After the revolution of 2011 and subsequent terror events, the annual numbers of tourists arriving in Tunisia dwindled sharply. Tourism has recently only slowly started growing again. Jewish tourists who attend the Ghriba pilgrimage were among the few reliable customers whose numbers cut against trend and have actually risen since 2011—despite the precarious security situation. This includes organized groups of Israeli tourists, who are visiting Jerba to attend the Ghriba in increasing numbers. While Tunisia and Israel have never established official diplomatic relations, Israeli citizens of Tunisian origin are permitted to enter the country in order to attend the Ghriba.⁷⁰

Groups of Israeli tourists I observed in Jerba remained largely at a distance from their surroundings and stayed among themselves. Yet, at the same time, I observed these same people roaming the market within the island's commercial and administrative center Homt as-Suq, feeling at ease speaking with vendors (Jews and Muslims) in local Arabic, boasting to friends and relatives back in Israel via cell phone video-link over how gorgeous ("magniv") they found what they encountered. For Mizrahi Jewish Israelis, whose Arab cultural background was devalued upon their arrival in Israel and who live in a society that is segregated along ethnoreligious lines, visiting Jerba during the Ghriba must be a challenging experience.⁷¹

An Israeli man from Ashkelon, whom I met at a local synagogue in the Jewish neighborhood of Homt as-Souk in 2017, expressed his adherence to a right-wing version of Israeli nationalism, though he also mentioned that he likes to spend some quiet months with his relatives on Jerba every year in order "to clean his head"—that is, to take a leave from the hardships of daily life in Israel.⁷² Tunisian Jews who migrated to Israel generally belonged to the lower and less educated strata of Tunisian society, while the more affluent and bourgeois among Tunisian Jewry preferred destinations in Europe or America. While some Jews of Tunisian origin have achieved prominence in Israel (e.g., Menachem Mazuz, Silvan Shalom, Ofer Lellouche), many live in peripheral regions or neighborhoods, and their status in Israeli society has remained comparatively low up to the present.[73] In his ambivalent narrative, the Israeli man I interviewed in Jerba in 2017 reflected upon his life experiences in Israel from his temporary retreat in Jerba.

My encounters with French people of Tunisian-Jewish origin during fieldwork in Tunisia reflected the socioeconomic differences that characterized Jewish emigration to Israel and France, and they displayed different patterns of interaction with Tunisian society. For example, in 2018, I met an elderly lady from Paris who had been born and raised in Tunis. After an initial absence of eleven years after her emigration in the 1960s, she has returned regularly for prolonged visits. After 2011, she wrote an autobiographical book and currently travels throughout Tunisia on a reading tour, encountering limited but highly interested audiences—some of whom approach her and welcome her "back home." She takes this as encouragement of her quest to raise consciousness in the Tunisian public concerning the story of Tunisian Jewry, which has been largely forgotten over the past few generations.[74]

In May 2018 I met a Parisian psychotherapist in her forties, whose parents left their native Tunisia in the 1960s. Upon our encounter at the Ghriba compound she expressed estrangement at the sight of what seemed to her like remnants of "humanity's childhood" (i.e., the superstition, the fertility rituals, the sticking of papers with prayers and wishes into a wall in the great synagogue, like at the Western Wall in Jerusalem). Yet, this woman nevertheless travels to Tunisia frequently, has attended the Ghriba twice in recent years, and supports the idea of establishing a Jewish Museum in Tunis. This second-generation emigrant retains an emotional attachment to "Jewish Tunisia" which serves as a reference point for her—even while her life is centered in a European metropolis and far removed in any sense from Jewish communal life in Tunisia. Nevertheless, she would like to see Tunisia's Jewish heritage acknowledged and visibly represented in contemporary Tunisia.[75]

In sum, the Ghriba is not only a traditional religious pilgrimage—it is an occasion when Jerba turns into a liminal space, where encounters and communications are possible that do not occur in Tunisia during the rest of the year. In Tunisia, where Jewish topics are otherwise largely invisible within the public sphere, the Ghriba is an opportunity for the Tunisian government to brand Tunisia as a tolerant and peaceful country—for celebrating the country's Jewish heritage and for highlighting the kind of cultural "Great Barrier Reef" that Jerba represents, with its mosaic of distinct communities which have been living on the island for ages. To some degree, indeed, Jerba during the Ghriba echoes a Middle East which has ceased to exist since the establishment of nation-states in the region, and more recently as a result of the weakening and fragmentation of those nation-states, and the rise of ethnosectarian violence that has come along with it.[76]

CONCLUSIONS

This study is in keeping with a "post-Area Studies" approach which avoids thinking in container entities such as "the Arab world" or "the Islamic(ate) world," or, for that matter, Israel as a perceived Jewish space that is set apart from anything Arab. Through my research in the Tunisian-Jewish context I encountered a multiplicity of partly interconnected cultural spaces or "arenas" in various local environments within and across regions. For a short period each year, the island of Jerba becomes a liminal space where all these arenas overlap and interact in a tangible way. Contemporary Tunisia allows us to study the intersections between the multifaceted meanings of Jewishness for people from vastly different backgrounds, including intersections between Jewishness, Israeliness, and Arabness.[77] Simultaneously, the case of "Jewish Tunisia" enables new perspectives and insights regarding the political and societal reconfigurations happening in Tunisia since the revolution of 2011.

In adding a Jewish dimension to scholarship on the modern and contemporary Middle East, the conceptual approach outlined in this chapter harks back to the intersections between Jewish and Arabic/Islamic Studies that once were a hallmark of German Oriental Studies. Scholarship related to Jewish topics within Middle Eastern philosophy, literature, and history or contemporary developments has become a sprawling field of inquiry in Anglo-Saxon academia, but is still largely neglected in Germany, and the same holds true regarding scholarship on contemporary Israel. By (re-)integrating Jewish and Israeli topics into a broader Middle East area studies framework, contemporary German academia would thus follow an international trend and simultaneously revise a scar that Nazi rule has left on this disciplinary field.

Meanwhile, Germany increasingly becomes an arena of encounter between Jews and Muslims—including Israelis and Arabs. The Israel-Palestine conflict, and the prevailing political culture within the countries of origin of many recent immigrants and refugees, are factors which complicate these interactions. Jewish and Muslim or Arab identities are often perceived as mutually exclusive, even while Jews and Muslims are the targets of different forms of the same racism on the part of German majority society.[78] Hence, scholarship along the approach outlined in this chapter intersects with research on Jewish-Muslim relations in Europe, scholarship on theological entanglements, and comparative religious studies.[79]

NOTES

1. Achim Rohde, "Ein Hamburger Koran und die Degradierung des Hebräischen in der christlichen Theologie des 17. Jahrhunderts," *Hamburger Schlüsseldokumente zur deutsch-jüdischen Geschichte* (2018), https://juedische-geschichte-online.net/beitrag/jgo:article-51; "400 Jahre Orientalistik/Hebraistik in Hamburg. Vom Akademischen Gymnasium zur Hamburger Universität," in *Das Akademische Gymnasium. Bildung und Wissenschaft in Hamburg 1613–1883*, Dirk Brietzke, Franklin Kopitzsch, and Rainer Nicolaysen (eds.) (Berlin/Hamburg: Dietrich Reimer Verlag, 2013), 195–212.

2. Ludmilla Hanisch, *Die Nachfolger der Exegeten: Deutschsprachige Erforschung des Vorderen Orients in der ersten Hälfte des 19. Jahrhunderts* (Wiesbaden: Harassowitz, 2003).

3. Suzanne L. Marchand, *German Orientalism in the Age of Empire* (Cambridge: Cambridge University Press, 2009); Ivan Davidson Kalmar, "Arabizing the Bible: Racial Supersessionism in Nineteenth Century Christian Art and Biblical Criticism," in *Orientalism Revisited*, Ian Netton (ed.) (London and New York: Routledge, 2012), 176–86.

4. Achim Rohde, "Der innere Orient: Orientalismus, Antisemitismus und Geschlecht im Deutschland des 18.-20. Jahrhundert," *Die Welt des Islams* 45, no. 3 (2005): 370–411.

5. Achim Rohde, "Asians in Europe. Reading German-Jewish History through a Post-Colonial Lens," in *Orientalism, Gender and the Jews. Literary and Artistic Transformations of European National Identity Discourses*, Ulrike Brunotte, Anna-Dorothea Ludewig, and Axel Stähler (eds.) (Berlin: De Gruyter, 2015), 17–32.

6. Ismar Schorsch, "Converging Cognates: The Intersection of Jewish and Islamic Studies in Nineteenth Century Germany," *Leo Baeck Institute Year Book* 55, no. 1 (2010): 3–36. The Corpus Coranicum project, located at the Berlin-Brandenburgische Akademie der Wissenschaften (www.corpuscoranicum.de), has acknowledged its roots in the *Wissenschaft des Judentums*. See Dirk Hartwig, Walter Homolka, and Michael J. Marx (eds.), *"Im vollen Licht der Geschichte": Die Wissenschaft des Judentums und die Anfänge der Koranforschung* (Würzburg: Ergon, 2008).

7. Ruchama Johnston-Bloom, "Analogising Judaism and Islam: Nineteenth and Twentieth-Century German–Jewish Scholarship on Islam," *Journal of Beliefs & Values*, 38, no. 3 (2017): 267–75; Susannah Heschel, "German-Jewish Scholarship on Islam as a Tool for De-Orientalizing Judaism," *New German Critique* 117 (2012): 91–107; Susannah Heschel, "Revolt of the Colonized: Abraham Geiger's Wissenschaft des Judentums as a Challenge to Christian Hegemony in the Academy," *New German Critique* 77 (1999): 61–85.

8. Ludmila Hanisch,"Akzentverschiebung—Zur Geschichte der Semitistik und Islamwissenschaft während des 'Dritten Reichs,'" *Berichte zur Wissenschaftsgeschichte* 18 (1995): 217–26; *Ausgegrenzte Kompetenz: Porträts Vertriebener Orientalisten Und Orientalistinnen 1933–1945. Eine Hommage Anlässlich des XXVIII. Deutschen Orientalistentags In Bamberg, 26.-30. März 2001* (Halle: Orientwissenschaftliches Zentrum der Martin-Luther-Universität Halle-Wittenberg, 2001).

9. Ekkehard Ellinger, *Deutsche Orientalistik zur Zeit des Nationalsozialismus, 1933–1945* (Edingen-Neckarhausen: Deux Mondes, 2006); Achim Rohde, "Elfenbeinturm Revisited. Zur Geschichte der Orientalistik im Nationalsozialismus. Das Beispiel der Hamburger Universität," *Orient* 41, no. 3 (2000): 435–60.

10. Achim Rohde, "Zur Geschichte der Abteilung Geschichte und Kultur des Vorderen Orients (Islamwissenschaft)," in *Vom Kolonialinstitut zum Asien-Afrika-Institut—100 Jahre Asien- und Afrikawissenschaften in Hamburg*, Ludwig Paul (ed.) (Gossenberg: Ostasienverlag, 2008), 128–49.

11. Jihan Jasmin S. Dean, "De-Orientalization of Jews after 1989 in Germany: The Relationship between Discourse and Subjects," in *Internal Outsiders—Imagined Orientals? Anti-*

semitism, Colonialism and Modern Constructions of Jewish Identity, Ulrike Brunotte, Jürgen Mohn, and Christina Späti (eds.) (Würzburg: Ergon, 2017), 201–12.

12. Mathias Berek, Kirsten Heinsohn, David Jünger, and Achim Rohde, "Vom Erfolg ins Abseits? Jüdische Geschichte als Geschichte der 'Anderen.' Ein Gespräch," *Medaon—Magazin für jüdisches Leben in Forschung und Bildung* 11 (2017): 1–17; Klaus Hödl, "'Jewish History' as Part of 'General History': A Comment," *Medaon—Magazin für jüdisches Leben in Forschung und Bildung* 12, no. 22 (2018): 1–4.

13. For an illustration of this, see program websites: http://www.nahoststudien.uni-halle.de/; https://www.naher-osten.uni-muenchen.de/studium_lehre/index.html.

14. For an illustration of this, see program website: https://www.zis.geschichte.uni-muenchen.de/ueber-uns/index.html.

15. For an illustration of this, see program website. https://www.uni-marburg.de/de/cnms. When the CNMS was founded in 2006 at the initiative of the Hessian regional government, it was initially suggested that Goethe University Frankfurt's Institute of Jewish Studies should move to Marburg and become part of the CNMS as well. Unsurprisingly, the Frankfurters resisted the idea with indignation, as they deal exclusively with Ashkenazi Jewry. Regarding the study of Israeli topics, scholars at the CNMS currently lack the necessary Hebrew language skills, and Israeli authorities have refused entry to a CNMS professor at Ben Gurion airport in 2016, thereby discouraging cooperation with Israeli colleagues. Author's interview with the acting director of the CNMS, Stefan Weninger, March 2018.

16. Stuart Elden, "How Should We Do the History of Territory?" *Territory, Politics, Governance* 1, no. 1 (2013): 5–20.

17. Béatrice von Hirschhausen, Hannes Grandits, Claudia Kraft, Dietmar Müller, and Thomas Serrier, *Phantomgrenzen. Räume und Akteure in der Zeit neu denken* (Göttingen: Wallstein, 2015).

18. Claudia Derichs, "Reflections: Normativities in Area Studies and Disciplines," *TRAFO—Blog for Transregional Research*, October 31, 2014, http://trafo.hypotheses.org/1372.

19. Derichs, "Reflections." See also Claudia Derichs, *Knowledge Production, Area Studies and Global Cooperation* (London/New York: Routledge, 2017).

20. Katja Mielke and Anna-Katharina Hornidge, "Crossroads Studies: From Spatial Containers to Interactions in Differentiated Spatialities," *Crossroads Asia Working Paper Series* 15 (2014), http://crossroads-asia.de/en/publications/working-papers.html.

21. Nile Green, "Rethinking the 'Middle East' after the Oceanic Turn," *Comparative Studies of South Asia, Africa and the Middle East* 34, no. 3 (2014): 556–64.

22. John Allen, *Lost Geographies of Power* (Oxford: Blackwell Publishers, 2003); Achim Rohde, "Mapping Reconfigurations: MENA and Europe post Arab Spring. Challenges for Scholarship and Politics," in *"Guests and Aliens": Re-Configuring New Mobilities in the Eastern Mediterranean After 2011—with a Special Focus on Syrian Refugees*, Elif Aksaz and Jean-Francois Pérouse (eds.), Les Dossiers de l'IFEA, 2016, http://books.openedition.org/ifeagd/1829.

23. Arjun Appadurai, "How Histories Make Boundaries: Circulation and Context in a Global Perspective," *Transcultural Studies* 1 (2010): 4–13. See also, Jörg Gertel, "Spatialities of Hunger: Post-National Spaces, Assemblages, Reliabilities," *Middle East—Topics & Arguments* 5 (2010): 25–34.

24. Baruch Kimmerling (ed.), *The Israeli State and Society. Boundaries and Frontiers* (New York: SUNYP, 1989); Baruch Kimmerling and Joel S. Migdal, *The Palestinian People: A History* (Cambridge: Harvard University Press, 2003); Adi Ophir, Michal Givoni, Sari Hanafi (eds.), *The Power of Inclusive Exclusion. Anatomy of Israeli Rule in the Occupied Palestinian Territories* (New York: Zone Books, 2009).

25. This is a long-established, though rarely practiced, approach to Israel Studies. See, for example, Marc A. Tessler, "The Identity of Religious Minorities in Non-Secular States: Jews in Tunisia and Morocco and Arabs in Israel," *Comparative Studies in Society and History* 20, no. 3 (1978): 359–73; Yusuf Sarfati, *Mobilizing Religion in Middle East Politics. A Comparative Study of Israel and Turkey* (London, New York: Routledge, 2013); Omar M. Dajani, "The Middle East's Majority Problems: Minoritarian Regimes and the Threat of Democracy," *Ethnic and Racial Studies* 38, no. 14 (2015): 2516–33.

26. *Ahl al-Dhimma* (protected people) is the Arabic term that designates the legal status of Christians, Jews, and other non-Muslims under Muslim rule in the Middle Ages. Dhimmitude is a neologism borrowed from the French language and popularized as a polemical term in analogy with servitude, in order to portray the status of non-Muslims under Muslim rule as inferior and oppressed.

27. For a broad overview see, "Round Table: Jewish Identities in the Middle East, 1876–1956," *International Journal of Middle East Studies* 46, no. 3 (2014): 577–605.

28. Gilles Deleuze and Félix Guattari, *Anti-Oedipus* (London: Continuum, 2004); Arjun Appadurai, *Modernity at Large. Cultural Dimensions of Globalization* (Minneapolis: University of Minnesota Press, 1996).

29. For the ongoing reform of history education in Tunisian schools, see Maria Lucenti, "La nouvelle reforme scolaire en tunisie: le defi democratique entre analyse des manuels et didactique," *Foro de Educación* 15, no. 23 (2017): 219–42; Oren Fliegelman, "The Question of Education in the 2014 Tunisian Constitution: Article 39 and Its Ambiguous Values," *Middle East Law and Governance* 8 (2016): 1–31. See also "Unterricht Macht Schule," *Goethe-Institut Tunisia*, https://www.goethe.de/ins/tn/de/kul/sup/tup/ums.html. For an interview with Sihem Ben Sedrine, president of the Tunisian Truth and Dignity Commission, see Sarah Mersch, "Interview with Sihem Bensedrine," *Quantara.de*, December 11, 2016, https://en.qantara.de/node/25750. The commission's mandate has been extended until the end of 2018, see "Tunisie: Sihem Bensedrine et l'IVD poursivent leur activité," *Kapitalis*, May 24, 2018, http://kapitalis.com/tunisie/2018/05/24/tunisie-sihem-bensedrine-et-livd-poursuivent-leur-activite/.

30. Paul Patton, *Deleuzian Concepts: Philosophy, Colonization, Politics* (Stanford: Stanford University Press, 2010).

31. Homi K. Bhabha, *The Location of Culture* (London: Routledge, 1994).

32. Patton, *Deleuzian Concepts*, 52.

33. Akhil Gupta and James Ferguson, "Beyond 'Culture': Space, Identity, and the Politics of Difference," in *Culture, Power, Place. Explorations in Critical Anthropology*, Akhil Gupta and James Ferguson (eds.) (Durham: Duke University Press, 1997), 33–51.

34. Paul Sebag, *Histoire des Juifs de Tunisie des Origines à nos Jours* (Paris: L'Harmattan, 1991); Jacques Taïeb, *Sociétés juives du Maghreb moderne (1500–1900). Un monde en mouvement* (Paris: Maisonneuve et Larose, 2000).

35. Elia Boccara, *La saga des Sépharades portugais: Tunis, un havre pour les familles fuyant l'Inquisition* (Paris: Tchou, 2012).

36. Habib Kazdaghly, "Les Communautés dans l'Histoire de la Tunisie Moderne et Contemporaine," in *Les Communautés Méditerranéennes de Tunisie. Hommage au Doyen Mohamed Hédi Cherif*, Faculté des Lettres, des Arts et des Humanités de Manouba (ed.), (Tunis: Centre de Publication Universitaires, 2006), 59–75. For more detail, see Lionel Lévy, *La nation juive portugaise: Livourne, Amsterdam, Tunis, 1591–1951* (Paris: L'Harmattan, 1999); Nadia Gallico Spano, *Mabruk. Ricordi di un'inguaribile ottimista* (Cagliari: AM&D edizioni, 2005).

37. Daniel Carpi, *Between Mussolini and Hitler: The Jews and the Italian Authorities in France and Tunisia* (Hanover: University Press of New England, Brandeis University Press, 1994); Jacob André Guez, *Au Camp de Bizerte: journal d'un juif tunisien interné sous l'Occupation allemande, 1942–1943* (Paris: Harmattan, 2001).

38. Claude Nataf, "Les Mutations du Judaisme Tunisien Après la Seconde Guerre Mondiale," *Archives Juives* 39, no. 1 (2006): 125–36; Dorsaf Nehdy, *Die Spannungen der jüdisch-muslimischen Beziehung in Tunesien während des 20. Jahrhunderts und ihr Zusammenhang mit der massiven Auswanderung der Juden aus diesem Land* (Dissertationsschrift, FU Berlin, 2010). https://refubium.fu-berlin.de/handle/fub188/7404; Lucette Valensi, "Espaces Publics, Espaces Comunautaires aux XIXe et XXe Siècles," *Printemps* 10 (1994): 97–109.

39. For a scenic article, see, for instance, Elizabeth Bryant, "Ancient Tunisian Jewish Community Faces Uncertain Future," *Religion News Service*, June 20, 2016, https://religionnews.com/2016/06/20/ancient-tunisian-jewish-community-faces-uncertain-future/. For in depth studies, see Yaron Tsur, *Sipur tarbut: Yehude Tunisyah ya-aratsot Muslemiyot aḥerot* [The Evolution of a Culture: The Jews of Tunisia and Other Muslim Countries] (Jerusalem: Merkaz Zalman Shazar le-toldot Yiśra'el, 2003); Mikha'el M. Laskier, *North African Jewry in the Twentieth Century: The Jews of Morocco, Tunisia, and Algeria* (New York: New York

University Press, 1994); Abraham L. Udovitch and Lucette Valensi, *The Last Arab Jews: The Communities of Jerba, Tunisia* (Chur: Harwood Academic Publishers, 1984); Mark A. Tessler and Linda L. Hawkins, "The Political Culture of Jews in Tunisia and Morocco," *International Journal of Middle East Studies* 11 (1980): 59–86; Nataf, "Les mutations du judaïsme tunisien," 125–36.

40. For example, weeks after the Israeli air force had bombed the PLO headquarters in Tunis in 1985, a Tunisian policeman went on a shooting spree on the Ghriba compound in Jerba, killing three and wounding twenty people. See also Raouf Saïd, "Bombardement israélien de Hammam-Chott: La Tunisie devant le Conseil de Sécurité ou la conduite d'un débat," *Leaders*, October 15, 2018, http://www.leaders.com.tn/article/25706-raouf-said-bombardement-israeli en-de-hammam-chott-la-tunisie-devant-le-conseil-de-securite-ou-la-conduite-d-un-debat.

41. Thus, history school textbooks issued during the 1980s and 1990s analyzed by the author presented Tunisia as an Arab and Muslim country, with no mention of Jews or other marginal groups. See also, "Pour l'intégration des minorités religieuses dans les manuels scolaires tunisiens," *Kapitalis*, November 21, 2016, http://kapitalis.com/tunisie/2016/11/21/pour-lintegration-des-minorites-religieuses-dans-les-manuels-scolaires-tunisiens/.

42. Interview with Dorsaf Nehdy, Tunis, November 2017. Nehdy received a grant by the Tunisian government to study Jewish Studies in Germany in the 1990s. She eventually received her PhD from the Free University Berlin with a study on Jewish-Muslim relations in post-1945 Tunisia. Interview with Moncef Ben Abdeljelil, Frankfurt a. M., July 2018. Abdeljelil is a historian from the University of Sousse who served as council to the Minister of Education in the early 1990s. See Sarah J. Feuer, *Regulating Islam. Religion and the State in Contemporary Morocco and Tunisia* (Cambridge: Cambridge University Press, 2018).

43. Claude Hagège and Bernard Zarca, "Les Juifs et La France en Tunisie. Les Bénéfices d'une Relation Triangulaire," *Le Mouvement Social* 197, no. 4 (2001): 9–28.

44. Colette Bismuth-Jarrassé and Dominique Jarrassé, *Synagogues de Tunisie. Monuments d'une Historie et d'une Identité* (Éditions Esthetiques du Divers, 2010); Dora Carpenter-Latiri, "Visites de la synagogue de La Goulette: la synagogue Beith Mordechai, rue Khaznadar, témoin et miroir d'une minorité de Tunisie," *Expressions Maghrebines* 13, no. 2 (2014): 79–98.

45. Stéphanie Poussel, "The Democratic Turn in Tunisia: Civic and Political Redefinition of Canons of Cultural Diversity," *Nationalism and Ethnic Politics* 22, no. 1 (2016): 50–70; Nadia Marzouki, "Interview with Stéphanie Pouessel: Pluralism and Minorities in Post-Revolutionary Tunisia," *Middle East Law and Governance* 6 (2014): 53–62.

46. Filippo Petrucci and Marisa Fois, "Attitudes towards Israel in Tunisian political debate: from Bourguiba to the new constitution," *The Journal of North African Studies* 21, no. 3 (2016): 392–410.

47. For a video covering the damage, see https://www.facebook.com/AsTuSoMi/videos/vb.358222207646312/1200825683385956/?type=2&theater.

48. "Naissance de la Licra Tunisie pour lutter contre le racisme." *Kapitalis*, November 6, 2018, http://kapitalis.com/tunisie/2018/11/06/naissance-de-la-licra-tunisie-pour-lutter-contre-le-racisme/.

49. Ahmed Abbes, "Non à la LICRA Tunisie! Soutien à TACBI-BDS! Lettre ouverte à Habib Kazdaghli, ancien Doyen de la Faculté des Lettres, des Arts et des Humanités de la Manouba," http://tacbi.org/node/79, November 16, 2018.

50. Najat Abdulhaq, *Jewish and Greek Communities in Egypt: Entrepreneurship and Business before Nasser* (London: IB Tauris, 2016); Sarah Irving, "Gender, Conflict, and Muslim-Jewish Romance: Reading 'Ali al-Muqri's *The Handsome Jew* and Mahmoud Saeed's *The World through the Eyes of Angels*," *Journal of Middle East Women's Studies* 12, no. 3 (2016): 343–62. See also various papers presented at the international conference "Jews in Muslim Majority Countries—History and Perspectives" held at the Jewish Museum Berlin in October 2017, https://www.jmberlin.de/en/jews-in-muslim-majority-countries.

51. Statement made by the Tunisian Minister of Cultural Affairs during a symposium at the occasion of the Grhiba, Jerba, May 2017, author's observation.

52. Author's observation, Jerba, May 2018. Plans to open a second Jewish museum in Morocco were announced in summer 2018—see Amina Kaabi, "A New Jewish Museum Is Set

to Open in Fes Bringing Judeo-Moroccan History to the Forefront," *Mille*, July 26, 2018, http://www.milleworld.com/jewish-museum-fes/.

53. "#Culture—Un musée juif ouvrira bientôt à Tunis," *CRIF*, 24 April 2018. http://www.crif.org/fr/revuedepresse/culture-un-musee-juif-ouvrira-bientot-tunis; Mélinée Le Priol, "Les juifs de Tunisie veulent valoriser leur patrimoine," *La Croix*, June 12, 2018, https://www.la-croix.com/Religion/Judaisme/juifs-Tunisie-veulent-valoriser-leur-patrimoine-2018-06-12-1200946389.

54. The Tunisian parliament is composed of altogether 217 seats, but not all members attended the session. "René Trabelsi: une journée historique pour moi et pour la Tunisie," *Kapitalis*, November 13, 2018, http://kapitalis.com/tunisie/2018/11/13/rene-trabelsi-une-journee-historique-pour-moi-et-pour-la-tunisie/.

55. Igal Avidan, "Ich hatte Glück. Der andere starb. Perez Trabelsi überlebte zwei Attentate. Ein Gespräch mit dem Präsidenten der Synagoge auf Djerba, Tunesien, über antijüdische Attentate," *Chrismon Plus*, July 3, 2014, https://chrismon.evangelisch.de/personen/perez-trabelsi-21722.

56. Mohamed Haddad, "Yassine Ayari, un ancien blogueur de la révolution tunisienne devient député," *Le Monde*, February 7, 2018, https://www.lemonde.fr/afrique/article/2018/02/07/yassine-ayari-un-ancien-blogueur-de-la-revolution-tunisienne-devient-depute_5253144_3212.html.

57. But his predecessor as minister of tourism, Selma Elloumi-Rekkik, is an entrepreneur, too, and no one has disputed her government post in court. See "Yassine Ayari fera appel en justice contre la nomination de René Trabelsi," *Kapitalis*, November 6, 2018, http://kapitalis.com/tunisie/2018/11/06/yassine-ayari-fera-appel-en-justice-contre-la-nomination-de-rene-trabelsi/.

58. Stéphanie Poussel, "Les marges renaissantes: Amazigh, Juif, Noir. Ce que la révolution a changé dans ce 'petit pays homogène par excellence' qu'est la Tunisie," *L'Année du Maghreb* 8 (2012): 143–60; Mohamed Amine Jelassi, *Les Minorités en Tunisie* (Thèse de Doctorat en Droit, Université de Carthage, Faculté des sciences juridiques, Tunis, 2018); Hasib Jeridi, *At-Ta'adudiyya ath-thaqafiyya fi-l-Jama'a al-Wataniyya. Al-'Aqaliyat fi Tunis. Al-Berber wa-l-Yahud wa-s-Suwad* [Cultural Diversity in the National Community. Minorities in Tunisia: Amazigh, Jews, and People of Colour] (Tunis: Al-Badawi lil Nasher, 2016); Abdelhamid Largueche, "La Minorité Noire de Tunis au XIXe Siècle," *Annuaire de l'Afrique du Nord* 30 (1991): 135–53.

59. Indeed, despite its overall gains in these elections, in Monastir an-Nahda did not receive sufficient votes for Slama to enter the municipal council. For press reports, see, "Tunisie-Monastir: un juif tête de liste d'Ennahdha aux municipales," *Kapitalis*, February 19, 2018, http://kapitalis.com/tunisie/2018/02/19/tunisie-ennahdha-choisit-un-juif-tunisien-pour-participer-aux-municipales/. For an analysis of the municipal elections, see Arab Center for Research and Policy Studies, *Situation Assessment: Municipal Election Results and Their Repercussions in Tunisia*, https://www.dohainstitute.org/en/PoliticalStudies/Pages/Municipal-Elections-in-Tunisia-Results-and-Implications.aspx, May 15, 2018. For a broader view, see Francesco Cavatorta, "Salafism, Liberalism, and Democratic Learning in Tunisia," *The Journal of North African Studies* 20, no. 5 (2015): 770–83; Fabio Merone, "Enduring Class Struggle in Tunisia: The Fight for Identity beyond Political Islam," *British Journal of Middle Eastern Studies* 42, no. 1 (2015): 74–87.

60. Syrine Attia, "Festival international de Carthage: la venue de Michel Boujenah fait polémique," *Jeune Afrique*, July 5, 2017, https://www.jeuneafrique.com/454574/societe/festival-international-de-carthage-venue-de-michel-boujenah-menacee/; "Michel Boujenah très ému au Festival de Carthage," *Tribune Juive*, July 20, 2017, https://www.tribunejuive.info/spectacles/michel-boujenah-tres-emu-au-festival-de-carthage.

61. See facebook group, https://www.facebook.com/groups/SHJTUNISIE/. See also Efrat Rosen-Lapidot and Harvey Goldberg, "The Triple Loci of Jewish-Maghribi Ethnicity: Voluntary Associations in Israel and in France," *The Journal of North African Studies* 18, no. 1 (2012): 1–19.

62. Debbie Barnard, "How Art Assuages History: Nostalgia in Judeo-Tunisian Literature," *The Journal of North African Studies* 21, no. 2 (2016): 199–212; Robert Watson, "Secondhand

Memories: Franco-Tunisian Jewish Women and the Predicament of Writing Return," *Life Writing* 10, no. 1 (2013): 25–46.

63. https://harissa.com/news555/fr. See also, Facebook groups like https://www.facebook.com/JewsOfTunisia.

64. Anat Feldman, "In the Realms of Ethnicity, Religion and Emigration: New Communities of Memory in Israel," *Review of Religious Research* 57, no. 2 (2015): 171–89.

65. Daniel Speck, "Tunis: Orient für Freunde," *Die Zeit* 47/2018, November 15, 2018, https://www.zeit.de/2018/47/tunis-tunesien-nordafrika-kultur-tourismus-reise. See also the artist's homepage, http://rafram.com/junction/.

66. Dora Carpenter-Latiri, "The Ghriba Pilgrimage in the Island of Jerba: The Semantics of Otherness," in *Pilgrimages Today: Based on Papers Read at the Symposium on Pilgrimages Today Held at Åbo, Finland, on 19–21 August 2009,* Tore Ahlbäck and Björn Dahla (eds.) (Åbo: Donner Institute for Research in Religious and Cultural History, 2010), 38–55.

67. Habib Trabelsi, "Ghriba 2017: une kermesse riche en promesses," *Kapitalis*, May 15, 2017. http://kapitalis.com/tunisie/2017/05/15/ghriba-2017-une-kermesse-riche-en-promesses/.

68. Dora Carpenter-Latiri, "The Ghriba in the Island of Jerba (or Jerba) or the Re-invention of a Shared Shrine as a Metonym for a Multicultural Tunisia," in *Sharing the Sacra: the Politics and Pragmatics of Inter-communal Relations around Holy Places*, G. Bowman (ed.) (London: Berghahn, 2012), 118–38. See also a special exhibition at the *Musée du Bardo* in 2016/17, entitled *Lieux Saints Partagés*, https://www.youtube.com/watch?v=xpGK5qYOIgI.

69. I. Cortés-Jiménez, J.-J. Nowak, and M. Sahli, "Mass Beach Tourism and Economic Growth: Lessons from Tunisia," *Tourism Economics* 17, no. 3 (2011): 531–47, https://doi.org/10.5367/te.2011.0047.

70. Jacob Abadi, "Tunisia and Israel: Relations under Stress," *Middle Eastern Studies* 53, no. 4 (2017): 507–32; Samuel Ghiles-Meilhac, "Tunisia's Relations with Israel in a Comparative Approach," *Bulletin du Centre de recherche français à Jérusalem* 25 (2014).

71. Yehouda Shenhav and Hannan Hever, "'Arab Jews' after Structuralism: Zionist Discourse and the (De)formation of an Ethnic Identity," *Social Identities* 18, no. 1 (2012): 101–18.

72. Author's interview with protagonist, Jerba, May 2017.

73. Sami Shalom Chetrit, *Intra-Jewish Conflict in Israel: White Jews, Black Jews* (London, New York: Routledge, 2010); Harvey E. Goldberg and Chen Bram, "Sephardic/Mizrahi/Arab-Jews: Reflections on Critical Sociology and the Study of Middle Eastern Jewries within the Context of Israeli Society," *Studies in Contemporary Jewry* 22 (2007): 227–56.

74. Author's interview with protagonist, Jerba, May 2018.

75. Author's interview with protagonist, Jerba, May 2018.

76. Doing fieldwork in Tunisia on this particular topic might be considered an act of grieving Middle Eastern cosmopolitanism. William Hanley, "Grieving Cosmopolitanism in Middle East Studies," *History Compass* 6, no. 5 (2008): 1346–67.

77. Nomi Stone, "Al-Bilad al-Haqaniya? Otherness and Homeland in the Case of Djerban Jewry," *Journal of Modern Jewish Studies* 6, no. 3 (2007): 257–72.

78. Ozan Zakariya Keskinkılıç and Armin Langer (eds.), *Fremdgemacht und Reorientiert. Jüdisch-muslimische Verflechtungen* (Berlin: Verlag Yilmaz-Günay, 2018).

79. Catherine Keller, *Cloud of the Impossible. Negative Theology and Planetary Entanglement* (New York: Columbia University Press, 2014).

BIBLIOGRAPHY

"#Culture—Un musée juif ouvrira bientôt à Tunis." *CRIF*. April 24, 2018. http://www.crif.org/fr/revuedepresse/culture-un-musee-juif-ouvrira-bientot-tunis.

Abadi, Jacob. "Tunisia and Israel: Relations under Stress." *Middle Eastern Studies* 53, no. 4 (2017): 507–32.

Abbes, Ahmed. "Non à la LICRA Tunisie! Soutien à TACBI-BDS! Lettre ouverte à Habib Kazdaghli, ancien Doyen de la Faculté des Lettres, des Arts et des Humanités de la Manouba." http://tacbi.org/node/79. November 16, 2018.

Abdulhaq, Najat. *Jewish and Greek Communities in Egypt: Entrepreneurship and Business before Nasser.* London: IB Tauris, 2016.

Allen, John. *Lost Geographies of Power.* Oxford: Blackwell Publishers, 2003.

André Guez, Jacob. *Au Camp de Bizerte: journal d'un juif tunisien interné sous l'Occupation allemande, 1942–1943.* Paris: Harmattan, 2001.

Appadurai, Arjun. "How Histories Make Boundaries: Circulation and Context in a Global Perspective." *Transcultural Studies* 1 (2010): 4–13.

———. *Modernity at Large. Cultural Dimensions of Globalization.* Minneapolis: University of Minnesota Press, 1996.

Arab Center for Research and Policy Studies. *Situation Assessment: Municipal Election Results and Their Repercussions in Tunisia.* https://www.dohainstitute.org/en/PoliticalStudies/Pages/Municipal-Elections-in-Tunisia-Results-and-Implications.aspx, May 15, 2018.

Attia, Syrine. "Festival international de Carthage: la venue de Michel Boujenah fait polémique." *Jeune Afrique.* July 5, 2017. https://www.jeuneafrique.com/454574/societe/festival-international-de-carthage-venue-de-michel-boujenah-menacee/.

Avidan, Igal. "Ich hatte Glück. Der andere starb. Perez Trabelsi überlebte zwei Attentate. Ein Gespräch mit dem Präsidenten der Synagoge auf Djerba, Tunesien, über antijüdische Attentate." *Chrismon Plus.* July 3, 2014. https://chrismon.evangelisch.de/personen/perez-trabelsi-21722.

Barnard, Debbie. "How Art Assuages History: Nostalgia in Judeo-Tunisian Literature." *The Journal of North African Studies* 21, no. 2 (2016): 199–212.

Berek, Mathias, Kirsten Heinsohn, David Jünger, and Achim Rohde. "Vom Erfolg ins Abseits? Jüdische Geschichte als Geschichte der 'Anderen.' Ein Gespräch." *Medaon—Magazin für jüdisches Leben in Forschung und Bildung* 11 (2017): 1–17.

Bhabha, Homi K. *The Location of Culture.* London: Routledge, 1994.

Bismuth-Jarrassé, Colette, and Dominique Jarrassé. *Synagogues de Tunisie. Monuments d'une Historie et d'une Identité.* Éditions Esthetiques du Divers, 2010.

Boccara, Elia. *La saga des Sépharades portugais: Tunis, un havre pour les familles fuyant l'Inquisition.* Paris: Tchou, 2012.

Bryant, Elizabeth. "Ancient Tunisian Jewish Community Faces Uncertain Future." *Religion News Service.* June 20, 2016. https://religionnews.com/2016/06/20/ancient-tunisian-jewish-community-faces-uncertain-future/.

Carpenter-Latiri, Dora. "The Ghriba in the Island of Jerba (or Jerba) or the Re-invention of a Shared Shrine as a Metonym for a Multicultural Tunisia." In *Sharing the Sacra: The Politics and Pragmatics of Inter-communal Relations around Holy Places*, edited by G. Bowman, 118–38. London: Berghahn, 2012.

———. "The Ghriba Pilgrimage in the Island of Jerba: The Semantics of Otherness." In *Pilgrimages Today: Based on Papers Read at the Symposium on Pilgrimages Today Held at Åbo, Finland, on 19–21 August 2009*, edited by Tore Ahlbäck and Björn Dahla, 38–55. Åbo: Donner Institute for Research in Religious and Cultural History, 2010.

———. "Visites de la synagogue de La Goulette: la synagogue Beith Mordechai, rue Khaznadar, témoin et miroir d'une minorité de Tunisie." *Expressions Maghrebines* 13, no. 2 (2014): 79–98.

Carpi, Daniel. *Between Mussolini and Hitler: The Jews and the Italian Authorities in France and Tunisia.* Hanover: University Press of New England, Brandeis University Press, 1994.

Cavatorta, Francesco. "Salafism, Liberalism, and Democratic Learning in Tunisia." *The Journal of North African Studies* 20, no. 5 (2015): 770–83.

Chetrit, Sami Shalom. *Intra-Jewish Conflict in Israel: White Jews, Black Jews.* London, New York: Routledge, 2010.

Cortés-Jiménez, I., J.-J. Nowak, and M. Sahli. "Mass Beach Tourism and Economic Growth: Lessons from Tunisia." *Tourism Economics* 17, no. 3 (2011): 531–47.

Dajani, Omar M. "The Middle East's Majority Problems: Minoritarian Regimes and the Threat of Democracy." *Ethnic and Racial Studies* 38, no. 14 (2015): 2516–33.

Dean, Jihan Jasmin S. "De-Orientalization of Jews after 1989 in Germany: The Relationship between Discourse and Subjects." In *Internal Outsiders—Imagined Orientals? Antisemit-*

ism, Colonialism and Modern Constructions of Jewish Identity, edited by Ulrike Brunotte, Jürgen Mohn, and Christina Späti, 201–12. Würzburg: Ergon, 2017.

Deleuze, Gilles, and Félix Guattari. *Anti-Oedipus*. London: Continuum, 2004.

Derichs, Claudia. *Knowledge Production, Area Studies and Global Cooperation*. London/New York: Routledge, 2017.

———. "Reflections: Normativities in Area Studies and Disciplines." *TRAFO—Blog for Transregional Research*. October 31, 2014. http://trafo.hypotheses.org/1372.

Elden, Stuart. "How Should We Do the History of Territory?" *Territory, Politics, Governance* 1, no. 1 (2013): 5–20.

Ellinger, Ekkehard. *Deutsche Orientalistik zur Zeit des Nationalsozialismus, 1933–1945*. Edingen-Neckarhausen: Deux Mondes, 2006.

Feldman, Anat. "In the Realms of Ethnicity, Religion and Emigration: New Communities of Memory in Israel." *Review of Religious Research* 57, no. 2 (2015): 171–89.

Feuer, Sarah J. *Regulating Islam. Religion and the State in Contemporary Morocco and Tunisia*. Cambridge: Cambridge University Press, 2018.

Fliegelman, Oren. "The Question of Education in the 2014 Tunisian Constitution: Article 39 and Its Ambiguous Values." *Middle East Law and Governance* 8 (2016): 1–31.

Gertel, Jörg. "Spatialities of Hunger: Post-National Spaces, Assemblages, Reliabilities." *Middle East—Topics & Arguments* 5 (2010): 25–34.

Ghiles-Meilhac, Samuel. "Tunisia's Relations with Israel in a Comparative Approach." *Bulletin du Centre de recherche français à Jérusalem* 25 (2014).

Goldberg, Harvey E., and Chen Bram. "Sephardic/Mizrahi/Arab-Jews: Reflections on Critical Sociology and the Study of Middle Eastern Jewries within the Context of Israeli Society." *Studies in Contemporary Jewry* 22 (2007): 227–56.

Green, Nile. "Rethinking the 'Middle East' after the Oceanic Turn." *Comparative Studies of South Asia, Africa and the Middle East* 34, no. 3 (2014): 556–64.

Gupta, Akhil, and James Ferguson. "Beyond 'Culture': Space, Identity, and the Politics of Difference." In *Culture, Power, Place. Explorations in Critical Anthropology*, edited by Akhil Gupta and James Ferguson, 33–51. Durham: Duke University Press, 1997.

Haddad, Mohamed. "Yassine Ayari, un ancien blogueur de la révolution tunisienne devient député." *Le Monde*. February 7, 2018. https://www.lemonde.fr/afrique/article/2018/02/07/yassine-ayari-un-ancien-blogueur-de-la-revolution-tunisienne-devient-depute_5253144_3212.html.

Hagège, Claude, and Bernard Zarca. "Les Juifs et La France en Tunisie. Les Bénéfices d'une Relation Triangulaire." *Le Mouvement Social* 197, no. 4 (2001): 9–28.

Hanisch, Ludmila. "Akzentverschiebung—Zur Geschichte der Semitistik und Islamwissenschaft während des 'Dritten Reichs.'" *Berichte zur Wissenschaftsgeschichte* 18 (1995): 217–26.

———. *Ausgegrenzte Kompetenz: Porträts Vertriebener Orientalisten Und Orientalistinnen 1933–1945. Eine Hommage Anlässlich des XXVIII. Deutschen Orientalistentags In Bamberg*, 26–30. März 2001. Halle: Orientwissenschaftliches Zentrum der Martin-Luther-Universität Halle-Wittenberg, 2001.

———. *Die Nachfolger der Exegeten: Deutschsprachige Erforschung des Vorderen Orients in der ersten Hälfte des 19. Jahrhunderts*. Wiesbaden: Harassowitz, 2003.

Hanley, William. "Grieving Cosmopolitanism in Middle East Studies." *History Compass* 6, no. 5 (2008): 1346–67.

Hartwig, Dirk, Walter Homolka, and Michael J. Marx (eds.). *"Im vollen Licht der Geschichte": Die Wissenschaft des Judentums und die Anfänge der Koranforschung*. Würzburg: Ergon, 2008).

Heschel, Susannah. "German-Jewish Scholarship on Islam as a Tool for De-Orientalizing Judaism." *New German Critique* 117 (2012): 91–107.

———. "Revolt of the Colonized: Abraham Geiger's Wissenschaft des Judentums as a Challenge to Christian Hegemony in the Academy." *New German Critique* 77 (1999): 61–85.

Hödl, Klaus. "'Jewish History' as Part of 'General History': A Comment." *Medaon—Magazin für jüdisches Leben in Forschung und Bildung* 12, no. 22 (2018): 1–4.

Irving, Sarah. "Gender, Conflict, and Muslim-Jewish Romance: Reading 'Ali al-Muqri's *The Handsome Jew* and Mahmoud Saeed's *The World through the Eyes of Angels.*" *Journal of Middle East Women's Studies* 12, no. 3 (2016): 343–62.
Jelassi, Mohamed Amine. *Les Minorités en Tunisie.* Thèse de Doctorat en Droit, Université de Carthage. Faculté des sciences juridiques. Tunis, 2018.
Jeridi, Hasib. *At-Ta'adudiyya ath-thaqafiyya fi-l-Jama'a al-Wataniyya. Al-'Aqaliyat fi Tunis. Al-Berber wa-l-Yahud wa-s-Suwad* [Cultural Diversity in the National Community. Minorities in Tunisia: Amazigh, Jews, and People of Colour]. Tunis: Al-Badawi lil Nasher, 2016.
Johnston-Bloom, Ruchama. "Analogising Judaism and Islam: Nineteenth and Twentieth-century German–Jewish Scholarship on Islam." *Journal of Beliefs & Values*, 38, no. 3 (2017): 267–75.
Kaabi, Amina. "A New Jewish Museum Is Set to Open in Fes Bringing Judeo-Moroccan History to the Forefront." *Mille.* July 26, 2018. http://www.milleworld.com/jewish-museum-fes/.
Kalmar, Ivan Davidson. "Arabizing the Bible: Racial Supersessionism in Nineteenth Century Christian Art and Biblical Criticism." In *Orientalism Revisited*, edited by Ian Netton, 176–86. London and New York: Routledge, 2012.
Kazdaghly, Habib. "Les Communautés dans l'Histoire de la Tunisie Moderne et Contemporaine," In *Les Communautés Méditerranéennes de Tunisie. Hommage au Doyen Mohamed Hédi Cherif*, edited by Faculté des Lettres, des Arts et des Humanités de Manouba, 59–75. Tunis: Centre de Publication Universitaires, 2006.
Keller, Catherine. *Cloud of the Impossible. Negative Theology and Planetary Entanglement.* New York: Columbia University Press, 2014.
Keskinkılıç, Ozan Zakariya, and Armin Langer (eds.). *Fremdgemacht und Reorientiert. Jüdisch-muslimische Verflechtungen.* Berlin: Verlag Yilmaz-Günay, 2018.
Kimmerling, Baruch (ed.). *The Israeli State and Society. Boundaries and Frontiers.* New York: SUNYP, 1989.
Kimmerling, Baruch, and Joel S. Migdal. *The Palestinian People: A History.* Cambridge: Harvard University Press, 2003.
Largueche, Abdelhamid. "La Minorité Noire de Tunis au XIXe Siècle." *Annuaire de l'Afrique du Nord* 30 (1991): 135–53.
Laskier, Mikha'el M. *North African Jewry in the Twentieth Century: The Jews of Morocco, Tunisia, and Algeria.* New York: New York University Press, 1994.
Lévy, Lionel. *La nation juive portugaise: Livourne, Amsterdam, Tunis, 1591–1951.* Paris: L'Harmattan, 1999.
Lucenti, Maria. "La nouvelle reforme scolaire en Tunisie: le defi démocratique entre analyse des manuels et didactique." *Foro de Educación* 15, no. 23 (2017): 219–42.
Marchand, Suzanne L. *German Orientalism in the Age of Empire.* Cambridge: Cambridge University Press, 2009.
Marzouki, Nadia. "Interview with Stéphanie Pouessel: Pluralism and Minorities in Post-Revolutionary Tunisia." *Middle East Law and Governance* 6 (2014): 53–62.
Merone, Fabio. "Enduring Class Struggle in Tunisia: the Fight for Identity beyond Political Islam." *British Journal of Middle Eastern Studies* 42, no. 1 (2015): 74–87.
Mersch, Sarah. "Interview with Sihem Bensedrine." *Quantara.de.* December 11, 2016. https://en.qantara.de/node/25750.
"Michel Boujenah très ému au Festival de Carthage." *Tribune Juive.* July 20, 2017. https://www.tribunejuive.info/spectacles/michel-boujenah-tres-emu-au-festival-de-carthage.
Mielke, Katja, and Anna-Katharina Hornidge. "Crossroads Studies: From Spatial Containers to Interactions in Differentiated Spatialities." *Crossroads Asia Working Paper Series* 15 (2014). http://crossroads-asia.de/en/publications/working-papers.html.
"Naissance de la Licra Tunisie pour lutter contre le racisme." *Kapitalis*, November 6, 2018, http://kapitalis.com/tunisie/2018/11/06/naissance-de-la-licra-tunisie-pour-lutter-contre-le-racisme/.
Nataf, Claude. "Les Mutations du Judaisme Tunisien Après la Seconde Guerre Mondiale." *Archives Juives* 39, no. 1 (2006): 125–36.

Nehdy, Dorsaf. *Die Spannungen der jüdisch-muslimischen Beziehung in Tunesien während des 20. Jahrhunderts und ihr Zusammenhang mit der massiven Auswanderung der Juden aus diesem Land*. Dissertationsschrift, FU Berlin, 2010. https://refubium.fu-berlin.de/handle/fub188/7404.

Ophir, Adi, Michal Givoni, and Sari Hanafi (eds.). *The Power of Inclusive Exclusion. Anatomy of Israeli Rule in the Occupied Palestinian Territories*. New York: Zone Books, 2009.

Patton, Paul. *Deleuzian Concepts: Philosophy, Colonization, Politics*. Stanford: Stanford University Press, 2010.

Petrucci, Filippo, and Marisa Fois. "Attitudes towards Israel in Tunisian Political Debate: From Bourguiba to the New Constitution." *The Journal of North African Studies* 21, no. 3 (2016): 392–410.

"Pour l'intégration des minorités religieuses dans les manuels scolaires tunisiens." *Kapitalis*. November 21, 2016. http://kapitalis.com/tunisie/2016/11/21/pour-lintegration-des-minorites-religieuses-dans-les-manuels-scolaires-tunisiens/.

Poussel, Stéphanie. "Les marges renaissantes: Amazigh, Juif, Noir. Ce que la révolution a changé dans ce 'petit pays homogène par excellence' qu'est la Tunisie." *L'Année du Maghreb* 8 (2012): 143–60.

———. "The Democratic Turn in Tunisia: Civic and Political Redefinition of Canons of Cultural Diversity." *Nationalism and Ethnic Politics* 22, no. 1 (2016): 50–70.

Priol, Mélinée Le. "Les juifs de Tunisie veulent valoriser leur patrimoine." *La Croix*. June 12, 2018, https://www.la-croix.com/Religion/Judaisme/juifs-Tunisie-veulent-valoriser-leur-patri
moine-2018-06-12-1200946389.

"René Trabelsi: une journée historique pour moi et pour la Tunisie." *Kapitalis*. November 13, 2018. http://kapitalis.com/tunisie/2018/11/13/rene-trabelsi-une-journee-historique-pour-moi-et-pour-la-tunisie/.

Rohde, Achim. "400 Jahre Orientalistik/Hebraistik in Hamburg. Vom Akademischen Gymnasium zur Hamburger Universität." In *Das Akademische Gymnasium. Bildung und Wissenschaft in Hamburg 1613–1883*, edited by Dirk Brietzke, Franklin Kopitzsch, and Rainer Nicolaysen, 195–212. Berlin/Hamburg: Dietrich Reimer Verlag, 2013.

———. "Asians in Europe. Reading German-Jewish History through a Post-Colonial Lens." In *Orientalism, Gender and the Jews. Literary and Artistic Transformations of European National Identity Discourses*, edited by Ulrike Brunotte, Anna-Dorothea Ludewig, and Axel Stähler, 17–32. Berlin: De Gruyter, 2015.

———. "Der innere Orient: Orientalismus, Antisemitismus und Geschlecht im Deutschland des 18.-20. Jahrhundert." *Die Welt des Islams* 45, no. 3 (2005): 370–411.

———. "Ein Hamburger Koran und die Degradierung des Hebräischen in der christlichen Theologie des 17. Jahrhunderts." *Hamburger Schlüsseldokumente zur deutsch-jüdischen Geschichte* (2018). https://juedische-geschichte-online.net/beitrag/jgo:article-51.

———. "Elfenbeinturm Revisited. Zur Geschichte der Orientalistik im Nationalsozialismus. Das Beispiel der Hamburger Universität." *Orient* 41, no. 3 (2000): 435–60.

———. "Mapping Reconfigurations: MENA and Europe post Arab Spring. Challenges for Scholarship and Politics." In *"Guests and Aliens": Re-Configuring New Mobilities in the Eastern Mediterranean after 2011—with a Special Focus on Syrian Refugees*, edited by Elif Aksaz and Jean-Francois Pérouse. Les Dossiers de l'IFEA, 2016. http://books.openedition.org/ifeagd/1829.

———. "Zur Geschichte der Abteilung Geschichte und Kultur des Vorderen Orients (Islamwissenschaft)." In *Vom Kolonialinstitut zum Asien-Afrika-Institut—100 Jahre Asien- und Afrikawissenschaften in Hamburg*, edited by Ludwig Paul, 128–49. Gossenberg: Ostasienverlag, 2008.

Rosen-Lapidot, Efrat, and Harvey Goldberg. "The Triple Loci of Jewish-Maghribi Ethnicity: Voluntary Associations in Israel and in France." *The Journal of North African Studies* 18, no. 1 (2012): 1–19.

"Round Table: Jewish Identities in the Middle East, 1876–1956." *International Journal of Middle East Studies* 46, no. 3 (2014): 577–605.

Saïd, Raouf. "Bombardement israélien de Hammam-Chott: La Tunisie devant le Conseil de Sécurité ou la conduite d'un débat." *Leaders*. October 15, 2018. http://www.leaders.com.tn/article/25706-raouf-said-bombardement-israelien-de-hammam-chott-la-tunisie-devant-le-conseil-de-securite-ou-la-conduite-d-un-debat.
Sarfati, Yusuf. *Mobilizing Religion in Middle East Politics. A Comparative Study of Israel and Turkey*. London, New York: Routledge, 2013.
Schorsch, Ismar. "Converging Cognates: The Intersection of Jewish and Islamic Studies in Nineteenth Century Germany." *Leo Baeck Institute Year Book* 55, no. 1 (2010): 3–36.
Sebag, Paul. *Histoire des Juifs de Tunisie des Origines à nos Jours*. Paris: L'Harmattan, 1991.
Shenhav, Yehouda, and Hannan Hever. "'Arab Jews' after Structuralism: Zionist Discourse and the (De)formation of an Ethnic Identity." *Social Identities* 18, no. 1 (2012): 101–18.
Spano, Nadia Gallico. *Mabruk. Ricordi di un'inguaribile ottimista*. Cagliari: AM&D edizioni, 2005.
Speck, Daniel. "Tunis: Orient für Freunde." *Die Zeit* 47/2018. November 15, 2018. https://www.zeit.de/2018/47/tunis-tunesien-nordafrika-kultur-tourismus-reise.
Stone, Nomi. "Al-Bilad al-Haqaniya? Otherness and Homeland in the Case of Djerban Jewry." *Journal of Modern Jewish Studies* 6, no. 3 (2007): 257–72.
Taïeb, Jacques. *Sociétés juives du Maghreb moderne (1500–1900). Un monde en mouvement*. Paris: Maisonneuve et Larose, 2000.
Tessler, Marc A. "The Identity of Religious Minorities in Non-Secular States: Jews in Tunisia and Morocco and Arabs in Israel." *Comparative Studies in Society and History* 20, no. 3 (1978): 359–73.
Tessler, Mark A., and Linda L. Hawkins. "The Political Culture of Jews in Tunisia and Morocco." *International Journal of Middle East Studies* 11 (1980): 59–86.
Trabelsi, Habib. "Ghriba 2017: une kermesse riche en promesses." *Kapitalis*. May 15, 2017. http://kapitalis.com/tunisie/2017/05/15/ghriba-2017-une-kermesse-riche-en-promesses/.
Tsur, Yaron. *Sipur tarbut: Yehude Tunisyah ya-aratsot Muslemiyot aḥerot* [The Evolution of a Culture: The Jews of Tunisia and Other Muslim Countries]. Jerusalem: Merkaz Zalman Shazar le-toldot Yiśra'el, 2003.
"Tunisie: Sihem Bensedrine et l'IVD poursivent leur activité." *Kapitalis*. May 24, 2018. http://kapitalis.com/tunisie/2018/05/24/tunisie-sihem-bensedrine-et-livd-poursuivent-leur-activite/.
"Tunisie-Monastir: un juif tête de liste d'Ennahdha aux municipals." *Kapitalis*. February 19, 2018. http://kapitalis.com/tunisie/2018/02/19/tunisie-ennahdha-choisit-un-juif-tunisien-pour-participer-aux-municipales/.
Udovitch, Abraham L., and Lucette Valensi. *The Last Arab Jews: The Communities of Jerba, Tunisia*. Chur: Harwood Academic Publishers, 1984.
"Unterricht Macht Schule." *Goethe-Institut Tunisia*. https://www.goethe.de/ins/tn/de/kul/sup/tup/ums.html.
Valensi, Lucette. "Espaces Publics, Espaces Comunautaires aux XIXe et XXe Siècles." *Printemps* 10 (1994): 97–109.
Von Hirschhausen, Béatrice, Hannes Grandits, Claudia Kraft, Dietmar Müller, and Thomas Serrier. *Phantomgrenzen. Räume und Akteure in der Zeit neu denken*. Göttingen: Wallstein, 2015.
Watson, Robert. "Secondhand Memories: Franco-Tunisian Jewish Women and the Predicament of Writing Return." *Life Writing* 10, no. 1 (2013): 25–46.
"Yassine Ayari fera appel en justice contre la nomination de René Trabelsi." *Kapitalis*. November 6, 2018. http://kapitalis.com/tunisie/2018/11/06/yassine-ayari-fera-appel-en-justice-contre-la-nomination-de-rene-trabelsi/.

Chapter Eleven

Methodological Canaanism

The Case for a Rupture between Jewish Studies and Israel Studies

Johannes Becke

> To you, the Hebrew homeland is truly and literally a homeland—not as a vision, a desire, or a metaphor; not as a solution to the Jewish problem, not as a solution to global problems, and not as a solution for the psychological complexes of those struck by the Diaspora. To you, the Hebrew language is truly and literally your language; the language of your mother, your culture and your soul; the one and only language of your thought and emotion. To you, the Hebrew reality is the reality which has shaped your character and your thought, the landscape of your soul is the landscape of the homeland, and your past is but the past of the homeland. (Letter to the Hebrew Youth, Yonatan Ratosh)[1]

This chapter introduces the concept of methodological Canaanism, an approach which calls for a systematic rupture between the research fields of Jewish Studies and Israel Studies. Building on the writings of the Canaanites (Young Hebrews),[2] the chapter argues that the field of Jewish Studies is unequipped to explore the reality of Israeli politics, culture, and society. Instead of reading Israeli history exclusively through the lens of Jewish survival (Diasporism) or the dialectic of Zionist prowess and Palestinian suffering (Palestinocentrism), methodological Canaanism explores the rise of a Jewish-Israeli nation as an integral element of nation-building and state formation in the Middle East and North Africa. Whereas Jewish Studies focuses on the history, culture, and religion of an ethnosectarian Diaspora, Israel Studies as a field studies the national movement and the nation-state which emerged from and *against* this Diaspora. While the two research fields are linked by Hebrew as a common language, the historical rupture of the Zionist project in Jewish history calls for a disciplinary rupture between scholars of a stateless Diaspora and scholars of an anti-Diasporic state project. For the emerging field of Israel Studies, this insight calls for a systematic integration of Israel Studies into the broader field of Middle East Studies: Students who specialize in Israeli politics, culture, and society should be trained in advanced Hebrew *and* Arabic; courses on Israel should systematically integrate the Israeli case into a larger set of Middle Eastern states and societies; and graduates of these programs should receive a degree in Middle East Studies instead of Jewish Studies or Israel Studies.

THE SHTETL IN THE JUNGLE: ISRAEL STUDIES AS ENCLAVE STUDIES

In its idiosyncratic dualism of exceptionalism and parochialism, the emerging research field of Israel Studies closely mirrors the historical trajectory of the Zionist project. After its exodus from the Comparative Politics of Western nation-states, Israel Studies gazes toward Jewish Studies in a peculiar combination of denial, ambivalence, and nostalgia. Having failed to integrate into Middle East Studies, the research field has long begun its retreat into post-post-Zionist localism,[3] an approach which might ultimately threaten to turn the field of Israel Studies into a form of Afula Studies.

This trend toward *Israel Studies as Enclave Studies* is driven both by donor politics and an enduring legacy of methodological exceptionalism. From a perspective of donor institutions, the establishment of single-issue or in fact single-country professorships and research centers seems to guarantee maximal impact and attaching Israel Studies to Jewish Studies promises to bring Israel Studies closer to its target demographic—the increasingly unattached Jewish youth of the West. At the same time, this curious separation of Israel from the region of the Middle East as a proverbial villa in the jungle (or perhaps a shtetl in the jungle) reflects a profound disconnect of the Jewish-Israeli experience from regional history: as a modern revenant of Allosemitism,[4] the methodological exceptionalism behind the approach of Israel Studies as Enclave Studies understands Zionism and the State of Israel as "a nationalist movement and a nation-state radically different from all the others, needing separate concepts to describe and comprehend them and special treatment in all or most social intercourse."[5] A look at the major Israel Studies conferences throughout the last decade reveals the continuity of what Michael Barnett famously described as the "politics of uniqueness."[6] Within the research field of Israel Studies, Israeli politics, culture, and society are almost exclusively studied within a single-case research design, thereby treating Israel as an idiosyncratic case, unfit for comparative theory-building and global history alike. Instead of overcoming methodological exceptionalism, the rapid growth of Israel Studies threatens to entrench it. Within the emerging network of new research centers, professorships, journals, academic associations and specialized degrees in "Israel Studies," the "politics of uniqueness" (Barnett) has long become hegemonic.

The rise of methodological exceptionalism within Israel Studies is closely related to the decline of the settler-colonial paradigm. Comparisons between European settler-colonialism and the Zionist project were always somewhat tendentious, but at least they proposed a strongly comparative framework. Once this approach had atrophied into a degenerating research program (Lakatos), its withdrawal into the Israel-obsessed academic niche of "Settler-Colonial Studies" (with its *own* conferences and academic journals) cleared the path for Allozionism, a multilayered pattern of exceptionalism within Israel Studies. The secret to the success of this paradigm might be found in its connectivity to a wide range of discursive formations, ranging from messianic *Heilsgeschichte* (redemptive history) to outright demonization. Both Zionists and anti-Zionists will agree on the *moral* exceptionalism of the Zionist project; both Philosemites and Antisemites will emphasize the *unique* characteristics of Israeli statehood which seem to set it apart from its neighbors; Israel Studies scholars in both India and Germany will emphasize the *special* nature of German-Israeli or Indian-Israeli ties.

At first sight, the close integration of Israel Studies into Jewish Studies promises to overcome this methodological exceptionalism. By studying Israel as a *Jewish* state,[7] the enclave situation of the research field might be overcome by studying the continuity between Jewish-Diasporic and Jewish-Israeli culture. Didn't Herzl write his books in German instead of Hebrew? Didn't Diaspora Jews have *other* forms of self-government before 1948? Shouldn't the most radical forms of Israeli nativism, including Canaanism itself, best be understood as a paradoxical continuity of Jewish-Diasporic thought, as Baruch Kurzweil famously argued?[8]

In contrast, methodological Canaanism argues for a systematic rupture between Jewish Studies and Israel Studies. Any integration of the two fields will invariably reproduce a Zionist or a Diasporist teleology, thereby reading either Jewish-Diasporic or Jewish-Israeli life as exceptional—if not both. While Jewish Studies has already produced a rich set of historiographic and theoretical tools to study Jewish-Diasporic life in its complex interaction with non-Jewish environments, Israel Studies still faces the challenge of doing the same in a different context: Despite the fantasy of Israel as an isolated colonial villa or an Ashkenazi shtetl in the jungle, the country has long become *part* of the region of the Middle East and North Africa, whether by Mizrahi-Jewish immigration or by Israel's interactions with its neighbors.[9]

THE NEGATION OF THE LEVANT

Canaanism, whether in its radical (Yonatan Ratosh), revisionist (Uri Avnery) or pragmatic form (Aharon Amir),[10] has been interpreted as the most radical form of the Zionist "negation of the Diaspora,"[11] a "total alternative that would sever Israelism from Judaism and would adapt only the elements of nativist affiliation; . . . a complete severance from exilic Jewish history."[12] By proclaiming a new Hebrew nation, shaped by the Hebrew language and the Hebrew homeland,[13] Canaanism (especially as an artistic and poetic phenomenon) built on a long line of "Nietzschean artistic consciousness"[14] found in the works of Shaul Tchernichovsky and Micha Josef Berdichewsky. Nonetheless, despite anxious displays of sons-of-the-soil nativism, Canaanism was profoundly shaped by Jewish-Diasporic culture and Zionist ideology. Canaanite *Herrenmenschentum* breathed the Zionist ethos of creating the "first Hebrews" out of the "last Jews," Canaanite factionalism echoed the *Luftmenschentum* of Jewish-Diasporic radicalism, and the puzzling obsession with anti-Zionist countermyths struggled to belie its origins in Zionist mythmaking. In addition to the negation of the Diaspora, the historiosophical speculations by Adya Gur Horon about an ancient Hebrew past[15] of the *entire* Middle East formed the basis for another pattern of denial—the negation of Palestinian-Arab identity. Given this twofold denial of the Jewish-Diasporic past and the Palestinian-Arab present—why should methodological Canaanism be a fruitful approach for Israel Studies? Wouldn't the "religionization" (Hebrew: *hadata)* of Israeli society prove that "all the possibilities of the Canaanite option have been exhausted in the discourse on Israeli identity"?[16]

Indeed, the integration of Jewish Studies and Israel Studies promises to overcome the negation of the Diaspora—but only at the price of a systematic *negation of the Levant*, defined as the negation of the dynamics of indigenization, Creolization, and Levantinization, which have shaped contemporary Jewish-Israeli culture, politics, and society. The Canaanites may have erred in their two-pronged attack on the windmills of Zionism and Arabism, but they were the first to grasp the revolutionary impact of indigenization on Jewish-Israeli life in the Middle East—even if they might have preferred the terms "the Land of the Euphrates" or "the Semitic Space." In this sense, methodological Canaanism as a form of historiographic indigenization marks the paradigmatic shift from a society of immigrants to a society of natives. Consider this from Israel Bartal:

> For this society, it goes without saying that the experience of the land, its past, its landscapes and its population are part of the natural experience of the native son. He can ask all the tough questions, openly deal with "sensitive" subjects, belittle the question of what the nations of the world may think and uncover

the complexity of his research objects, their relativity and the ambiguity of the sources under investigation.[17]

The negation of the Levant, especially the systematic denial of historical, cultural, and political parallels between Israel and its neighbors, finds its origins in the "great chain of Orientalism."[18] Despite a profound ambivalence toward European culture,[19] powerful forces within the Zionist project sought to Westernize, modernize, enlighten, and indeed *whiten* the new Hebrew. Despite a profound Levantinization of Israel's cuisine, popular culture, and political system, the denial of the Levant forms part of the methodological exceptionalism of Israel Studies. Within Israeli academia, Israel Studies and Middle East Studies remain institutionally segregated.[20] In fact, the growth of Israel Studies (often based on international students who come to Israel for two-year MA programs) has exacerbated the tendency toward Israel Studies as Enclave Studies. In the case of Ben Gurion University, Israel Studies (at the Sde Boker campus) and Middle East Studies (at the Be'er Sheva campus) are separated by 56km of geographical distance.

The *pragmatic* reasons for this gap between Israel Studies and Middle East Studies are relatively easy to locate. On Israeli campuses, the freezing of the peace process has led to a substantial decline of firsthand knowledge about the region; Arabic language training at Israeli schools is security-oriented and focuses on Modern Standard Arabic instead of the Palestinian Arab dialect;[21] antinormalization efforts and the BDS movement have put additional pressure on people-to-people contacts between Israeli scholars and their colleagues in the Arab world. The same is true about Israel Studies *outside* of Israel, of course, especially in the Anglosphere—faithful disciples of Saidian orthodoxy will struggle to reconcile their own commitment to the Palestinian cause with the presence of an Israel Studies professorship in their department of Middle East Studies.

Within Zionist discourse, however, the negation of the Levant represents a denial of indigenization, a pattern described by Israel Bartal as "a characteristic display of insecurity, of estrangement to the land and its past and a profound need to apologize."[22] Scholars have described the trajectory of the Zionist project from a Western state project with a Middle Eastern infrastructure to a Middle Eastern state with a Western infrastructure[23] as a form of Levantinization,[24] Creolization,[25] or Arabization,[26] a process which calls for a critical review of Orientalist clichés about the region and Occidentalist clichés about Israel.[27] In the words of Atalia Omer, it is "misleading and ahistorical to refer to fourth- and fifth-generation Israelis as persistently European, even if they are Ashkenazi."[28]

Perhaps, the persistent negation of the Levant touches a deeper anxiety about the loss of Jewish-Diasporic exceptionalism. While the decidedly Middle Eastern nature of Israeli cuisine may be an appealing element of nation branding, the ongoing Levantinization (or rather Lebanonization) of Israeli politics calls into question the Zionist mission of creating a *model state* for a *model society*. For cultural Zionists like Nahum Goldmann, the normalizing effect of indigenization represented a crucial threat to the Zionist project, which might risk becoming "some kind of second Lebanon, or a second Syria, even if it were to reach a somewhat higher quality, for as such it will not be able to fulfill its historical mission. The State of Israel needs to serve as a tool to fulfil the unique Jewish ideas and not just preach them, ranging from the prophets onward to Achad Ha'Am, Martin Buber, and A.D. Gordon."[29] In this context, a core element of Israel's political assimilation to the Middle East might have been the capture and military rule over the occupied territories, creating a political regime of coercive rule not very different from the *mukhabarat* state among its Arab neighbors.[30] In retrospect, this scenario of authoritarian spill-over followed the prophetic warning of Yeshayahu Leibowitz after the Six Day War. According to Leibowitz, Israeli expansionism—not unlike Maronite expansionism in the case of Greater Lebanon[31] — would turn the country from a Jewish state into a "'Canaanite' state," "concerned only with the specific problems of rule and administration of this state—the problem of ruling over both Jews and Arabs. Its situation would be much like that of the state of Lebanon, perplexed as it is with the relations between Maronite Christians, Moslems, and Druzes."[32]

METHODOLOGICAL CANAANISM: ISRAEL STUDIES AS MIDDLE EAST STUDIES

While political Canaanism proclaimed the birth of a "new Hebrew nation in the Land of Israel," methodological Canaanism translates this premise into the analysis of Zionist thought and Israeli reality by studying this new nation as an "independent and separate entity" with crucial "ties to World Jewry," but nonetheless firmly "implanted in the Semitic Space" as a member of the "society of self-liberating peoples" in the postcolonial world.[33] This regional-comparative approach of integrating Israel Studies into Middle East Studies struggles first and foremost against methodological exceptionalism, an approach which threatens to turn the research field (in classical Canaanite parlance) into an "isolationist entity," bound by "chains which restrain its development and its self-determination" and "permanently depending on the support of the Jewish Diaspora."[34] As a radical alternative to Israel Studies as Enclave Studies, methodological Canaanism emphasizes Israel's geographic location and political nature as an integral element of the Middle East and North Africa—without denying its close ties to the Jewish Diaspora or the entanglement of the Zionist project into the "colonial system."[35] In other words, methodological Canaanism writes Israel into the study of the Middle East—and the Middle East into the study of Israel.

Studying Israel as a part of the Middle East recognizes the dual rupture of indigenization: the rupture with the European origins of Zionism, and the rupture with the politics, culture, and history of the Jewish Diaspora. In contrast to the isolationist logic of Zionism and the exclusionary logic of Arabism, this regional-comparative approach puts special emphasis on the dynamics of "taking root in the region."[36] While political Canaanism proposed various schemes of regional integration (ranging from confederationism to "de-Zionization"),[37] methodological Canaanism recognizes the fact that Israel has long *become* a part of the region and calls for its systematic inclusion into the study of the Middle East. This aspect of exploring Israel in a Middle Eastern setting may be particularly relevant for the religious counterrevolution or "religionization" in Israeli society. While political Canaanism struggled for a secular alternative against ethnosectarianism, methodological Canaanism recognizes that Israel's religionization[38] might simply be another element of indigenization. After all, in a region shaped by irredentism, militarism, and religious nationalism, the isomorphic dynamics and feedback effects of "taking root in the region" might take on a much darker side than the playful Creolization of Israeli cuisine.

By emphasizing the rupture between Jewish-Diasporic state evasion and Jewish-Israeli state formation,[39] methodological Canaanism calls for the application of a different set of theoretical and historiographic tools to the study of Zionism and Israel. While Jewish Studies has long developed sophisticated concepts to study the history, culture, and religion of a dispersed, acephalous, and segmented community, Israel Studies requires its own approaches to explore the transition of this very community toward centralized state control through a process of indigenization, territorialization, and nationalization. In contrast to the strong philological tradition within Jewish Studies, Israel Studies looks toward the Social Sciences to explore the dynamics of nationalism, state formation, and ethnic conflict. This methodological rupture with Jewish Studies becomes particularly relevant for the question of theory-guided comparison. Comparative approaches within Jewish Studies will look for similar forms of religious practice, ritual, and interpretive tradition; in contrast, comparative approaches within Israel Studies will search for comparable patterns of settlement, statehood, and militarization.

In this comparative endeavor, the Zionist project may of course be fruitfully compared with national movements outside of the Middle East, including Greek and Armenian Diaspora nationalism,[40] the war financing of the Viet Cong,[41] or ethnoreligious minority nationalism in British India.[42] Nonetheless, comparative case studies within a Middle Eastern setting might be the best research strategy to explore the dual rupture of indigenization. Instead of comparing the Zionist project to European settler-colonialism or

Jewish-Diasporic self-rule, methodological Canaanism privileges intraregional comparisons between Israel and its neighbors, whether in the domain of state formation,[43] territorial expansion,[44] or state-Diaspora relations.[45]

As an emerging research field, Israel Studies is still in a state of flux. In the words of Zeev Tzahor, it is still "unclear whether the history of Israel should be linked to the history of the Jews and Judaism or whether it will be linked to the history of the Middle East by cutting the link to Judaism and global Jewry."[46] Given the alignment of donor interests and Israeli political culture toward methodological exceptionalism (Israel Studies as Enclave Studies), the counterhegemonic research agenda of methodological Canaanism will have to emphasize the advantages of a regional-comparative approach (Israel Studies as Middle East Studies). Alternatively, the integration of Israel Studies into Jewish Studies would perpetuate the negation of the Levant—and well-meaning attempts to create a field of "Israel/Palestine Studies" would first and foremost respond to the Palestinocentric anxieties of American-Jewish Post-Zionism instead of exploring Jewish-Israeli indigenization in the Middle East and North Africa. In contrast, Israel Studies will thrive if it can be established as an integral element of a comparative discipline of Middle East Studies—without repeating the twofold mistakes of political Canaanism, the negation of the Jewish-Diasporic past and the Palestinian-Arab present.

PUTTING METHODOLOGICAL CANAANISM INTO PRACTICE

If methodological Canaanism calls for a rupture between Jewish Studies and Israel Studies, how should this rupture be implemented on the ground? Four elements might be crucial for a more sophisticated study of Jewish-Israeli indigenization in the Middle East—evading the fallacy of self-Orientalization, learning from the settler-colonial paradigm, specifying the advantages of intraregional case studies, and systematically including Israel into comparative research and teaching on the Middle East. First, the fallacy of self-Orientalization consists in an exclusive reading of Middle Eastern Jewish (Mizrahi) culture as "indigenous" to the region while European Jewish (Ashkenazi) culture continues to be interpreted as "foreign," "settler-colonial," or "white." In fact, both Ashkenazi-Jewish and Mizrahi-Jewish Israelis went through similar processes of flight and expulsion, immigration and settlement, Hebraization, and finally indigenization. In contrast to the retroactive invention of "Arab-Jews" by Iraqi-Israelis academics, most Middle Eastern Jews did *not* undergo a systematic process of cultural Arabization—and even if they did, Arabic-speaking Jews from Morocco were as foreign to the Land of Israel/Palestine as Russian-speaking Jews from Odessa. Instead of replicating Orientalist clichés about Umm Kulthum and Shakshouka in Israeli culture, the more intriguing research approach might be a regional-comparative focus on the *Occidentalized* features of the Zionist project. For instance, scholars might explore the dynamics of "Third World colonialism"[47] in the Middle East by comparing Greater Israel to Greater Morocco, study secularism as a form of elite-driven nation-building in Tunisia and Israel or compare the impact of high modernist developmentalism on Israeli and Egyptian statecraft.

Second, methodological Canaanism would be well-advised to learn from the settler-colonial paradigm. Even if its parallelization between European expansion and Zionist settlement was somewhat tendentious, it derived its analytical leverage from its succinct reduction of complexity. Regional-comparative approaches should emulate this focus on elements of the Zionist project which are clearly distinctive, yet fully comparable. One example might be the transformative shift from state evasion to state formation, which calls for a more systematic comparison between Jewish, Kurdish, and Berber nationalism.[48] Another example would be the indivisibility of ethnicity and religion, which could serve as the basis for a structured comparison between Zionism and other forms of ethnosectarianism by minority groups (for instance Assyrian and Aramean nationalism by Aramaic-speaking Christians).[49] A third example can be found in what Michael Walzer has called the "paradox of liberation,"[50] the phenomenon of religious counterrevolutions against secularizing state projects. Walzer himself compares the Israeli case to India and Algeria, but secular Zionist *mamlakhtiyut* might also be compared to the state-building ideologies of two other Middle Eastern countries (both of which used to be close allies of Israel), namely Kemalism in Turkey and modern Iranian nationalism under the Pahlavi dynasty.

Third, to specify the advantages of comparative case studies *within* the Middle East, case selection should be expanded beyond highly similar cases like Turkey as a militarized ethnic democracy or Armenia as a Diaspora-driven minority state with a strong pattern of irredentist expansionism. Instead, the Zionist project might also be compared to more *dissimilar* cases of Middle Eastern state formation, including proto-states which have failed to cross the threshold of statehood (the Sahrawi Arab Democratic Republic), ephemeral states (like the Rif Republic), postrevolutionary states controlled by religious nationalists (Iran), or nonstate national movements (like the various factions of Kurdish nationalism). In addition, comparative case studies which systematically include Israel into a Middle Eastern sample will need to make the case for a theory-guided specification of regional boundaries which go beyond a vague sense of regional belonging. Promising examples for such an approach might be found in a historical-institutionalist focus on shared institutional legacies, whether in terms of Ottoman rule, colonial law, or postcolonial high modernism.

Fourth, in order to systematically include Israel into comparative research and teaching on the Middle East, Israel Studies should be offered as a specialization in a Middle East Studies program instead of isolating it as a stand-alone degree (like an MA in "Israel Studies"). Instead of teaching classes about Israel (without the Middle East) or classes about the Middle East (without Israel), scholars should incorporate Israel as a case study into comparative classes about the modern Middle East, whether the class focuses on state formation, gender relations, or language politics. In addition, if seminars are cotaught for instance by Israel Studies and Turkish Studies faculty, they should be complemented with specialized reading classes which focus on primary documents in Hebrew or Turkish. In this context, the approach of encouraging Israel Studies to take root within Middle East Studies also concerns the question of language teaching itself. Students who specialize in Israel Studies will require a significantly higher level of Modern Hebrew than students who focus on Jewish Studies. While degrees in Jewish Studies rarely require a language proficiency which goes beyond one or two years of Hebrew (reaching level *Aleph* or respectively level *Bet*), students who specialize in the field of Israel Studies should have three years of Modern Hebrew within a BA program, and five years within a full MA program. At the same time, they should be systematically required to study Modern Standard Arabic (minimum of two years) and, wherever possible, acquire at least a basic familiarity with spoken Palestinian Arabic (at least one year).

This focus on Jewish-Israeli indigenization in the Middle East should not result in an artificial negation of the Jewish-Diasporic past and present. After all, one of the most deplorable features of political Canaanism might have been its sectarian radicalism, resulting in bizarre slogans such as "Zionists out of the State of Israel!" (at a Canaanite protest against the World Zionist Congress in 1951[51]) or Shlomo Sand's astounding failure to recognize that *How and when did I stop being a Jew?*[52] might perhaps be the most, well, *Jewish* book title in the history of the Canaanite movement. Students who specialize in Israel Studies will need an advanced understanding of modern Jewish-Diasporic history, including Jewish religious law, Jewish philosophy, and Jewish art—both to appreciate the *rupture* of the Zionist project and to recognize the many continuities between Jewish-Diasporic and Jewish-Israeli culture. Israel has long moved away from MAPAI-style secular biblicism, and any introductory class on Israeli politics and society will necessarily have to talk about the Temple Mount, the messianism of the settler movement, and the process of religionization within the IDF. In this context, by including Israel into classes on state and religion in the Middle East, the role of *halacha* and *shari'a* in modern Middle Eastern societies could be discussed in a comparative framework. Alternatively, classes on state and religion in Israeli society could be cotaught by Israel Studies faculty and specialists in Jewish Studies. For pragmatic reasons of language teaching alone, Israel Studies positions will continue to rely systematically on the infrastructure of Jewish Studies, even if the natural home of an Israel Studies professorship will always be a pluralistic department of Middle East Studies. Israel Studies *without* the teaching of Modern Hebrew and *without* the analysis of primary sources in the classroom would be mere window-dressing. The Canaanite movement was right in its analysis that the Hebraization of Jewish-Diasporic culture represented a primary turning point in the history of Jewish-Israeli indigenization. This transformational experience can only be conveyed to students based on primary sources in Hebrew itself—even if contemporary Israeli society might look very different from the aggressively secular, distinctly post-Jewish, and proudly anti-Zionist "Homeland of the Hebrews" which the Canaanites once imagined.

CONCLUSION: AFTER POST-POST-ZIONISM

After the nationalist myth-making of early Zionist historiography, the critical backlash of Post-Zionism and the localism of Post-Post-Zionism,[53] methodological Canaanism might be a helpful tool against methodological exceptionalism in the field of Israel Studies, not least by including the historiography of the Zionist project into a regional-comparative perspective on nationalism and state formation in the modern Middle East and North Africa. Methodological Canaanism emphasizes the rupture of Jewish-Israeli indigenization in the Middle East. Students of a dispersed, acephalous, and segmented Diaspora will need very *different* tools and comparative approaches than students of a state project which invested tremendous resources into nationalization, territorialization, and centralization. While Israel Studies relies critically on the expertise and infrastructure of Jewish Studies, especially for advanced classes of Modern Hebrew, students who specialize in Zionist thought and Israeli reality will need an advanced knowledge of the modern Middle East, including a substantial knowledge of Modern Standard Arabic and ideally of spoken Palestinian Arabic. Israel Studies without Jewish Studies will consist of mere window dressing, perhaps as a continuation of the Zionist (and Canaanite) negation of the Diaspora. In contrast, Israel Studies without Middle East Studies would perpetuate the negation of the Levant, the negation of the dynamics of indigenization, Creolization, and Levantinization which have shaped contemporary Jewish-Israeli culture, politics, and society.

While some faculty of Jewish Studies tend to fear that Israel Studies will eat into their limited number of students, the campus reality on the ground looks very different. Classes in Israel Studies, especially if they are well-integrated into a program of Middle East Studies, attract an *additional* student audience which rarely would have thought of attending courses in Jewish Studies. Students are well aware that the two research fields overlap, but that a focus on modern Israeli society will require a different specialization and prepare them for a different job market than the option of Jewish Studies. Instead of forcing the two research fields onto a Procrustean bed, whether of a Zionist or a Diasporist making, Israel Studies should therefore be encouraged to take roots in the domain of Middle East Studies to become, as Uri Avnery would have said, a "free partner in its shape and future."[54]

NOTES

1. Yonatan Ratosh, "Ktav El Ha-Noar Ha-Ivri (Letter to the Hebrew Youth)," in *Reshit Ha-Yamim* [The First of Days] (Tel Aviv: Hadar, 1982), 32–37. All translations by the author unless otherwise indicated.
2. For an overview, James S. Diamond, *Homeland or Holy Land? The Canaanite Critique of Israel* (Bloomington and Indianapolis: Indiana University Press, 1986).
3. On Post-Post-Zionism, see Assaf Likhovski, "Post-Post-Zionist Historiography," *Israel Studies* 15, no. 2 (2010): 1–23.
4. Zygmunt Bauman, "Allosemitism: Premodern, Modern, Postmodern," in *Modernity, Culture and "the Jew,"* Bryan Cheyette and Laura Marcus (eds.) (Polity Press, 1998), 143–56.
5. Johannes Becke, "Beyond Allozionism: Exceptionalizing and De-Exceptionalizing the Zionist Project," *Israel Studies* 23, no. 2 (2018): 168–93, 169.
6. Michael N. Barnett, "The Politics of Uniqueness: The Status of the Israeli Case," in *Israel in Comparative Perspective. Challenging the Conventional Wisdom*, Michael N. Barnett (ed.) (Albany: State University of New York Press, 1996), 3–25.
7. Derek Jonathan Penslar, "Is Israel a Jewish State?" in *Israel in History. The Jewish State in Comparative Perspective* (London and New York: Routledge, 2007), 65–89.
8. Baruch Kurzweil, "Mahuta U-Mekoroteha Shel Tnuat 'Ha-Ivrim Ha-Tze'irim' ('ha-Kna'anim')" [Essence and Origins of the Movement of the 'Young Hebrew' ('Canaanites')], in *Sifrutenu Ha-Chadasha—Hemshech o Mahapecha?* [Our New Literature: Continuity or Revolution] (Tel Aviv: Schocken, 1959).
9. Atalia Omer, "Hitmazrehut or Becoming the East: Re-Orienting Israeli Social Mapping," *Critical Sociology* 43, no. 3 (2017): 949–76.
10. Diamond, *Homeland or Holy Land? The Canaanite Critique of Israel*, 95.
11. Yaacov Shavit, *The New Hebrew Nation. A Study in Israeli Heresy and Fantasy* (London: Frank Cass, 1987), 11.
12. David Ohana, "The Israeli Identity and the Canaanite Option," in *The Gift of the Land and the Fate of the Canaanites in Jewish Thought*, Katell Berthelot, Joseph E. David, and Marc Hirshman (eds.) (Oxford: Oxford University Press, 2014), 311–52, 311.
13. A. G. Horon, "Eretz Ha-Kedem" [The Land of Kedem], in *Mi-Nitzachon Le-Mapolet* [From Victory to Crash], Yonatan Ratosh (ed.) (Tel Aviv: Hadar, 1976), 40; Uri Avnery, *Ha-Minshar Ha-Ivri* [The Hebrew Manifesto] (Tel Aviv: Ha-Pe'ula Ha-Shemit, 1959).
14. Elliott Rabin, "'Hebrew' Culture: The Shared Foundations of Ratosh's Ideology and Poetry," *Modern Judaism* 19, no. 2 (1999): 119–32, 127.
15. A. G. Horon, *Kedem Va-Erev: Kna'an—Toldot Eretz Ha-Ivrim* [East and West: Canaan—The History of the Land of the Hebrews] (Tel Aviv: Dvir, 2000).
16. Ohana, "The Israeli Identity and the Canaanite Option," 311.
17. Israel Bartal, "'Am' ve-'aretz' Be-Reshit Ha-Elef Ha-Shlishi: Sikum Beinayim" ['People' and 'Land' at the Turn of the Third Millenium: An Intermediate Summary], *Cathedra* 100 (2001): 21–26, 26.
18. Aziza Khazzoom, "The Great Chain of Orientalism: Jewish Identity, Stigma Management, and Ethnic Exclusion in Israel," *American Sociological Review* 68, no. 4 (2003): 481–510.
19. Jehuda Reinharz and Yaacov Shavit, *Glorious, Accursed Europe. An Essay on Jewish Ambivalence* (Waltham, MA: Brandeis University Press, 2010).

20. Elie Podeh, "Israel in the Middle East or Israel and the Middle East: A Reappraisal," in *Arab-Jewish Relations. From Conflict to Resolution? Essays in Honour of Professor Moshe Ma'oz*, Elie Podeh and Asher Kaufman (eds.) (Brighton and Portland: Sussex Academic Press, 2006), 93–113.

21. Yonatan Mendel, *The Creation of Israeli Arabic. Political and Security Considerations in the Making of Arabic Language Studies in Israel* (New York: Palgrave Macmillan, 2014).

22. Bartal, "'Am' ve-'aretz' Be-Reshit Ha-Elef Ha-Shlishi: Sikum Beinayim," 26.

23. Many thanks to Orit Rozin for this pithy observation.

24. Jacqueline Kahanoff, "What about Levantinization?" *Journal of Levantine Studies* 1, no. 1 (2011): 13–22.

25. Johannes Becke, "Dismantling the Villa in the Jungle: Matzpen, Zochrot, and the Whitening of Israel," *Interventions: International Journal of Postcolonial Studies* (2019). (Forthcoming).

26. Avi Shilon, "Ha-Arabisatziya Shel Israel ve-Ha-Piyus She-Miri Regev Asuya Lecholel" [Israel's Arabization and the Reconciliation Which Miri Regev Could Bring About], *Ha'aretz*, June 9, 2018.

27. Johannes Becke, "Towards a De-Occidentalist Perspective on Israel: The Case of the Occupation," *Journal of Israeli History* 33, no. 1 (2014): 1–23.

28. Omer, "Hitmazrehut or Becoming the East," 949–76, 952.

29. Nahum Goldmann, *Be-Darkei Ami* [On the Paths of My People] (Jerusalem: HaSifriya HaZionit, 1968), 176. Many thanks to Orit Rozin for directing my attention to this passage.

30. Ilan Pappé, "The Mukhabarat State of Israel: A State of Oppression Is Not a State of Exception," in *Thinking Palestine*, Ronit Lentin (ed.) (London and New York: Zed Books, 2008), 148–69.

31. Oren Barak, *State Expansion and Conflict: In and between Israel/Palestine and Lebanon* (Cambridge: Cambridge University Press, 2017).

32. Yeshayahu Leibowitz, "The Territories [1968]," in *Judaism, Human Values and the Jewish State*, Eliezer Goldman (ed.) (Cambridge: Harvard University Press, 1992), 223–28, 225.

33. Avnery, *Ha-Minshar Ha-Ivri*, 7.

34. Avnery, *Ha-Minshar Ha-Ivri*, 8.

35. Avnery, *Ha-Minshar Ha-Ivri*.

36. Avnery, *Ha-Minshar Ha-Ivri*, 9.

37. Oded Pilavsky, "De-Zionisaziya: Mai Ka Mashma Lan?" [De-Zionization: What Does It Mean?]" *Matzpen* 53 (1970).

38. Yoav Peled and Horit Herman Peled, *The Religionization of Israeli Society* (London and New York: Routledge, 2018).

39. James C. Scott, *The Art of Not Being Governed: An Anarchist History of Upland Southeast Asia* (New Haven, CT: Yale University Press, 2009).

40. Anthony D. Smith, "Diasporas and Homelands in History: The Case of the Classic Diasporas," in *The Call of the Homeland: Diaspora Nationalisms, Past and Present*, Allon Gal, Athena S. Leoussi, and Anthony D. Smith (eds.) (Leiden and Boston: Brill, 2010), 3–26.

41. Derek Jonathan Penslar, "Rebels without a Patron State: How Israel Financed the 1948 War," in *Purchasing Power. The Economics of Modern Jewish History*, Rebecca Kobrin and Adam Teller (eds.) (Philadelphia: University of Pennsylvania Press, 2015), 171–91.

42. Faisal Devji, *Muslim Zion. Pakistan as a Political Idea* (Cambridge: Harvard University Press, 2013).

43. Michael N. Barnett, *Confronting the Costs of War* (Princeton: Princeton University Press, 1993); Joel S. Migdal, *Strong Societies and Weak States* (Princeton, NJ: Princeton University Press, 1988).

44. Becke, "Towards a De-Occidentalist Perspective on Israel"; Oded Haklai and Neophytos Loizides (eds.), *Settlers in Contested Lands. Territorial Disputes and Ethnic Conflicts* (Stanford: Stanford University Press, 2015); Barak, *State Expansion and Conflict*.

45. Moshe Ma'oz and Gabriel Sheffer (eds.), *Middle Eastern Minorities and Diasporas* (Brighton: Sussex Academic Press, 2002).

46. Zeev Tzahor, "Toldot Medinat Israel: Akademia ve-Politika" [History of the State of Israel: Academia and Politics], *Cathedra* 100 (2001): 378–94, 394. Many thanks to Rona Yona for directing my attention to this passage.

47. Awet Tewelde Weldemichael, *Third World Colonialism and Strategies of Liberation. Eritrea and East Timor Compared* (Cambridge: Cambridge University Press, 2013).

48. Ofra Bengio and Bruce Maddy-Weitzman, "Mobilised Diasporas: Kurdish and Berber Movements in Comparative Perspective," *Kurdish Studies* 1, no. 1 (2013): 65–90.

49. Adam H. Becker, *Revival and Awakening. American Evangelical Missionaries in Iran and the Origins of Assyrian Nationalism* (Chicago and London: Chicago University Press, 2015).

50. Michael Walzer, *The Paradox of Liberation. Secular Revolutions and Religious Counterrevolution* (New Haven: Yale University Press, 2015).

51. Diamond, *Homeland or Holy Land?*, 64.

52. Shlomo Sand, *Eich Ve-Matai Chadalti Lihiyot Yehudi? Mabat Israeli* [How and When Did I Stop Being a Jew? An Israeli Perspective] (Tel Aviv: Dvir, 2013).

53. Likhovski, "Post-Post-Zionist Historiography."

54. Avnery, *Ha-Minshar Ha-Ivri*, 9.

BIBLIOGRAPHY

Avnery, Uri. *Ha-Minshar Ha-Ivri* [The Hebrew Manifesto]. Tel Aviv: Ha-Pe'ula Ha-Shemit, 1959.

Barak, Oren. *State Expansion and Conflict: In and between Israel/Palestine and Lebanon*. Cambridge: Cambridge University Press, 2017.

Barnett, Michael N. "The Politics of Uniqueness: The Status of the Israeli Case." In *Israel in Comparative Perspective. Challenging the Conventional Wisdom*, edited by Michael N. Barnett, 3–25. Albany: State University of New York Press, 1996.

———. *Confronting the Costs of War*. Princeton, NJ: Princeton University Press, 1993.

Bartal, Israel. "'Am' ve-'aretz' Be-Reshit Ha-Elef Ha-Shlishi: Sikum Beinayim" ['People' and 'Land' at the Turn of the Third Millenium: An Intermediate Summary]. *Cathedra* 100 (2001): 21–26.

Bauman, Zygmunt. "Allosemitism: Premodern, Modern, Postmodern." In *Modernity, Culture and "the Jew,"* edited by Bryan Cheyette and Laura Marcus, 143–56. Polity Press, 1998.

Becke, Johannes. "Beyond Allozionism: Exceptionalizing and De-Exceptionalizing the Zionist Project." *Israel Studies* 23, no. 2 (2018): 168–93.

———. "Dismantling the Villa in the Jungle: Matzpen, Zochrot, and the Whitening of Israel." *Interventions: International Journal of Postcolonial Studies* (2019). (Forthcoming).

———. "Towards a De-Occidentalist Perspective on Israel: The Case of the Occupation." *Journal of Israeli History* 33, no. 1 (2014): 1–23.

Becker, Adam H. *Revival and Awakening. American Evangelical Missionaries in Iran and the Origins of Assyrian Nationalism*. Chicago and London: Chicago University Press, 2015.

Bengio, Ofra, and Bruce Maddy-Weitzman. "Mobilised Diasporas: Kurdish and Berber Movements in Comparative Perspective." *Kurdish Studies* 1, no. 1 (2013): 65–90.

Devji, Faisal. *Muslim Zion. Pakistan as a Political Idea*. Cambridge: Harvard University Press, 2013.

Diamond, James S. *Homeland or Holy Land? The Canaanite Critique of Israel*. Bloomington and Indianapolis: Indiana University Press, 1986.

Goldmann, Nahum. *Be-Darkei Ami* [On the Paths of My People]. Jerusalem: HaSifriya HaZionit, 1968.

Haklai, Oded, and Neophytos Loizides (eds.). *Settlers in Contested Lands. Territorial Disputes and Ethnic Conflicts*. Stanford: Stanford University Press, 2015.

Horon, A. G. "Eretz Ha-Kedem" [The Land of Kedem]. In *Mi-Nitzachon Le-Mapolet* [From Victory to Crash], edited by Yonatan Ratosh. Tel Aviv: Hadar, 1976.

———. *Kedem Va-Erev: Kna'an—Toldot Eretz Ha-Ivrim* [East and West: Canaan—The History of the Land of the Hebrews]. Tel Aviv: Dvir, 2000.

Kahanoff, Jacqueline. "What about Levantinization?" *Journal of Levantine Studies* 1, no. 1 (2011): 13–22.
Khazzoom, Aziza. "The Great Chain of Orientalism: Jewish Identity, Stigma Management, and Ethnic Exclusion in Israel." *American Sociological Review* 68, no. 4 (2003): 481–510.
Kurzweil, Baruch. "Mahuta U-Mekoroteha Shel Tnuat 'Ha-Ivrim Ha-Tze'irim' ('ha-Kna'anim')" [Essence and Origins of the Movement of the 'Young Hebrew' ('Canaanites')]. In *Sifrutenu Ha-Chadasha—Hemshech o Mahapecha?* [Our New Literature: Continuity or Revolution]. Tel Aviv: Schocken, 1959.
Leibowitz, Yeshayahu. "The Territories [1968]." In *Judaism, Human Values and the Jewish State*, edited by Eliezer Goldman, 223–28. Cambridge: Harvard University Press, 1992.
Likhovski, Assaf. "Post-Post-Zionist Historiography." *Israel Studies* 15, no. 2 (2010): 1–23.
Ma'oz, Moshe, and Gabriel Sheffer (eds.). *Middle Eastern Minorities and Diasporas*. Brighton: Sussex Academic Press, 2002.
Mendel, Yonatan. *The Creation of Israeli Arabic. Political and Security Considerations in the Making of Arabic Language Studies in Israel*. New York: Palgrave Macmillan, 2014.
Migdal, Joel S. *Strong Societies and Weak States*. Princeton: Princeton University Press, 1988.
Ohana, David. "The Israeli Identity and the Canaanite Option." In *The Gift of the Land and the Fate of the Canaanites in Jewish Thought*, edited by Katell Berthelot, Joseph E. David, and Marc Hirshman, 311–52. Oxford: Oxford University Press, 2014.
Omer, Atalia. "Hitmazrehut or Becoming the East: Re-Orienting Israeli Social Mapping." *Critical Sociology* 43, no. 3 (2017): 949–76.
Pappé, Ilan. "The Mukhabarat State of Israel: A State of Oppression Is Not a State of Exception." In *Thinking Palestine*, edited by Ronit Lentin, 148–69. London and New York: Zed Books, 2008.
Peled, Yoav, and Horit Herman Peled. *The Religionization of Israeli Society*. London and New York: Routledge, 2018.
Penslar, Derek Jonathan. "Is Israel a Jewish State?" In *Israel in History. The Jewish State in Comparative Perspective*, 65–89. London and New York: Routledge, 2007.
———. "Rebels without a Patron State: How Israel Financed the 1948 War." In *Purchasing Power. The Economics of Modern Jewish History*, edited by Rebecca Kobrin and Adam Teller, 171–91. Philadelphia: University of Pennsylvania Press, 2015.
Pilavsky, Oded. "De-Zionisaziya: Mai Ka Mashma Lan?" [De-Zionization: What Does It Mean?]. *Matzpen* 53 (1970).
Podeh, Elie. "Israel in the Middle East or Israel and the Middle East: A Reappraisal." In *Arab-Jewish Relations. From Conflict to Resolution? Essays in Honour of Professor Moshe Ma'oz*, edited by Elie Podeh and Asher Kaufman, 93–113. Brighton and Portland: Sussex Academic Press, 2006.
Rabin, Elliott. "'Hebrew' Culture: The Shared Foundations of Ratosh's Ideology and Poetry." *Modern Judaism* 19, no. 2 (1999): 119–32.
Ratosh, Yonatan. "Ktav El Ha-Noar Ha-Ivri" [Letter to the Hebrew Youth]." In *Reshit Ha-Yamim* [The First of Days]. Tel Aviv: Hadar, 1982.
Reinharz, Jehuda, and Yaacov Shavit. *Glorious, Accursed Europe. An Essay on Jewish Ambivalence*. Waltham, MA: Brandeis University Press, 2010.
Sand, Shlomo. *Eich Ve-Matai Chadalti Lihiyot Yehudi? Mabat Israeli* [How and When Did I Stop Being a Jew? An Israeli Perspective]. Tel Aviv: Dvir, 2013.
Scott, James C. *The Art of Not Being Governed: An Anarchist History of Upland Southeast Asia*. New Haven, CT: Yale University Press, 2009.
Shavit, Yaacov. *The New Hebrew Nation. A Study in Israeli Heresy and Fantasy*. London: Frank Cass, 1987.
Shilon, Avi. "Ha-Arabisatziya Shel Israel ve-Ha-Piyus She-Miri Regev Asuya Lecholel" [Israel's Arabization and the Reconciliation Which Miri Regev Could Bring About]. *Ha'aretz*. June 9, 2018.
Smith, Anthony D. "Diasporas and Homelands in History: The Case of the Classic Diasporas." In *The Call of the Homeland: Diaspora Nationalisms, Past and Present*, edited by Allon Gal, Athena S. Leoussi, and Anthony D. Smith, 3–26. Leiden and Boston: Brill, 2010.

Tzahor, Zeev. "Toldot Medinat Israel: Akademia ve-Politika" [History of the State of Israel: Academia and Politics]. *Cathedra* 100 (2001): 378–94.

Walzer, Michael. *The Paradox of Liberation. Secular Revolutions and Religious Counterrevolution*. New Haven: Yale University Press, 2015.

Weldemichael, Awet Tewelde. *Third World Colonialism and Strategies of Liberation. Eritrea and East Timor Compared*. Cambridge: Cambridge University Press, 2013.

Part V

The Future of Israel Studies

Chapter Twelve

Thinking Big

Connecting Classical Jewish Studies,
Jewish Studies Past, Present, Presence, and Israel Studies

Dani Kranz

This essay focusses on the genealogy of Jewish Studies in post-1945 (West) Germany.[1, 2] It attests to the dynamics in the field of Jewish Studies, which stand in direct connection to societal dynamics, the increasing distance to the Shoah, Jewish migration to Germany, and *Realpolitik*. It depicts that within the structures of classical Jewish Studies (CJS), historical studies of Jews up to 1945—including pre-1933 Jewish histories—antisemitism, and the Shoah, as well as cultural and literature studies, dominate. Owing to the diversifying Jewish population in the country, a new manner of Jewish Studies, which I shall coin as "Jewish Studies past, present, presence" (JSPPP), has been developing since the early 2000s. Research within JSPPP covers the past in the present, present issues of Jewish life in Germany, but also Jewish—agentic—presences, and its scholarly output spans issues of migration, memorial culture, and identity politics; it comes from academic areas inclusive of management or comparative legal sciences. Oftentimes it touches on Jewish/non-Jewish relations as well as Israel. JSPPP intersects and connects with Israel Studies, and scholars of JSPPP might be active in both areas. While some Israel Studies are adjacent to CJS structures, most Israel Studies as well as JSPPP are conducted within different settings, and as part of a specific discipline. These structures are specific to Germany and owes to German/Jewish as well as German/Jewish/Israeli relations. Yet, I will argue that CJS, JSPPP, and Israel Studies would benefit from being thought—and being taught—together to increase the appreciation of the entanglements and complexities at hand, which I will outline in this chatper. I will begin with the politics of Jewish Studies, move on to CJS, then to JSPPP and to Israel Studies—making a detour to the discussions about the Jewish Museum Berlin (JMB), which bears witness to existing tensions, followed by my conclusion arguing for the need to think entangled, transregional, transcultural, and transreligious—in other words to think big.

My data is based on ongoing ethnographic fieldwork (since 2002) as an anthropologist of Jews, Israelis, Germans, and "others"—mainly Palestinians, Arabic speakers, and individuals with backgrounds in Turkey and the MENA (Middle East and North Africa) region within Germany. Data has also been derived through my status as an anthropologist who teaches within the area of JSPPP and Israel Studies, attends (academic) conferences and meetings. But who also regularly participates on public panels, and within discussions—places and circumstances which are well-suited for data collection. Furthermore, my ethnography relates to my applied anthropological work, which includes cooperation with museums, political consulting, and political education. As I delved into the history of my own discipline—for a lack of a better term—I drew on discussions and encounters with my colleagues; issues of any kind about Jewish Studies and current affairs form part of our interactions. I follow the logic of a multisited ethnography in and of the world-system, which furthermore connects macro-, meso-, and micro-levels.[3] My data collection is opportunistic.[4] For anthropologists everything is data and thus of interest to understanding intersections of structures, categories, and in this specific case the boundaries between academic research areas and genealogies of knowledge production. It is characteristic of the anthropological *pensée* to think holistically, conflated, and transdisciplinary, as generalists anthropologists are invested in the multivocality of their research fields.[5]

"FRAUGHT STUDIES" OR THE POLITICS OF JEWISH STUDIES

Franziska Becker attested that research relating to Jews is fraught and political.[6] Her ethnographic study focused on quota-refugees, and their settling in and adjustment processes in Germany. Becker's key finding concerns that Russian[7] Jews adjust their biographical narratives to fit with the hegemonic local master narrative of Jews in Germany post-1945. This master narrative, which is shared by Jews and non-Jews alike, defines Jews as victims. It stands in conflict with the Russian master narratives of Russians, including Jews, as victors over Nazi Germany. Becker's finds ruffled feathers as it lifts the discourse of Jewish/non-Jewish relationships, it makes a known, yet hidden, discourse visible: it is located by default in a fraught area, hence my notion "fraught studies." Her work incidentally covers much broader ground than just Russian Jewish migration to Germany: it outlines the framing of Jewish/non-Jewish relations and dynamics by way of Russian Jewish incomers who had to learn the local, German, discourse. The output of Y. Michal Bodemann, which prefigures Becker's work, caused similar reactions.[8] Bodemann analyzed Jewish/non-Jewish relations in Germany, and outlined that Jews have a specific, symbolic function within non-Jewish German society: they are vital in the construction of the new, post-Shoah Germany which is ritualistically enacted in German memorial culture—which differs from Jewish memorial culture.[9]

More than two decades after Bodemann's seminal study, and nearly two decades after Becker's equally important work, studies on "all things Jewish" remain political. Studies of the Jewish Museum Berlin, the Holocaust Memorial (HM) in Berlin, as well as Israelis—standing in for Jewish Israelis in mainstream discourse—can be added to the canon of "fraught studies" in Germany.[10] Indeed, these topics coincide by way of intersections, which easily turn into intersecting minefields as the concept of the "Jew" always relates to the past as well as the past in the present in Germany. "Jew" always relates to "Israeli" even though both/either are not necessarily the same.[11] However, a Jew can also be an Israeli, and an Israeli can be a Jew, but not all Jews are Israelis and not all Israelis are Jews—categories which Bishop Kendzia and Kranz found to be regularly conflated during ethnographic fieldwork.

"German Jew" connotes to the much-fabled *Requiem Germani*, which stresses the achievements of German Jews.[12] It somehow distracts from the recurrent violence against Jews, which also took place when Jews had already entered the center of society during the Weimar Republic.[13] "Jews" also connotes to terror and persecution under the Nazis, which culminated in the mass murder of Jews (Shoah). The Shoah was part of the multiple genocides of the Holocaust, which also targeted Sinti and Roma (who refer to "their" genocide as Porajmos), Yenish people, and also was aimed at political dissidents, homosexuals, and individuals who were deemed unworthy of living by Nazi definitions—individuals who lived in Nazi conquered territories might also be deported and murdered at a whim.[14] "Jews" remain central in the German as well as European history of othering.[15] This is an allocated role they share with Muslims, although Jews and Muslims are positioned differently in present-day Germany.[16] "Israelis" are positioned yet differently within this matrix, and they stand right on the ambivalent intersection of "Jew," that is the past and the past in the present, and "Israeli," which is the present despite its past entanglements—with all the forces which clash at this intersection.[17]

While pre-Shoah Jewish history and the pursuant murderous history, experiences, and narratives of survivors, evidence against collaborators and the mechanisms of genocide, restitution praxes, and medical/trauma have been covered in both academic and popular writing—less is known about Jewish presence postwar, and even less about the Jewish present. This issue, the ample research on Jewish history, the Shoah, and antisemitism as opposed to living Jews is an expression of the aftermaths of genocide and Jewish/Jewish relations, but also part of *Vergangenheitsbewältigung* [coming to terms with the past] and part of a German mourning process, which—as Jackie Feldman and Anja Peleikis evidence—turns Jews into ultimate others. This scenario is part of a division of labor between non-Jewish Germans and Jews in Germany that I will follow up on in the next section.[18]

However, the research arena is dynamic, and researchers are somehow children of their own time. With timely distance to the Shoah, but also owing up to a diversifying and more approachable Jewish population, historical research began to incorporate post-Shoah history as well as oral history, while more empirical research on the Jews presently living in Germany has also been carried out.[19] Still, a bias persists toward historical studies and research—JSPPP is carried out rarely within the area of CJS, instead being found primarily in the fields of anthropology, European ethnology, and sociology. It is at this junction where I wish to begin my analysis of disjunctures and intersections of the broad areas of CJS, JSPPP, and Israel Studies—as the prevailing structures and divisions need to be located within their historical context. It is my contention that, by way of the academic structures that came into being in this situation, CSJ and JSPPP as well as Israel Studies are set apart despite being conflated and despite these areas being beset with the identity investments of postwar German society. It is also my contention that these structures replicate societal and social structures, which show tensions concerning the connections of the strands "Jew" and "Israeli."[20]

I will begin my analysis with a short history of CJS as opposed to JSPPP and continue to Israel Studies. I will cover what is being studied, and move on to the ongoing debates, discussions, and disagreements concerning the Jewish Museum Berlin (JMB). These debates must be seen as located within competing discourses about national, yet transnationally infused, discourses concerning CJS and JSPPP—which directly relate to Israel Studies. Israel Studies—that is, studies that research any angle of Israel or Israelis—necessarily intersects with JSPPP because Jews and Israel have a complex relationship with one another even if some diasporic Jews wish to part ways with Israel for good.[21] The case of the JMB is such a fitting example because it seems to be the most debated and contentious Jewish museum, which was furthermore born within the postunification self-finding process of Germany, which, as the debates evidence, is ongoing but which meanwhile includes transnational features. The JMB is also so central within debates of past, present, and presence possibly because it is located in the capital of reunited Germany, which is also the capital of memories; Berlin is a place of yearning in German as well as in Jewish, German Jewish, and Israeli history. The city also infuses present-day imagination. Berlin is replete with museums, memorials, and *aides mémoires*. History is haptic in Berlin. This feature—the "touchability"' of history—is central to the notion of the "new Berlin." The JMB links Jewish past and present, and Israeli past and present. Building on the notion of the capital of memories, Jerusalem can be described as the capital of all Abrahamic religions—spanning peace, war, coexistence, and recurring violence. As well as being central in the Israeli/Palestinian conflict, it also is a space of imaginations. By that token, I will argue that the exhibition *Welcome to Jerusalem* ventures precisely into the intersecting minefield that impacts JSPPP and Israel Studies in the present: that of Jewish/non-Jewish, and of German/Jewish/Israeli relations, the German Middle East conflict, and underlying (unreflected) identity investments within these topics.[22] The dynamics and tensions within and between CJS, JSPPP, and Israel Studies are part of societal dynamics, which cannot be divorced from one another, and which must be seen as a conflated and conflicted (mine)field.

CLASSICAL JEWISH STUDIES IN GERMANY

While Jewish Studies and/or Judaic Studies had been continuously extant in English-speaking countries, CJS—and its further development JSPPP—faced particular challenges within post-Shoah Germany. There were hardly Jews left, and those Jews who had survived in Germany, or who had come to what became the Federal Republic of Germany, were concerned with the building of structures of communities, restitution, and mere survival; places to study things Jewish, or Judaism from within the Jewish community that existed pre-Shoah, had been destroyed. This situation made the social scientific study of Jews unduly harder, and contributed to the development of CJS, which mainly focused on historical Jewish life up to 1933, and the Nazi era until 1945, and within *Judaistik* on Judaism, philology, early, or early modern Jewish history as well as Biblical Hebrew. Both broad areas are not empirical.[23]

The lack of research in the country had already received criticism decades ago, and that criticism must be seen as an expression of postgenocidal intergroup relations.[24] It stands in direct relation to trauma and boundary management for the surviving Jews, who—understandably—harbored mistrust toward their non-Jewish surroundings.[25] It must also be located within the specific distance that German non-Jews kept from Jews, and the wishful obliviousness of the German mainstream.[26] The existing output leads to the paradox that this wishful obliviousness and the notion of *Wir haben von nichts gewusst* [We didn't know of anything] fed into one another for about forty years post-Shoah: Jews were a thing of the past, and thus fell under the auspices of historians, literature scholars or *Judaisten*.[27] The very limited willingness to engage in restitution from the German side certainly contributed to the negative perceptions from the Jewish side.[28] Problematically, this praxis remains an issue, and doubt has been cast on testimonies throughout.[29] In consequence, a significant number of Jews had no interest in being the subject of study, however well-intentioned the researcher.[30]

Non-Jewish researchers who were interested in JSPPP might be perceived as threats by Jews, limiting the field primarily to Jews themselves. As a word of caution: how many researchers approached Jews for research purposes is not known, and accordingly it is not known either whether German, non-Jewish, researchers had any interest in this research area within empirical sciences—or if they avoided work within JSPPP altogether. What is known is that researchers who are Jews reported difficulties concerning access to their research participants, and that their own Jewishness could function as an "entry ticket."[31] To complicate matters further, not many Jews were interested in what was to become CJS or JSPPP.[32] JSPPP including Jewish communal studies, Jewish sociology, and anthropology, or demography remained a near lacuna until well into the 2000s—the works of Harry Maor (1961), Jakob Oppenheimer (1967), Doris Kuschner (1977) were exceptions—and all these were conducted by Jews from within Jewish communities and on Jews that were part of the Jewish communities.[33] The edited volume *Juden in Deutschland nach 1945* [Jews in Germany after 1945] can be seen as a turning point in 1988, which introduced JSPPP on a wider scale. While Y. Michal Bodemann criticized that this essay collection also came from Jewish authors, it covers the wider Jewish population, which had been inaccessible to previous researchers who focused on Jews who were members of the Jewish communities.[34] Given the dynamics of post-Nazi Germany, persistent trauma amongst the Jewish population, and Jewish/non-Jewish relationships remaining tense—this scenario is unsurprising, but it needs also to be appreciated as an expression of its time.[35]

Yet, "things to do with Jews" are substantial for German postwar identities. On the one hand, the allies had outlined to the West German government that how it treated its remaining Jews, and how it behaved toward the Jewish State—Israel—was decisive if Germany was ever being admitted into the company of civilized nations again.[36] Frank Stern argued that this demand led to an outward philosemitism which was spiked by prevailing, latent antisemitism.[37] Pól O'Dochartaigh linked to this line of argument by defining philozionism as a political code for German foreign policy, with "no way to maneuver."[38] While Stern and O'Dochartaigh raise contentious points, I would argue that a heartfelt desire exists among parts of the German, non-Jewish population to make good for the past and that genuine scientific interest exists in "things Jewish" and also "things Israeli." At the same time, the Shoah has different long-term effects for Jews, and non-Jews, in the country. O'Dochartaigh attests that for Jews it persists, while (some) non-

Jews can convince themselves that it is the past, a phenomenon I have referred to as "traumatized time."[39]

Given such fraught background, it is unsurprising that CJS is dominated by historical studies, literature, cultural studies, and art history—and by the specific branch of *Judaistik* (disciplines—and I do not mean to sound cynical—for which a living Jewish presence is not necessarily needed). Thus, the structures of CJS inclusive of *Judaistik* bear witness to aftermaths of genocide on location.[40] Jews were studied in the past tense and in the past, producing a plethora of research that covers facets of the Jewish/German Jewish past in the greatest detail possible. This situation created a specific division of labor within CJS and JSPPP: the former was dominated by German non-Jews, while the latter was dominated by Jews.[41] Gabriel Geis coined the term *Gegenwartsbewältigung* [coming to terms with the present] in regard to the Jewish present and the Jewish presence in the country as his participants experienced it, which he contrasts with his coined term *Vergangenheitsbewältigung* of the German non-Jewish population.[42] This insightful analysis directly relates to Kathryn Freker's psychoanalytically based study on young Jews in Germany. She found that there was no neutral ground between locally raised Jews and German non-Jews in a research situation, attesting further to the limited options of JSPPP.[43]

MULTIKULTI, JEWISH CULTURE, AND BERLIN REPUBLIC

Despite this tense situation and division of labor, which has been reified in academic structures, an interest in things Jewish remained—emerging in full force during the mid-1990s. In the euphoria concerning the "new Germany," the "new Berlin," and "*Multikulti*," but also in the wake of the arrival of Russian Jewish immigrants—however difficult their settling in was—a vivid interest in Jewish culture (whatever that is) awakened.[44] Potentially this interest expresses a yearning for something that had been lost: Jewish life, culture, presence, and present, an issue that would finally come out in full force, and which might be coined *Gegenwartsbewältigung*, from a German, non-Jewish perspective.

A phenomenon came into existence that was conceptualized as "Jewish space"—a space in which Jews and non-Jews encounter each other and engage in "things Jewish," which is a continuation of the "Judaizing milieu."[45] While the participants of the Judaizing milieu are more concerned with memory politics, the contributors of the Jewish space are somewhat more interested in things Jewish which are less politically encumbered, and which can be experienced together, in the present, such as "Jewish music." Liliane Weissberg tackled this phenomenon in 2003, and relates it directly to what I have coined CJS. She outlines that (classical) Jewish Studies and "things

Jewish" are of significant interest to German non-Jews but that they do not necessitate a Jewish presence. This argument is central both in her assessment of the *Hochschule für Jüdische Studien* in Heidelberg (founded in 1979)—which attracts many non-Jewish students—and in her later analysis of Jewish Studies in 2008. Weissberg observed that Jewish Studies is in search of its subject; in this sense she is my harbinger in thought. Weissberg underlines the identity investments within the area: she underscores that the *Hochschule* might even produce Jews,[46] as opposed to scholars of (classical) Jewish Studies, or JSPPP experts. Tellingly, a position that covers JSPPP, Jewish sociology, or Jewish anthropology—in other words the diasporic presence in Germany lacked at the time of her analysis, and this remains a lacuna in Heidelberg in as much as in other CJS centers. Weissberg's analysis of the situation of Jewish Studies builds on her long-term—ethnographic—observations of "the Jewish space." She attests to a dialectic of academic and societal developments. Her observations of the situation in the 1990s and early 2000s underscore the performative tropes of imaginations about Jews, an issue assessed in depth in her monography Fake Jews (*Falsche Juden*).[47] Weissberg outlined that oftentimes non-Jews perform Jewish art—in particular klezmer—for non-Jewish audiences.[48] She refers to this phenomenon as "Jews at play," who perform palatable parts of Jewish history—as opposed to their living, Shoah-encumbered tribes' people.[49] This scenario leads to the situation in regard to Jewish Studies that I have described above: CJS is biased toward historical studies as Jews were difficult/impossible to access, and, at the same time, those who could access them—Jews themselves—were often not interested in research on them, and to complicate matters "things Jewish" were a minefield haunted by trauma. An early Israeli (re)migrant to Germany expressed during my PhD research "They are living with 6 million ghosts, Jews and Germans alike. That is too much for everybody."[50] In front of this background it is unsurprising that German non-Jews had a desire for something "Jewish-lite" such as (non-political) Jewish art, and in particular klezmer. Yet, Jews did not necessarily share this desire—as I found across nearly two decades as an anthropologist. The most avid listeners of klezmer were German non-Jews. The Israeli mentioned descends from a *Yekke* family; our conversation during a casual stroll through Cologne sprang back to mind by way of a line of the Berlin-based Israeli artist Adi Liraz: "In my grandmother's house, no Yiddish was spoken, nor klezmer music heard."[51] Like her, he had not grown up with Yiddish and neither with klezmer. German non-Jews, Jews born and raised in Germany, as well as Israelis, might have very different notions of palatable bits of the past, but more so of the present and their presence.

JEWISH STUDIES PAST, PRESENT, PRESENCE: BEYOND THE REALMS OF CLASSICAL JEWISH STUDIES

While CJS and JSPPP covered different grounds, research with a focus on Russian Jews had begun to appear from the mid-1990s. Around the same time Jewish culture, or versions of it, became hip, and discussions about a Holocaust memorial and a Jewish museum were regular news items; the presence of Russian Jews in Germany was noted. This admixture substantiated JSPPP, as not all was history and trauma, and more so, living Jews made news at the same time that memory debates became mainstream debates. These debates were not free of tensions and indicated that German non-Jews and Jews continued to experience the long shadow of the Shoah, and Jewish/non-Jewish relations, differently. Lea Rosh, the German, non-Jewish initiator of the Holocaust Memorial, took the German publisher of the American (Jewish) historian Ruth Gay to court for the author's claim that she adopted a Jewish name to appear Jewish, while indeed she was not a Jew.[52] This lawsuit is indicative of a much wider, and ongoing, power struggle about "German memorial culture," which is dominated by German non-Jews and relegates Jews to perform specific roles, which Jews might increasingly refuse: these are Jews who express agency.[53]

Furthermore, internal Jewish quarrels made and make the news. They are possibly overreported due to a specific interest in "things Jewish" and a hunger for Jewish life in Germany. Jews seemed exotic. They had been seen as history until recently, or a secluded and reclusive minority that only very few knew. Russian Jews fast became an interest of social scientists, as the early works of Julius Schoeps, Willy Jasper, and Bernhard Vogt, Yvonne Schütze, or Franziska Beckerindicate.[54] Yet, besides Schoeps, Jasper, and Vogt, none of these scholars—or those who would follow—came from CJS. With the arrival of Russian Jews, the investment into *multikulti* and the craving for Jewish culture JSPPP gained decisive momentum, and the confines of CJS were too limiting. Alphabetically, Becker is an anthropologist, so is Julia Bernstein; Y. Michal Bodemann is a sociologist; Alina Gromova is a European ethnologist; Eszter Gantner is a historian at the crossroads of history and anthropology; Kurt Grünberg is a psychoanalyst; Victoria Hegner is a European ethnologist; Lena Inowlocki is a sociologist, so is Karen Körber.[55] Dani Kranz is an anthropologist, Jeffrey Peck is a literature scholar cum ethnographer, Yvonne Schütze is a sociologist.[56] Susanne Spülbeck who wrote an ethnographically based meta-analysis of the figure of the Jew—very much ahead of its time—is also an anthropologist, while Liliane Weissberg is a literature and cultural studies scholar who publishes vivid, ethnographically based papers.[57] Breaking with the alphabetical order is Micha Brumlik, one of the most prolific writers on the Jewish presence, who joined a CJS center only upon his retirement. While he is now mainly interested in Jewish philosophy, history, and religion—thus fitting with CJS—Brumlik was a professor for pedagogics, and thus located in JSPPP during his "active service."[58]

The background of these anthropologists and sociologists are also indicative of societal shifts. They constitute Jews who grew up in Germany, Hungary, Russia, the United States, or who have transnational, multilocal backgrounds, while others are non-Jewish Germans. A shift had occurred by way of further temporal distance from the Shoah, and also by way of a much larger Jewish presence in Germany. Yet, things to do with Jews, their presence in Germany, as well as museums and memory politics—the past in the present, negotiations and interpretations—remain political, as the works of Irit Dekel, Jackie Feldman and Anja Peleikis, and Victoria Bishop Kendzia, a sociologist and three anthropologists, respectively, evidence.[59] Unlike most of their historian colleagues, these scholars publish in English as well as in German, making their work less accessible in Germany, and marginalizing them in the local German language discourse that dominates the CJS chairs, departments, and centers. Another difference lies in their education—about half of them were educated abroad and thus outside of German discourses; some of them remain based abroad but affiliated with German research centers; while the absolute majority consists of migrants from, or to, Germany. By default, they access different repertoires. Furthermore, their output might depict difficult bits of a Jewish presence that assumes Jewish agency: these are not "Jews at play," as JSPPP by definition touches raw nerves and ventures into (discursively) difficult terrain—it is political.

Hand in hand with the scholarly activities within academic JSPPP, more Jews added their voices by way of nonfiction writing.[60] A shared concern of all tropes of JSPPP is the figure of the Jews, which creates a permanent situation of abnormality.[61] Max Czollek argued polemically that the German, non-Jewish, majority cannot expect of Jews to be stand-in experts for "antisemitism, the holocaust and Israel," and to be willing to render specific performances within a German theater of memories.[62] Czollek bases his argument on the works of Y. Michal Bodemann who had put forward that ethnic groups are vital in the construction of nation-states.[63] He had stressed that Jews perform a specific, prescribed role for the German, non-Jewish, public—they conduct ideological labor for German non-Jews.[64] Jael Geis had identified this phenomenon as a "division of labor" that reaches back into the early years of postwar Germany, and that has remained in place ever since—she defines it as fatal.[65] Indeed, the continuing fatality comes out in the writings of various of the JSPPP scholars who reflect on their own Jewishness in the research situation or use their ethnographic "I" as a resource.[66] Drawing on Michael Rothberg I had described my work as an anthropologist as that of a deeply implicated subject; an issue that most of the JSPPP crowd mentions in different nuances.[67] "We" are impacted by a sticky matrix we cannot shake off.⁶⁸ even as the research situation mellowed compared to previous decades. The differences between CJS and JSPPP need to be seen in the context of Jewish/non-Jewish relations post-Shoah, which also comes to the fore as JSPPP directly relates to Israel Studies.

ISRAEL STUDIES:
BY SHEER NECESSITY ISRAEL
STUDIES PAST, PRESENT, PRESENCE

Comparatively, Israel Studies is a younger field than *Judaistik* and classical Jewish Studies. Mirroring the developments of JSPPP, research within the broad area of Israel Studies is not necessarily conducted within the realms of a chair of Israel Studies, or within the very few Israel Studies centers. All Israel Studies professorships and centers are adjacent to CJS centers or seminars, but they run on a much smaller scale. At the time of writing, more than twenty professorships, institutes, centers, or research clusters exist that are dedicated to CJS. A mere four Israel studies professorships exist, none of which is tenured, three of which (Mainz, Munich, Potsdam) are guest professorships which oftentimes house an Israeli academic for a term up to the maximum of three years. Research clusters exist at independent (Stiftung Wissenschaft und Politik Berlin, SWP) or university-affiliated institutes (GIGA Hamburg), yet these aim at providing research at the juncture of political consulting, which is aimed at the political classes. Research on Israel—and Israelis—is conducted within JSPPP, indicating how strongly JSPPP and Israel Studies are intersecting: anthropologists, legal scholars, management scholars, political scientists, social psychologists, sociologists all contribute.⁶⁹ Interestingly, colleagues from these areas did not necessarily see themselves as related to JSPPP and "that identity business" (Fieldnotes, January 2, 2019) while clearly acknowledging that they do have expertise in "identity business" but stressing their specialization in Israeli identity business, plus their home discipline (Fieldnotes, December 5, 2018).⁷⁰

Contributions from disciplines that dominate CJS (history, cultural studies, literature, and religious studies) nearly lack. The work of Jenny Hestermann on German/Israeli diplomatic relations, or Dan Diner on German/Israeli restitutions negotiations, constitute exceptions.⁷¹ These two studies, and the project series on the knowledge transfer between Germany and Israel indicate an ongoing oddity: they are wedged between German Jewish history (as with *The Historical Archive of the Hebrew University: German-Jewish Knowledge and Cultural Transfer, 1918–1948*) and German Israeli history (as with *German-Israeli Research Cooperation in the Humanities (1970–2000): Studies on Scholarship and Bilaterality*—indicating the foundation of the State of Israel in 1948 as *the* turning point while for CJS in Germany 1933 is oftentimes *the* turning point.[72]

The issue is that of a turning point, but also structural: centers and funding for German Jewish history exist within CJS, but less so for Israeli history, putting it into a bracket with JSPPP. Israel Studies, like Israeli German history, share another parameter with JSPPP. All three tropes have quite some Jewish contributors, and Israel Studies has a significant catchment with Israelis: they bring with them the major advantage of knowledge of Hebrew. While equally important, Arabic speakers and Palestinian citizens of Israel are underrepresented in this mix—replicating the majority/minority situation in Israel itself. However, this issue contributes to an ongoing lacuna in academic research within Israel Studies: we obtained a grant of the German-Israeli Foundation for Scientific Development (GIF 1186) to understand *The Migration of Israeli Jews to Germany since 1990* (2014–2018), while Stephan Hagemann and Robby Nathanson researched attitudes of Jewish Israelis toward Germany.[73] Research on Palestinian citizens of Israel, and Palestinians in Germany, all but lacks entirely, and to date no research on the attitudes of Palestinians citizens of Israel—or Palestinians in the West Bank or Gaza—of Germany exists despite clear evidence that Germany, historical links, and politics impact on them too.[74]

"Things to do with Israel" are subject to specific, contradictory, investments in Germany. The figure of the Israeli, like the figure of the Jew, carries specific significance within German majority society.[75] Hagemann and Nathanson evidenced in their sociological, quantitative study—which was not conducted within the realm of CJS or Israel studies structures—that Israel, and Israelis, are perceived as increasingly negative by the German majority.[76] On the contrary, the Israeli Jewish majority sees Germans and Germany as increasingly positive. Somewhat ironically, the past creates a bridge between Israelis, Jews, and Germans, while the present makes for a divide according to Dan Diner.[77] This divide pertains to the social and societal levels, while the political level exists in an equilibrium of prescribed structures.[78] It is precisely the social and societal levels that set CJS and JSPPP/Israel studies apart: one branch concerns the past, which is mainly European dominated, while the other branch is concerned with the present, which is transnational, often less European, and thus demanding different tools of research including Hebrew and/or Arabic. Regarding Israel itself, Israel is maturing as a Jewish majority state, and a society that is not free of tension. An Israeli-style Jewishness has come to dominate socially, societally, culturally, legally, and politically, and relationship to those who are defined as ethnoreligious others are complicated. This mix of factors impacts on international relations too. Israel Studies, and by extension the work within JSPPP that concerns German/Israeli relations, make it difficult-to-listen-to *Requiem Yisraeli*. These realities tap into areas which can be described as highly fraught, as the discussions and disagreements about the exhibition *Welcome to Jerusalem* in the JMB indicate.

WELCOME TO JERUSALEM: BUT TO WHICH ONE?

While Jews remain a touchy and political topic in Germany, opinions about Israel, the Israeli/Palestinian conflict, and the wider MENA region, diverge considerably among the German resident population. JSPPP and Israel Studies are not free from these tensions, and reactions to researchers can be rather impassioned. Using my own ethnographic "I," reactions to publications are revealing. Whatever I publish about Israel, and Israelis, causes the strongest reactions and can culminate into emails which demand to know if I am a Jew, and what nationality I hold; in contrast—my output on Germany never caused anybody to ask me if I am Christian.[79] Fellow researchers reported similar reactions, and some debates spill over onto social media. By this token, the JMB—which lies at the crossroads of CSJ, JSPPP, and Israel Studies—resembles a "perfect storm." Discussion about a national Jewish museum had begun in the early 1990s alongside debates about a Holocaust memorial: a Jewish museum, homed in the same building as the Jewish community existed already in the shape of the *Stiftung Neue Synagoge: Centrum Judaicum*. This museum can be regarded as the collected memories of the Jewish community of Berlin because besides exhibitions and events it also houses a comprehensive archive. Yet, it is clearly a Jewish space and not a Jewish national museum, putting these two museums at odds with each other and evidencing further the different memory cultures.

Output on the JMB and the HM, both facilities which aim at remembering, commemorating, (re)presenting Jewish—or German?—history and its aftermath, exist across local and national newspapers, social media, and within academic and popular writing. Bodemann gives an early summary, Jeffrey M. Pecka later one, and Victoria Bishop Kendzia added the latest book to the academic canon.[80] The journalist Thomas Lackmann depicts the discussions and politics surrounding the creation of the JMB in the popular science book *Jewrassic Park*.[81] Plenty of sources exist on the Libeskind-Bau while others encircle the JMB within the wider memorial sphere of Berlin.[82] In other words, the process from the initial debates to the opening and up to the present never lost their intrigue on academics, journalists, politicians, and the wider public alike.

Similar to the academic surroundings of CJS, JSPPP, and Israel Studies, the JMB fulfils an educational function—it is a site of "political education."[83] According to its self-definition it does not limit itself to memorialization and remembrance, it is inclusive of issues of diversity and current German society, indicating its clear link to JSPPP. While it houses artifacts of

Jewish—German Jewish—history, it also tackles the Shoah and post-Shoah Jewish life in Germany. It houses exhibitions about current issues of the Jewish present and German society at large, such as circumcision (*Haut ab!* ran from October 24, 2014, until March 1, 2015), or with women's (un)covering (*Cherchez la femme* ran from March 31 until August 27, 2017), and of course *Welcome to Jerusalem*.[84] The JMB indicates an investment into comparative perspectives of issues that relate to Jews, but also to Muslims, both as the two historical and present "others" to the Christian majority society of Germany. One might argue that the JMB employs the religious triangle as its vantage point. Since the airing of *Welcome to Jerusalem*, it ventures strongly into the area of Israel Studies, stressing the link between JSC, JSPPP, and Israel Studies—academically speaking. The exhibition indicates that Jerusalem can be perceived from different perspectives historically and presently, and it attempts to show these. This approach fits with previous exhibitions, which approached the Jewish experience by way of a comparative angle. The JMB can be described as transnational, transcultural, and transreligious, and it is precisely this triple nexus which causes friction.

The JMB and its adjacent academy have received ample attention from local, and national German language media, some favorable, some critical. *Welcome to Jerusalem* triggered international attention, and drew attention to the museum and its academy. The exhibition approaches Jerusalem as a city that is central to Judaism, Christianity, and Islam, thus attempting to unravel intricate historical and current links within the city, which have much wider ramifications. Following a German language report in the left-liberal *taz* in early December 2018, the English language version of the left, liberal Israeli daily *Haaretz* reported that the Israeli Prime Minister had demanded of the German chancellor Angela Merkel to pull funding from the JMB and a number of other institutions.[85] According to the report, the museum is deemed to present "a Muslim-Palestinian perspective of the city [Jerusalem]."[86] This report did not go unnoticed within Germany, and *taz* published a letter on the same day in German, and in English, in which Israeli artists demanded to counter the shrinking of spaces within the realm of cultural productions, which the governing forces aim at in Israel, and also abroad.[87] An internal-Israeli debate spilled over to Germany again, because funding from Germany for specific NGOs and projects had attracted criticism from the Israeli side before.[88] By way of its makeup, the exhibition necessarily ventures into the Israeli/Palestinian conflict as it depicts Jerusalem as a historically and presently mixed city, that includes non-Jews too, it includes different perspectives of the same space, and reveals the conceptualization of Jerusalem. The presentation of Jerusalem within this comprehensive scope, including Palestinian citizens of Israel and Palestinian residents of Jerusalem,[89] attracted a rebuke by the Israeli foreign ministry, which published in the New York Times: "The purpose and the reason of existence of the Jewish

Museum is to preserve and show Jewish life in Germany throughout the centuries, and not to deal with the Israeli-Palestinian conflict, and *certainly not to take sides*."[90] *Welcome to Jerusalem* is political and transnational in scope like JSPPP as well as Israel Studies. Neither can be limited to history, art, or literature, but either includes realpolitik by definition, and the impact of the past on the present. Following its logic of being an institution of political education, the JMB with this specific exhibition is relevant to the discussion of the dynamics within CJS, JSPPP, and Israel Studies: it deals with the past, the present and presences. My point is not to condone or condemn the exhibition, my point is that it is somewhat ironic that the branches of the Israeli administration followed the same logic as the German non-Jewish audience at a klezmer event: a craving for Jewish culture, and history—but only the palatable bits, please.

THINKING BIG: PAST, PRESENT, PRESENCES

I aimed at an overview of the genealogy of Jewish Studies in Germany post-1945, and to put these developments into their sociohistorical context. What I also aimed at is to indicate how academic structures create divisions between CJS, JSPPP, and Israel Studies, and that these divisions must be understood in terms of the history of knowledge production within a specific, fraught setting. Continuing in this vein of a meta-analysis, it would be a worthy endeavor to analyze "Jewish Studies" in the broadest sense, and from various angles. It would also be fruitful to research the researchers themselves and to build on the (self-) reflective output that began to tackle the personal within research CJS, JSPPP, and the area of Israel Studies: researchers and research operate in time, they might be the (wicked) children of their time.[91] Taking this wider approach would lift hidden discourses and make use of the very valuable resource of the ethnographic "I," as any scholar is intimately linked to their field of research.[92]

The debates concerning the JMB generally—and about *Welcome to Jerusalem* specifically—indicate that CJS, JSPPP, and Israel Studies are entangled and enmeshed. The intersections between CJS, JSPPP, and Israel Studies come to the fore when these three tropes are considered on an ongoing timescale, transnationally, and inclusive of various "breaking points": 1933, 1945, 1948, 1949, 1952, 1967, 1973, 1987, 1989, 1993, 2000, and 2005. The years 1933, 1945, 1949, 1952, and 1989 might appear logical if one thinks of German and German Jewish history, while 1948 is a key date for Israeli history. Yet, I would argue that 1967 (which marks the year of the Six Day War and the beginning of the Israeli occupation of the West Bank), 1987 and 1993 (the beginning and end of the First Intifada and Oslo Treaty, respectively), and 2000 and 2005 (which mark the beginning of the Second

Intifada, its end and the disengagement from Gaza, respectively), are also key years that need to filter in because they carry significant meaning within public discourse in Germany, in Israel, as well as Palestinian society and beyond it—they turn German residents into implicated subjects and give vivid expression to multidirectional memory as well as attitudes which are formative concerning Israel/Palestine, and which impact on local Jewish/non-Jewish relations.[93] By this token, German, Jewish, Israeli, and Palestinian history ought to be thought together, as the current issues are impacted by the past in the present, presences, and agency on all sides.[94]

I am arguing in favor of approaching CJS, JSPPP, and Israel Studies as intimately related, as inseparable triplets as the—incomplete—number crunching indicates: events relate to one another. Needless to say, it is fallacious to think history from the present to the past and to see historical events as logically following as they might do in hindsight. Yet, the past, mainly covered within CJS, impacts on the present as the various authors within JSPPP indicate. Their work indicates tensions of interpretative acts, and power struggles concerning representations of the past, and the past in the present. Indeed, the issues at bay demand to think big, that is to relate past, present, and presence, and to connect Germany—and Europe—with Israel, the Middle East/MENA to understand the intricate links, to break artificial disciplinary boundaries, and to approach complex and entangled interreligious/interethnic relations. This is to say: the triplet needs to be shifted in focus away from Germany and into a more transnational location. It also needs to enter transreligious terrain, because—as *Welcome to Jerusalem* indicates—Christian/Jewish/Muslim relations are as much linked as German/Israeli/Palestinian relations. Yet, a limitation to the religious triangle, or a simplification to the three, obvious, actors would be an oversimplification: multisited ethnographic approaches would be key to incorporate.

Returning to the locality, Germany, which was my starting point, this approach seems rather timely as Jews/Israelis and Muslims/Palestinians must be thought together to be detangled.[95] Both groups constitute "significant others" within contemporary German society, they are subject to the process of alloism.[96] Alloism is a specific process of othering that allows for the creation of significant, but malleable, others; within the German, and European context, these were Jews, and Muslims.[97] This othering has spilled over into specific German investments in Israel/Palestine that reach up to the present, but which draw on the past.[98] Thus, it is key to connect the historical areas covered by CJS to the area of JSPPP and Israel Studies—research on Jews, and by extension Israel, is political, and it is fraught, and precisely for this reason researchers, academics, and scholars should contribute their knowledge as sensitive expert educators.

NOTES

1. I would like to thank the editors for their patience, acceptance that I could not attend the workshop in person, and for still incorporating my thoughts in this volume. Alphabetically, my gratitude goes to Micha Bodemann, Irit Dekel, Lina Nikou, Till van Rahden, and Liliane Weissberg for their feedback, input, and for pointing me to more and new sources.

2. *Gedenkstätten* and *Mahnmale*, both of which translate into memorials in English, are beyond the scope of this endeavor. It should be noted that Jewish history and political education is mediated through them; a colleague outlined the overt presence of the past in the present "The first encounter with Jews is through the Shoah" (Fieldnotes, October 18, 2017). See also Irit Dekel, *Mediation in the Holocaust Memorial* (New York: Palgrave Macmillan, 2013); "Jews and Other Others at the Holocaust Memorial in Berlin," *Anthropological Journal of European Cultures* 23, no. 2 (2014): 71–84; "Subjects of Memory? On Performing Holocaust Memory in Two German Historical Museums," *Dapim: Studies on the Holocaust* 30, no. 3 (2016): 296–314. By this token, *Gedenkstätten* and *Mahnmale* fall within the area of CJS and touch on JSPPP; given their popularity with Israelis they also relate to Israel Studies. See Jackie Feldman, *Between the Death Pits and the Flag: Youth Voyages to Holocaust Poland and the Performance of Israeli National Identity* (New York and Oxford: Berghahn Press, 2010). Educational and research projects, which might be housed on a project basis in universities or universities of applied science, and which might be under the auspices of the Bundeszentrale für politische Bildung (bpb, Federal Agency for Civic Education), or projects of independent agents (*Träger*)—such the Bundesverband für NS-Verfolgte, Stiftung Erinnerung, Verantwortung, Zukunft (EVZ), or which fall within the Bundesprogramm (Federal Programme) Demokratie Leben! (Live democracy!)—are beyond scope of this chapter. See https://www.demokratie-leben.de/?tx_projectmap_pi1%5Bproject%5D=484andtx_projectmap_pi1%5Baction%5D=showandtx_projectmap_pi1%5Bcontroller%5D=Projectandcontrast=1. Indeed, the projects, programs, and actors are so plentiful that they would necessitate several research projects to understand the various intersections, disjunctures, overlaps, and synergies.

3. See George E. Marcus, "Ethnography in/of the World System: The Emergence of Multi-Sited Ethnography," *Annual Review of Anthropology* 24 (1995): 95–117.

4. See Bridget Anderson, *Us & Them? The Dangerous Politics of Immigration Control* (Oxford: Oxford University Press, 2013).

5. See Ruth Landes, *The City of Women* (Albuquerque: University of New Mexico Press, 1947).

6. See Franziska Becker, *Ankommen in Deutschland* (Berlin: Dietrich Reimer Verlag, 2001).

7. Becker, *Ankommen*. Becker uses the terms Russian Jews, which is commonly used in local German discourse for Jewish immigrants who entered Germany as quota refugees (*Kontingentflüchtlinge*). As Victoria Hegner outlined, Jews from countries of the former Soviet Union were defined according to the local, hegemonic discourse. In the United States 'Russian' Jewish were referred to as Soviet Jews, the emphasis lay on the political system. I will use the term Russian Jews in this chapter to make it more readable; however, by far not all Russian Jews are Russians, despite the Russian language being a unifying parameter. See Victoria Hegner, "I Am What I Am. Identitätskonzepte russischsprachiger Juden in Chicago," in *Russisch-jüdische Gegenwart in Deutschland*, Karen Körber (ed.) (Göttingen: Vandenhoek & Ruprecht, 2015), 82–106.

8. See Y. Michal Bodemann, "Staat und Ethnizität: Der Wiederaufbau der Jüdischen Gemeinden im Kalten Krieg," in *Jüdisches Leben in Deutschland seit 1945*, Micha Brumlik, Doron Kiesel, Cilly Kugelmann, and Julius Schoeps (eds.) (Frankfurt am Main: Jüdischer Verlag bei Athenaeum, 1988), 49–69; "The State in the Construction of Ethnicity and Ideological Labor. The Case of German Jewry," *Critical Sociology* 17, no. 3 (1991): 35–46; *Gedächtnistheater: Die jüdische Gemeinschaft und ihre Deutsche Erfindung* (Hamburg: Rotbuch Verlag, 1996).

9. See Bodemann, *Gedächtnistheater: Die jüdische Gemeinschaft und ihre Deutsche Erfindung*; See also Y. Michal Bodemann, *In den Wogen der Erinnerung: Jüdische Existenz in Deutschland* (Munich: Deutscher Taschenbuch Verlag, 2002); "Introduction: The Return of the

European Jewish Diaspora," in *The New German Jewry and the European Context*, Y. M. Bodemann (ed.) (Basingstoke and New York: Palgrave Macmillan, 2008), 1–12; Micha Brumlik and Petra Kunik (eds.), *Reichsprogromnacht* (Frankfurt am Main: Brandes und Apsel, 1988).

10. On the JMB see Victoria Bishop Kendzia, "'Jewish' Ethnic Options in Germany between Attribution and Choice: Autoethnographic Reflection at the Jewish Museum in Berlin," *Anthropological Journal of European Cultures* 23, no. 2 (2014): 60–70; Victoria Bishop Kendzia, *Visitors to the House of Memory: Identity and Political Education at the Jewish Museum Berlin* (New York: Berghahn, 2018). On the HM, see Dekel, *Mediation in the Holocaust Memorial*; Dekel, "Jews and Other Others at the Holocaust Memorial in Berlin"; Irit Dekel, "On the Unknown Soldier Symbol in Israeli Culture," *Studies in Judaism, Humanities, and the Social Sciences* 1, no. 1 (2017): 85–100. On Israelis see Dani Kranz, "Where to Stay and Where to Go? Ideas of Home and Homelessness amongst Third Generation Jews Who Grew up in Germany," in *In the Shadows of the Shadows of the Holocaust. Narratives of the Third Generation*, Esther Jilovsky, Jordy Silverstein, and David Slucki (eds.) (London: Vallentine Mitchell, 2015), 179–208; "Forget Israel—The Future Is in Berlin! Local Jews, Russian Immigrants and Israeli Jews in Berlin and across Germany," *Shofar* 34, no. 4 (2016): 5–28; "Navigating Mythical Time. Israeli Jewish Migrants and the Identity Play of Mirrors," in *The Future of the German Jewish Past. Festschrift of the Centre of German-Jewish Studies of the University of Sussex*, G. Reuveni (ed.) (West Lafayette: Purdue University Press, Forthcoming).

11. See Bodemann, *In den Wogen der Erinnerung: Jüdische Existenz in Deutschland*.

12. See Amos Elon, *Requiem Germani* (Tel-Aviv: Keter, 2002), [Hebrew].

13. See Avraham Barkai, *"Wehr Dich!" Der Centralverein deutscher Staatsbürger jüdischen Glaubens (C. V.) 1893–1938* (Munich: C.H. Beck, 2002). See also Cornelia Hecht, *Deutsche Juden und Antisemitismus in der Weimarer Republik* (Bonn: J.H.W. Dietz, 2003). A problem of these historical studies overall is the 'elite' focus. Elites left more documents. The person who serves as the subject of historical research replicates the position held during their lifetime, as Sally Cole found. See Sally Cole, *Ruth Landes: A Life in Anthropology* (Lincoln: University of Nebraska Press, 2004). Focusing on the life and legacy of the anthropologist Ruth Landes, she outlined that unlike Landes's male, married, anthropology colleagues—whose wives supported them and managed their inheritance—Landes lacked such privilege. I would argue the same holds for elite Jews versus Jewish commoners: elite Jews appear overrepresented as they had an array of helpers and support that allowed them to leave a specific kind of inheritance. See George E. Marcus, "The Problem of the Unseen World of Wealth for the Rich: Toward an Ethnography of Complex Connections," *Ethos* 17, no. 1 (1989): 114–23.

14. As a side point, the Shoah remains often represented Eurocentrically within German discourse, which is another local feature of JCS and Jewish historical studies. Much less is written about the impact on say, Algerian, Libyan, or Tunisian Jews who were subject to persecution due to the collaboration of Vichy France and Fascist Italy with Nazi Germany. A rare fictional account that approaches this issue is *Piccola Sicilia* by Daniel Speck (Frankfurt: Fischer, 2018).

15. Jackie Feldman and Anja Peleikis, "Performing the Hyphen: Engaging German Jewishness at the Jewish Museum in Berlin," *Anthropological Journal of European Cultures* 23, no. 2 (2014): 43–59; Dani Kranz, "Ein Plädoyer für den Alloismus: Historische Kontinuitäten, Zeitgeist und transkultureller Antisemitismus," in *Flucht ins Autoritäre—Rechtsextreme Dynamiken in der Mitte der Gesellschaft*, Oliver Decker and Elmar Brähler (eds.) (Leipzig: Universität Leipzig, 2018), 177–92; Zygmunt Bauman, "Allosemitism. Premodern, Modern, Postmodern," in *Modernity, Culture, and "the Jew,"* Bryan Cheyette and Laura Marcus (eds.) (Cambridge: Polity Press, 1998), 143–56; Daniel Chirot and Anthony Reid, *Essential Outsiders: Chinese and Jews in the Modern Transformation of Southeast Asia and Central Europe* (Seattle: University of Washington Press, 1998).

16. Gil Anidjar, *The Jew, the Arab. A History of the Enemy* (Stanford: Stanford University Press, 2003); Matti Bunzl, "Between Anti-Semitism and Islamophobia: Some Thoughts on the New Europe," *American Ethnologist* 32, no. 4 (2005): 499–508; Zakariya Keskinkılıç and Ármin Langer (eds.), *Fremdgemacht & Reorientiert—jüdisch-muslimische Verflechtungen*

(Berlin: Verlag Yılmaz-Günay, 2018); Kranz, "Ein Plädoyer für den Alloismus: Historische Kontinuitäten, Zeitgeist und transkultureller Antisemitismus."

17. Kranz, "Ein Plädoyer für den Alloismus: Historische Kontinuitäten, Zeitgeist und transkultureller Antisemitismus."

18. See Bodemann, "Staat und Ethnizität: Der Wiederaufbau der Jüdischen Gemeinden im Kalten Krieg."

19. Tamar Lewinsky, *Displaced Poets: Jiddische Schriftsteller im Nachkriegsdeutschland, 1945–1951* (Göttingen: Vandenhoek & Ruprecht, 2008); Lina Nikou, *Einladungen in die alte Heimat. Besuchsprogramme deutscher Großstädte für Verfolgte des Nationalsozialismus*, PhD dissertation, Forschungsstelle für Zeitgeschichte in Hamburg, FZH, Universitaet Hamburg, 2017.

20. See Kendzia, "'Jewish' Ethnic Options in Germany between Attribution and Choice"; Dani Kranz, "Anthropological Perspectives on German NGOs in Israel/the Palestinian Territories," in *German NGOs in Israel and the Palestinian Territories*, Anna Abelmann and Katharina Konarek (eds.) (Berlin: Springer, 2018), 53–64.

21. Judith Butler, *Parting Ways: Jewishness and the Critique of Zionism* (New York: Columbia University Press, 2013).

22. Jüdisches Museum Berlin, *Welcome to Jerusalem*, 2017. https://www.jmberlin.de/ausstellung-welcome-to-jerusalem.

23. See Till Van Rahden, "History in the House of the Hangman: How Postwar Germany Became a Key Site for the Study of Jewish History," in *The German-Jewish Experience Revisited*, Steven E. Aschheim and Vivian Liska (eds.) (Berlin: De Gruyter, 2015), 171–92.

24. See Pnina Lave Levinson, "Religiöse Richtungen und Entwicklungen in den Gemeinden," in *Jüdisches Leben in Deutschland seit 1945*, Micha Brumlik, Doron Kiesel, Cilly Kugelmann, and Julius Schoeps (eds.) (Frankfurt am Main: Jüdischer Verlag bei Athenäum, 1988), 140–71; also Bodemann, *Gedächtnistheater: Die jüdische Gemeinschaft und ihre Deutsche Erfindung*.

25. Kurt Grünberg, "Folgen des Holocaust bei Kindern von Überlebenden in der Bundesrepublik Deutschland," in *Reichsprogromnacht: Vergangenheitsbewältigung aus jüdischer Sicht*, Micha Brumlik and Petra Kunik (eds.) (Frankfurt am Main: Brandes und Apsel, 1988), 59–75; Doris Kuschner, *Die jüdische Minderheit in der Bundesrepublik: Eine Analyse*, unpublished PhD dissertation, Faculty of Philosophy, University of Cologne, 1977; also Bodemann, *Gedächtnistheater: Die jüdische Gemeinschaft und ihre Deutsche Erfindung*.

26. Peter Longerich, *"Davon haben wir nichts gewusst!": Die Deutschen und die Judenverfolgung 1933–1945* (Munich: Siedler, 2006).

27. Longerich, *"Davon."*

28. Jael Geis, "Gehen oder Bleiben? Der Mythos von der 'Liquidationsgemeinde,'" in *Gedächtnistheater: Die jüdische Gemeinschaft und ihre Deutsche Erfindung*, Y. M. Bodemann (ed.) (Hamburg: Rotbuch Verlag, 1996), 56–79.

29. Kristin Platt, *Bezweifelte Erinnerung, verweigerte Glaubhaftigkeit. Überlebende des Holocausts in den Ghettorenten-Verfahren* (München: Wilhelm Fink, 2012).

30. Dani Kranz, *Shades of Jewishness: The Creation and Maintenance of a Liberal Jewish Community in Post-Shoah Germany*, PhD dissertation, University of St. Andrews, 2009. For an instance in the United States, see Walter E. Mitchell, "The Goy in the Ghetto," in *Between Two Worlds: Ethnographic Essays on American Jewry*, Jack Kugelmass (ed.) (Ithaca, NY: Cornell University Press, 1988), 225–39.

31. Kuschner, *Die jüdische Minderheit in der Bundesrepublik: Eine Analyse*, 7–8.

32. Liliane Weissberg, "Jewish Studies or Gentile Studies: A Discipline in Search of Its Subject," in *The New German Jewry and the European Context*, Y. Michal Bodemann (ed.) (Houndsmill: Palgrave Mcmillan, 2008), 101–10.

33. Harry Maor, *Über den Wiederaufbau der jüdischen Gemeinden in Deutschland seit 1945*, PhD dissertation, Philosophy Department, University of Mainz, 1961, http://harrymaor.com/download.htm#item1.

34. See Bodemann, *Gedächtnistheater: Die jüdische Gemeinschaft und ihre Deutsche Erfindung*.

35. See Grünberg, "Folgen des Holocaust bei Kindern von Überlebenden in der Bundesrepublik Deutschland"; Kurt Grünberg, "Bedrohung durch Normalität," in *Sozio-Psycho-Somatik: Gesellschaftliche Entwicklungen und psychosomatische Medizin*, W. Soellner, W. Wesiack, and B. Wurm (eds.) (Hamburg: Springer Verlag, 1989), 127–34; "Contaminated Generativity: Holocaust Survivors and Their Children in Germany," *The American Journal of Psychoanalysis* 67 (2007): 82–97; Lena Inowlocki, "Normalität als Kunstgriff. Zur Traditionsvermittlung jüdischer DP-Familien in Deutschland," in *Überlebt und Unterwegs. Jüdische Displaced Persons in Nachkriegsdeutschland: Jahrbuch des Fritz Bauer Instituts* (Frankfurt: Campus, 1997); *Traditionalität als reflexiver Prozeß: Großmütter, Mütter und Töchter in jüdischen Displaced-Persons-Familien. Eine biographieanalytische und wissenssoziologische Untersuchung* (Berlin: Philo-Verlag, 2002); Pol O'Dochartaigh, "Philo-Zionism as a German Political Code. Germany and the Israeli-Palestinian Conflict since 1987," *Debatte* 15, no. 2 (2007): 233–55; *Germans and Jews since the Holocaust* (London: Palgrave, 2016).

36. George Lavy, *Germany and Israel: Moral Debt and National Interest* (Portland, OR: F. Cass, 1996); Kenneth M. Lewan, "How West Germany Helped to Build Israel," *Journal of Palestine Studies* 4, no. 4 (1975): 41–64; Angelika Timm, "Der Faktor USA in der Entwicklung deutsch-israelischer Beziehungen während des Kalten Krieges," *Comparativ* 16, no. 2 (2006): 46–63.

37. Cited in Bodemann, *Gedächtnistheater: Die jüdische Gemeinschaft und ihre Deutsche Erfindung*, 129.

38. O'Dochartaigh, "Philo-Zionism as a German Political Code"; *Germans and Jews since the Holocaust*, 192.

39. O'Dochartaigh, *Germans and Jews since the Holocaust*; see also Kranz, "Navigating Mythical Time. Israeli Jewish Migrants and the Identity Play of Mirrors."

40. Studies on Sinti and Roma are similarly problematic, as fieldwork access is difficult to obtain, and trauma persists; to the best of my knowledge there is no ethnography of the Sinti and Roma in Germany.

41. Stephanie Schüler-Springorum, "Non-Jewish Perspectives on German-Jewish History in a Generational Project?" *The German-Jewish Experience Revisited*, Steven E. Aschheim and Vivian Liska (eds.) (Berlin/Boston: De Gruyter, 2015), 192–205; Van Rahden, "History in the House of the Hangman."

42. Gabriel Geis, *"Gegenwartsbewältigung" nach 1945 geborenen Juden in der Bundesrepublik Deutschland* (Hamburg: Psychologisches Institut, 1986).

43. Lynn Rapaport (1997), a U.S. American Jew who conducted a sociological study among Germany-raised Jews indicates some of these tensions, but the tensions were less than between Frerker who was German born and raised, and her also German born and raised research participants. See Kathryn Frerker, *Junge Juden in Deutschland: Lebensentwürfe im Schatten des Holocaust*, unpublished master's thesis, Department of Psychology, University of Cologne, 1998, 51.

44. The discourse concerning *multikulti*, short for multiculturalism, has meanwhile changed. In the 1990s and early 2000s *multikulti* was widely regarded as positive and as standing in for a new, diverse Germany. However, at the same time that *multikulti* was hyped, significant parts of the population shifted to the right, and pogrom-like violence against asylum seekers as well as long-term, Turkish, residents took place in several places in Germany in the 1990s. See Jude Bloomfield, "'Made in Berlin': Multicultural Conceptual Confusion and Intercultural Reality," *International Journal of Cultural Policy* 9, no. 2 (2003): 167–83; John Borneman, "Multikulti or Schweinerei in the Year 2000," *German Politics & Society* 20, no. 2 (2002): 93–114; Joseph Cronin, "Wladimir Kaminer and Jewish Identity in 'Multikulti' Germany," *Skepsis* 9/10 (2018): 65–77.

45. All translations from German and Hebrew into English are my own. See Bodemann, *Gedächtnistheater: Die jüdische Gemeinschaft und ihre Deutsche Erfindung*, 48–55.

46. Sandra Anusiewic-Baer (2017) echoes this find in her research on the Moses Mendelsohn Oberschule in Berlin. Some of the non-Jewish pupils converted to Judaism. See Sandra Anusiewicz-Baer, *Die jüdische Oberschule in Berlin* (Bielefeld: Transcript, 2017); See also Diana Pinto "Are There Jewish Answers to Europe's Questions?" *European Judaism: A Journal for the New Europe* 39, no. 2 (2006): 47–57; Eszter Gantner and Jay (Koby) Oppenheim,

"Jewish Space Reloaded: An Introduction," *Anthropological Journal of European Cultures* 23, no. 2 (2014): 1–10.

47. Nike Thurn, *Falsche Juden: Performative Identität in der deutschsprachigen Literatur von Lessing bis Walser* (Göttingen: Wallstein, 2015).

48. Liliane Weissberg, "Reflecting the Past, Envisioning the Future: Perspectives for German-Jewish Studies," *GHI Bulletin* 35 (2004): 11–32, 12.

49. Weissberg, "Reflecting the Past, Envisioning the Future," 2; See also Kranz, *Shades of Jewishness: The Creation and Maintenance of a Liberal Jewish Community in Post-Shoah Germany*, 145.

50. Fieldnotes, October 5, 2004.

51. Adi Liraz, *Blog—Adi Liraz*, 2018. https://adi-liraz.squarespace.com/blog/.

52. Sabine Deckwerth, "Autorin darf auf Namensänderung hinweisen: Lea Rosh verliert vor Gericht gegen einen Buchverlag," *Berliner Zeitung*, May 29, 2002, https://www.berlinerzeitung.de/autorin-darf-auf-namensaenderung-hinweisen-lea-rosh-verliert-vor-gericht-gegen-einen-buchverlag-16314910.

53. Max Czollek, *Desintegriert Euch!* (München: Carl Hanser, 2018); see also Bodemann, *Gedächtnistheater: Die jüdische Gemeinschaft und ihre Deutsche Erfindung*. Also see Weissberg, "Reflecting the Past, Envisioning the Future: Perspectives for German-Jewish Studies."

54. Julius Schoeps, Willy Jasper, and Bernhard Voght (eds.), *Russische Juden in Deutschland: Integration und Selbstbehauptung in einem fremden Land* (Weinheim: Beltz Althenaum, 1996); Yvone Schütze, "Warum Deutschland und nicht Israel?" *BIOS* 2 (1997): 186–208; Becker, *Ankommen in Deutschland*.

55. See Julia Bernstein, "Russian Food Stores as Transnational Enclave? Coping with the Reality of Immigration in Israel and Germany," in *Essenskulturen*, G. Engel and S. Scholz (eds.) (Berlin: Trafo Verlag, 2008), 41–62; *Food for Thought* (Frankfurt: Campus, 2013); "Dichte und Dichtung der neuen Lebenswelten: Das Bolschoi Theater in der Aldi-Tüte," in *Russisch-jüdische Gegenwart in Deutschland*, Karen Körber (ed.) (Göttingen: Vandenhoek & Ruprecht, 2015), 134–51; Bodemann, "The State in the Construction of Ethnicity and Ideological Labor"; Bodemann, *Gedächtnistheater: Die jüdische Gemeinschaft und ihre Deutsche Erfindung*; Bodemann, *In den Wogen der Erinnerung*, Alina Gromova, *Generation »koscher light«. Urbane Räume und Praxen junger russischsprachiger Juden in Berlin* (Bielefeld: Transcript, 2013); "Jewish Dating or Niche-making? A Topographical Representation of Youth Culture," *Anthropological Journal of European Cultures* 23, no. 2 (2014): 11–25; "Jüdische Vergemeinschaftung als Praxis der Distinktionen. Auf den Spuren der kulturellen Praktiken und sozialen Positionierungen in der Migrationsgesellschaft," in *Russisch-jüdische Gegenwart in Deutschland*, Karen Körber (ed.) (Göttingen: Vandenhoek & Ruprecht, 2015), 60–81; Eszter Gantner, "Interpreting the Jewish Quarter," *Anthropological Journal of European Cultures* 23, no. 2 (2014): 26–42; "Jewish Quarter as Urban Tableaux," in *Jewish and Non-Jewish Spaces in Urban Context*, Alina Gromova, Felix Heinert, and Sebastian Voigt (eds.) (Neofelis: Berlin, 2015), 197–213; "Vom Scheunenviertel zum Schmelztigel. Das jüdische Erbe Berlins zwischen Erinnerungspolitik und urbanem Marketing," in *In Guter Gesellschaft? Die Rolle der Denkmalpflege in Stadtmarketing und Tourismus*, Bernhard Serra and Martina Ullrich (eds.) (Dresden: Thelem, 2015), 130–40; Grünberg, "Folgen des Holocaust bei Kindern von Überlebenden in der Bundesrepublik Deutschland"; "Bedrohung durch Normalität"; Kurt Grünberg, *Liebe nach Auschwitz: Die Zweite Generation* (Tuebingen: Edition Diskord, 2000); Grünberg, "Contaminated Generativity: Holocaust Survivors and Their Children in Germany"; Victoria Hegner, *Gelebte Selbstbilder: Gemeinden russisch-jüdischer Migranten in Chicago und Berlin* (Frankfurt/Main: Campus, 2008); Hegner, "I Am What I Am. Identitätskonzepte russischsprachiger Juden in Chicago"; Inowlocki, "Normalität als Kunstgriff. Zur Traditionsvermittlung jüdischer DP-Familien in Deutschland"; Inowlocki, *Traditionalität als reflexiver Prozeß*; Karen Körber, *Juden, Russen, Emigranten: Identitätskonflikte jüdischer Einwanderer in einer ostdeutschen Stadt* (Frankfurt: Campus, 2005); "Zäsur, Wandel oder Neubeginn: Russischsprachige Juden in Deutschland zwischen Recht, Repäsentation und Neubeginn," in *Russisch-jüdische Gegenwart in Deutschland*, Karen Körber (ed.) (Göttingen: Vandenhoek & Ruprecht, 2015), 13–36.

56. This list is necessarily incomplete despite basing it on literature searches, searches in university departments, and also consultation with librarians and other researchers. See Kranz, *Shades of Jewishness*; "Where to Stay and Where to Go?"; "Forget Israel—The Future Is in Berlin!"; "Ein Plädoyer für den Alloismus"; Jeffrey M. Peck, *Being Jewish in the New Germany* (Piscataway, NJ: Rutgers University Press, 2006); Schütze, "Warum Deutschland und nicht Israel?"; Weissberg, "Reflecting the Past, Envisioning the Future: Perspectives for German-Jewish Studies"; "Jewish Studies or Gentile Studies."

57. There are of course more scholars who are based abroad and who fall within CJS or JSPPP. Bodemann, Peck, and Weissberg are homed at North American universities, but they held fellowships at German universities and institutes; they took part in, and impacted on German discourse also in the local, German, language. This sets their output apart from "English only" output of other, academically no less important scholars who did not reach German-speaking audiences. See Susanne Spülbeck, *Ordnung und Angst: Russische Juden aus Sicht einer Ostdeutschen Dorfes nach der Wende* (Frankfurt/Main: Campus, 1997);

58. For example, see Brumlik and Kunik (eds.), *Reichsprogromnacht*.

59. Dekel, *Mediation in the Holocaust Memorial*; "Jews and Other Others at the Holocaust Memorial in Berlin"; "Subjects of Memory?"; Feldman and Peleikis, "Performing the Hyphen: Engaging German Jewishness at the Jewish Museum in Berlin"; Kendzia, "'Jewish' Ethnic Options in Germany between Attribution and Choice"; *Visitors to the House of Memory*.

60. Dmitrij Belkin, *Germanija: Wie ich in Deutschland jüdisch und erwachsen wurde* (Frankfurt: Campus, 2016); Czollek, *Desintegriert Euch!*; Dimitrij Kapitelman, *Das Lächeln meines unsichtbaren Vaters* (München: Carl Hanser, 2018); Yascha Mounk, *Stranger in My Own Country* (New York: Farrar, Straus and Giroux, 2014); Channah Trzebiner, *Die Enkelin* (Frankfurt: Weissbooks, 2013).

61. Kranz, "Ein Plädoyer für den Alloismus."

62. Czollek, *Desintegriert Euch!*

63. See Bodemann, "The State in the Construction of Ethnicity and Ideological Labor"; *Gedächtnistheater: Die jüdische Gemeinschaft und ihre Deutsche Erfindung*; *In den Wogen der Erinnerung*.

64. Bodemann, "The State in the Construction of Ethnicity and Ideological Labor."

65. Geis, "Gehen oder Bleiben?," 68.

66. Kendzia, "'Jewish' Ethnic Options in Germany between Attribution and Choice"; Gromova, "Jewish Dating or Niche-making?"; Kranz, "Where to Stay and Where to Go?"; "Ein Plädoyer für den Alloismus."

67. Michael Rothberg, "Multidirectional Memory and the Implicated Subjects: On Sebald and Kentridge," in *Performing Memory in Art and Popular Culture*, Liedeke Plate and Anneke Smelik (eds.) (London: Routledge, 2013), 39–58; Kranz, "Navigating Mythical Time."

68. Kranz, "Navigating Mythical Time."

69. See Dani Kranz, "Almost Like Jews: Children of Foreign, Non-Jewish Mothers and Israeli Jewish Fathers in the State of Israel," in *Stop! No Borders*, Ra'anan Lipshitz and Hani Zubida (eds.) (Tel Aviv: Yediot, 2017), 493–506 [Hebrew]; Marcus Gick, *Die EMRK und Israel* (Munich: Beck, 2019); Guy Katz, *Intercultural Negotiations: The Unique Case of Germany and Israel* (Norderstedt: Books on Demand, 2011); Stephan Stetter, "Illusion: Die Zwei-Staaten-Lösung ist nicht zu retten," *Internationale Politik und Gesellschaft*, October 22, 2018, https://www.ipg-journal.de/schwerpunkt-des-monats/illusionen/artikel/detail/illusion-die-zwei-staaten-loesung-ist-nicht-zu-retten-3056/; Maya Hadar, *Ends and Means: How Outcomes of Political Violence Affect Social and National Identities—The Case of Israel*, PhD dissertation, Department of Social Sciences, Leipzig University, 2019; Dekel, "On the Unknown Soldier Symbol in Israeli Culture," 85–100.

70. Fieldnotes, January 2, 2019; Fieldnotes, December 5, 2018.

71. Jenny Hestermann, *Inszenierte Versöhnung. Reisediplomatie und deutsch-israelische Beziehungen von 1957–1984* (Frankfurt am Main: Campus, 2016); Dan Diner, *Rituelle Distanz. Israels deutsche Frage* (Munich: Deutsche Verlags-Anstalt, 2015).

72. https://rosenzweig.huji.ac.il/book/german-jewish-knowledge-and-cultural-transfer-1918-1948; http://gih.vanleer.org.il/pages/about-us/.

73. Stefan Hagemann and Roby Nathanson, *Deutschland und Israel heute. Verbindende Vergangenheit, trennende Gegenwart?* (Gütersloh, Germany: Bertelsmann Foundation, 2015), https://www.bertelsmann-stiftung.de/fileadmin/files/BSt/Publikationen/GrauePublikationen/Studie_LW_Deutschland_und_Israel_heute_2015.pdf, 10.

74. See Shahd Wari, *Palestinian Berlin* (Berlin: LIT, 2017); see also the edited volume Anna Abelmann and Katharina Konarek (eds.), *German NGOs in Israel and the Palestinian Territories* (Berlin: Springer, 2018).

75. Dani Kranz, "Anthropological Perspectives on German NGOs in Israel/the Palestinian Territories."

76. Hagemann and Nathanson, *Deutschland und Israel heute*.

77. Diner, *Rituelle Distanz. Israels deutsche Frage*.

78. O'Dochartaigh, *Germans and Jews since the Holocaust*.

79. Email to author, December 22, 2017.

80. Bodemann, *Gedächtnistheater: Die jüdische Gemeinschaft und ihre Deutsche Erfindung*; Peck, *Being Jewish in the New Germany*; Kendzia, *Visitors to the House of Memory*.

81. Thomas Lackmann, *Jewrassic Park. Wie baut man (k)ein Jüdisches Museum in Berlin* (Berlin and Wien: Philo, 2000).

82. Bloomfield, "'Made in Berlin': Multicultural Conceptual Confusion and Intercultural Reality"; Feldman and Peleikis, "Performing the Hyphen: Engaging German Jewishness at the Jewish Museum in Berlin"; Sabine Offe, "Sites of Remembrance? Jewish Museums in Contemporary Germany," *Jewish Social Studies, New Series* 3, no. 2 (1997): 77–89.

83. Kendzia, *Visitors to the House of Memory*, 19.

84. Jüdisches Museum Berlin, *Haut ab! Haltungen zur rituellen Beschneidung*, 2014, https://www.jmberlin.de/ausstellung-haut-ab; *Cherchez la femme*, 2017, https://www.jmberlin.de/ausstellung-cherchez-la-femme.

85. Noa Landau, "Israel Demanded Germany Cut Funding to Jewish Museum in Berlin, Report Says," *Haaretz*, December 9, 2008, https://www.haaretz.com/world-news/europe/report-israel-demanded-germany-cut-funding-to-jewish-museum-in-berlin-1.6726205/.

86. Landau, "Israel."

87. Anonymous, "Ein offener Brief . . . israelischer Künstler*innen gegen schrumpfende Räume in der Kultur," *taz*, December 9, 2018, http://www.taz.de/Streit-um-Juedisches-Museum-Berlin/!5561765/?fbclid=IwAR25G6lR8u4HhiAY7Mfu87t8G4r0kQSNdVptW0uKbPDN45fY3QGfn9PgClA.

88. Kranz, "Anthropological Perspectives on German NGOs in Israel/the Palestinian Territories."

89. Self-ascribed Palestinians are not monolithic; they also hold widely different opinions.

90. Melissa Eddy and Isabel Kershner, "Jerusalem Criticizes Berlin's Jewish Museum for 'Anti-Israel Activity,'" *NY Times*, December 23, 2018, https://www.nytimes.com/2018/12/23/arts/design/berlin-jewish-museum-israel-bds-welcome-to-jerusalem.html?fbclid=IwAR2SyLo2Rsj5HlQqXJoi3zkM_tIKgSVrPMrQzcuvY4946c0MyA6kgRfw7l8. (Emphasis added.)

91. Nancy D. Munn, "The Cultural Anthropology of Time: A Critical Essay," *Annual Review of Anthropology* 21 (1992): 93–123.

92. For a U.S. case study, see Gelya Frank, "Jews, Multiculturalism and Boasian Anthropology," *American Anthropologist* 4 (1997): 731–45. For an Israeli case study, see Ariel Handel and Ruthi Ginsburg, "Israelis Studying the Occupation: An Introduction," *Critical Inquiry* 44 (2018): 331–42.

93. Rothberg, "Multidirectional Memory and the Implicated Subjects." For a U.K. example, see Adam Groves, "From Gaza to the Streets of Britain. British Social Media Coverage of the 2014 Israel-Gaza Conflict," *Jewish Culture and History* 18, no. 3 (2017): 331–49.

94. I am grateful to Lina Nikou for stressing this very important point from her perspective as a historian.

95. Kranz, "Ein Plädoyer für den Alloismus."

96. Kranz, "Ein Plädoyer für den Alloismus."

97. Anidjar, *The Jew, the Arab. A History of the Enemy*; Bauman, "Allosemitism"; Bunzl, "Between Anti-Semitism and Islamophobia."

98. O'Dochartaigh, "Philo-Zionism as a German Political Code"; *Germans and Jews since the Holocaust.*

BIBLIOGRAPHY

Abelmann, Anna, and Katharina Konarek (eds.). *German NGOs in Israel and the Palestinian Territories.* Berlin: Springer, 2018.
Anderson, Bridget. *Us & Them? The Dangerous Politics of Immigration Control.* Oxford: Oxford University Press, 2013.
Anidjar, Gil. *The Jew, the Arab. A History of the Enemy.* Stanford: Stanford University Press, 2003.
Anonymous. "Ein offener Brief . . . israelischer Künstler*innen gegen schrumpfende Räume in der Kultur." *taz.* December 9, 2018. http://www.taz.de/Streit-um-Juedisches-Museum-Berlin/!5561765/?fbclid=IwAR25G6lR8u4HhiAY7Mfu87t8G4r0kQSNdVptW0uKbPDN4 5fY3QGfn9PgClA.
Anusiewicz-Baer, Sandra. *Die jüdische Oberschule in Berlin.* Bielefeld: Transcript, 2017.
Barkai, Avraham. *"Wehr Dich!" Der Centralverein deutscher Staatsbürger jüdischen Glaubens (C. V.) 1893–1938.* Munich: C.H. Beck, 2002.
Bauman, Zygmunt. "Allosemitism. Premodern, Modern, Postmodern." In *Modernity, Culture, and "the Jew,"* edited by Bryan Cheyette and Laura Marcus, 143–56. Cambridge: Polity Press, 1998.
Becker, Franziska. *Ankommen in Deutschland.* Berlin: Dietrich Reimer Verlag, 2001.
Belkin, Dmitrij. *Germanija: Wie ich in Deutschland jüdisch und erwachsen wurde.* Frankfurt: Campus, 2016.
Bernstein, Julia. "Russian Food Stores as Transnational Enclave? Coping with the Reality of Immigration in Israel and Germany." In *Essenskulturen,* edited by G. Engel and S. Scholz, 41–62. Berlin: Trafo Verlag, 2008.
———. *Food For Thought.* Frankfurt: Campus, 2013.
———. "Dichte und Dichtung der neuen Lebenswelten: Das Bolschoi Theater in der Aldi-Tüte." In *Russisch-jüdische Gegenwart in Deutschland,* edited by Karen Körber, 134–51. Göttingen: Vandenhoek & Ruprecht, 2015.
Bishop Kendzia, Victoria. "'Jewish' Ethnic Options in Germany between Attribution and Choice: Autoethnographic Reflection at the Jewish Museum in Berlin." *Anthropological Journal of European Cultures* 23, no. 2 (2014): 60–70.
———. *Visitors to the House of Memory: Identity and Political Education at the Jewish Museum Berlin.* New York: Berghahn, 2018.
Bloomfield, Jude. "'Made in Berlin': Multicultural Conceptual Confusion and Intercultural Reality." *International Journal of Cultural Policy* 9, no. 2 (2003): 167–83.
Bodemann, Y. Michal. "Staat und Ethnizität: Der Wiederaufbau der Jüdischen Gemeinden im Kalten Krieg." In *Jüdisches Leben in Deutschland seit 1945,* edited by Micha Brumlik, Doron Kiesel, Cilly Kugelmann, and Julius Schoeps, 49–69. Frankfurt am Main: Jüdischer Verlag bei Athenaeum, 1988.
———. "The State in the Construction of Ethnicity and Ideological Labor. The Case of German Jewry." *Critical Sociology* 17, no. 3 (1991): 35–46.
———. *Gedächtnistheater: Die jüdische Gemeinschaft und ihre Deutsche Erfindung.* Hamburg: Rotbuch Verlag, 1996.
———. *In den Wogen der Erinnerung: Jüdische Existenz in Deutschland.* Munich: Deutscher Taschenbuch Verlag, 2002.
———. "Introduction: The Return of the European Jewish Diaspora." In *The New German Jewry and the European Context,* edited by Y. M. Bodemann, 1–12. Basingstoke and New York: Palgrave Macmillan, 2008.
Borneman, John. "Multikulti or Schweinerei in the Year 2000." *German Politics & Society* 20, no. 2 (2002): 93–114.
Brumlik, Micha, and Petra Kunik (eds.). *Reichsprogromnacht.* Frankfurt am Main: Brandes und Apsel, 1988.

Bundesministerium für Familie, Senioren, Frauen und Jugend. *Demokratie Leben!* n.d. https://www.demokratie-leben.de/?tx_projectmap_pi1%5Bproject%5D=484&tx_projectmap_pi1%5Baction%5D=show&tx_projectmap_pi1%5Bcontroller%5D=Project&contrast=1.

Bunzl, Matti. "Between Anti-Semitism and Islamophobia: Some Thoughts on the New Europe." *American Ethnologist* 32, no. 4 (2005): 499–508.

Butler, Judith. *Parting Ways: Jewishness and the Critique of Zionism*. New York: Columbia University Press, 2013.

Chirot, Daniel, and Anthony Reid. *Essential Outsiders: Chinese and Jews in the Modern Transformation of Southeast Asia and Central Europe*. Seattle: University of Washington Press, 1998.

Cole, Sally. *Ruth Landes: A Life in Anthropology*. Lincoln: University of Nebraska Press, 2004.

Cronin, Joseph. "Wladimir Kaminer and Jewish Identity in 'Multikulti' Germany." *Skepsis* 9/10 (2018): 65–77.

Czollek, Max. *Desintegriert Euch!* München: Carl Hanser, 2018.

Deckwerth, Sabine. "Autorin darf auf Namensänderung hinweisen Lea Rosh verliert vor Gericht gegen einen Buchverlag." *Berliner Zeitung*. May 29, 2002. https://www.berliner-zeitung.de/autorin-darf-auf-namensaenderung-hinweisen-lea-rosh-verliert-vor-gericht-gegen-einen-buchverlag-16314910.

Dekel, Irit. *Mediation in the Holocaust Memorial*. New York: Palgrave Macmillan, 2013.

———. "Jews and Other Others at the Holocaust Memorial in Berlin." *Anthropological Journal of European Cultures* 23, no. 2 (2014): 71–84.

———. "Subjects of Memory? On Performing Holocaust Memory in Two German Historical Museums." *Dapim: Studies on the Holocaust* 30, no. 3 (2016): 296–314.

———. "On the Unknown Soldier Symbol in Israeli Culture." *Studies in Judaism, Humanities, and the Social Sciences* 1, no. 1 (2017): 85–100.

Diner, Dan. *Rituelle Distanz. Israels deutsche Frage*. Munich: Deutsche Verlags-Anstalt, 2015.

Eddy, Melissa, and Isabel Kershner. "Jerusalem Criticizes Berlin's Jewish Museum for 'Anti-Israel Activity.'" *NY Times*. December 23, 2018. https://www.nytimes.com/2018/12/23/arts/design/berlin-jewish-museum-israel-bds-welcome-to-jerusalem.html?fbclid=IwAR2SyLo2Rsj5HlQqXJoi3zkM_tIKgSVrPMrQzcuvY4946c0MyA6kgRfw7l8.

Elon, Amos. *Requiem Germani*. Tel-Aviv: Keter, 2002. [Hebrew]

Feldman, Jackie. *Between the Death Pits and the Flag: Youth Voyages to Holocaust Poland and the Performance of Israeli National Identity*. New York and Oxford: Berghahn Press, 2010.

Feldman, Jackie, and Anja Peleikis. "Performing the Hyphen: Engaging German Jewishness at the Jewish Museum in Berlin." *Anthropological Journal of European Cultures* 23, no. 2 (2014): 43–59.

Frank, Gelya. "Jews, Multiculturalism and Boasian Anthropology." *American Anthropologist* 4 (1997): 731–45.

Frerker, Kathryn. *Junge Juden in Deutschland: Lebensentwürfe im Schatten des Holocaust*. Unpublished Master's Thesis. Department of Psychology, University of Cologne, 1998.

Gantner, Eszter. "Interpreting the Jewish Quarter." *Anthropological Journal of European Cultures* 23, no. 2 (2014): 26–42.

———. "Jewish Quarter as Urban Tableaux." In *Jewish and Non-Jewish Spaces in Urban Context*, edited by Alina Gromova, Felix Heinert, and Sebastian Voigt, 197–213. Neofelis: Berlin, 2015.

———. "Vom Scheunenviertel zum Schmelztigel. Das jüdische Erbe Berlins zwischen Erinnerungspolitik und urbanem Marketing." In *In Guter Gesellschaft? Die Rolle der Denkmalpflege in Stadtmarketing und Tourismus*, edited by Bernhard Serra and Martina Ullrich, 130–40. Dresden: Thelem, 2015.

Gantner, Eszter, and Jay (Koby) Oppenheim. "Jewish Space Reloaded: An Introduction." *Anthropological Journal of European Cultures* 23, no. 2 (2014): 1–10.

Geis, Gabriel. *"Gegenwartsbewältigung" nach 1945 geborenen Juden in der Bundesrepublik Deutschland*. Hamburg: Psychologisches Institut, 1986.

Geis, Jael. "Gehen oder Bleiben? Der Mythos von der 'Liquidationsgemeinde.'" In *Gedächtnistheater: Die jüdische Gemeinschaft und ihre Deutsche Erfindung*, edited by Y. M. Bodemann, 56–79. Hamburg: Rotbuch Verlag, 1996.
German-Israeli Research Cooperation in the Humanities. *German-Israeli Research Cooperation in the Humanities (1970–2000): Studies on Scholarship and Bilaterality*. 2015. http://gih.vanleer.org.il/pages/about-us/.
Gick, Marcus. *Die EMRK und Israel*. Munich: Beck, 2019.
Gromova, Alina. *Generation »koscher light«. Urbane Räume und Praxen junger russischsprachiger Juden in Berlin*. Bielefeld: Transcript, 2013.
———. "Jewish Dating or Niche-making? A Topographical Representation of Youth Culture." *Anthropological Journal of European Cultures* 23, no. 2 (2014): 11–25.
———. "Jüdische Vergemeinschaftung als Praxis der Distinktionen. Auf den Spuren der kulturellen Praktiken und sozialen Positionierungen in der Migrationsgesellschaft." In *Russischjüdische Gegenwart in Deutschland*, edited by Karen Körber, 60–81. Göttingen: Vandenhoek & Ruprecht, 2015.
Groves, Adam. "From Gaza to the Streets of Britain. British Social Media Coverage of the 2014 Israel-Gaza Conflict." *Jewish Culture and History* 18, no. 3 (2017): 331–49.
Grünberg, Kurt. "Folgen des Holocaust bei Kindern von Überlebenden in der Bundesrepublik Deutschland." In *Reichsprogromnacht: Vergangenheitsbewältigung aus jüdischer Sicht*, edited by Micha Brumlik and Petra Kunik, 59–75. Frankfurt am Main: Brandes und Apsel, 1988.
———. "Bedrohung durch Normalität." In *Sozio-Psycho-Somatik: Gesellschaftliche Entwicklungen und psychosomatische Medizin*, edited by W. Soellner, W. Wesiack, and B. Wurm, 127–34. Hamburg: Springer Verlag, 1989.
———. *Liebe nach Auschwitz: Die Zweite Generation*. Tuebingen: Edition Diskord, 2000.
———. "Contaminated Generativity: Holocaust Survivors and Their Children in Germany." *The American Journal of Psychoanalysis* 67 (2007): 82–97.
Hadar, Maya. *Ends and Means: How Outcomes of Political Violence Affect Social and National Identities—The Case of Israel*. PhD Dissertation. Department of Social Sciences, Leipzig University, 2019.
Hagemann, Stefan, and Roby Nathanson. *Deutschland und Israel heute. Verbindende Vergangenheit, trennende Gegenwart?* Gütersloh, Germany: Bertelsmann Foundation, 2015. https://www.bertelsmann-stiftung.de/fileadmin/files/BSt/Publikationen/GrauePublikationen/Studie_LW_Deutschland_und_Israel_heute_2015.pdf.
Handel, Ariel, and Ruthi Ginsburg. "Israelis Studying the Occupation: An Introduction." *Critical Inquiry* 44 (2018): 331–42
Hecht, Cornelia. *Deutsche Juden und Antisemitismus in der Weimarer Republik*. Bonn: J.H.W. Dietz, 2003.
Hegner, Victoria. *Gelebte Selbstbilder: Gemeinden russisch-jüdischer Migranten in Chicago und Berlin*. Frankfurt/Main: Campus, 2008.
———. "I Am What I Am. Identitätskonzepte russischsprachiger Juden in Chicago." In *Russisch-jüdische Gegenwart in Deutschland*, edited by Karen Körber, 82–106. Göttingen: Vandenhoek & Ruprecht, 2015.
Hestermann, Jenny. *Inszenierte Versöhnung. Reisediplomatie und deutsch-israelische Beziehungen von 1957–1984*. Frankfurt am Main: Campus, 2016.
Inowlocki, Lena. "Normalität als Kunstgriff. Zur Traditionsvermittlung jüdischer DP-Familien in Deutschland." In *Überlebt und Unterwegs. Jüdische Displaced Persons in Nachkriegsdeutschland: Jahrbuch des Fritz Bauer Instituts*. Frankfurt: Campus, 1997.
———. *Traditionalität als reflexiver Prozeß: Großmütter, Mütter und Töchter in jüdischen Displaced-Persons-Familien. Eine biographieanalytische und wissenssoziologische Untersuchung*. Berlin: Philo-Verlag, 2002.
Jüdisches Museum Berlin. *Haut ab! Haltungen zur rituellen Beschneidung*. 2014. https://www.jmberlin.de/ausstellung-haut-ab.
———. *Cherchez la femme*. 2017. https://www.jmberlin.de/ausstellung-cherchez-la-femme.
———. *Welcome to Jerusalem*. 2017. https://www.jmberlin.de/ausstellung-welcome-to-jerusalem.

Kapitelman, Dimitrij. *Das Lächeln meines unsichtbaren Vaters.* München: Carl Hanser, 2018.
Katz, Guy. *Intercultural Negotiations: The Unique Case of Germany and Israel.* Norderstedt: Books on Demand, 2011.
Keskinkılıç, Zakariya, and Ármin Langer (eds.). *Fremdgemacht & Reorientiert—jüdisch-muslimische Verflechtungen.* Berlin: Verlag Yılmaz-Günay, 2018.
Körber, Karen. *Juden, Russen, Emigranten: Identitätskonflikte jüdischer Einwanderer in einer ostdeutschen Stadt.* Frankfurt: Campus, 2005.
———. "Zäsur, Wandel oder Neubeginn: Russischsprachige Juden in Deutschland zwischen Recht, Repäsentation und Neubeginn." In *Russisch-jüdische Gegenwart in Deutschland*, edited by Karen Körber, 13–36. Göttingen: Vandenhoek & Ruprecht, 2015.
Kranz, Dani. *Shades of Jewishness: The Creation and Maintenance of a Liberal Jewish Community in Post-Shoah Germany.* PhD Dissertation. University of St. Andrews, 2009.
———. "Where to Stay and Where to Go? Ideas of Home and Homelessness amongst Third Generation Jews Who Grew up in Germany." In *In the Shadows of the Shadows of the Holocaust. Narratives of the Third Generation*, edited by Esther Jilovsky, Jordy Silverstein, and David Slucki, 179–208. London: Vallentine Mitchell, 2015.
———. "Forget Israel—The Future Is in Berlin! Local Jews, Russian Immigrants and Israeli Jews in Berlin and across Germany." *Shofar* 34, no. 4 (2016): 5–28.
———. "Almost Like Jews: Children of Foreign, Non-Jewish Mothers and Israeli Jewish Fathers in the State of Israel." In *Stop! No Borders*, edited by Ra'anan Lipshitz and Hani Zubida, 493–506. Tel Aviv: Yediot, 2017. [Hebrew]
———. "Anthropological Perspectives on German NGOs in Israel/the Palestinian Territories." In *German NGOs in Israel and the Palestinian Territories*, edited by Anna Abelmann and Katharina Konarek, 53–64. Berlin: Springer, 2018.
———. "Ein Plädoyer für den Alloismus: Historische Kontinuitäten, Zeitgeist und transkultureller Antisemitismus." In *Flucht ins Autoritäre—Rechtsextreme Dynamiken in der Mitte der Gesellschaft*, edited by Oliver Decker and Elmar Brähler, 177–92. Leipzig: Universität Leipzig, 2018.
———. "Navigating Mythical Time. Israeli Jewish Migrants and the Identity Play of Mirrors." In *The Future of the German Jewish Past. Festschrift of the Centre of German-Jewish Studies of the University of Sussex*, edited by G. Reuveni. West Lafayette: Purdue University Press, Forthcoming.
Kuschner, Doris. *Die jüdische Minderheit in der Bundesrepublik: Eine Analyse.* Unpublished PhD Dissertation. Faculty of Philosophy, University of Cologne, 1977.
Lackmann, Thomas. *Jewrassic Park. Wie baut man (k)ein Jüdisches Museum in Berlin.* Berlin and Wien: Philo, 2000.
Landes, Ruth. *The City of Women.* Albuquerque: University of New Mexico Press, 1947.
Landau, Noa. "Israel Demanded Germany Cut Funding to Jewish Museum in Berlin, Report Says." *Haaretz.* December 9, 2008. https://www.haaretz.com/world-news/europe/report-israel-demanded-germany-cut-funding-to-jewish-museum-in-berlin-1.6726205/.
Lavy, George. *Germany and Israel: Moral Debt and National Interest.* Portland, OR: F. Cass, 1996.
Levinson, Pnina Lave "Religiöse Richtungen und Entwicklungen in den Gemeinden." In *Jüdisches Leben in Deutschland seit 1945*, edited by Micha Brumlik, Doron Kiesel, Cilly Kugelmann, and Julius Schoeps, 140–71. Frankfurt am Main: Jüdischer Verlag bei Athenäum, 1988.
Lewan, Kenneth M. "How West Germany Helped to Build Israel." *Journal of Palestine Studies* 4, no. 4 (1975): 41–64.
Lewinsky, Tamar. *Displaced Poets: Jiddische Schriftsteller im Nachkriegsdeutschland, 1945–1951.* Göttingen: Vandenhoek & Ruprecht, 2008.
Liraz, Adi. *Blog—Adi Liraz.* 2018. https://adi-liraz.squarespace.com/blog/.
Longerich, Peter. *"Davon haben wir nichts gewusst!": Die Deutschen und die Judenverfolgung 1933–1945.* Munich: Siedler, 2006.
Maor, Harry. *Über den Wiederaufbau der jüdischen Gemeinden in Deutschland seit 1945.* PhD Dissertation. Philosophy Department, University of Mainz, 1961. http://harrymaor.com/download.htm#item1.

Marcus, George E. "The Problem of the Unseen World of Wealth for the Rich: Toward an Ethnography of Complex Connections." *Ethos* 17, no. 1 (1989): 114–23.

———. "Ethnography in/of the World System: The Emergence of Multi-Sited Ethnography." *Annual Review of Anthropology* 24 (1995): 95–117.

Mitchell, Walter E. "The Goy in the Ghetto." In *Between Two Worlds: Ethnographic Essays on American Jewry*, edited by Jack Kugelmass, 225–39. Ithaca, NY: Cornell University Press, 1988.

Mounk, Yascha. *Stranger in My Own Country*. New York: Farrar, Straus and Giroux, 2014.

Munn, Nancy D. "The Cultural Anthropology of Time: A Critical Essay." *Annual Review of Anthropology* 21 (1992): 93–123.

Nikou, Lina. *Einladungen in die alte Heimat. Besuchsprogramme deutscher Großstädte für Verfolgte des Nationalsozialismus*. PhD Dissertation. Forschungsstelle für Zeitgeschichte in Hamburg, FZH, Universitaet Hamburg, 2017.

O'Dochartaigh, Pol. "Philo-Zionism as a German Political Code. Germany and the Israeli-Palestinian Conflict since 1987." *Debatte* 15, no. 2 (2007): 233–55.

———. *Germans and Jews since the Holocaust*. London: Palgrave, 2016.

Offe, Sabine. "Sites of Remembrance? Jewish Museums in Contemporary Germany." *Jewish Social Studies, New Series* 3, no. 2 (1997): 77–89.

Oppenheimer, Walter W. J. *Jüdische Jugend in Deutschland*. Munich: Juventa, 1967.

Peck, Jeffrey. M. *Being Jewish in the New Germany*. Piscataway, NJ: Rutgers University Press, 2006.

Pinto, Diana. "Are There Jewish Answers to Europe's Questions?" *European Judaism: A Journal for the New Europe* 39, no. 2 (2006): 47–57

Platt, Kristin. *Bezweifelte Erinnerung, verweigerte Glaubhaftigkeit. Überlebende des Holocaust in den Ghettorenten-Verfahren*. München: Wilhelm Fink, 2012.

Rapaport, Lynn. *Jews and Germans after the Holocaust*. Cambridge: Cambridge University Press, 1997.

Rothberg, Michael. "Multidirectional Memory and the Implicated Subjects: On Sebald and Kentridge." In *Performing Memory in Art and Popular Culture*, edited by Liedeke Plate and Anneke Smelik, 39–58. London: Routledge, 2013.

Schoeps, Julius, Willy Jasper, and Bernhard Voght (eds.). *Russische Juden in Deutschland: Integration und Selbstbehauptung in einem fremden Land*. Weinheim: Beltz Althenaum, 1996.

Schüler-Springorum, Stephanie. "Non-Jewish Perspectives on German-Jewish History in a Generational Project?" *The German-Jewish Experience Revisited*, edited by Steven E. Aschheim and Vivian Liska, 192–205. Berlin/Boston: De Gruyter, 2015.

Schütze, Yvonne. "Warum Deutschland und nicht Israel?" *BIOS* 2 (1997): 186–208.

Speck, Daniel. *Piccola Sicila*. Frankfurt: Fischer, 2018.

Spülbeck, Susanne. *Ordnung und Angst: Russische Juden aus Sicht einer Ostdeutschen Dorfes nach der Wende*. Frankfurt/Main: Campus, 1997.

Stetter, Stephan. "Illusion: Die Zwei-Staaten-Lösung ist nicht zu retten." *Internationale Politik und Gesellschaft*. October 22, 2018. https://www.ipg-journal.de/schwerpunkt-des-monats/illusionen/artikel/detail/illusion-die-zwei-staaten-loesung-ist-nicht-zu-retten-3056/.

The Franz Rosenzweig Minerva Research Center. *The Historical Archive of the Hebrew University: German-Jewish Knowledge and Cultural Transfer, 1918–1948*. 2019. https://rosenzweig.huji.ac.il/book/german-jewish-knowledge-and-cultural-transfer-1918-1948.

Thurn, Nike. *Falsche Juden: Performative Identität in der deutschsprachigen Literatur von Lessing bis Walser*. Göttingen: Wallstein, 2015.

Timm, Angelika. "Der Faktor USA in der Entwicklung deutsch-israelischer Beziehungen während des Kalten Krieges." *Comparativ* 16, no. 2 (2006): 46–63.

Trzebiner, Channah. *Die Enkelin*. Frankfurt: Weissbooks, 2013.

Van Rahden, Till. "History in the House of the Hangman: How Postwar Germany Became a Key Site for the Study of Jewish History." In *The German-Jewish Experience Revisited*, edited by Steven E. Aschheim and Vivian Liska, 171–92. Berlin: De Gruyter, 2015.

Wari, Shahd. *Palestinian Berlin*. Berlin: LIT, 2017.

Weissberg, Liliane. "Reflecting the Past, Envisioning the Future: Perspectives for German-Jewish Studies." *GHI Bulletin* 35 (2004): 11–32.
———. "Jewish Studies or Gentile Studies: A Discipline in Search of Its Subject." In *The New German Jewry and the European Context*, edited by Y. Michal Bodemann, 101–10. Houndsmill: Palgrave Mcmillan, 2008.

Chapter Thirteen

Intersections of Jewish Studies and Israel Studies

Israeli Haredim

Tryce Hyman

A great deal of ink has been spilled about the intersections between—and the ostensible future of—Jewish Studies and Israel Studies. Arguments range from a full integration of each into the other to firm declarations that the fields must be divorced from one another (even within the present volume). Most would agree that there will always be a certain overlap, and that Israel Studies will always have need of some recourse to Jewish Studies. In truth, both fields study essentially the same phenomena on different scales. Jewish Studies looks at the internal dynamics of Jewish communities and their interface with majority society, while Israel Studies looks at the internal dynamics of the state and its interface with the international order.

Moreover, many topics of focus within Israel Studies would be (and in some instances have been) largely unintelligible without reference to Jewish Studies. As a high-profile for instance: the infighting of members of the Israeli intelligentsia such as Benny Morris and Ilan Pappé on the international stage must be understood as an extension of the impassioned (and often ad-hominem) identity discourse of the nineteenth-century *Wissenschaft des Judentums* milieu from which the Israeli academe (and Jewish Studies besides) arose.[1] Indeed, the debate within Israel, and internationally, about the meaning of a "Jewish state" or a "state of Jews" and how or if such a state can be a part of the international order—with broad-ranging Diaspora combatants (your Norman Finkelsteins and Alan Dershowitzes)—are all Jewish Studies topics writ large, and in fact, precede Israeli statehood.[2] Moreover, even the "special relationship" between Israel and the United States defies understanding outside of a Jewish Studies framework. It is not enough to see the matter as solely something so banal as effective lobbying or *Realpolitik*—though both of course are factors. You must understand both the long history of deliberate Jewish communal utility to the hegemon as a survival strategy, *and* the particularities of the history of Jews in America.[3]

As fields, Jewish Studies and Israel Studies each have their origins as responses to crises surrounding the existential legitimacy of Jewishness (however defined) in a particular realm—citizenship and statehood, respectively—as the contributions in this volume of Shlomit Attias and Aron Kleiman well illustrate. Both likewise remain heavily activist in nature, replete with disciplinary proclamations and bold calls to action, even within this very volume. This is a trait each carries from their common nineteenth-century roots in the *Wissenschaft des Judentums*. Years of academic overlap and coordinated activism among those engaged in the two fields, whatever their stance on Zionism or place in the broader discourse, have made it impossible to disentangle the fields. This is a simple fact, and one which obviates debate about whether they *should* be disentangled. There is even a certain irony inherent to such an endeavor, as bringing together academics to debate the matter can only serve to entangle the two fields further (as the conference which generated this volume effectively demonstrates). Moreover, the intersections and entanglements of Jewish Studies and Israel Studies are *themselves* worthy topics of study in each field, because they have an impact on each other as well as their objects of study: Diaspora Jewry and the State of Israel. To such an end, what are these intersections? What are their limits? How might the tools of one field be effectively deployed within the other?

With the above in mind, this chapter will examine a particular critique offered by a Jewish Studies scholar, Yoel Finkelman, to his counterparts within a specific Israel Studies subfield: Harediology. Scholarship on Israeli Haredim operates under the paradigm of *Israelization*; that, across time, "Israeliness" has worked its way into the Haredi enclave and brought large portions of the community to terms with features of mainstream Israeli culture such as Zionism.[4] The idea is that Haredim will ultimately reach a level of *Israelization*, bringing all but the most radical Haredi communities into mainstream culture. While Haredim as yet maintain strict practices in forms of dress and a gendered society, increased Haredi use of modern technologies and Hebrew as an everyday language are considered to be indicative of the *Israelization* process.[5]

Yoel Finkelman expresses his reservations on the subject in a 2014 article appearing in *Israel Studies* and titled "The Ambivalent Haredi Jew," where he favors models of ambivalence in explaining Haredi engagement with Israel—similar to his effective and illuminating approach to American Haredim in works such as *Strictly Kosher Reading*.[6] Following a survey of

Finkelman's dissenting article, an exploration of relevant social studies on Israeli Haredim checks his critique for broader applicability. In so doing, an intersection between Jewish Studies and Israel Studies, as well as its limits, shall be identified: while useful, ambivalence is no more adequate a paradigm than *Israelization* for explaining Haredi responses to and engagement with Israeli society. Rather, any approach that seeks to understand changes among Haredim in their engagement with Israeli society must account for changes within Israeli society itself as a majority *Jewish* society.

FINKELMAN AND HAREDI AMBIVALENCE

Yoel Finkelman argues against the *Israelization* narrative of Haredi society dominating academic approaches to Israeli Haredim, contending that *Israelization* is inadequate as an explanatory model for the Haredi encounter with the State of Israel. Finkelman suggests that "ambivalence" is central to understanding this encounter.[7] Haredi ambivalence results from contradictory impulses in Haredi society—in general, the clash between dogmatic isolationism, official Haredi ideology, the attractiveness of majority Israeli society, and what Finkelman terms a "collective social control that prevents people from saying what they really think."[8]

Finkelman suggests that the sociology of ambivalence offers several useful models for examining these contradictory impulses: commonplace ambivalence, Merton's structural ambivalence, and Bauman's discursive ambivalence.[9] Finkelman elaborates on these ambivalence models by highlighting their presence in Haredi print media.[10]

Commonplace ambivalence is a virtually universal attempt by people/ groups to balance competing values and desires—or, as a variant: when a community or individual does not practice what it preaches.[11] Finkelman finds that mainstream Haredi media goes to great lengths to hide this particular ambivalence by refraining from reporting on instances of Haredi corruption or illegal behavior.[12] Another example of this is ambivalence in Haredi media toward internet use, where it is simultaneously condemned by articles and promoted by features such as tech columns.[13]

Robert Merton's structural ambivalence seeks out the social roots of ambivalence as the competition between two competing ideals.[14] This ambivalence can be built into a group's social statuses and roles, to the extent that a society can no longer function without these contradictory pulls.[15] Finkelman identifies such structural ambivalence operating in Haredi media: the political party Shas's *Yom Leyom* newspaper seeks its Middle East analysis from an academic outside the Haredi community, while the magazine *Mishpacha* (a Haredi publication geared toward all streams of Haredi Judaism) acknowledges that "unchanging" Haredi Judaism must necessarily change to meet the community's needs and interests.[16] Finkelman makes special note that such ambivalences are operatively functional only from the perspective of the Haredi community itself, while majority Israeli culture perceives such ambivalence as an indicator of the extreme dysfunctionality of Haredi society.[17]

Zygmunt Bauman's discursive ambivalence (which is the model Finkelman appears to favor) occurs when a group's distinctions of insider/outsider or friend/enemy are confused or rendered inadequate by the presence of what Bauman calls the *stranger* or the *undecided*.[18] Finkelman tweaks Bauman's categories in applying them to Haredi media, noting the correlation that the ambivalence expresses therein results from the fact that the extreme black-and-white outlook of Haredi ideology continues to confront an increasingly complex and gray Israeli Haredi reality.[19] Finkelman notes that the content of Israel's leading Haredi weekly *Mishpacha* is so ambivalent that the magazine has provoked an ambivalent response from its own broad Haredi readership.[20] Despite a sense that its readership considers the content of *Mishpacha* to be ideologically and religiously problematic, the magazine retains the highest rates of circulation.[21] Finkelman identifies this phenomenon as a perfect example of Bauman's discursive ambivalence, wherein ambivalent Haredim read an ambivalent magazine, ambivalently published, by ambivalent Haredim, ambivalently.[22] The circularity of this paradigm is the hallmark of discursive ambivalence, examples for which Finkelman repeatedly pulls from the pages of *Mishpacha* at some length—positing that such ambivalence is ultimately subconscious and can lead to communal paralysis.[23] Finkelman asserts that this paralysis stymies public discourse and has contributed to a lack of outward progress in the Haredi community.[24]

Finkelman turns his attention to the proponents of *Israelization* as a model of Haredi social change. While he acknowledges some level of truth to the *Israelization* narrative, Finkelman expresses misgivings about the anthropological nature of this narrative—and the overall lack of historical tools applied to the model.[25] He takes issue with certain aspects of the *Israelization* narrative, such as the concept of Haredi "post-fundamentalism," because there is a lack of historiographical work behind making this identification—which is to say that comparisons have yet to be made for how Haredi isolation and openness have changed over the decades.[26] Most significantly, Finkelman criticizes the assumption of the *Israelization* narrative that Haredi society is moving in one primary direction, without accounting for the multidirectional pulls within Haredi society which models of ambivalence readily and abundantly identify.[27] For this reason, Finkelman feels that the paradigm of ambivalence is an improvement over the narrative of *Israelization*, which will allow for a more complete picture of Haredi society and the various directional pulls animating it from within.[28] Finkelman concludes his article with a call for using the paradigm of ambivalence to open up lines of future research, based around his strong suspicion that ambivalence extends beyond just the pages of Haredi newspapers and magazines and into virtually every aspect of Haredi life.[29]

SEEKING AMBIVALENCE IN THE ISRAELI HAREDI POPULATION AT LARGE

Yoel Finkelman's suspicions will be taken to task by looking at sociological studies of Haredi society, topically, both in an area Finkelman's article does not touch on—contemporary health practices—as well as some that he does—technology, Zionism, and military service. Following an examination of these topics and Haredi response at the popular level, a discussion will follow which calls into question the applicability of both *Israelization* and Finkelman's proposed transition to an ambivalence research paradigm.

Contemporary Medicine—Autism, Prenatal Testing, Social Work, and Counseling

There has been a gradual growth recently in Haredi engagement with special education and modern approaches to disability.[30] Michael Shaked and Yoram Bilu find that among Haredi families with autistic children, diagnoses are initially sought outside the community from medical doctors.[31] In seeking these diagnoses, Haredi mothers use secular medical language in the cause of expediency, refraining from using any religious terminology (possession, etc.)—though mothers express a level of ambivalence toward the doctors they sought out.[32]

In the pursuit of treatment for their afflicted children, Shaked and Bilu find that Haredi mothers readily employ a combination of cutting-edge medical treatments and traditional religious approaches to illness.[33] While seeking modern medical treatment for their autistic children, Haredi mothers tend to reformulate these treatments to correspond to traditional Haredi frameworks.[34] For example, the Option method—a treatment of choice for autism at the time of the study—is described by one of the mothers in Shaked and Bilu's study as thoroughly Jewish:

> Do you think that Option is a new idea? Whoever really wants to live his life by that we call *musar* (ethics), according to the dictates of our books of ethics ... has Option in the palm of his hand. I can give you some examples. In *Pirke Avot* ("Saying of the Father") it is said: "Judge every man by the scale of merit," "Who is rich? He who rejoices in his portion." ... All this is Option from both the child's perspective and from the perspective of the family and caretakers.[35]

This tendency to formulate modern treatments in traditional terms is joined by an attribution of greater effectiveness to mystical methods and rabbinic knowledge over modern treatments.[36]

Shaked and Bilu also find that Haredi mothers express the conviction that the autism of their children is ordained by God for some profound and divine purpose.[37] A majority of the Haredi mothers interviewed included the concept of the transmigration of souls, reasoning that their children are high-souled people reborn with pure minds who must only cleanse themselves of minor spiritual flaws before they can reach the highest heaven.[38] The authors note that this view that autistic "children were holy and had special souls" has an analog in Western popular culture such as "fairy children" or "idiot savant," similarly with mystical or quasi-mystical sources.[39]

Because of this tendency to view autism as a sign of the spiritual purity of the children afflicted, and the extreme difficulty that often comes along with caring for an autistic child, Haredi mothers conceptualize their motherhood of these children as a distinctive test of faith.[40] Within this conceptualization, Shaked and Bilu find that Haredi mothers adopt stories of historical Jewish suffering as analogs—both from the biblical narrative and from the horrors of the Shoah.[41] Haredi mothers seek to emulate the exemplary conduct of such figures as Abraham, Job, and faithful Shoah survivors by facing the trial of caring for their afflicted children while accepting autism as God's divine will.[42]

The authors also find themselves fascinated by the manner in which the Haredi have integrated Facilitated Communication (a treatment which uses a facilitator to physically assist autistic patients in communication) into the Haredi religious framework.[43] There is a phenomenon among activists of this treatment option in the Haredi community portraying the method as a form of divination, operating from the standpoint that autistic children are specially touched by the divine presence.[44] In this manner, the authors conclude that autism has been transformed within the Haredi community; whereas it was once an aberrant taboo, the disorder is now a dramatic metaphysical validation of the normative Haredi worldview.[45]

The growing receptiveness of Israeli Haredim to contemporary medicine extends to pregnancy care. In their study on Haredi engagement with prenatal testing, Tsipy Ivry, Elly Teman, and Ayala Frumkin find—contrary to popular perceptions among academics—that Haredi women do not insist upon, nor pursue, demedicalized pregnancies.[46] Rather, Haredi women are permissive of prenatal testing procedures that are not overly-invasive upon their persons.[47] The authors discover that mothers from different Haredi groups take a broad range of stances on prenatal testing; while all reject especially invasive methods like maternal serum screening tests and amniocentesis, attitudes toward various ultrasound scans—especially full-anatomy scans—vary widely.[48] This is largely a reflection of rabbinic opinions within particular Haredi communities, ranging from a broad allowance of all such scans, to prohibitions (as among the Lubavitch) against all scans without clear medical necessity.[49]

Ivry et al. find that Haredi women exhibit the kind of ambivalence Finkelman describes, which expresses itself as a personal religious dilemma when prenatal testing presents evidence of fetal complications.[50] Expectant Haredi mothers face the danger of knowing that they will give birth to deformed or disabled children, which puts them at risk of resenting or despairing of the motherhood which is their highest religious purpose.[51] This danger is exacerbated by the reality that women in Haredi communities often bear upward of six children after age forty, which substantially increases the statistical probability of bearing children with disabilities such as Down syndrome.[52] The fear of this danger among Haredi mothers is thoroughly articulated by one of Ivry et al.'s interviewees:

> I hope the Lord will always choose me to have healthy and good children, but if once He chooses me for something else then it is probably my fated duty. Pregnancy for me is a God-given duty (*tafkid*) so I will do the task that has been prescribed for me.... If I am chosen I must be suitable for the task and I can handle it. I pray a lot that this won't happen. There is a special prayer that we say: "Please do not test my faith."[53]

Because of this prevalent view that bearing and raising an unhealthy child is a test of faith, and because fetal anomalies are seen as being in the hands of God, knowing or trying to know about them beforehand through prenatal testing can be religiously problematic (though it has not decreased the prevalence of such testing).[54] This potential religious danger to Haredi women from prenatal testing, and a desire by Haredi authorities to prevent the proliferation of disabled children, has led to a marked increase in the practice of genetic screening of couples prior to marriage and even in the acceptability of contraception as a practice among some Haredi communities.[55] There has also been a rise in rabbinic permissions to terminate pregnancies where severe disability may result, though Haredi women often feel that even when given such permission, they have still failed the test of faith that God has placed upon them.[56]

This sense of failure is exacerbated by the growing public acceptance and even venerability of disabled children in the Haredi community as conduits of divination (as Shaked and Bilu similarly found) and the vessels of especially pure souls.[57] For these reasons, prenatal testing has become an excursion into modernity that Haredi women take as a test of their righteousness, against Haredi standards of gendered piety, resulting in a sort of ranking system in the community based upon their navigation of this ordeal.[58] Ivry et al. conclude that prenatal testing among Haredi women exposes them to a sense of social and spiritual risk far beyond having unknowingly carried a disabled child, since the possibility of knowing has made Haredi women "terrified of being frightened."[59]

Rachel L. Erhard and Dana Erhard-Weiss find in their study on counseling service use among the Haredim that the number of counselors at Haredi schools has experienced relatively explosive growth, from nonexistent to over three hundred in a short time frame.[60] Despite this growth, school counselors are often given another title (such as "supervisor" or "principal's assistant") because of the stigma that is still attached to seeking nonhalakhic solutions to personal problems—especially those in the realm of family life and children.[61]

This stigma, and the Haredi social mores of gender segregation, causes a level of isolation from the professional counseling community—making it impossible for Haredi counselors to attend professional meetings, seminars, or conferences.[62] This truncates the possibilities of thoroughly extensive training for Haredi counselors, as there are no Haredi-friendly programs that confer an academic degree. Further, Erhard and Erhard-Weiss found that male Haredi counselors face an additional roadblock to successful counseling: because such men do not represent the highest ideal of the Haredi biblical scholar, they are not considered to be viable male role models for Haredi boys.[63] Despite these issues, and general suspicions found by the authors to non-Haredi normative counseling methods, the authors find that the community demand for counseling services is exceptionally high—to the extent that school rabbis and principals are demanding that Israeli governmental agencies provide more counseling services.[64] Erhard and Erhard-Weiss conclude that this demand reflects a growing recognition within the Haredi community of social ills that were previously considered taboo topics of discussion.[65]

Anat Freund and Toa Band-Winterstein's study on "social work related change processes" shows similar findings in the increase of recognition of social ills within the Haredi community and the social acceptability of seeking help.[66] Notably, receptiveness is not homogenous—different Haredi groups are more or less open to such help (similarly to receptiveness to prenatal ultrasounds found by Ivry et al.).[67] The growth of openness to the benefits of seeking out social workers has been facilitated by the establishment of nonprofit organizations that cater exclusively to the Haredi community.[68]

Freund and Band-Winterstein find that much of this growth in receptiveness to seeking help is related to the fact that externalization of social problems, especially child maltreatment, has come to be seen as legitimate.[69] Haredi families have come to see seeking care as more relevant than family reputations of marriage suitability (which may be related also to the developing conception of the sacral nature of disabled children) and therefore do not attempt to hide such children as was common in the past.[70] This change also contains a generational component, where the younger generation of Haredim are now far more likely to report problems such as physical and sexual abuse than the generation before them.[71]

Another substantial change in the Haredi community is the legitimization of marriage-related issues leading to divorce, family breakdown, or miscarriage—as one of the study's social worker interviewees elaborates:

> In the past, the divorce process in the ultra-orthodox society was intricate and complex; it took time until the ultraorthodox family dared to even think about other options. . . . Today, divorce has gained a certain legitimization in this society as well, so that more and more families have decided to break the traditional family unit. . . . I believe that, nowadays, women will be more encouraged to get a divorce if their lives become unbearable. . . . Some believe that divorce has become a trend. . . . You can always break up the family if something doesn't seem quite right. In my opinion, this is a very positive characteristic of the ultra-orthodox society—divorce is now accepted, but people still struggle and do their best to reconcile.[72]

This openness has grown to the point that in many Haredi communities, such as Bnai Brak, rabbis refer people to social workers, while the educators and administrators of Haredi schools regularly report on cases.[73] Whereas in the past, social work was seen by the Haredim at large as an interfering threat to Haredi family life—today, Haredi communities are actively involved in a range of social aid services.[74] The older stereotype of a "conspiracy of silence" that purposely hid issues of family strife and abuse is found to exist only among certain groups anymore, while social work professionals servicing Haredi communities are increasingly drawn from the Haredi community itself.[75]

Freund and Band-Winterstein note that this new openness is not due entirely to changes within Haredi society. Rather, they emphasize the significance of changes in the approach social work professionals use in servicing the Haredi community.[76] While in the past, social workers among Haredim attempted to impose mainstream Israeli mores onto those few Haredim who did seek care, more recently, social workers have taken an approach that deliberately engages in cultural sensitivity to Haredi society.[77] This newer approach focuses on the general areas where the goals of social work and Haredi mores overlap and results in a change that, while still in its infancy, shows a dramatic uptick in positive Haredi engagement with social work.[78]

Technology—Internet Use among Haredi Women, Cellular Phones and the Yetser Hara

Finkelman's discussion on Haredi ambivalence toward internet and cellular technologies in print media notes completely opposite representations of these technologies in the pages of *Yated Ne'eman*.[79] While the newspaper often publishes about the excessive danger of the "ravages of technology" and cites prominent rabbis who prohibit internet or smartphone use, *Yated Ne'eman* also publishes a weekly tech page that contains product reviews and information about computer-maintenance, along with the disclaimer that technology should only be used with rabbinic supervision.[80] From Finkelman's perspective of ambivalence, these contradictions emphasize the gap between ideological purity and reality. A closer look at this "gap" will focus specifically on internet usage and the cellular phone.

The Haredi response to the internet is complex. Historically, Haredi leadership have denounced most forms of modern communications technology as vectors of secularism and idolatry.[81] While the internet is perceived to be similarly threatening by rabbinic authorities, the internet represents substantial socioeconomic opportunity for the Haredim that is seen as increasingly necessary in the changing job market.[82] This has created considerable ambiguity within the Haredi population toward the internet, with official responses ranging from an outright ban on the web to rulings that internet use is legitimate so long as such use is restricted to professional or religious purposes.[83] Due to the fact that women are the primary breadwinners of Haredi households, computer and internet-based occupations have become very popular work-from-home options.[84]

The dilemma faced by Haredim over the internet is generally articulated as a tension between the variety of "possibilities" and "dangers" internet use presents to the community.[85] In their study, Oren Livio and Keren Tenenboim Weinblatt's interviewees tend to view internet use as not particularly dangerous to themselves individually, but consider that most dangers posed by the internet are applicable to the Haredi community as a whole.[86] Interestingly, these women consider themselves as something of an *avant-garde* of the community and therefore above the danger of outsider influence from the internet on the community as a whole.[87] While the possibilities presented by the internet are taken as primarily applicable to the individual woman, in terms of socioeconomic opportunity and learning, there is a sense that the dangers of the internet are largely male-centric.[88] One of Livio and Weinblatt's subjects expresses this sense explicitly:

> It's more about men and less about women, because women are not that hysterical and pictures don't get stuck in their heads that much. They get less excited by things that are supposedly immodest. . . . I don't know, it's woman's nature. . . . She thinks more about feelings and less about the sexual expression of feelings. They look more for relations than physical stimulation.[89]

This particular gendering of internet usage's "possibilities" and "dangers" form the basis by which Haredi women construct what Livio and Weinblatt call "discursive dichotomies" that legitimize internet use.[90]

These dichotomies juxtapose the internet against the highly virulent, in the Haredi view, influence of television. For example: in the technology/ content dichotomy, the internet is approached as tool rather than as the aggregate of its content.[91] This separation of the internet from its content (as opposed to television, which is viewed as synonymous with its content) allows the "dangers" of the internet to be open to selective avoidance.[92] This dichotomy is joined by choice/coercion, which Livio and Weinblatt identify as being a means of legitimizing the internet as explicitly distinct from television.[93] The general idea is that while an internet user must actively navigate to whatever content is viewed, a television viewer is subject to whatever content is being broadcast.[94] Notably, this dichotomy of legitimization goes so far as to take metaphysical distinctions into its argument, identifying television as a visual medium (and therefore related to profane sensuality) while asserting that the internet is a verbal medium whose attendant reading is thus related to religious learning and divinity.[95] This use of religious interpretations to legitimize internet use is part of a broader attempt by the women of Livio and Weinblatt's study to present the activity as falling within the realm of normative Haredi Judaism.[96]

The authors find that among the women they interviewed, the tentative (which is to say nonubiquitous) rabbinic approval of religious and work-related internet usage is used as a platform to legitimize much broader usage in practice.[97] That initial internet usage is for religious or work purposes is seen as justification of subsequent use beyond these realms.[98] These extraneous activities are asserted by the women in Livio and Weinblatt's study to be in reality not a threat to the traditional Haredi social structure, contrary to rabbinic assertion.[99] Rather, internet use by Haredi women is self-described as safeguarding mores in an economy that increasingly forces these women into the work force:

> If it's for work it will always increase ultra-Orthodox women's use of the internet.... If I can sit home and do it, why wouldn't I? I want to be at home, I want to be with my kids. But it will always, always have a higher cause.... (An ultra-Orthodox woman) won't sit at home and work on the internet and ... you know, just because she doesn't feel like going to work. It'll be because she wants to be with her kids, because she wants, I don't know, to make lunch for her husband. It will always have added value.[100]

Not only is the use of the internet by Haredi women seen to be an avenue to insulate the community, as expressed above, it is also seen as merely a continuation of a reality in which the venturing of Haredi women into the workforce has not undermined Haredi social mores.[101] Livio and Weinblatt note that while this justification may appear to be counterintuitive, and that new communication technologies would inexorably alter gendered social mores, recent scholarship shows that this is in fact not the case even in non-religious communities.[102]

The authors come to the conclusion that any assessment of the examination of Haredi society's relationship with the internet would be better served from the point of view of the user rather than that of the official discourse of the rabbinic leadership and approved media (as Finkelman does).[103] Notably, in the seven years since Livio and Weinblatt's study, computer and internet use has become an even more pronounced Haredi niche—even amongst Haredi males forced into the labor market by the economy and those who opt to serve in the military.[104] Even in the military, use of Haredi soldiers as "cyberwarriors" is taken as a means to safeguard Haredi social (specifically gender) mores while they serve, clearly reflecting the findings of Livio and Weinblatt.[105]

While Haredi response to the internet has been complex, their response to the cellular phone has been even more so. In his article on the topic, Nathaniel Deutsch notes that the danger of the cellular phone (as an object that embodies *yetser hara* [the evil inclination]) is taken by some of the rabbinic leadership to be so profound that it is actively preventing the advent of the Messianic Age.[106] While initially the cellular phone was determined by Haredi authorities to be no more or less dangerous than traditional telephones, this changed radically with the advent and increasing ubiquity of internet-capable cellular phones.[107] In 2004, Haredi authorities began to pressure Israeli telecom companies to develop and make available Haredi-friendly, or "kosher," cellular phones, while forbidding Haredim from purchasing "non-kosher" devices or service plans.[108]

"Kosher" devices and plans are essentially a downgrade to older cellular phone functionality and service—Haredi users can make and receive calls but are denied access to the internet, text messaging service, and camera/video capability.[109] Notably, this ultimately renders cellular phones into an analog of the cordless home telephone set. "Kosher" service plans carry additional restrictions, such as blocking numbers for forbidden services (dating, phone sex, etc.) as well as billing higher rates for any calls that were not "kosher-to-kosher," and dedicated kosher network number sequences.[110] These efforts by Haredi authorities, along with various decrees that Haredim are religiously obligated to use "kosher" cellular phones, officially integrated them into the *halakhic* universe of Haredi Judaism.[111]

Deutsch finds that while the collaboration between Israeli telecoms and Haredi authorities on the "kosher" cellular phone was successful and their use by Haredim relatively widespread, rabbinic authorities struggle with compliance among community members.[112] Many Haredim continue to keep and use their old cellular phones and plans after having purchased a "kosher" model, and the authorities have come to realize a need to explicitly ban anything but the exclusive use of "kosher" phones.[113] Haredi leadership has felt compelled to resort to particularly coercive methods, such as prohibiting the administrators of all Haredi schools from accepting any student whose parents own "non-kosher" cellular phones.[114]

Deutsch concludes from this disparity between policy and practice, that the Haredim do not ubiquitously reject new technology out of hand (as they ostensibly used to), nor are they fully convinced by the stance their leadership has taken on cellular phones.[115] This is notably similar to the findings of Livio and Weinblatt on internet usage among Haredi women. This is perhaps unsurprising, as the overall sentiment found by Livio and Weinblatt is that internet usage is not as dangerous to the community as authorities asserted it to be, and the current hardline stance among rabbinic authorities is in regard to internet usage on phones. Another similar phenomenon between the two studies is beginning with approved activity (using the internet for work or religious purpose or using a "kosher" phone) that expand beyond such ("secular" nonwork use of the internet or *also* using "nonkosher" phones) in such a way that is contrary to official rabbinic discourse.

Popular Haredi Masculinity and Zionism, the Military, and Haredi Response to Terrorism

In Finkelman's article on Haredi ambivalence, he discusses the process by which Haredim have come to terms with Zionism. He notes that Haredi ideological arguments against Zionism have largely faded into the background, and all but the most extreme groups take the existence of the Jewish State of Israel for granted and even hesitantly celebrate it.[116] Within mainstream Haredi publications, especially those meant to clarify Haredi Judaism to the larger Israeli public, the topic of Zionism as a political and national ideology is left alone almost entirely.[117] The majority of Haredi writing, then, both for internal and external consumption, has moved beyond the previous Haredi attitude of anti-Zionism.[118] Finkelman also notes that the Haredi media defends Israel from international criticism and celebrates its national accomplishments.[119]

Haredi relations with the state have come to focus primarily on culture, specifically on the dangers of secularism, and revolve around protecting Haredim from secular influence.[120] Finkelman characterizes this as "surrounding them [Haredim] in the warm embrace of a totalizing Haredi enclave" that has developed into Haredi-only cities, a desire to eliminate government oversight of Haredi institutions such as education, and religious bodies such as the "Rabbinic Committee for the Character of Vacation Spots."[121]

Finkelman identifies the apparent contradictions between official Haredi ideology on military service and its depiction in Haredi media as the example of Haredi ambivalence *par excellence*.[122] While Haredi rabbinic authorities have pronounced the IDF as religiously dangerous and utterly inappropriate for God-fearing Jews, Haredi media regularly heap praise, and even adoration, on the accomplishments of the military, while glorifying its machismo.[123] Be that as it may, Finkelman notes that any attempt by the state to draft yeshiva students is treated by the Haredi media as a threat of catastrophic and existential proportions.[124] While Finkelman focuses upon the ambivalence displayed within the Haredi media (which are, ultimately, approved media sources), a look at Haredi engagement with military service at the popular level and its response to terrorism helps provide a wider vista of Haredi society at large.

Nurit Stadler notes in her study on Haredi conceptions of military service that the official Haredi stance on the military as depicted by leadership and the Haredi media is not homogenously reflected in the sentiments of the Haredi public. Such expressions of the official stance include items such as broadside depiction of the Haredi soldiers in the IDF as a stream of apostasy that threatens the very existence of the Haredi community.[125] Despite this official viewpoint of the army as a realm of transgression and sin, Stadler finds among her interviewees that there is a general change among male yeshiva students away from this to see the army instead as a site of religious trial and error—in which one might achieve the most spectacular feats of piety.[126] Stadler notes this shift as well as a growing self-criticism of Haredi exemptions from military conscription among the Ashkenazi Haredim she studies.[127]

In addition to the official view of Haredi leadership already mentioned, Stadler finds that her yeshiva student interviewees openly and consistently mock the idea that Torah study is elemental to Israeli military success.[128] Her respondents unanimously have significant misgivings about the sweeping prohibition from Haredi leadership against enlistment in the IDF.[129] Interviewees cite a variety of causes for these misgivings including not only practical concerns such as the dire economic state of the Haredi community, but also issues with fundamental elements of Haredi society itself—notably, the studious lifestyle that is imposed upon Haredi males.[130] The yeshiva students of Stadler's study view the studious model of lifetime study as an unrealistic vision of the founding generation of Israeli Haredim; it is a unique philosophy that cannot be implemented today.[131] There is even a growing sentiment that the stance of Haredi leadership against all male endeavor beyond Torah study is extra-*halahakic*, clearly expressed by one of the students:

> They [the Haredi authorities] presume to build a society with very unrealistic values; it is suitable for a specific handful, a handful of ascetics that enter a monastery and also decide not to marry. . . . But to take a society, a collective, without distinction, to say everybody . . . is part of this ideal, this is simply not

realistic, *this is not what is written in the scriptures, and it is not suitable for human nature.*[132]

Stadler identifies much of this criticism as stemming from a complete bottleneck of avenues for the expression of Haredi masculine virtuosity, with students pointing out that *halakha* for this reason clearly stipulates that *any* student who proves unsuited for study should cease his pursuit after five years and seek other endeavors.[133] This sentiment from yeshiva students indicates a desire for the relegitimization of "practical Judaism" within Haredi society.[134] This critical discourse against the exclusivity of the studious model for masculine validity has led to what Stadler describes as a fantasy in which her interviewees express a longing to serve in the army.[135]

Because restrictions against military enlistment are framed in the language depicting the IDF as a realm of impurity and sin, much of the fantasies of yeshiva students about entering the service tend to view that realm as one of adventurism which passing through "unscathed" would be a mark of spiritual fortitude.[136] There is also an idea that the boundless energy of yeshiva students is well suited to Israel's military endeavors, and that enforced enlistment by the state would ultimately swell Haredi voluntary enlistment:

> We want to see the world—to spend all our energy. The guys from the yeshivas have a lot of energy and nowhere to vent it, and if they vent it in war I am telling you, we will have a strong army. . . . The minute they recruit even a small amount by force, the recruiting office will be flooded with yeshiva students wanting to enlist.[137]

This fantasy is combined with another, that the rigors of yeshiva study predispose students to be excellent combat soldiers—military training and discipline are relatively mild in comparison.[138] Students express admiration for Haredi soldiers (in clear defiance of Haredi officialdom's stance) as an actualization of the fantasy that the Haredi masculinity of the scholar can and does translate into the larger Israeli masculinity of the soldier.[139] The view of the yeshiva students Stadler interviews directly contradicts the viewpoint expressed by Haredi rabbis: engagement with the military will serve as a great fortification of Haredi identity rather than its abandonment, as the battle against the *yetser hara* would be glorified through IDF experience.[140]

Stadler concludes that the military fantasies of her yeshiva student interviewees indicate a clear longing among young Haredi men for a new model of masculine religiosity that allows for different avenues to piety.[141] She offers this as an explanation for the recent large-scale Haredi enrollment in defense and aid organizations. She ends by noting that this aspect of Haredi *Israelization* will be slow-going on a large scale due to the Haredi community's continuing reliance on rabbis and their textual interpretations.[142]

In their study on Haredi responses to terrorism in Israel, Yael L. E. Ankri, Eytan Bachar, and Arieh Y. Shalev make note of the protective effect that a high degree of religiosity in an individual generally has against the development of post-traumatic stress disorder (PTSD).[143] The authors are surprised to find that, despite this, Haredim exhibit significantly higher rates of PTSD in response to terrorist attacks than Israeli society at large.[144] Haredim also display a much higher incidence and intensity of self-blaming, and an individual sense of isolation despite the close-knit nature of the Haredi community.[145] Ankri et al. suggest that manifestations of Haredi guilt in response to terror attacks constitutes a novel form of post-traumatic guilt, which the authors venture to call either *faith-preserving guilt* or *identity-preserving guilt*.[146] This particular form of guilt serves to preserve belief in the face of trauma, in correlation with the strong concept of divine providence within Haredi Judaism.[147] Interestingly, Haredi individuals who survived terror attacks transferred the Haredi normative concept of collective punishment to themselves individually—which could account for the apparent contradiction between Haredi instances of PTSD and the general trend of protection afforded by high religiosity.[148]

Ankri et al. close out their study with the recommendation that professionals treating Haredi PTSD sufferers recognize and acknowledge Haredi *faith/identity-preserving guilt* when they begin treating such patients, rather than risk the cost of challenging them prematurely.[149] The authors further note the importance for therapists of integrating such religious guilt into the therapeutic dialogue with patients, with a close eye on how that integration can facilitate resilience and recovery for each patient.[150] This consideration of Haredi sensibilities by Ankri et al., and others noted above, will be of great use in our discussion of Haredi *Israelization* versus Finkelman's dissent in favor of ambivalence.

DISCUSSION: ISRAELIZATION VERSUS AMBIVALENT ENCLAVISM

Based on the social studies surveyed, Finkelman's suspicion that ambivalence operates in various realms of Haredi society appears to have proven valid. Ambivalences of the kind that Finkelman discusses are indeed present in the various studies. Be that as it may, Finkelman's observations lack a certain depth. For instance, Finkelman's example of choice in his study of Haredi print media is the magazine *Mishpacha*. However, *Mishpacha* is not merely a print media operation—the publication maintains a robust website with content in a variety of languages.[151] In reality, then, *Mishpacha* is a multimedia outlet with global reach. This muddles Finkelman's assessment of the magazine as an expression of ambivalent enclavism.

Some of this lack of depth may be due to Finkelman's assertion that Haredi engagement is specifically one of ambivalent enclavism. For example, he makes wry note of the Rabbinic Committee for the Character of Vacation Spots, indicating a sense of the absurd.[152] Finkelman's wryness overlooks the possibility that the committee might actually be a *necessary* fixture of Haredi society rather than a bizarre instance of reactionary ambivalence. If the website for the company Sea Secret is any indication, the committee is rather necessary. Sea Secret is a company that sells modest swimwear aimed at Haredi women over the internet.[153] The apparel sold is long-sleeved, is modestly skirted, includes a matching hair covering, and is available in wide variety of stylish designs. The site ships globally, operates in three languages, and even has a dedicated page with a listing of the locations and schedules of gender-segregated beaches in Israel.[154] The clear indication here is that rather than existing as a Haredi reaction to the threat of secular licentiousness, the Rabbinic Committee for the Character of Vacation Spots simply reflects the reality (and apparent permissibility) of an Israeli Haredi beach culture.

As in the example above, some elements of Haredi engagement with Israeli society cannot be taken within a framework of Haredi ambivalence about their enclavism. Instances of anticonscription protests, or the glorification of yeshiva students arrested for draft-dodging are actions that take place far outside the Haredi enclave.[155] Perhaps more dramatically, an exposé on Israel's Channel 2 shows Haredim harassing their religious (but non-Haredi) neighbors and young girls in Beit Shemesh on issues of modesty and expressing the intent to make the city, and ultimately the entire country, Haredi.[156] These examples are far from ambivalent enclavism . . . they are activism. Interestingly, this activism qualifies as yet another alternative route to Haredi masculinity outside the yeshiva like the one Nurit Stadler discusses in her study on military fantasy—but in the opposite direction. This activism may be highly adversarial toward mainstream Israeli society, but it is also a dramatic entry of Haredim into the public sphere rather than an expression of ambivalent enclavism. Such activism also falls outside the *Israelizaton* narrative, considering its open and popular rebellion against the "Israeliness" that narrative insists Haredim are trending toward as a whole.

Leaving ambivalence aside for a moment, if *Israelization* is becoming increasingly inadequate to account for Haredi engagement with Israeli society, why does the *Israelization* narrative retain its primacy in scholarship? Yoel Finkelman has been actively criticizing the concept for a decade and a half, yet it remains the textbook paradigm.[157] Zvi Zameret discusses *Israelization* in his 1993 (translated into English in 2002) book *The Melting Pot in Israel*, noting that as a process *Israelization* has largely ceased to function in the state due to the growing plurality of Israeli society.[158] In his assessment, the continuing emphasis on *Israelization* has much to do with the frustration felt by secular Israelis due to their loss of hegemony over the state.[159] This has bled from politics into scholarship, as thoroughly exemplified in Charles S. Liebman's 1997 article in *Israel Studies* titled "Reconceptualizing the Culture Conflict among Israeli Jews." Liebman's article is alarmist, possibly to the point of panic, about the threat secular Judaism faces in Israel and calls for its protection.[160] He also insists that secular Judaism (as opposed to secular Jews) constitutes a silent majority in Israel.[161] *Israelization* in Liebman's view has been inadequate in neutralizing the threat Haredim pose to secular Judaism, and he implores "secular Judaism" to enter Israel's *kulturkampf* as a third party in between irreligion and Haredi radicalism (a call echoed in this very volume, though with an aim for diffusing tension, by Yossi Ben Harush).[162] Liebman's call represents an academic response to the failure of *Israelization* as a process, in the manner Zamaret describes. Notably, Liebman's assertions do not reflect statistical data, which shows that religiosity in Israel has been steadily rising . . . with secularism now in the minority.[163] This shift is important and will return to our discussion later. If *Israelization* is questionable moving forward as an operative concept, and Finkelman's ambivalence framework is also inadequate to account for Haredi activism within Israeli society, what exactly is happening in the Haredi community?

In Deutsch's study on Haredi response to cellular phones, he notes a moment of irony in which a rabbi inverts a Talmudic concept in arguing against the use of cellular phones.[164] The rabbi describes cellular phones as being as dangerous as bringing "*menuval* into the *'bes hamedresh*."[165] Deutsch notes that the irony of this statement is that this decontextualized formulation from the Talmud (BT Kiddushin 30b) is actually about the specific process of bringing dangerous things into the house of study (*beys medresh* . . . in this sense, into Judaism) in order to render their danger impotent.[166] While Deutsch doesn't give the matter any more attention in his study, it is of vital importance. This concept of bringing things into Judaism to render them nonthreatening is the single process at work, at the popular level, in every social study we have surveyed: internet usage has become a means to protect the Haredi family, modern medical practices have become a route to piety, public acknowledgement of autism and other birth defects has become a route to mystical experience and community prestige, cellular phones are made "kosher," rabbis refer Haredim to social workers, et cetera. All these things are part of a popular trend in Haredi society in which things from beyond the "enclave" have been "brought into the *beys medresh*" and reformulated into normative terms. Finkelman's ambivalence model is therefore most applicable in looking at a Haredi leadership which maintains a party line that no longer reflects Haredi popular practice. If *Israelization* cannot, as Finkelman would agree, account for this disparity between the theory and practice of Haredi society . . . why does this disparity exist?

Central to Finkelman's criticism of *Israelization* is that it does not account for Haredi engagement with Israeli society across time, the process of rolling acculturation which he has illustrated at work among American Haredim in works such as *Strictly Kosher Reading*. While such accounting is useful, it can and should also be directed toward *Israeli society's* engagement with Haredim across time as well. In the social studies surveyed, there is a common theme of greater sensitivity to Haredi society over past practices and an insistence that such sensitivity helps to account for engagement and therefore should continue. This paradigm shift is exemplified in one final study: Daphna Birenbaum-Carmeli work on the promotion of pregnancy spacing in Haredi communities. Birenbaum-Carmeli's, self-identifying as thoroughly secular, expected her program (ultimately in the form of a pamphlet) of promoting the health benefits of pregnancy spacing to meet with considerable opposition from the Haredi community.[167] She worked with nurses of Haredi extraction in an endeavor to present the material in as sensitive a manner as possible, yet still expected a negative response to the content—as pregnancy spacing is considered a dereliction of a Haredi woman's duties.[168] Ultimately, and to the bewilderment of Birenbaum-Carmeli, her pamphlet failed to illicit opposition from the Haredi community—but rather met with numerous positive responses.[169]

In this case of the pregnancy spacing pamphlet, it was the approach of a secular medical professional far more than the content of her message that dictated the response of the Haredi community. Such a correlation should be obvious, yet has gone largely unnoted in studies of Haredim because there has been no accounting for the changes in mainstream Israeli approaches to the Haredi community. These changes, and the shift of popular Haredi society away from enclavism, reflect the fact that the nature of Israeli society overall has changed considerably since the establishment of the state. The monolithic and secularist *Mamlakhtiyut* statism of Israel's earlier decades, and its attempt to shoehorn all of Israel into its own mold (unsuccessfully), is long gone. This change is implicit in the feeling among Stadler's yeshiva students that the Haredi party line has become an antiquated relic of the community's founding generation—not because they have been *Israelized*, but because Israel has changed in such a way that enclavism no longer makes sense to them. Rather than Haredim having been *Israelized* out of the enclave, the Israeli mainstream itself has moved closer to the Haredim.

If this is the case, why then has Haredi activism against the Israeli majority become more prevalent? During the period of greatest Israeli secularity, enclavism was a protective response against a majority with which Haredim had little core common ground. Now that Israel has significantly desecularized, there *is* common ground upon which Haredim can stand and struggle for control of an Israeli society they no longer feel utterly disconnected from. This emergent reality makes the conception of *Israelization* irrelevant. Moreover, it also obviates Finkelman's paradigm of ambivalent enclavism in a novel way. His scholarly focus on American Haredim can function in a more classical Jewish Studies model. American Haredim exist surrounded by a majority society which is never going to resolve *itself* as a source of ambivalence. The Israeli case is quite different. As we have seen, mainstream Israeli society has come be seen as having enough in common with Haredi society as to largely obviate the enclavism which has animated Haredi Judaism since its advent as a response to European modernity.

CONCLUSIONS

While Yoel Finkelman is correct in his criticism of the *Israelization* narrative employed in studying Israeli Haredim, his ambivalence paradigm, though much broader and more granular, is still inadequate for a paradigm with so fundamental a difference from that experienced by American Haredim. It is here that one of the many intersections between Jewish Studies and Israel Studies can be found and its limits elaborated. Israeli Haredim are a Jewish minority, and therefore Jewish Studies tools should (even must) be used in their study. However, the majority society they live under is *also* Jewish, a key factor which places Israeli Haredim outside the ken of any Jewish Studies topic—or at least any topic temporally newer than the Second Temple period. As we can see in this instance, Israel Studies essentially begins where the utility of Jewish Studies for the topic ends. While Jewish Studies is essential for identifying the phenomena at work among Israeli Haredim, the realities of Israel as a Jewish majority society and state make it necessary to employ the tools of Israel Studies to make meaning out of the phenomena a Jewish Studies approach identifies.

While there may be a certain appeal to the ostensible tidiness of providing a clearer dividing line between Jewish Studies and Israel Studies, such as the integration of Israel Studies into Middle Eastern Studies suggested by some of the contributors to the present volume, the extant realities of the fields in question and the objects under study make this impossible. As discussed in the pages above, there is too much scholarly and activist overlap and intersection between Jewish Studies and Israel Studies for the latter to be effectively disentangled and then folded into another field. Indeed, Israel Studies finds itself thoroughly engaged in the continuing discourse of Diaspora Jewish identity—as the contribution in this volume by Shlomit Attias illustrates, and the one from Aharon Klieman exemplifies—so much so that this engagement qualifies as a subtopic of Jewish Studies in its own right.[170]

There is, of course, another equally salient reality which prevents any dissolution of Israel Studies into broader Middle Eastern Studies: the interminable persistence of the Israel-Palestine conflict. Contemporary trends in

Middle Eastern Studies (and Postcolonial Studies overall) and the advent of Israel Studies are the direct result of this continuing conflict—and they remain the intellectual battlements of the conflict's parties *by design*.[171] This is true even where centers of Israel Studies and Middle Eastern Studies enjoy cordial relations and close collaboration, as they do at the University of Oklahoma (OU).[172] Yet even at OU, they are and remain necessarily separate by design; one is housed within the College of Arts and Sciences (as part of a joint center with Judaic Studies) and the other is housed within the College of International Studies. It is unlikely, if not impossible, that such a formal separation will end for as long as the Israel-Palestine Conflict continues.

This is not to say that the criticisms of those advocating for drastic changes to the intersections between Jewish Studies and Israel Studies are without merit. Quite the contrary, Johannes Becke's bold call in this volume for a "methodological Canaanism" makes many salient points about the need for a thematically broader and more regionalized scope in the study of Israel—however unlikely a "systematic rupture between the research fields of Jewish Studies and Israel Studies" might be. Such criticisms should be taken seriously and applied constructively to Israel Studies, even if calls to firmly separate the fields are left aside (as they ultimately must be). This can only serve to enrich Israel Studies (and Jewish Studies by extension) while also easing the reservations of those concerned about an intellectual bottleneck in the field. To wit, this contribution's example of an intersection between Jewish Studies and Israel Studies: Israeli Haredi engagement with a shifting, Jewish, Israeli majority society could only be fully contextualized by examining how Israel's regional location has contributed to this shift.

Finally, it is worth considering that the formal (and political) separation of Israel Studies from Middle Eastern Studies may not reflect the academic realities at hand, at least in certain environments. To offer some evidence for this, albeit personal and anecdotal, in 2018 the author of this chapter simultaneously completed two separate graduate degrees at the University of Oklahoma—both fell under the combined umbrellas of the Schusterman Center for Judaic and Israel Sudies *and* the Center for Middle Eastern Studies. The academic integration across my two programs was substantial. For example, Schusterman Center core faculty sat on my Middle Eastern Studies thesis committee and taught the majority of my Middle Eastern Studies coursework. I must stress that this was not a matter of desiring an Israel-centric thesis topic and having to resort to Schusterman Center faculty to do so—my topic was a write-up on the Islamic State's ideology through an elaborate qualitative analysis of its defunct *Dabiq* magazine.

Despite formal and political separation between Israel Studies and Middle Eastern Studies, a more organic and gradual academic integration may be occurring as emergent topical requirements demand it. As more broadly Middle Eastern Studies topics gain increasing relevance within Diaspora Jewish discourse, such topics become increasingly the purview of Jewish Studies as well. Quite naturally, without prompting, the intersections between all three fields are in fact widening. There is a certain symmetry to this. As Achim Rhode discusses in this volume, all three arise from an older scholarly framework of similar topical breadth.

NOTES

1. See Tryce Hyman, "Israel's New Historians and the Identity Discourse of the *Wissenschaft des Judentums*," *Phi Alpha Theta Conference*, Shawnee, OK, 2016. For an elaboration on the broad influence of the *Wissenschaft des Judentums*, see "Special Issue: Cultures of *Wissenschaft des Judentums* at 200," *PaRDes: Journal of the German Association of Jewish Studies* 24 (2018): 1–286.

2. These kinds of debate topics have been prevalent within Zionist circles and outside them since Theodor Herzl first published *Der Judenstaat* in 1896. For an example of Jewish opposition to Zionism from its earliest days, see Yaakov M. Rabkin, *A Threat from Within: A History of Jewish Opposition to Zionism* (London: Zed, 2006).

3. The collision of these two historical paradigms has increasingly become a site of discourse and tension among American Jewry. See, as one of a rolling series of examples: Batya Urgon-Sargon, "Seeking to Help Israel, American Jewish Institutions Sold Us Out," *The Forward*, February 4, 2019, https://forward.com/opinion/418721/seeking-to-help-israel-american-jewish-institutions-sold-us-out/. It is also notable that the conception of Jews in the persistent millenarianism of American Protestantism, so key to understanding the history of American Jewry, is also essential to the American-Israeli "special relationship."

4. Barry M. Rubin, *Israel: An Introduction* (New Haven: Yale University Press, 2012), 158.

5. Rubin, *Israel*, 162.

6. Yoel Finkelman, "The Ambivalent Haredi Jew," *Israel Studies* 19, no. 2 (2014): 264–93; see Yoel Finkelman, *Strictly Kosher Reading: Popular Literature and the Condition of Contemporary Orthodoxy* (Brighton, MA: Academic Studies Press, 2011).

7. Finkelman, "The Ambivalent Haredi Jew," 266.
8. Ibid.
9. Ibid., 266–67.
10. Ibid., 271.
11. Ibid.
12. Ibid.
13. Ibid.
14. Ibid., 272.
15. Ibid., 274.
16. Ibid.
17. Ibid., 276.
18. Ibid., 276–77.
19. Ibid., 277.
20. Ibid.
21. Ibid.
22. Ibid., 278.
23. Ibid., 279–84.
24. Ibid.
25. Ibid., 286.
26. Ibid., 287.
27. Ibid.
28. Ibid., 288.
29. Ibid.

30. Michal Shaked and Yoram Bilu, "Grappling with Affliction: Autism in the Jewish Ultraorthodox Community In Israel," *Culture, Medicine and Psychiatry* 30 (2006): 1–27, 4.
31. Ibid., 6.
32. Ibid.
33. Ibid., 7.
34. Ibid., 9.
35. Ibid.
36. Ibid., 10.
37. Ibid., 12.
38. Ibid., 13.
39. Ibid., 15–16.
40. Ibid., 17.
41. Ibid., 17–18.
42. Ibid., 19.
43. Ibid., 20.
44. Ibid.
45. Ibid., 22.
46. Tsipy Ivry, Elly Teman, and Ayala Frumkin, "God-sent Ordeals and Their Discontents: Ultra-Orthodox Jewish Women Negotiate Prenatal Testing," *Social Science & Medicine* 72 (2011): 1527–33, 1527.
47. Ibid.
48. Ibid., 1529.
49. Ibid.
50. Ibid., 1530.
51. Ibid.
52. Ibid.
53. Ibid.
54. Ibid., 1531.
55. Ibid.
56. Ibid., 1532.
57. Ibid., 1530.
58. Ibid., 1533.
59. Ibid.
60. Rachel L. Erhard and Dana Erhard-Weiss, "The Emergence of Counseling in Traditional Cultures: Ultra-Orthodox Jewish and Arab Communities in Israel," *International Journal for the Advancement of Counselling* 29 (2007): 149–58, 151.
61. Ibid., 155.
62. Ibid., 156.
63. Ibid.
64. Ibid., 157.
65. Ibid.
66. Anat Freund and Tova Band-Winterstein, "Between Tradition and Modernity: Social Work-Related Change Processes in the Jewish Ultra-Orthodox Society in Israel," *International Journal of Intercultural Relations* 37 (2013): 422–33, 426.
67. Ibid.
68. Ibid., 427.
69. Ibid.
70. Ibid.
71. Ibid., 428.
72. Ibid.
73. Ibid., 429.
74. Ibid.
75. Ibid., 430.
76. Ibid., 431.
77. Ibid.
78. Ibid.

79. Finkelman, "The Ambivalent Haredi Jew," 271.
80. Ibid.
81. Oren Livio and Keren Tenenboim Weinblatt, "Discursive Legitimation of a Controversial Technology: Ultra-Orthodox Jewish Women in Israel and the Internet," *The Communication Review* 10 (2007): 29–56, 31.
82. Ibid.
83. Ibid., 32.
84. Ibid.
85. Ibid., 35.
86. Ibid., 36.
87. Ibid.
88. Ibid., 40.
89. Ibid.
90. Ibid., 41.
91. Ibid.
92. Ibid., 42.
93. Ibid., 43.
94. Ibid.
95. Ibid., 44.
96. Ibid.
97. Ibid.
98. Ibid., 46.
99. Ibid., 47.
100. Ibid., 48.
101. Ibid., 49.
102. Ibid.
103. Ibid., 50.
104. Christina Case Bryant, "Israel's Newest Cyber Warriors: Ultra-Orthodox Jews," *The Christian Science Monitor*, June 1, 2014.
105. Ibid.
106. Nathaniel Deutsch "The Forbidden Fork, the Cell Phone Holocaust, and Other Haredi Encounters with Technology," *Contemporary Jewry* 29 (2009): 3–19, 6.
107. Ibid., 8.
108. Ibid.
109. Ibid., 9.
110. Ibid.
111. Ibid.
112. Ibid., 17.
113. Ibid.
114. Ibid.
115. Ibid., 18.
116. Finkelman, "The Ambivalent Haredi Jew," 267.
117. Ibid., 268.
118. Ibid.
119. Ibid.
120. Ibid.
121. Ibid., 269.
122. Ibid., 281.
123. Ibid.
124. Ibid.
125. Nurit Stadler, "Playing with Sacred/Corporeal Identities: Yeshiva Students' Fantasies of Military Participation," *Jewish Social Studies: History, Culture, and Society* 13, no. 2 (2007): 155–78, 156.
126. Ibid., 157.
127. Ibid., 159.
128. Ibid., 161–62.

129. Ibid., 165.
130. Ibid.
131. Ibid.
132. Ibid. (Emphasis mine.)
133. Ibid., 167.
134. Ibid.
135. Ibid.
136. Ibid., 168.
137. Ibid., 169.
138. Ibid., 170.
139. Ibid.
140. Ibid., 171.
141. Ibid., 172.
142. Ibid., 173.
143. Yael L. E. Andri, Eytan Bachar, and Arieh Y. Shalev, "Reactions to Terror Attacks in Ultra-Orthodox Jews: The Cost of Maintaining Strict Identity," *Psychiatry: Interpersonal and Biological Processes* 73 (2010): 190–97, 190.
144. Ibid., 193.
145. Ibid., 194.
146. Ibid., 195.
147. Ibid.
148. Ibid.
149. Ibid., 196.
150. Ibid.
151. See *Mishpacha Magazine*, http://www.mishpacha.com/.
152. Finkelman, "The Ambivalent Haredi Jew," 269.
153. "Modest Swimwear for Girls, Teens & Women by Sea Secret," Sea Secret, http://seasecret.biz/.
154. "Israeli Swimwear: Where Use Them in Israel?" Sea Secret, http://seasecret.biz/israeli-swimwear-where-use-them-israel.
155. Yair Ettinger, "Hundreds Protest Arrest of Haredi Draft-Dodger," *Haaretz*, August 18, 2014, http://www.haaretz.com/news/national/.premium-1.611017; "Yeshivah Bochur Released from IDF Prison 6; Tells the Media 'The IDF Will Not Break Us, We Will Not Serve,'" *The Yeshivah World*, March 25, 2014, http://www.theyeshivahworld.com/news/headlines-breaking-stories/223518/yeshivah-bochur-released-from-idf-prison-6-tells-the-media-the-idf-will-not-break-us-we-will-not-serve.html.
156. "Between the Suns (with Updated English Subtitles)," YouTube, December 27, 2011, http://youtu.be/I5HKtaaws-g; for the original broadcast in its entirety: http://www.mako.co.il/mako-vod-channel2-news/ulpan-shishi-2011/December/VOD-2755d4d47db6431006.htm.
157. Yoel Finkelman, "Review: Haredim Yisraelim: Hishtalvut BeLo Temi'ah? [Israeli Haredim: Integration without Assimilation?] by Kimmy Caplan; Emmanuel Sivan," *Modern Judaism* 27, no. 3 (2004): 296–300; see Rubin, *Israel: An Introduction*.
158. Zvi Zameret, *The Melting Pot in Israel: The Commission of Inquiry concerning Education in the Immigrant Camps during the Early Years of the State* (Albany: State University of New York Press, 2002), 157.
159. Zameret, *The Melting Pot*, 157.
160. Charles S. Liebman, "Reconceptualizing the Culture Conflict among Israeli Jews," *Israel Studies* 2, no. 2 (1997): 172–89, 186.
161. Liebman, "Reconceptualizing the Culture Conflict," 186.
162. Liebman, "Reconceptualizing the Culture Conflict," 187.
163. Asher Arian and Ayala Keissar-Sugarmen, *A Portrait of Israeli Jewry: Beliefs, Observances, and Values among Israeli Jews 2009: Highlights from an In-depth Study Conducted by the Guttman Center of the Israel Democracy Institute for the Avi Chai Foundation* (Jerusalem: Avi Chai, 2012), 30. Notably, what we have in this is yet more discourse on "proper" Jewishness internal to Israel, related ultimately to the state's standing in the international order, and thus, the matter is yet another Jewish Studies matter operating *within* Israel Studies.

164. Deutsch, "The Forbidden Fork," 6.
165. Deutsch, "The Forbidden Fork," 6.
166. Deutsch, "The Forbidden Fork," 6.
167. Daphna Birenbaum-Carmeli, "Your Faith or Mine: A Pregnancy Spacing Intervention in an Ultra-Orthodox Jewish Community in Israel," *Reproductive Health Matters* 16, no. 32 (2008): 185–91, 185.
168. Birenbaum-Carmeli, "Your Faith or Mine," 188.
169. Birenbaum-Carmeli, "Your Faith or Mine," 189.
170. On this particular paradigm, the scholarship of Derek J. Penslar comes to mind.
171. Notably, Edward Said's *Orientalism*, seminal for both contemporary Middle Eastern Studies and Post-Colonial Studies, was developed explicitly to provide the Palestinian cause with such an intellectual battlement. That Israel Studies would develop in response to its growing success is hardly surprising. See Edward W. Said, *Orientalism*, 25th Anniversary Edition (New York: Vintage Books, 1994 [1978]), 26–27.
172. For example, the Schusterman Center for Judaic and Israel Studies at the University of Oklahoma maintains cordial relations and many cosponsorships with the Center for Middle Eastern Studies and the Center for Persian Studies at the University of Oklahoma. They share affiliated faculty members from each other's core faculty, and for years at a time the Schusterman Visiting Professor from Israel taught many of the core courses for Middle Eastern Studies at the undergraduate and graduate level.

BIBLIOGRAPHY

Ankri, Yael L. E., Eytan Bachar, and Arieh Y. Shalev. "Reactions to Terror Attacks in Ultra-Orthodox Jews: The Cost of Maintaining Strict Identity." *Psychiatry: Interpersonal and Biological Processes* 73 (2010): 190–97.

Arian, Asher, and Ayala Keissar-Sugarmen. *A Portrait of Israeli Jewry: Beliefs, Observances, and Values among Israeli Jews 2009: Highlights from an In-depth Study Conducted by the Guttman Center of the Israel Democracy Institute for the Avi Chai Foundation*. Jerusalem: Avi Chai, 2012.

"Between the Suns (with Updated English Subtitles)." YouTube. November 27, 2011. http://youtu.be/I5HKtaaws-g.

Birenbaum-Carmeli, Daphna. "Your Faith or Mine: A Pregnancy Spacing Intervention in an Ultra-Orthodox Jewish Community in Israel." *Reproductive Health Matters* 16, no. 32 (2008): 185–91.

Bryant, Christina Case. "Israel's Newest Cyber Warriors: Ultra-Orthodox Jews." *The Christian Science Monitor*. June 1, 2014.

Deutsch, Nathaniel. "The Forbidden Fork, the Cell Phone Holocaust, and Other Haredi Encounters with Technology." *Contemporary Jewry* 29 (2009): 3–19.

Erhard, Rachel L., and Dana Erhard-Weiss. "The Emergence of Counseling in Traditional Cultures: Ultra-Orthodox Jewish and Arab Communities in Israel." *International Journal for the Advancement of Counselling* 29 (2007): 149–58.

Ettinger, Yair. "Hundreds Protest Arrest of Haredi Draft-Dodger." *Haaretz*. August 18, 2014. http://www.haaretz.com/news/national/.premium-1.611017.

Finkelman, Yoel. "The Ambivalent Haredi Jew." *Israel Studies* 19, no. 2 (2014): 264–93.

———. "Review: Haredim Yisraelim: Hishtalvut BeLo Temi'ah? [Israeli Haredim: Integration without Assimilation?] by Kimmy Caplan; Emmanuel Sivan." *Modern Judaism* 27, no. 3 (2004): 296–300.

———. *Strictly Kosher Reading: Popular Literature and the Condition of Contemporary Orthodoxy*. Brighton, MA: Academic Studies Press, 2011.

Freund, Anat, and Tova Band-Winterstein. "Between Tradition and Modernity: Social Work-Related Change Processes in the Jewish Ultra-Orthodox Society in Israel." *International Journal of Intercultural Relations* 37 (2013): 422–33.

Hyman, Tryce. "Israel's New Historians and the Identity Discourse of the *Wissenschaft des Judentums*." *Phi Alpha Theta Conference*. Shawnee, OK. 2016. https://www.academia.edu

/30362483/Is-rael_s_New_Historians_and_the_Identity_Discourse_of_the_Wissenschaft_des_Judentums.
"Israeli Swimwear: Where Use Them in Israel?" Sea Secret. http://seasecret.biz/israeli-swimwear-where-use-them-israel.
Ivry, Tsipy, Elly Teman, and Ayala Frumkin. "God-sent Ordeals and Their Discontents: Ultra-Orthodox Jewish Women Negotiate Prenatal Testing." *Social Science & Medicine* 72 (2011): 1527–33.
Liebman, Charles S. "Reconceptualizing the Culture Conflict among Israeli Jews." *Israel Studies* 2, no. 2 (1997): 172–89.
Livio, Oren, and Keren Tenenboim Weinblatt. "Discursive Legitimation of a Controversial Technology: Ultra-Orthodox Jewish Women in Israel and the Internet." *The Communication Review* 10 (2007): 29–56.
"Modest Swimwear for Girls, Teens & Women by Sea Secret." Sea Secret. http://seasecret.biz/.
Rabkin, Yakov M. *A Threat from Within: A History of Jewish Opposition to Zionism*. London: Zed, 2006.
Rubin, Barry M. *Israel: An Introduction*. New Haven: Yale University Press, 2012.
Said, Edward W. *Orientalism*. 25th Anniversary Edition. New York: Vintage Books, 1994 [1978].
Shaked, Michal, and Yoram Bilu. "Grappling with Affliction: Autism in the Jewish Ultraorthodox Community In Israel." *Culture, Medicine and Psychiatry* 30 (2006): 1–27.
"Special Issue: Cultures of *Wissenschaft des Judentums* at 200." *PaRDes: Journal of the German Association of Jewish Studies* 24 (2018): 1–286.
Stadler, Nurit. "Playing with Sacred/Corporeal Identities: Yeshiva Students' Fantasies of Military Participation." *Jewish Social Studies: History, Culture, and Society* 13, no. 2 (2007): 155–78.
Urgon-Sargon, Batya. "Seeking to Help Israel, American Jewish Institutions Sold Us Out." *The Forward*. February 4, 2019. https://forward.com/opinion/418721/seeking-to-help-israel-american-jewish-institutions-sold-us-out/.
"Yeshiva Bochur Released from IDF Prison 6; Tells the Media 'The IDF Will Not Break Us, We Will Not Serve'." *Yeshiva World News*. March 25, 2014. http://www.theyeshivaworld.com/news/headlines-breaking-stories/223518/yeshiva-bochur-released-from-idf-prison-6-tells-the-media-the-idf-will-not-break-us-we-will-not-serve.html.
Zameret, Zvi. *The Melting Pot in Israel: The Commission of Inquiry concerning Education in the Immigrant Camps during the Early Years of the State*. Albany: State University of New York Press, 2002.

Index

1967 War. *See* Six-Day War

Aayari, Yassine, 182
Abdulhadi, Rabab, 138
Academy of Sciences of the Soviet Union, 46
Agapov, Mikhail, 49, 59
Ahbar, Ka'ab al-, 78
Ahmadinejad, Mahmood, 86
Alt-Right, 15
Amar, Rabbi Shlomo Moshe, 5, 35
American Jews, 157–165, 166, 248
Ankara, 105
Ankri, Yael L. E., 262
Anti-Defamation League (ADL), 110
antisemitism, 15, 159–160, 165, 167, 176; college campuses and, 9, 143, 144; Germany, 176, 217, 220, 222, 226; Iranian, 85; Tunisia, 181; Turkey, 109, 110–112, 113; United States of America, 15, 143, 144, 160, 163, 165, 167. *See also* pogrom
anti-Zionism, 159–160, 165, 167, 259; among Jews, 122, 138, 139, 142, 143; college campuses and, 8, 134–150; intersectionality and, 137–140; Iran, diplomatic anti-Zionism, 81; Iran, ideological anti-Zionism, 79–80; Iran, strategic anti-Zionism, 80; Middle Eastern Studies and, 144; Soviet Union, 46; Tunisia, 181; Turkey, 109; United

States of America, 138–140, 143, 144, 150, 167
Appadurai, Arjun, 178
Arab Studies, 53
Arab-Israeli Conflict, 3, 4, 8, 47, 48, 49, 59, 73, 181
Arama, Rabbi Isaac Ben Moses, 5, 35–39
Arendt, Hannah, 128
Armstrong, Cherryl, 167
Ashton, John, 89
Association for Israel Studies (AIS), 1, 149
Association of the Study of Israel, 47
Australia, 8, 166
Avnery, Uri, 210

Baal Ha'Akeda. *See* Arama, Rabbi Isaac Ben Moses
Balat, 114
Balfour Declaration, 46, 50
Bali, Rifat N., 103
Balta, Evren, 112
Band-Winterstein, Toa, 254–255
Bani-Israel. *See* Jewish identity, perspective of Islam in Iran
Barnard College, 135
Barnett, Michael, 200
Bartal, Israel, 202–203
Basel, 126
Bauman, Zygmunt, 250
BDS (Boycott, Divestment and Sanctions) movement, 135, 136, 137, 139, 148,

203
Bechar, Eytan, 262
Becker, Franziska, 218, 225
Beit Shemash, 263
Belarus, 49
Ben Ali, Zine El Abidine, 181
Ben-Gurion, David, 5, 15–27, 92;
  admiration of Baruch Spinoza, 16;
  animosity toward Source Criticism, 25;
  bible as core of Jewishness, 20, 23–24;
  bible as creation of Jewish genius, 20, 23–27; bible as history, 26; bible as source of secular authority, 18–20;
  biblical humanism and, 21–23; biblical nationalism and, 21–23; biblical presentism, 21–23; conception of Arab-Jewish relations, 22; impact of literature on, 19; on biblical Joshua, 22; perception of biblical vs rabbinic authority, 18, 23, 24; perspective on Palestinian nationalism, 19; rivalry with Wladimir Ze'ev Jabotinsky, 19; Yehezkel Kaufmann and, 26
Ben-Gurion University, 124
Berdichevsky, M. Y., 21
Berdichewsky, Micha Josef, 202
Berlin, 2, 27, 219, 220, 223, 223–225, 227, 229
Bernstein, Julia, 225
Bhaba, Homi K., 180
bibliocentrism, 17
Bilgi University, 104
Bilkent University, 104
Bilu, 19
Bilu, Yoram, 251–252, 253
Birenbaum-Carmeli, Daphna, 265
Biton Commission, 16
Bnai Brak, 255
Bodemann, Y. Michal, 219, 222, 225, 226, 229
Boujenah, Michel, 183
Bourguiba, Habib, 181, 183
Brandeis University, 59
Bratkin, Dimitry, 58
Brenner, Michael, 90
Brenner, Yosef Hayim, 21, 124
British Mandate, 19
British Palestine Exploration Fund, 58
Brody Jewish Center-Hillel, 135

Brown, Benjamin, 34, 37
Brumlik, Micha, 225
Buber, Martin, 204

Canaanites. *See* Young Hebrews.
Canada, 112, 181
Catholic Church, 57
Center for Jewish Studies at Karl-Franzens University Graz, 1
Chahed Yousef, 182
Charles and Lynn Schusterman Family Foundation, 149
Christian Supersessionism, 15
Cohen, Steve, 15
Cologne, 223
colonialism, 85, 138, 201, 205, 207
Columbia University, 133, 135, 138, 149
Czollek, Max, 226

Daat Torah, 37–38, 38
Dekel, Irit, 226
Delulze, Gilles, 180
Dershowitz, Alan, 247
Deutsch, Nathaniel, 258–259
Diner, Dan, 227, 228
Dmitrevsky, Alexy, 60

Erhard, Rachel L., 254
Erhard-Weiss, Dana, 254
Eytan, Walter, 92
Ezra, 19

Far Left, 15
Fedorchenko, Andrey, 47, 49
Feldman, Jackie, 220, 226
Festival Carthage, 183
Finkelman, Yoel, 248, 248–251, 255, 259, 262–263, 265
Finkelstein, Norman, 247
Fontaine, Sheryl, 167
France, 181
Freker, Kathryn, 223
Fruend, Anat, 254–255
Frumkin, Ayala, 252–254

Gantner, Eszter, 225
Gaon, Rabbi Saadia, 124
Gay, Ruth, 225
Geis, Gabriel, 223

Geller, Steven, 25
George Washington University, 136
German-Israeli Foundation for Scientific Development, 228
Germany, 217–233; antisemitism in, 176, 217, 220, 222, 226; Israel-Palestine Conflict and, 221, 228, 229, 230; national identity and the Holocaust, 222, 223, 226; relationship with Jewish minority, 221–222, 223, 225–226; relations with Israel, 222, 228, 230
Gevaryahu, 27
Ghriba Pilgrimage, 182, 183–185
Goldman, Ralph, 48
Goldmann, Nahum, 204
Gordon, A. D., 204
Greece, 129
Gromova, Alina, 225
Grünberg, Kurt, 225
Guattari, Félix, 180
Guttstadt, Cory, 104

Ha'Am, Ahad, 5, 18, 21, 123, 204
Hadad, Rafram, 183
Hagemann, Stephan, 228
halacha. *See* Israel, "church" and state
Hamadan, 73
Haredim, 4, 10, 34, 248; ambivalent enclavism and, 248–251, 262–263; as a Jewish minority within Israel, 10, 266; as a Jewish Studies subject, 10, 266; as an Israel Studies subject, 10, 266; beach culture, 263; engagement with Israeli society, 35–37, 37, 263–265, 267; Israelization and, 248, 250–251, 263–264, 266; perspective on Zionism, 248; perspectives on Autism, 251–252; perspectives on cellular phones, 258–259; perspectives on counseling and mental health care, 254–255; perspectives on family planning, 265; perspectives on military service, 260–261; perspectives on prenatal care, 252–254; perspectives on terrorism, 262; perspectives on the internet, 256–258
Haredization. *See* Israel, "church" and state
Harry S. Truman Research Institute for the Advancement of Peace, 59

Haskalah, 3, 17, 158
Hasköy, 114
Hazaz, Hayim, 24
Hebrew University, 59, 227
Hegner, Victoria, 225
Heidelberg, 223
Herzl, Theodor, 94, 126, 201
Hestermann, Jenny, 227
Hezekiah, 16
Hill, Marc Lamont, 138
historiography, 16
Hochschule für Jüdische Studien, 223
Holocaust, 219; denial, 15, 86; memorialization, 225, 229–231
Holocaust Denial. *See* Holocaust, denial
Holocaust Memorial Berlin, 225, 229
Holy Land Studies, 45, 49–52, 54–58; Christian Arabs as paradigm, 57; definition, 52–55; descriptive model of, 56; history of, 54; neo-conservative model of, 57; postcolonial model of, 58; Russian use for interests in the Levant, 55–58, 60
Homt as-Suq, 184
Horon, Adya Gur, 202
Hughes, Aaron, 3
Hungary, 226

Iakimova, Elizaveta, 49
Ibn Munabbih, Wahb, 78
Ibn Salam, Abdullah, 78
Imperial Orthodox Palestine Society, 54, 55, 56, 58
Institute for Israel and Jewish Studies, 150
Institute for the Study of Asian and African Countries, 49
International Association for the Safeguarding of the Cultural Heritage of the Jews of Tunisia, 182
Iran, 73–95, 178; Arab-Israeli Conflict and, 73, 78, 79; constitution, 74; international relations of, 74–75, 79; Israel, relations with, 80, 88, 89; Israel-Palestine Conflict and, 74, 78, 79; Jewish minority, relations with, 86; messianism within, 74, 82–84; Mustazaf-Mustakber (oppressed-oppressor) concept, 74; nuclear program within, 80; political theology

within, 75, 84, 86; support of terrorism, 80
Iranian Jews, 85
Iranian Revolution, 73
Iranian Studies, 75
ISIS. *See* Islamic State
Islam, 73; apocalypticism in Iran, 74, 82–84; messianism in Iran, 86; perspective on Judaism in Iran, 73, 75–78; political Islam, 74, 84
Islamic Law, 75
Islamic Republic of Iran. *See* Iran
Islamic State, 74, 267
Islamic Studies, 75, 175
Israel: as a Jewish majority society/state, 10, 122, 125, 126, 128, 201, 228, 266; as a Middle Eastern state, 4, 9, 16–17, 48, 49, 137, 143, 150, 175–177, 186, 199–209, 266; as a "Western outpost," 4; Basic Law, 125; Bible and cultural identity in, 5, 17–18, 23–24; Bible and national identity in, 18, 20, 23; "church" and state, 32, 35, 35–37, 37, 127; culture and politics, 206; demographics, 125, 128; de-secularization, 265–266; education in, 16; history of, 5, 7, 16, 19, 21, 46, 123–124, 126, 127, 129, 158, 200, 220; impact upon Jewish identity, 122, 123, 124, 125, 126; messianism within, 74, 89–90; minorities within, 123, 125, 128; nationalism within, 128; perspective of American Jews on, 8, 35; perspective of Turkish Jews, 6, 101, 102, 104, 106–110, 111, 113; political theology within, 75, 86, 92; relations with Iran, 80, 85, 89; relations with post-Soviet Russia, 48, 49, 51, 55; religion and politics in, 5, 22; religion and society, 31–40; secularism in, 265; secular-religious status quo, 32–33, 35, 39, 122; statism, 18; view of Iran within, 74
Israel Education, 8, 157–165; Arab-Israeli Conflict and, 160; history of, 161, 163; Israel Engagement as, 163–164; Israel Peoplehood as, 164–165; Israel-Palestine Conflict and, 160; Jewish identity and, 162, 164, 165, 167; response to antisemitism, 160, 163, 165, 167; response to anti-Zionism, 160, 163, 165, 167
Israel Engagement. *See* Israel Education
Israel Institute, 149
Israel Peoplehood. *See* Israel Education
Israel Studies: Area Studies and, 9, 16, 60; definition of, 45, 50; donor support, 3, 48–70, 129, 146, 149–150, 228; entanglement between Jewish Studies and, 10, 247–248, 266–268; Eurocentrism and, 16; German academia, separation from Jewish Studies, 10, 177, 186, 228; Germany and, 227–228, 231–232; Global Studies and, 9; "harediology" within, 39, 248; history of, 2, 9, 46–47, 129, 167, 200–201, 247–248; Holocaust and, 230; Holy Land Studies and, 54, 58; Holy Land Studies as, 5; international politics and, 133; intersectionality and, 137–140; Iran and, 75, 95; Iranian Messianism Studies as, 6, 86; Israel and, 202–203; Israel Education as, 8, 157–158; Israeli exceptionalism and, 9; Israel-Palestine Conflict and, 10, 53, 134, 203, 229, 230, 231–232, 266–268; Israel-Palestine Conflict and, 144, 150, 266–267; Jewish Studies and, 248; language instruction and, 208, 209; methodology, 147–148, 200–201, 208; Middle Eastern Studies and, 9, 16, 49, 144, 177, 177–179, 186, 200–210, 266; Moscow School of, 5, 49; Nizhniy Novgorod School of, 5; objectivity in, 34; Odessa School of, 6; post-Soviet territories and, 45, 46, 47, 48, 49–51; rupture between Jewish Studies and, 9, 10, 15, 128, 145–150, 167–168, 199–209, 247, 266–268; Soviet Union, 46, 47; state support of, 1, 3, 48, 51, 54, 59, 60, 146, 228; structure, 147, 227; Turkey and, 102, 102–104, 112, 114
Israeli Declaration of Independence, 19
Israeli-Arab Conflict. *See* Arab-Israeli Conflict.
Israel-Palestine Conflict, 4, 19, 52–53, 59, 74, 78, 91, 110, 134, 181, 183, 186, 221; Israel Studies, relation to, 10, 53,

134, 203, 229, 230, 231–232; Middle Eastern Studies, in relation, 10, 266–268
Italy, 180
Ivry, Tsipy, 252–254

Jabotinsky, Vladimir Ze'ev, 5, 19, 22, 126
Jaoskowitz, Ari, 92
Jasper, Willy, 225
Jerba, 181, 182, 183–185
Jerusalem, 230
Jewish Agency, 4
Jewish Enlightenment. *See Haskalah*.
Jewish identity: American Jewish perspectives, 157, 160, 162, 163, 164, 165–166, 167; anti-Judaism and, 8; antisemitism and, 8; anti-Zionism and, 8; bible and, 20, 23–27; Diaspora and, 4, 10, 158, 162, 165, 165–166, 202, 226, 247; Germany and, 218–220, 230; Haredi conception of, 35, 38; Holocaust and, 7, 218–219, 223, 226; hybridity and, 4; identity politics and, 160, 163, 165, 167, 200; Islamic perspective in Iran, 6, 73, 75–78, 85, 91, 95; Israel and, 3, 4, 7, 8, 10, 122, 123, 124, 125, 134, 163, 164, 165, 166, 167, 206, 220, 227, 247; Israel Education and, 162, 164, 165, 167; perspective of Iranian Jews about, 6; perspective of Tunisian Jews on, 9; perspective of Turkish Jews, 6, 102, 106, 113; Source Criticism and, 25; Tunisia and, 181–183; Turkish majority perspective, 102, 110–111; United States of America and, 140–141, 143; Zionism and, 8, 122, 123, 125, 127, 247
Jewish Museum Berlin, 220, 229–231, 231
Jewish Studies: centers of, 1; China and, 127; donor support of, 3, 128, 146, 228; entanglement between Israel Studies and, 10, 247–248, 266–268; Eurocentrism and, 16; Germany and, 217–227, 231–232; "harediology" within, 39, 248; history of, 2, 4, 9, 34, 128–129, 158, 161, 167, 175–176, 186, 247–248, 268; Holocaust and, 221, 226; India and, 127; Iran and, 75, 95; Iranian Messianism Studies as, 6, 95; Israel and, 159; Israel Studies and, 248; Israel-Palestine Conflict and, 230, 231; Israel-Palestine Conflict and, 145; Japan and, 127; Korea and, 127; Middle Eastern Studies and, 9, 177, 186; minority studies and, 102, 103, 112, 114; objectivity in, 34; oral history within, 105; post-Soviet territories, 46, 47, 48; rupture between Israel Studies and, 9, 10, 15, 128, 145–150, 167–168, 199–209, 247, 266–268; separation from Israel Studies in German academia, 10, 177, 186, 228; shaper of Jewish identity and culture, 40; state support of, 1, 3, 146, 228; textual analysis and, 31; Tunisia and, 183; Turkey and, 102, 102–104, 112, 114; Turkish "minority studies" as, 6; use in statecraft, 32, 39; varieties of, 217, 231
Jewish Theological Seminary, 25
Jews: American. *See* American Jews: Iranian; Iranian Jews: Russian; Russian Jews: Tunisian; Tunisian Jews: Turkish; Turkish Jews
Jorhomi, Ubaid ben Shadhia, 78
Josephus, Flavius, 16
Judaism: impact of Israel on, 122, 125; messianism, 87–88, 89, 93–94; perspective of Islam in Iran, 73, 75–78, 91, 95; secularism, 126, 127
Judaistik. *See* Jewish Studies, in Germany
Jüdische Hochschule, 177

Kalimis. *See* Jewish identity, perspective of Islam in Iran
Kaplan, Mordechai, 164
Kaplanow, Rashid, 48
Kapsutin Antonin, 56, 57
Kariv, Avraham, 24
Kashrut, 36–37, 38
Katz, Ethan B., 92
Kaufmann, Yehezkel, 25–26
Kendzia, Victoria Bishop, 219, 226, 229
Keren, Michael, 18
Khitrovo, Vasily, 60
Khomeini, Ayatollah Ruhollah, 74, 84
Kiev, 46, 49–50
Klatzkin, Jakob, 90
Klier, John, 48

Kolobov, Oleg, 49
Kornilov, Alexander, 49
Kosach, Grigory, 59
Kotel. *See* Western Wall Plaza
Kotel Affair. *See* Western Wall Plaza, controversy
Kotzin, Michael, 3
Krylov, Alexander, 49
Kuschner, Doris, 222

Lackmann, Thomas, 229
Lag BaOmer, 183
Lalehzar, Hamami, 89
Lapid, Nadav, 1
Lapid, Yair, 17
Lebanon, 79, 201
LeBlanc, Thomas, 136
Leibowitz, Yeshayahu, 24, 124, 201
Lellouche, Ofer, 184
Levtzion, Nehemia, 48
LICRA, 181
Lieberman, Avigdor, 51
Liraz, Adi, 223
Lisovoy, Nikolay, 57
Livio, Oren, 256, 259
Luzhkov, Yury, 54

Machover, Moshe, 94
Mahdaviat, 6, 82–84, 86
Mahdi. *See* Islam, messianism in Iran
Mainz, 227
Maira, Sunaina, 138
Mamlakhtiyut. *See* Israel, statism
Maor, Henry, 222
Mapu, Abraham, 19
Marburg University, 177
Marburg University Centre for Near and Middle Eastern Studies, 177
Maryasis, Dmitry, 49
Mashiach. *See* Judaism, messianism
Massuto, Umberto Moshe David, 25
Matsikh, Leonid, 48
Mazuz, Menachem, 184
Meged, Aharon, 18
Mendelssohn, Moses, 16, 25
Mendes-Flohr, Paul, 16
Merkel, Angela, 230
Merton, Robert K., 249–250
messianism, 86

Messianism Studies, 85
Meta-Halacha, 32, 34, 35, 39
Meyer, Michael, 85
MGIMO University, 49, 59
Michael and Elaine Sterling Institute for Jewish Studies and Modern Israel, 150
Michigan State University, 150
Middle Eastern Studies, 49, 175, 186; departments of, 3, 138; Israel Studies as, 9, 16, 49, 144, 177, 177–179, 186, 200–210, 266; Israel-Palestine Conflict and, 10, 138, 144, 203, 266–267; Jewish Studies as, 9, 177, 186
Minsk, 46
Mishpacha Magazine, 250, 262
Mochalova, Victoria, 48
Monastir, 183
Morocco, 126, 178, 206
Morris, Benny, 247
Moscow, 46, 48, 49, 51, 59
Moscow Center for University Teaching of Jewish Civilization (*Sefer*), 48, 49
Moscow Center of Jewish Studies, 48–49, 59
Moshav Etan, 183
Munich, 227
Musevi. *See* Turkish Jews

Nadim, Sanaa, 135
Nathanson, Robby, 228
National Institute of Strategic Studies of Ukraine, 49
nationalism/transnationalism, 4, 19, 21–23, 125, 127, 128, 129, 178, 179, 180, 181, 200, 205, 207, 209, 223, 226, 231
New York University, 136, 139
Neyzi, Leyla, 103
Nizhny Novgorod, 51, 59
Nosenko, Tatyana, 49

O'Dochartaigh, Pól, 222
Odessa, 46, 49, 51, 126, 206
Odessa University, 49
Omsk State University, 49
Oppenheimer, Jakob, 222
Oriental Studies, 46, 51, 175
Özlem, Altan-Olcay, 112

Pahlavi, Mohammad Rezah Shah, 84

Palestine Studies, 45, 52–53; definition, 52; Israel-Palestine Conflict, relation to, 53
Palestinian Authority, 55–56
Pappé, Ilan, 247
Paris, 182, 183, 185
Partow, Negar, 90
Patton, Paul, 180
Peck, Jeffrey M., 225, 229
Peighambrieyeh mausoleum, 73
Peleikis, Anja, 220, 226
Perestroika, 47
Persian Gulf States, 74
Picard, Ariel, 34
Pitzer College, 136
pogrom: September 1955 Pogrom, 107; Thrace Pogrom, 107. *See also* antisemitism
Poland, 129
Political Islam. *See* Islam, political Islam
Porath, Rabbi Jonathan, 48
Potsdam, 227
Primakov, Yevgeny, 54
Pritsak, Omelyan, 46
Protestantism, 57
Puar, Jasbir, 138
Pyrlin, Yevgeny, 53, 58

Qazvin, 73
Qu'ran, 73; Jews within, 73, 75–77

Rabbinic Committee for the Character of Vacation Spots, 263
Rabin, Yitzhak, 159
Rashi, 20, 23
Reinharz, Jehuda, 16
Rekhes, Elie, 3
Rifat Publishing, 103
Rockaway, Robert, 167
Rosh, Lea, 225
Rothberg, Michael, 226
Rouhani, Hassan, 86
Rumania, 129
Rumyantsev, Vladimir, 49
Russia, 46, 49, 226; Israel-Palestine Conflict and, 55–58; Palestinian Authority, relations with, 55–56
Russian Department of American Jewish Joint Distribution Committee, 48
Russian Empire, 126
Russian Jews in Germany, 225
Russian Orthodox Church, 54, 55, 57
Rutgers University, 138

Said, Edward, 138, 203
Salmon, Yosef, 90
Sand, Shlomo, 94, 208
San Francisco State University, 135, 138
Sarna, Nahum, 25
Schoeps, Julius, 225
scholarship versus advocacy, 3, 4, 32, 33, 39–40, 125, 162–163
Scholem, Gershom, 78, 93
Schusterman Center for Judaic and Israel Studies, 1, 15, 149, 267
Schütze, Yvonne, 225
Science of Judaism. *See* Jewish Studies, history of
Sde Boker, 21, 27
Second Aliyah, 18, 19
Secular Judaism. *See* Judaism, secularism
Segal, Moshe Zvi, 25
Shahak, Israel, 91
Shaked, Michael, 251–252, 253
Shalev, Arieh Y., 262
Shalom, Silvan, 184
Shamir, Yitzhak, 91
Shapira, Anita, 22
Shapovalov, Mikhail, 49
Shariah. *See* Islamic Law
Shas, 249
Shi'ite Studies, 75
Shiism. *See* Islam (Iranian topics)
Shinan, Avigdor, 17
Shush, 73, 85
Sibera, 49
Siege of Jerusalem, 16
Six-Day War, 3, 204, 231
Slama, Simon, 183
Smith, George P., 138
Smolenskin, Peretz, 17
Société d'Histoire des Juifs de Tunisie, 183, 185
Source Criticism, 25–27
Spätjudentum. *See* Source Criticism
Spinoza, Baruch, 20, 25
Spülbeck, Susanne, 225
St. Petersburg, 51, 56

Stadler, Nurit, 260–261, 263
Stampfer, Shaul, 48
Stern, Frank, 222
Stiftung Wissenschaft und Politik Berlin, 227
Stony Brook University, 135
Stowe, Harriet Beecher, 19
students: Jewish, 140–143; non-Jewish, 1, 3, 4
Students for Justice in Palestine, 135, 137
Styria, 1
Sukenik, Eliezer, 25
Summer Institute for Israel Studies, 59
Swarthmore College, 134
Syria, 79, 204

Tabenkin, Israel, 18, 19
Tchernichovsky, Shaul, 202
Tehran Jewish Committee, 85
Tel Aviv, 19, 127
Tel Aviv Museum, 19
Tel Aviv University, 136
Teman, Elly, 252–254
Temple University, 138
Teveth, Shabtai, 17
Thrace, 107
Ting-Tooney, Stella, 162
Tomb of Daniel, 73, 85
Tomb of Esther and Mordechai, 73
Tomb of Habakkuk, 73
Tomsk State University, 49
Trabelsi, René, 182
transnationalism. *See* nationalism/transnationalism
Tufts University, 137
TÜKAM - Research and Application Center of Turkey's Cultures, 104
Tunis, 183
Tunisia, 178; antisemitism within, 181; Arab-Israeli Conflict and, 181; Ghriba Pilgrimage and tourism, 184; Israel, relations with, 184; Israel-Palestine Conflict and, 181; Jewish minority, relationship with, 180, 181, 182
Tunisian Jews, 180–185; Arab-Israeli Conflict and, 181; diaspora of, 180–181, 182, 183, 184–185; history of, 180–181; Israel-Palestine Conflict and, 181; migration to Israel, 181, 183, 184
Turkey, 101–114, 178, 207; antisemitism within, 109, 110–112, 113; Israel-Palestine Conflict and, 110; Jewish minority, relations with, 101, 106, 107, 110–112; relations with Israel, 110
Turkish Jews, 101–114; demographics, 101, 102, 105; Holocaust, perspective on the, 106; Israel, perspective on, 101, 102, 104, 106–110, 111, 113; Istanbul, Turkish Jews of, 102, 105; migration to Israel, 101, 107–110, 113; migration to Spain and Portugal, 112; migration to the Unites States of America, 101, 106, 112
Tuyserkan, 73
Tzahor, Zeev, 206

UCLA, 136
Ukraine, 46, 49
Ukrainian Academy of Science, 46
Ukrainian Institute of Oriental Studies, 46
Ultra-Orthodox Jews. *See* Haredim
United States of America, 79, 89, 226; antisemitism within, 15, 143, 144, 160, 163, 165, 167; Israel, relationship with, 247
University of California, 133, 136, 138
University of Graz, 1
University of Haifa, 136
University of Illinois at Champaign-Urbana, 135
University of Michigan, 133, 136
University of Missouri, 138
University of Nizhny Novgorod, 49
University of Oklahoma, 1, 15, 149, 267
University of Tyumen, 49
University of Virginia, 135
Uspenski, Porfiri, 56

Vienna, 126
Vogt, Bernhard, 225
Vorobyova, Irina, 56
Vorotnyuk, Marina, 49

Walzer, Michael, 207
War of 1967. *See* Six-Day War
Washington, DC, 1, 136
Weinblatt, Keren Tenenboim, 256, 259

Weissberg, Liliane, 223
Weizman, Ezer, 46
Wellhausen, Julius, 25
Western Wall Plaza, 35; controversy, 35, 38–39
Wissenschaft des Judentums. *See* Jewish Studies, history of

Yamilinets, Boris, 57
Yanukovich, Victor, 50
YATOÇ - Community of Jewish Studies, 104
Young Hebrews, 9, 17, 21, 26, 199, 202, 204

Zakharchenko, Alla, 50
Zakovitch, Yair, 17
Zameret, Zvi, 263
Zarif, Mohammad Javad, 86
Zevi, Sabbatai, 78
Zionism: American Jewish education and, 8, 157–165; Australian Jewish education and, 8, 157–165; bible as history in, 21, 26; Christian Zionism, 91; history of, 5, 7, 16, 19, 21, 46, 123–124, 126, 127, 129, 158, 200; Iranian conception of, 6; Jewish identity, impact on, 122, 123, 125, 127; messianism and, 74, 82–84, 88–90, 92–93, 94; nationalism and, 125, 127, 200; negation of the Diaspora and, 7, 17, 145, 202, 203; negation of the Levant and, 203; perspective of Islam in Iran, 78–81, 90; response to Source Criticism, 25; secular redemption and, 20; UN resolutions on, 47
Zunz, Leopold, 2, 34
Zvyagelskaya, Irina, 49

About the Contributors

Shlomit Attias, PhD, lived in the United States for nearly twenty-seven years and four years in Australia. During these years she studied and taught in universities and Jewish schools. Between 2003–2015 she focused in her research on Israel Education for which she received both an MA from Emory University (2005) and a PhD from the University of Haifa (2016). At present she works at the Center of Educational Technology in Israel, where she develops Hebrew curricula for English-speaking schools. She also teaches at the Levinsky International College of Education in Israel.

Johannes Becke, PhD, teaches as assistant professor for Israel and Middle East Studies at the Heidelberg Center for Jewish Studies (Hochschule für Jüdische Studien Heidelberg), where he specializes in the Comparative Politics of Israel and the Middle East. After graduating from Freie Universität Berlin with a PhD in political science, he was granted a postdoctoral fellowship at the University of Oxford. His research has been published in *Israel Studies*, the *Journal of Israeli History*, *Jewish Studies Quarterly*, *Interventions*, and *Political Geography*. He is currently conducting a research project on the intellectual history of Israel Studies in the Arab World.

Yossef Yaacov (Yossi) Ben-Harush has an MA and BA from the Hebrew University in Jewish Thought. His Master's research focused on Aharon Roth, the founder of the closed Ultra-Orthodox Toldot Aharon community. Yossi recently submitted his graduate thesis on "R' Aharle Roth and the Radical Hasidism in His Writings." He lives and works in Jerusalem, and is an educator and lecturer at the Shalom Hartman Institute and in various other institutes within his city.

Klaus Hödl, PhD. is a historian at the Center for Jewish Studies at the University of Graz in Austria. His current research deals with Jewish and non-Jewish relations in Central Europe at the turn of the twentieth century. He teaches the history of Israel and related topics at Graz University. His latest book *Jews in Viennese Popular Culture around 1900* will be published in late 2019.

Tryce Hyman holds a BA in Judaic Studies, an MA in History, and an MA in International Studies from the University of Oklahoma, with research foci on the history of Zionism and the ideology of the Islamic State. His most recent publication, in *Small Wars Journal*, is an elaboration on use of the SWORD Model of Counterinsurgency as a tool for historical analysis, utilizing the Jewish Insurgency in Mandatory Palestine as a case study. Mr. Hyman is an independent academic copy editor and serves as the administrative assistant for the Schusterman Center for Judaic and Israel Studies at the University of Oklahoma.

Özgür Kaymak, PhD, completed her doctoral degree at Istanbul University in July 2016, her dissertation was titled *The Socio-Spatial Construction of Istanbul's Rum, Jewish and Armenian Communities*. She worked as a teaching assistant at Istanbul University, Women's Research and Education Center. She is the author of a book titled *İstanbul'da Az(ınlık) Olmak: Gündelik Hayatta Rumlar, Yahudiler, Ermeniler* [Being a Minority in Istanbul: Rums, Jews, Armenians in the Daily Life], published in 2017. She is currently working on a project in collaboration with Bremen University and the Mercator Foundation about Gender and Women's Research Centers at Universities in Turkey. She is also actively involved in the activities of the Women's Library and Information Center Foundation in Istanbul. Her academic interest areas are ethnoreligious minorities, collective memory, migration sociology, gender and feminist theories.

Aharon Klieman, PhD, is a Dr. Nahum Goldmann Professor Emeritus in Diplomatic Studies at Tel Aviv University; founding director of the Abba Eban Graduate Program in Diplomatic Studies; and a member of the Department of Political Science. Klieman serves as senior editor of *The Israel Journal of Foreign Affairs* and also chairs The International Political Science Association's Research Committee on Geopolitics. His doctorate is from The Johns Hopkins University's School of Advanced International Studies, with an M.A. from the School of International Affairs at Columbia University in Middle Eastern history and politics. A former senior associate of the Institute for National Security Studies (INSS) in Tel-Aviv, he has held visiting appointments in International Relations and Israel Studies at Georgetown University, The University of Chicago, The University of Denver, The University of Michigan, U.C.L.A., and The Watson Institute for International Studies at Brown University, and Trinity College, Dublin. Aharon Klieman's current research traces alternative traditions of "Israel among the Nations" and Jewish statecraft from biblical times through the long period of intercessors and Court Jews ("shtadlanim") in the Diaspora to modern Zionist diplomacy and contemporary Israeli foreign relations. He is also, together with Stuart Cohen, the author of *The Routledge Handbook on Israeli Security* (2018). An edited collection of essays entitled *Great Powers & Geopolitics in a Rebalancing World*, was published by Springer in 2015.

Dani Kranz, PhD, is the director of Two Foxes Consulting, senior research fellow at Bergische University Wuppertal, Germany, and an external research affiliate of the Zelikovitz Center for Jewish Studies, Carleton University, Ottawa, Canada. Trained in anthropology, social psychology, and history, her thematic expertise covers migration, ethnicity, law, the state/ stateliness, political life, and organizations. She has been conducting long-term fieldwork in Europe and the Middle East. Her current work concerns the trialectic Jews, Muslims, and Christians in Germany as well as the perceptions of Israeli Jewish and Palestinian/Arab Muslim migrants against the backdrop of German history, and the Middle East conflict.

Alan T. Levenson, PhD, is Schusterman/Josey Chair of Jewish History and director of the Schusterman Center for Judaic and Israel Studies at the University of Oklahoma. He is the author of *The Making of the Modern Jewish Bible: How Scholars in Germany, Israel, and America Transformed an Ancient Text* (2011); *Between Philosemitism and Antisemitism Defenses of Jews and Judaism in Germany, 1871–1932* (2004); *An Introduction to Modern Jewish Thinkers: From Spinoza to Soloveitchik* (2006); and *Joseph: Portraits through the Ages* (2016). He is also editor of *The Wiley-Blackwell History of Jews and Judaism* (2012).

Yakov M. Rabkin, PhD, is professor of history at the University of Montreal. He has been associated with CERIUM, Centre for Research on International Relations and has held visiting positions at several universities in France, Israel, Japan, and the United States. He is the author of *Science between the Superpowers*, a study of Soviet-American relations in science and technology (1988), coeditor of and contributor to *Interaction between Scientific and Jewish Cultures* (1995) and *Diffusion of New Technologies in the Post-Communist World* (1997). His book *A Threat from Within: A Century of Jewish Opposition to Zionism* (2006) is now available in fifteen languages. His most recent book is *What is Modern Israel?* (2016), also published in French, Japanese, and Russian. His current work focuses on demodernizing tendencies in history, with a book titled *De-modernization: A*

Future in the Past (2018). His areas of interest include the history of science, studies of modernization and demodernization, as well as contemporary Jewish history.

Amir Rezaeipanah, PhD, completed his doctoral degree in political science at the University of Shahid Beheshti (former Melli-Tehran). He is the author of *Identity, Discourse and Elections in Iran* (2016) and has contributed in the selection and translation of the book *Political Discourse Analysis* (2018). Rezaeipanah has cotranslated the book *Subjects and Simulations* (2019) coedited by Anne O'Byrne and Hugh J. Silverman. He is the author of *The History of the Post-Revolutionary Iran* (2019) and his PhD thesis engaged in a comparative analysis of the notion of messianism in the foreign policy of Iran an Israel. His research interests include political sociology, rereading Iran's contemporary history, especially studying the Islamic Revolution and its aftermath, Middle East studies, studying Israel from different perspectives, mainly its policy toward Iran, and working on Iran's presidential and parliamentary elections.

Achim Rohde, PhD, is Islamic scholar and scientific coordinator of the research network "Re-Configurations: History, Memory and Transformation Processes in the Middle East and North Africa" at the Center for Near and Middle East Studies at Philipps-University Marburg. He has published numerous essays on the history of German-speaking Oriental Studies. His current book project explores the reconstruction of Tunisia after the 2011 revolution, incorporating a previously neglected Jewish dimension. Rohde was co-organizer of the conference "Jews in Muslim Societies. History and Prospects," held in October 2017 at the Jewish Museum Berlin. His most recent publication with Mathias Berek, Kirsten Heinsohn, and David Jünger is "Vom Erfolg ins Abseits? Jüdische Geschichte als Geschichte der 'Anderen'. Ein Gespräch." Medaon 11, no. 20 (2017).

Carsten Schapkow, PhD, is L. R. Brammer Jr. Presidential Professor in History at the University of Oklahoma, where he also serves as the director of the Center for the Study of Nationalism. His research is on German-Jewish history and Sephardic history, which he has explored in numerous books and articles. His most recent book is *Role Model and Countermodel: The Golden Age of Iberian Jewry and German-Jewish Culture during the Era of Emancipation* (2016). He is currently working on a book titled *The Question of Loyalty in German-Jewish Culture (1754–1933)*.

Dzmitry Shavialiou, PhD, is a lecturer of international relations in the Department of International Relations, Belarusian State University. He is the author of the monograph *Perepiska Mak-Magona—Huseyna 1915–1916 i* *vopros o Palestine* [The McMahon—Hussein Correspondence, 1915–1916, and the question of Palestine] (2008). In 2010–2016, he published the Belarusian annual of Jewish Studies 'Tsaytshrift' / 'Časopis' (Vilnius). He is a member of the Council of European Association of Middle Eastern Studies.

Yaacov Yadgar, PhD, is Stanley Lewis Professor of Israel Studies, School of Interdisciplinary Area Studies and Department of Politics and International Relations Fellow at St. Anne's at Oxford University. His research revolves around issues of Jewish identity, religion, politics, and secularism. He focuses on placing Israel in theoretical and epistemological frameworks that bear obvious relevance beyond the specific case history. His scholarship is multidisciplinary, encompassing Jewish, political, cultural, religious, and media studies. He concentrates on Israeli sociopolitics (especially Israeli Judaism) and on the epistemological, historical, and political dimensions of Israeli identity. His main publications are *Sovereign Jews: Israel, Zionism, and Judaism* (2017), *Beyond Secularism: Traditionism and the Critique of Israeli Secularism* (2012 [Hebrew]), and *Secularism and Religion in Jewish-Israeli Politics: Traditionists and Modernity* (2011).